Where Are Poor People to Live?

Cities and Contemporary Society

Series Editors: Richard D. Bingham and Larry C. Ledebur,
Cleveland State University

Sponsored by the
Maxine Goodman Levin College of Urban Affairs
Cleveland State University

This new series focuses on key topics and emerging trends in urban policy. Each volume is specially prepared for academic use, as well as for specialists in the field.

SUBURBAN SPRAWL
Private Decisions and Public Policy
Wim Wiewel and Joseph J. Persky, Editors

THE INFRASTRUCTURE OF PLAY
Building the Tourist City
Dennis R. Judd, Editor

THE ADAPTED CITY
Institutional Dynamics and Structural Change
H. George Frederickson, Gary A. Johnson, and Curtis H. Wood

CREDIT TO THE COMMUNITY
Community Reinvestment and Fair Lending Policy
in the United States
Dan Immergluck

PARTNERSHIPS FOR SMART GROWTH
University-Community Collaboration for Better Public Places
Wim Wiewel and Gerrit-Jan Knaap, Editors

REVITALIZING THE CITY
Strategies to Contain Sprawl and Revive the Core
*Fritz W. Wagner, Timothy E. Joder, Anthony J. Mumphrey, Jr.,
Krishna M. Akundi, and Alan F.J. Artibise*

THE UNIVERSITY AS URBAN DEVELOPER
Case Studies and Analysis
David C. Perry and Wim Wiewel

PEOPLE AND COMPETITIVE ADVANTAGE OF PLACE
Building a Workforce for the 21st Century
Shari Garmise

Where Are Poor People to Live?

Transforming Public Housing Communities

Larry Bennett, Janet L. Smith,
and Patricia A. Wright
editors

M.E.Sharpe
Armonk, New York
London, England

Library of Congress Cataloging-in-Publication Data

Where are poor people to live? : transforming public housing communities / edited by
Larry Bennett, Janet L. Smith, and Patricia A. Wright.
    p. cm. — (Cities and contemporary society)
Includes bibliographical references and index.
ISBN 0-7656-1075-2 (cloth : alk. paper) — ISBN 0-7656-1076-0 (pbk. : alk. paper)
    1. Public housing—Illinois—Chicago. 2. Low-income housing—Illinois—Chicago.
3. Public housing—Government policy—United States. I. Bennett, Larry, 1950–
II. Smith, Janet L., 1962 III. Wright, Patricia A., 1949– IV. Series.

HD7288.78.U52C495 2006
363.5′850977311—dc22   2006003661

Printed in the United States of America

The paper used in this publication meets the minimum requirements of
American National Standard for Information Sciences
Permanence of Paper for Printed Library Materials,
ANSI Z 39.48-1984.

∞

BM (c)   10   9   8   7   6   5   4   3   2   1
BM (p)   10   9   8   7   6   5   4   3   2   1

Our Fight Must Go On
By Rene Maxwell (1949–2003)

Let no one tell you different
Until all injustices are erased
And people's needs are met
Until broken promises are kept
And it hasn't happened yet
Our fight, it must go on.

There are too many injustices
We the people face today.
And wishful thinking
I'm telling ya
Will not make them go away.
We have to stand together
Our purpose is all the same.
People's issues must be addressed
If not, our country will never change.
We have nothing to lose here
Everything in the world to gain.
We've been passive far too long,
That's why injustices still remain.
The call for action is now!
Our backs are against the wall!
It's the only civil thing we can do
Before the curtain falls.
So, let me hear the voices that separate right from wrong.
Let the world know we are here!
Come on, sing this song!

Contents

Tables and Figures

Tables

Figures

Preface

Where Are Poor People to Live?: Transforming Public Housing Communities is the product of many years of labor. Each of the editors has been involved in public housing research and advocacy since the 1990s, and the contributors to this volume possess a comparable wealth of experience working on public housing issues. The focus of this book is the reshaping of public housing in Chicago, which by the early 1990s had achieved the unenviable reputation as the worst in the United States. Although a number of factors speak to the uniqueness of Chicago's circumstances—the sheer size of the Chicago Housing Authority's (CHA) property inventory, the extreme racial segregation of its residents and, for many years, the highly politicized nature of the agency's operations—the effort to turn around public housing in this particular city has national implications.

The most significant of these implications centers on the processes that have been put in place to disperse former CHA residents and, in turn, the degree of benefit achieved for this population by way of what is called in public policy circles "deconcentration." The other important policy questions raised by Chicago's mode of reforming public housing center on the nature of the new "mixed-income communities" rising on the site of old-style public housing developments. Chicago's municipal government and the CHA have vigorously promoted mixed-income neighborhood plans, even in the face of public housing resident opposition and much uncertainty regarding the ultimate character of these new neighborhoods.

Both of these sets of policy questions are pertinent to public housing restructuring as it occurs across the United States. They are also of salience to the longstanding debates within the city planning profession concerning how to effectively and fairly involve residents in the development and implementation of revitalization strategies affecting their communities. The creation of these mixed-income communities is also of interest to policy makers and scholars attempting to understand contemporary trends in metropolitan development, especially the emergence of more residential and leisure activity-oriented central cities. In short, there is much that is local in the understanding of public housing transformation in Chicago, but this transformation is not simply a function of local factors. Readers of this volume will also note that several chapters link national policy trends—in particular, the evolution and national implementation of the federal government's HOPE VI program—to events in Chicago.

We wish to express our thanks to two members of the community of public housing policy analysts, researchers, and advocates whose work and personal insights have especially informed our own examination and interpretation of public housing issues: Sudhir Venkatesh of Columbia University and Lawrence Vale of the Massachusetts Institute of Technology. At M.E. Sharpe, Harry Briggs has been the most supportive of editors. As this book moved into production, Laurie Lieb did a terrific job of sorting out our sometimes awkward prose and frequently clashing citation methods. In overseeing production, Henrietta Toth combined precision and good humor.

Larry Bennett wishes to acknowledge research assistance that he has received from three former undergraduate students—Mike McDermott, Jamie Smith, and Matt Kitson—each having gone on either to graduate or law school. He also thanks Bill Sites for his helpful comments on an earlier version of Chapter 11.

Janet Smith wishes to acknowledge help with background research provided by Barbara Sherry, who is completing her PhD in Urban Planning at the University of Illinois at Chicago (UIC), Martha Glass, currently economic development planner at the UIC Voorhees Center and alumna of the Master of Urban Planning Program, and Daniel Cooper, who is currently a Master of Urban Planning student. Also, she thanks the UIC Great Cities Institute, where she was a Faculty Scholar in 1999–2000, for its support, encouragement, and space to research HOPE IV and begin documenting Chicago's plan to transform its public housing.

Pat Wright thanks Esteleta Cameron, program aide for the UIC Center for Urban Economic Development, Yittayih Zelalem, codirector of the UIC Voorhees Center, Martha Glass and Kelsa Rieger, alumna of the UIC Master of Urban Planning Program, for their assistance. She is also grateful to the following individuals whose commitments of time and insight contributed substantially to her writing of Chapter 6: Pamela Alfonso, James Field, Sarita Gupta, John LeFlore, Deidre Matthews, Rene Maxwell, Regina McGraw, Ethan Michaeli, Calvin Morris, Daniel Romero, Edward Shurna, Carol Steele, Lydia Taylor, Beauty Turner, Kate Walz, and Bill Wilen.

We could not have completed this project without the steadfastness of our spouses, Gwyn Friend, Jim Loellbach, and Dave Ranney, respectively. Thanks to all three of you! Finally, we dedicate this book to Wardell Yotaghan, departed colleague, friend, and continuing inspiration.

Where Are Poor People to Live?

Introduction

Larry Bennett, Janet L. Smith, and Patricia A. Wright

On January 6, 2000, the Chicago Housing Authority (CHA)—the third-largest public housing agency in the United States—released the final version of its "Plan for Transformation," an imposing set of documents laying out the ambitious new course of action that the long-troubled housing agency proposed to pursue over the next decade. The main provisions of the "Plan for Transformation" are the following. The CHA, whose housing portfolio had at one time approached 43,000 units, during the current decade plans to demolish 18,000 apartments, including all fifty-one of the agency's remaining "family" (that is, multiple-bedroom apartment) high-rise buildings. By 2010 the CHA housing stock is anticipated to number 25,000 units, all of which will be in sound physical condition—either renovated or newly constructed during the transformation process. The newly built public housing, rather than being clustered in low-income "projects," will form a component of "mixed-income" developments rising on the sites of some of the CHA's most notorious properties, such as the North Side Cabrini-Green complex. The Plan for Transformation is estimated to cost $1.5 billion and will necessitate the relocation of approximately 6,000 families.[1] By 2010 the CHA will be something akin to a public housing holding company: day-to-day property management and the provision of social services will be contracted out to private vendors.

The Plan for Transformation's program of action is currently well under way. In the last five years several thousand units of public housing have been demolished in Chicago, most notably at developments such as Robert Taylor Homes and Stateway Gardens, until recently prime components of the city's "State Street corridor" of public housing. Where once stood more than two dozen high-rise apartment buildings, stretching for approximately a mile south from Thirty-fifth Street on Chicago's South Side, there are now fewer than a half dozen buildings punctuating a huge, rectangular expanse of cleared land. Less visibly, the CHA has rehabilitated several thousand units of public housing reserved for senior citizens and issued housing vouchers to a somewhat smaller number of families seeking apartments in Chicago's private housing market.

For a decade and more, the CHA's internal problems and resulting struggles to upgrade the security of its resident population and to physically restore its properties have drawn the attention of politicians, policy experts, and social scientists across the United States. Moreover, journalistic accounts of life in public housing developments such as the Henry Horner and Robert Taylor Homes, as well as social science research conducted in the shadows of several of Chicago's major public housing complexes, have shaped national debates over such related topics as the "urban underclass," "concentrated poverty," and the "social isolation" of poor, racial minority populations.[2] Although for several reasons—including the degree of racial segregation experienced by its residents and the heavily politicized nature of its internal operations—the CHA has long been one of the extreme cases among U.S. public housing agencies (PHAs), its current approach to transformation, like its past failures, will resonate well beyond Chicago's municipal limits. In effect, by privatizing property management, pushing ahead with mixed-income residential redevelopment strategies, and increasingly depending on housing vouchers to assist low-income households, the CHA is forging a template for public housing redevelopment as it is likely to be pursued in the coming years by municipal and public housing officials across the country.

The principal aim of the editors and contributors to this volume is to provide a detailed account of how the CHA's Plan for Transformation is reshaping the lives of public housing residents in Chicago, defining a new vision of neighborhood development, and contributing to an associated restructuring of space in central Chicago. Apart from the vision expressed by the "Plan for Transformation" documents, nearly five years of experience with its implementation—which, in turn, have followed several years of preparatory planning and redevelopment work at particular CHA complexes—have provided a substantial knowledge base for assessing the Plan for Transformation's likely long-term impact on both Chicago's low-income renting population and its neighborhoods. Close inspection of the CHA's current drive to downsize, upgrade, and deconcentrate reveals flaws both in agenda and execution. Among the evident problems that have hampered the implementation of the Plan for Transformation have been conflicts between the CHA and the resident leadership at various of its developments and the geographic clustering (in effect, the resegregation) of CHA relocatees seeking private sector housing via federal Housing Choice (formerly Section 8) vouchers. Indeed, for the past decade—and well before the unveiling of the Plan for Transformation—a citywide Coalition to Protect Public Housing, founded by CHA residents, has sought to highlight the shortcomings of the CHA's approach to reorganizing its internal management, resident relations, and the general oversight of its developments. For readers having some familiarity with the checkered history of the CHA, these current points of conflict will not be surprising. Nevertheless, before we present the thematic propositions that structure the analysis offered in our subsequent chapters, as well as provide an overview of the chapters to come, we think that it is useful to offer a portrait of the life and times of this most troubled of local public housing agencies.

A Brief History of a Controversial Agency

The Chicago Housing Authority was the product of the Illinois General Assembly's Housing Authorities Act of 1937, a measure that was passed in response to that year's U.S. congressional action authorizing the public housing program.[3] During the late 1930s and early 1940s, the CHA built low-rise residential developments in a variety of locations on the city's North, West, and South Sides, while also taking over the management of developments such as the Jane Addams Houses, which had been built by the federal Public Works Administration.[4] During this period a significant portion of the CHA's tenants were workers in war-related industries.

The relative tranquility of the CHA's first decade was broken in the years just after World War II, during which "Chicago endured a pattern of urban guerilla warfare that was less related to ideological currents than to the ebb and flow of populations."[5] During the late 1940s and 1950s Chicago—whose housing stock had not grown appreciably since the 1920s, but whose population had spiked in response to the wartime industrial production boom—experienced a serious housing shortage. For its part, the CHA sought to provide accommodations for returning veterans and their families, which in some instances meant placing African Americans in white neighborhoods. In a series of incidents that began in 1946 at a temporary housing site near Midway Airport on the city's Southwest Side, white mobs, converging on the dwellings of African-American families, harassed and in some cases physically attacked the occupants. The CHA's executive director, Elizabeth Wood, was nevertheless committed to a program of racial integration within the agency's properties. Even as grassroots white resistance to residential integration spread across Chicago, becoming a matter of great concern for both ward-level politicians and municipal officials, the CHA followed a "neighborhood composition" standard in distributing units in its newly constructed developments. In effect, the CHA permitted the proportion of African-American residents within its developments to mirror the larger neighborhood's racial distribution. Although Wood's racial progressiveness aimed to work within the parameters of the locally acceptable, the growing restiveness of the city's Democratic Party leadership led to her ouster as head of the CHA in 1954.[6]

During the next fifteen years, the CHA pursued a program of sustained project development, building the huge Robert Taylor Homes complex (4,415 units) and completing other large projects, such as the approximately 3,500-dwelling Addams, Brooks, Loomis, and Abbott (ABLA) and Cabrini-Green developments. On the city's South and West Sides, many of the newly available residential units were filled with individuals and families displaced by the city's ongoing urban redevelopment initiatives. Even more critically, though, the vast majority of the CHA's "family" public housing units were constructed in African-American neighborhoods. Having won the right to review CHA siting plans in the late 1940s, Chicago's white city council members, by the mid-1950s, were systematically excluding new CHA developments from their wards.[7]

The beginning of the end of the CHA's era of mammoth project construction occurred on August 9, 1966, when a group of the agency's tenants sued it for violating federal constitutional and statutory civil rights protections by willfully segregating public housing residents.[8] In 1969, district judge Richard B. Austin ruled in favor of the *Gautreaux* plaintiffs, the first of a series of rulings that yielded the CHA's extremely dilatory efforts at scattered-site public housing construction in the 1970s and 1980s, but more consequentially, the Gautreaux Assisted Housing Program. This initiative, directed by a nonprofit organization, the Leadership Council for Metropolitan Open Communities, between the late 1970s and 1998—by way of the Section 8 housing voucher program—placed over 7,000 public housing–eligible families in racially mixed neighborhoods throughout Chicago and its suburbs.[9]

In the aftermath of Judge Austin's initial ruling, the CHA effectively ceased constructing public housing. Whereas the CHA had built more than 1,000 apartments annually from the mid-1950s until the end of the 1960s, from 1969 to 1980 the CHA's total production of residential units was 114.[10] Apart from the CHA's abrupt withdrawal from apartment construction, the 1960s also marked the point at which the quality of life within the agency's residential developments began its decades-long decline. A critical source of CHA housing deterioration in the 1960s was to be found in its rush to build units in the preceding years. At developments such as the Robert Taylor Homes, the number of residents on site—notably the legions of children overwhelming the development's corridors, elevators, and outdoor public spaces—quickly yielded an unceasing demand for building repairs.[11] And to make matters worse, the U.S. Congress's well-intentioned Brooke amendment of 1969, which capped resident rents at 25 percent of monthly income, undermined the CHA's already shaky fiscal well-being.[12] The Brooke amendment, of course, affected PHAs across the United States, but in Chicago the attenuation of revenue streams was coupled with extremely ineffective internal management. From the mid-1960s until the early 1980s, the person most closely associated with CHA operations was the politically connected real estate entrepreneur and chair of the CHA board of directors, Charles Swibel. Swibel's CHA bore little resemblance to a Weberian bureaucracy: executive positions were dominated by Democratic Party–affiliated personnel, internal accounting was erratic, and, favoritism in apartment assignments and responses to repair requests was used to pacify the resident population.[13]

Public attention to the failures of the CHA dates to at least the mid-1960s. In April of that year a prominent local journalist, M.W. Newman, published a week-long exposé of CHA problems in the *Chicago Daily News*.[14] In July 1970 two Chicago police officers were shot and killed on the grounds of Cabrini-Green, an incident that, according to residents, at first produced an intensive police crackdown, but was succeeded by years of systematic nonintervention while local gang conflict escalated.[15] By the early 1980s the U.S. Department of Housing and Urban Development (HUD) officials initiated a management audit of CHA operations and sought to remove Charles Swibel as chair of the CHA Board.[16] In late 1986, the CHA was added to HUD's list of "severely troubled" local public housing agencies.

The current era of CHA transformation can be dated from 1988 when Mayor Eugene Sawyer appointed Vincent Lane to head the CHA. Lane was a private real estate developer who had considerable experience running subsidized housing projects. From 1988 until his removal as chair of the CHA board in June 1995, Lane sought to reverse the fortunes of his agency through various measures: winning the CHA's first HOPE VI redevelopment grants, enforcing a controversial security crackdown in several of the agency's high-crime developments, and rehabilitating two CHA high-rise buildings as the mixed-income Lake Parc Place development (for very poor and working poor residents). However, during Lane's tenure at CHA a member of his management team was indicted for misuse of employee pension funds, and Lane himself was criticized for authorizing contracts with the Nation of Islam to provide building security services.[17] In 1991 Lane's CHA was sued by residents of the West Side Henry Horner Homes, who claimed that the public housing agency had withheld maintenance work to establish a pretext for closing down their development.[18] Four years later the plaintiffs and CHA reached a settlement providing for "one-for-one" replacement of public housing units as demolition of the Henry Horner high-rise structures proceeded. Moreover, despite much discussion of the agency's newfound commitment to project redevelopment via the mixed-income model, at major CHA developments such as Cabrini-Green, during the Lane years, little headway was made in actually producing workable redevelopment plans.

On May 31, 1995, Vincent Lane was joined at a press conference by Chicago mayor Richard M. Daley and HUD secretary Henry Cisneros to announce HUD's takeover of the CHA and, coincidentally, Lane's resignation as chair of the CHA board. From 1995 until 1999, the CHA was headed by a former HUD official, Joseph Shuldiner. Shuldiner committed himself to improving the CHA's internal management regime and advanced an ambitious, neighborhood-wide redevelopment proposal for Cabrini-Green and its surrounding area.[19] Also, as a result of congressional mandates attached to the Omnibus Consolidated Rescissions and Appropriations Act (OCRA) of 1996, the Shuldiner CHA performed "viability assessments" of developments holding nearly 19,000 housing units to determine if repairs were economically feasible.[20] The scale of demolitions that would have resulted from the direct implementation of the OCRA specifications undoubtedly set the stage for the adoption of the Plan for Transformation once control of the CHA returned to local hands in mid-1999. In the latter months of that year, CHA officials sought approval from the Clinton administration for their plan to initiate a complete overhaul of public housing operations in Chicago, even as they made the rounds of local public hearings and other civic forums to promote their vision of the new CHA.

In a letter to the *Chicago Tribune* in early 2000, CHA board chair Sharon Gilliam and agency CEO Phillip Jackson described the aims of the Plan for Transformation:

> Under the plan we submitted to the U.S. Department of Housing and Urban Development on Jan. 7, more than 24,000 new or completely rehabbed public housing units will be built in Chicago, enough to accommodate every current lease-compliant family. The plan also offers better access to needed services, which can help public housing residents get jobs, and dramatic increases in spending on property management to improve the everyday quality of life for residents. Included is some $350 million in improvements to senior housing, better security in partnership with the Chicago Police Department, private property management, less bureaucracy and an open and inclusive planning process that gives residents more direct input than they have ever had before in the redevelopment of public housing.[21]

These are indeed substantial claims. Five years into the implementation of the Plan for Transformation, and more than a decade beyond the CHA's initial efforts to redevelop major projects such as Cabrini-Green, it is time to take stock of the aims of public housing transformation in Chicago, as well as to assess how effectively public housing transformation has been implemented to this point.

Where Are Poor People to Live? Themes and Propositions

The national debates over the impoverishment of inner-city populations and the presumed failure of New Deal initiatives such as Aid to Families with Dependent Children and public housing have, for the most part, been structured by a group of theoretical perspectives and empirical assumptions emphasizing individual responsibility for a variety of social ills such as economic dependency, family disorder, and crime.[22] Coincidentally, a widespread perception of public bureaucratic failure—often tied to a conviction that private enterprise represents an inherently disciplined vehicle for structuring complex human initiatives and delivering "customer services"—has paved the way for institutional reforms expected to economize in the provision of social services while humanizing the link between government and citizen.[23]

These broadly framed assumptions, when applied to the restructuring of public and assisted housing programs in American cities, have produced a contemporary conventional wisdom that promotes the "devolution" of power from the federal government to localities, the "deconcentration" of former public housing residents, the privatization of public housing management functions, and the virtues of mixed-income neighborhood development.[24] It is our conviction that frequently in practice, and typically in principle, these assumptions are based on fundamental misunderstandings of why people in our society are poor, as well as poorly housed.[25] We offer the following set of alternative propositions to guide our readers in their investigation of the case studies and analytical perspectives offered in this volume's subsequent chapters, and as a challenge to other analysts of public housing reform in America. In the latter instance, it is our aim to suggest that an acceptance of the on-the-ground reality of the physical deterioration of public housing, as well as the broader phenomenon of inner-city economic collapse, does not necessarily yield the set of policy prescriptions that have become the new conventional wisdom of welfare reform and public housing restructuring.

(1) The emergent conventional wisdom of public housing reform objectifies public housing residents, and more broadly poor people, via the use of questionable characterizations such as "urban underclass" and through the application of dubious analytical perspectives such as "social isolation."[26]

One direct consequence of this objectification of public housing residents is the presumption by many policy experts and public housing "reformers" that in order to improve the lives of public housing residents, these individuals must be "acted upon" by progressive policy action: removed from deteriorated public housing neighborhoods, "treated" via programs inculcating better household and workplace skills, and relocated to ameliorative neighborhood environments.[27] Such initiatives can, furthermore—and quite appropriately—be implemented without engaging in serious consultation with public housing residents. In Chicago, the breakdown in consultation between the CHA and tenants has meant that an overwhelmingly African-American resident constituency has been relegated to a secondary and typically reactive role in the planning processes that have preceded the development of the new mixed-income communities that are replacing the old public housing.

The approach to public housing residents revealed by these policy preconceptions is reminiscent of the 1950s-era planners' attitude toward inner-city dwellers, who—in the words of political scientist James Q. Wilson— as "private regarding" individuals were not morally capable of playing a constructive consultative role in the design of neighborhood improvements.[28] Nor should the contemporary observer of public housing restructuring forget that the expert view of inner-city residents manifested by urban renewal advocates was linked to an excessive faith in the social and hygienic improvement of poor and working-class people that would result from the physical makeover of their neighborhoods. Urban renewal's physical utopia was high-rise modernism. In the case of contemporary public housing restructuring, the article of architectural faith is "new urbanism."[29]

(2) The process of policy devolution—delegating what had once been federal government initiatives and policy responsibilities to state and local governments—as reflected in public housing restructuring threatens the very foundation of what has been a long-standing national policy aspiration, to provide decent shelter for every American. Within the new mixed-income communities that are replacing conventional public housing developments, the need to use market-rate, housing-derived surpluses to fund their assisted housing components has already emerged as an ironclad justification for holding down the production of public housing units. More generally, the funding constraints that will certainly be associated with state and local government's newly inherited role as chief producer of affordable housing will lead to a diminution in the stock of publicly controlled affordable housing across America.

Nor is the optimistic vision offered by some advocates of public housing transformation—of affordable housing more widely distributed across the nation's metropolitan regions—guaranteed to follow in the wake of the federal government withdrawal from public housing production. Despite much talk of a new era in regional cooperation, multiple jurisdictional boundaries continue to divide the vast majority of metropolitan areas in the United States, and the popular sentiments driving land-use regulation in most suburban communities will also continue to resist the introduction of significant numbers of affordable rental housing units.[30] Practically speaking, as PHAs such as the Chicago Housing Authority transform and scale down their operations, neither the direct institutional means nor the requisite habits of interjurisdictional cooperation are in place to expand the choices of low-income residents seeking commodious, job-proximate shelter beyond the city limits.

(3) It is a remarkable juxtaposition of events that even as PHAs across America demolish residential units, offering their displaced former tenants housing vouchers to find shelter in the private market, in the nation's major metropolitan areas a growing affordable housing gap has emerged. In part, the undersupply of affordable rental housing is a function of local housing dynamics that reach back several decades: the slowing to a trickle of rental housing development for other than the high-end market, apartment-to-condominium conversions in gentrifying neighborhoods, and the abandonment or demolition of apartment buildings in deteriorating residential areas. But beyond housing market trends in major metropolitan areas, over the last generation there has been the concurrent leveling off of income growth among working-class and poor populations. Indeed, since the 1970s there has been a decline in the proportion of national income earned by the poorest 20 percent of Americans.[31] Or, to express the nature of this personal income or personal income/rental cost gap in another fashion, over the same period of time the incomes of renting Americans have increased by 6 percent. Among homeowners, income growth has been a substantially more robust 25 percent.[32]

Given the foregoing reality, the scaling down of the public housing program as a component of America's social safety net represents a cruel and destructive strategy. The editors and contributors to this volume are in agreement that a new era of affordable housing development and maintenance is long overdue. Nevertheless, in order to ensure that there will be an adequate supply of affordable housing widely available across urban America, the public sector must play a strong role either as the direct producer of affordable housing or as fiscal enabler and regulator of the affordable housing initiatives implemented by nonprofit and for-profit organizations.

(4) As we also demonstrate in the coming chapters, the majority of public housing residents in Chicago are neither passive victims of ill-conceived public policy nor social marginals whose character and aspirations need to

be uplifted by the efforts of forward-thinking policy makers. Indeed, the persistence and creativity revealed by Chicago's Coalition to Protect Public Housing (CPPH)—even as it has labored to communicate with constituents, who, due to the ongoing demolition and relocation activities of the CHA, are subject to substantial disruptions of their day-to-day lives—demonstrate that among the underutilized resources available to the decision makers seeking to remake public housing in Chicago are the experience and wisdom of CHA residents.

Nevertheless, the barriers confronting the CPPH as it moved beyond agenda setting and mobilization into the arenas of policy framing and implementation have been substantial. The group's public actions receive but limited media attention, and although it has forged an impressive number of interorganizational alliances, the CPPH has confronted a policy consensus that appears to be set in stone. Although there are vocal critics of the conventional wisdom of public housing salvation by public housing downsizing, a formidable coalition of public officials, civic leaders, foundation officers, and social scientists has maintained an unflinching commitment to the main provisions of the Plan for Transformation. This solid front in support of the particular mode of public housing rejuvenation selected in Chicago—even in the face of critical research and direct observation of various planning breakdowns at particular CHA developments—has, in effect, become a crucial means of disarming critics of the Plan for Transformation.

Looking Ahead

This volume is meant to break through the seemingly unyielding policy consensus driving public housing transformation in Chicago. The chapters that follow include contributions by activists, policy experts, and academic observers who examine both Chicago's chosen mode of public housing rejuvenation and the national context that has shaped the last decade's revolution in public housing. In reference to Chicago and its public housing residents and communities, the contributors focus on how mixed-income redevelopment and resident dispersal are likely to impact the lives of the city's low-income residents and reshape its network of residential neighborhoods.

In Part I of *Where Are Poor People to Live?* our contributors discuss the national forces that have shaped the Chicago Housing Authority's Plan for Transformation. Janet Smith, in Chapter 1, provides an account of national public housing policy and its twists and turns over the last decade and a half. In Chapter 2, Yan Zhang and Gretchen Weismann focus specifically on the federal government's HOPE VI program, interpreting the somewhat serendipitous political and policy convergences which, in the mid-1990s, recast an effort at public housing rehabilitation into a much more ambitious vision of public housing demolition and low-income neighborhood revitalization. Susan Popkin's Chapter 3 provides an overview of HOPE VI implementation across the United States, with a particular emphasis on the impact of new public housing environments and relocation from public housing on low-income families.

Our volume's second part focuses on the Chicago experience with HOPE VI, as well as the implementation of the CHA's Plan for Transformation. This section begins with Janet Smith's analysis in Chapter 4 of the ongoing Plan for Transformation. Chapter 5, by Pat Wright, is a detailed account of the emergence and evolution of the Coalition to Protect Public Housing, the CHA resident-led movement that has sought to respond to and modify the implementation of public housing downsizing in Chicago. Chapters 6 through 8 focus on the redevelopment processes at three major CHA complexes. In Chapter 6, Patricia Wright, Richard Wheelock, and Carol Steele discuss the contested redevelopment process at Cabrini-Green, whose local tenants, via the effective use of litigation, have won a considerable degree of oversight in reference to the neighborhood redevelopment of Cabrini-Green and adjoining properties. In Chapter 7, Larry Bennett, Nancy Hudspeth, and Patricia Wright discuss the rather different road to project transformation at the West Side ABLA Homes, where a compliant tenant leadership has largely acceded to a CHA and city of Chicago–driven redevelopment process. In Chapter 8, attorneys William Wilen and Rajesh Nayak discuss the stringent requirements that prospective low-income residents of mixed-income developments in Chicago must meet and contrast the experience of public housing residents affected by the Plan for Transformation with that of Henry Horner Homes residents. Like the Cabrini-Green residents, residents of the Horner Homes, due to a legal settlement reached in the 1990s, have managed to win a degree of influence over redevelopment processes (in this particular instance, resident relocation protocols) that is uncharacteristic of CHA transformation projects across the city.

The chapters in Part III of *Where Are Poor People to Live?* seek to derive lessons from the Chicago experience, examine issues that are likely to emerge as other cities pursue similar programs of public housing redevelopment, and offer insights toward the forging of more humane as well as more effective tools for developing and preserving affordable housing. In Chapter 9 William Wilen and Wendy Stasell address one of the most challenging public policy dilemmas posed by any concerted effort to rejuvenate public housing: the relative emphasis to be placed on maximizing access to decent quality housing as opposed to giving primacy to the racial integration of subsidized housing residents. In Chapter 10 Janet Smith discusses the design philosophy, new urbanism, that is so closely associated with HOPE VI–sponsored redevelopments in Chicago and across the United States. Smith examines the community-building philosophy advanced by new urbanist designers and the likelihood that this physical design model, as it is being applied to the CHA's new mixed-income developments, will in fact exercise a significant influence on the day-to-day interactions of neighborhood residents, locally based merchants, and neighborhood visitors. Larry Bennett, in Chapter 11, views the current redevelopment of public housing in Chicago against the longer arc of central city redevelopment efforts in this city and across the country. *Where Are Poor People to Live?* closes with an Epilogue, in which we discuss the most important lessons that are so far derivable from Chicago's ambitious campaign to revamp its public housing. The Epilogue also identifies a set of guiding principles and some promising alternative strategies that ought to be considered by progressive public officials, planners, and neighborhood activists seeking to develop socially equitable methods of inner-city rejuvenation and effective provision of shelter for low-income Americans.

Notes

1. Chicago Housing Authority, "Plan for Transformation," January 6, 2000.

2. Among the most important items in this literature, see Alex Kotlowitz, *There Are No Children Here* (New York: Doubleday, 1991); Nicholas Lemann, *The Promised Land* (New York: Vintage, 1992); Susan J. Popkin, Victoria E. Gwiasda, Lynn M. Olson, Dennis P. Rosenbaum, and Larry Buron, *The Hidden War: Crime and the Tragedy of Public Housing in Chicago* (New Brunswick, NJ: Rutgers University Press, 2000); Sudhir Alladi Venkatesh, *American Project* (Cambridge, MA: Harvard University Press, 2002); William Julius Wilson, *The Truly Disadvantaged* (Chicago: University of Chicago Press, 1987); and *When Work Disappears* (New York: Knopf, 1996).

3. Martin Meyerson and Edward C. Banfield, *Planning, Politics, and the Public Interest: The Case of Public Housing in Chicago* (New York: Free Press, 1964), p. 36.

4. Devereux Bowly Jr., *The Poorhouse: Subsidized Housing in Chicago, 1895–1976* (Carbondale: Southern Illinois University Press, 1978), pp. 17–54.

5. Arnold R. Hirsch, *Making the Second Ghetto: Race and Housing in Chicago, 1940–1960* (New York: Cambridge University Press, 1983), p. 41.

6. Roger Biles, *Richard J. Daley: Politics, Race, and the Governing of Chicago* (DeKalb: Northern Illinois University Press, 1995), pp. 87–88; Hirsch, *Making the Second Ghetto,* pp. 234–238.

7. Hirsch, *Making the Second Ghetto,* pp. 241, 257.

8. Leonard S. Rubinowitz and James E. Rosenbaum, *Crossing the Class and Color Lines: From Public Housing to White Suburbia* (Chicago: University of Chicago Press, 2000), pp. 23–24.

9. Rubinowitz and Rosenbaum, *Crossing the Class and Color Lines.*

10. Hirsch, *Making the Second Ghetto,* p. 265.

11. Venkatesh, *American Project,* pp. 21–29.

12. Susan J. Popkin, Larry F. Buron, Diane K. Levy, and Mary K. Cunningham, "The Gautreaux Legacy: What Might Mixed-Income and Dispersal Strategies Mean for the Poorest Public Housing Tenants?" *Housing Policy Debate* 11, no. 4 (2000): 915.

13. Steven Gittelson, "The Battle Over Charlie Swibel," *Chicago Magazine,* July 1982, pp. 101–103, 128–132; D. Bradford Hunt, "Anatomy of a Disaster: Designing and Managing the Second Ghetto," paper presented at the American Historical Association Annual Convention, Chicago, January 9, 2000.

14. Venkatesh, *American Project,* pp. 44–45.

15. Steve Bogira, "Prisoners of the War Zone," *Chicago Reader,* October 3, 1986.

16. Gittelson, "The Battle Over Charlie Swibel."

17. Sandy Banisky, "Chicago Housing Authority Watches Its Best Efforts Fail," *Baltimore Sun,* June 18, 1995.

18. Cory Oldweiler, "Horner Moves at Faster Pace, But Much Work Remains," *Chicago Reporter,* March 1998 (www.chicagoreporter.com/). See also Chapter 8 of this volume.

19. Larry Bennett and Adolph Reed, "The New Face of Urban Renewal: The Near North Redevelopment Initiative and the Cabrini-Green Neighborhood," in *Without Justice for All,* ed. Adolph Reed Jr., pp. 175–211 (Boulder, CO: Westview Press, 1999).

20. Harold Henderson, "There Goes Their Neighborhood," *Chicago Reader,* May 29, 1998.

21. Sharon Gilliam and Phillip Jackson, "CHA Strives for Positive Image," letter to the *Chicago Tribune,* February 2, 2000.

22. Michael B. Katz, *The Undeserving Poor* (New York: Pantheon Books, 1989), pp. 185–235; Alice O'Connor, *Poverty Knowledge: Social Science, Social Policy, and the Poor in Twentieth Century U.S. History* (Princeton, NJ: Princeton University Press, 2001), pp. 242–283.

23. Stephen Goldsmith, *The Twenty-first Century City* (Lanham, MD: Rowman & Littlefield, 1999); David Osborne and Ted Gaebler, *Reinventing Government* (Reading, MA: Addison-Wesley, 1992).

24. Henry G. Cisneros, "Urban Entrepreneurialism and National Economic Growth," Washington, DC, U.S. Department of Housing and Urban Development, September 1995; City of Chicago, "Holistic Urban Redevelopment: The ABLA Homes Model," n.d.; Mark Alan Hughes, "A Mobility Strategy for Improving Opportunity," *Housing Policy Debate* 6, no. 1 (1995): 271–295.

25. The following discussion of current social policy in the United States reflects the views of this volume's three editors.

26. Jeff Crump, "Deconcentration by Demolition: Public Housing, Poverty, and Urban Policy," *Environmental and Planning D: Society and Space* 20 (2002): 581–596; Bennett and Reed, "New Face of Urban Renewal"; O'Connor, *Poverty Knowledge,* pp. 266–272.

27. Edward G. Goetz, *Clearing the Way: Deconcentrating the Poor in Urban America* (Washington, DC: Urban Institute Press, 2003), pp. 21–88.

28. James Q. Wilson, "Planning and Politics: Citizen Participation in Urban Renewal," in *Urban Renewal: The Record and the Controversy,* ed. James Q. Wilson, pp. 407–421 (Cambridge, MA: M.I.T. Press, 1966).

29. Blair Kamin, "Can Public Housing Be Reinvented?" *Architectural Record,* February, 1999, pp. 84–89.

30. Peter Dreier, John Mollenkopf, and Todd Swanstrom, *Place Matters: Metropolitics for the Twenty-first Century* (Lawrence: University Press of Kansas, 2001), pp. 99–102; Goetz, *Clearing the Way,* pp. 101–105, 183–186. Also see Trine Tsouderos, "North Shore Dwellers Target Housing Law," *Chicago Tribune,* August 2, 2004.

31. Dreier, Mollenkopf, and Swanstrom, *Place Matters,* p. 15; Frank Levy, *The New Dollars and Dreams* (New York: Russell Sage Foundation, 1998), p. 50. See also David Leonhardt, "More Americans Were Uninsured and Poor in 2003, Census Finds," *New York Times,* August 27, 2004.

32. Joint Center for Housing Studies of Harvard University, *The State of the Nation's Housing 2002,* 2002, p. 19.

Part I

NATIONAL AND LOCAL CONTEXT FOR PUBLIC HOUSING TRANSFORMATION

1

Public Housing Transformation

Evolving National Policy

Janet L. Smith

Are we now at a third turning point:
dismantling the federal role in housing?

Always a tentative player on the American housing scene, the federal government might be best described as "reluctant" when it comes to public housing. Built on an unstable foundation, public housing was made possible by the Wagner-Steagall Housing Act of 1937, which allowed government to fund, build, and own homes to rent to its poor citizens. At the time, it was pitched as a way not only to improve abhorrent living conditions but also to stimulate the economy by creating jobs in construction and related industries. Despite the potential economic benefits—clearly important in the 1930s—members of the housing industry as well as Congress were concerned that publicly owned housing went beyond the purview of the U.S. government. Whether they feared "creeping socialism" or too much government intervention in the private market, or just believed that housing was a "local problem," many people insisted that housing development was not a function of government.[1]

Now, more than sixty years later, public housing policy stands at a crossroad. The federal government has been called "the largest slumlord in the nation," and many critics have declared public housing an embarrassment if not a mistake. At this third turning point, as Peter Dreier has christened the current state of U.S. housing policy, the original debate over whether or not we should even have public housing is being revisited.[2] After first getting government involved in the regulation of housing for the poor about a hundred years ago via tenement laws (first turning point) and then formally with enactment of the 1937 Housing Act (second turning point), federal lawmakers have recently devolved a great deal of authority and responsibility to local government and the private sector in order to deal with the public housing problem. Driving this decision is the view that the concentration of poor people in public housing, which is associated with a whole range of other social problems including high rates of crime, drug and alcohol abuse, domestic violence, and unemployment, is no longer appropriate. The solution, as mandated by current policy, is to "transform public housing" by spending billions of public dollars to tear down more than 100,000 units—most in high-rise towers built in the 1950s and 1960s—and replace most but not all of them with lower-density, low-rise, mixed-income developments. Residents are being relocated either permanently or temporarily with housing assistance vouchers as redevelopment takes place. The private sector is playing a prominent role in the process, with for-profit developers getting into the business of public housing redevelopment.

Transformation is both promising and controversial. On one hand, it provides an opportunity and the resources to improve the terrible, often uninhabitable living conditions of many public housing residents. On the other, these efforts stand to significantly reduce the number of permanent public housing units, disrupt the lives of residents at many sites, and cost millions of tax dollars with little guarantee or evidence that the outcome will fully meet the social goals of the program. This latter point is particularly problematic. Current national policy supports "the intentional mixing of incomes and working status of residents"[3] on the grounds that it will "promote the economic and social interaction of low-income families within the broader community, thereby providing greater opportunities for the upward mobility of such families."[4] While this goal sounds promising, we have virtually no evidence affirming its likelihood.[5] Despite the lack of evidence, policy now aims to make up for previous mistakes in the design and development of public housing that led to the social isolation of very low-income families, mostly African-American, and to redress the negative externalities that public housing has produced in surrounding communities.

Like welfare, public housing is being reinvented and represented as "new and improved." This chapter looks back at the historical roots of U.S. public housing policy in order to explain current efforts to transform and dismantle it, preparing a broader context for the dramatic change that is taking place in Chicago. Using the same turning points as Peter Dreier, the following provides an overview of legislative history, focusing on landmark decisions that affect where poor people live now and that, in turn, will probably determine where they can live in the future.

Origins

The first turning point marking government involvement in housing for the poor came in the late 1890s when activists worked to enact some of the first tenement laws defining health and safety minimums for slum buildings (e.g., see New York City Tenement House Act of 1901). Advocates like Alice Griffith in San Francisco hoped that light, air, and space standards would lead to construction of better living conditions for the throngs of immigrants coming to work in cities. Social reformers, such as Jane Addams and Mary Simkovitch, saw these laws fitting into a larger effort to civilize cities and, depending on your point of view, either uplift the masses or keep them under control.[6]

Although there were some successful attempts by philanthropists to build affordable homes for slum dwellers, the profitability of the "slum business" made these efforts the exception rather than the norm.[7] Furthermore, efforts to make tenement law federal policy failed since most legislators viewed regulation in general as "market interference" and housing specifically as a problem for local rather than national government. Why then is this period a turning point in federal public housing policy? The answer has less to do with the actual creation of legislation and more to do with three precedents set. First, the period introduced formal mechanisms by which government could regulate the development of housing to protect the health and safety of its poor citizens. While not necessarily successful at the time in getting private developers to comply, these regulations did get government involved. As a result, quality standards to offset threats to life and health have become a mainstay of all local and national housing policy in the United States. Moreover, these regulations have become fairly standard, initially through development of uniform building codes adopted by cities looking to not re-invent the wheel, and then through various federal policies over the years that required meeting minimum quality standards in exchange for resources.

Second, this time period affirmed early on the sacrosanct role of local government in providing housing for the poor. In part, this sentiment is driven by the fundamental federalist principle that in certain matters, local government is the best level at which to determine and implement policy since it can be more responsive than federal government to specific concerns. However, the politics of welfare policy in the United States has also given local government control over the design and implementation of programs for the poor; rather than mandating participation, each jurisdiction can choose to participate in the public housing program. This approach gave local elected officials the ability to assess the value of social welfare in terms of political capital and the prospect of the citizenry expressing its view directly at the polls or with their feet.

Third, atrocious living conditions in the late nineteenth century made it a lightning rod for social experimentation in the design and development of housing for the poor. Many people believed in "physical determinism"—just as controversial now as it was then—the theory that the design of buildings and open space can produce desired behavior such as reducing criminal activity or building community among residents. Whether driven by utopian visions of a just world, a civil society, or a beautiful city, the justification a hundred years ago was not that different from now: we have no excuse in this modern world, given the advances in technology and knowledge; we should be able to construct places that will benefit the poor living in them and inevitably all of society. Then and now, these ideas often come from a small set of activists and the reform-minded middle class whose vision for improving the slums appeals to our desire to perfect society or at least to rid cities of unsightly buildings and unsafe tenements.

The second turning point in U.S. housing policy is marked by the formal involvement of the federal government in the 1930s with passage of two distinct yet inextricably linked pieces of legislation. As already noted, the 1937 Public Housing Act brought government into the production and ownership of housing. Specifically, the law established (1) a permanent federal agency to deal with subsidized housing, (2) a method for transferring federal money to local authorities, (3) slum clearance as a public function, (4) the principle of charging rent relative to income, (5) the principle of using federal subsidies to make up the differential between operating costs and rents paid by low-income tenants, (6) a policy of local tax exemption of property to further subsidize rents, and (7) the principle that planning, building, and managing was the responsibility of local government. Clearly, this was a significant piece of legislation since it created a means for the federal government to provide funds and "authority" to local governments wishing to remove substandard housing in the private sector and replace it with new quality housing for the poor built by the public sector. However, local government per se would not necessarily own the properties; instead, a public housing authority (PHA) would be created. Each PHA would have a clearly defined mandate and geography in which to realize the legislative goal to "remedy the unsafe and unsanitary housing conditions and the acute shortage of decent, safe, and sanitary dwellings for families of lower income."[8]

A key feature of this legislation was making participation optional—local government could choose to but did not have to participate in the public housing program. As a result, the Chicago Housing Authority (CHA) was created in order to borrow federal funds to build and then operate public housing. As with any district that has fiscal responsibilities, housing authorities were enabled through state legislation, and each one had to be authorized by the jurisdiction (usually a city or county) in which it operated. In Chicago, this meant that elected city officials annually granted the CHA the right to operate in its jurisdiction. Also, since federal law required any property containing public housing to be tax-exempt, a written agreement to forgo property tax along with other requirements of the exchange, including who has final say on siting decisions, was produced as a legally binding document that had to be approved by elected officials in the local government forgoing taxes. From the start, then, the housing authority was dependent on local and federal government. Without the federal government, there were no funds to develop buildings and without local government there really was no ability to put those funds to use.

While monumental, the Wagner-Steagall Act came on the heels of legislation that many scholars consider really at the heart of modern housing policy in the United States. The National Housing Act of 1934 created the Federal Housing Administration (FHA), which made it possible for government to underwrite and insure mortgages so that more families could purchase homes. Before this time, purchasing a home required a great deal of money up front (often 50 percent of the value) and then quick repayment that ballooned at the end of five years. FHA mortgages fully amortized both the principle and the interest over the life of the loan, which made it possible to mortgage more of the actual home value. This feature was obviously a benefit to the purchaser; meanwhile, the lender had the federal government backing the loan in case of default (an obvious concern given the high numbers of mortgage defaults in the early 1930s). To further offset this risk, the government created a secondary market, the Federal National Mortgage Association (Fannie Mae), to buy the mortgages from lenders so they could keep more money liquid, thereby levering more loans to individual buyers.

As with public housing, the creation of the FHA was expected to stimulate the economy by changing the way people borrowed money to buy homes. Unlike public housing, this policy created demand rather than merely responding to it, sparking development that in turn created employment opportunities in the construction, real estate, and banking industries. The immediate effect was an increase in housing starts for the first time since the mid-1920s that continued until World War II. The long-term effect, whether intended or not, was the shift from a country primarily of renters to one dominated by homeowners.

When looked at together, the housing acts of 1934 and 1937 launched the modern housing system, helping to transform methods of production and consumption for all. However, as Gail Radford describes in her book *Modern Housing for America: Policy Struggles in the New Deal Era*, they also marked the beginning of a two-tiered system of housing policy—a means-tested program that directly produced public housing for poor people to rent and a targeted program that indirectly produced private housing for middle-income families to buy.[9] Not only did this system divide public and private sector roles in the production of housing, it changed the urban landscape and determined where poor people lived. In general, cities contain most of the public housing in the United States while most of the FHA-insured homes are in the suburbs. This pattern, which many scholars believe exacerbated economic and racial segregation in urban areas across the country, has clear roots in the ability of local government to choose whether or not to be part of the federal public housing system.[10]

Partisan politics at the federal level reinforced a bifurcated system of housing production over the years with each side supporting different and even opposing strategies to expand the supply of affordable housing for poor people. Generally speaking, Republicans have favored *distributive* programs that stimulate economic growth through private sector activity while Democrats have promoted direct assistance and intervention in the market via *redistributive* programs.[11] Distributive programs like the FHA, while not directly benefiting the poor, were presumed to help via "filtering," freeing up older homes as families moved into newer ones. In contrast, poor people directly benefited from public housing; however, it was considered expensive to taxpayers when compared to filtering, which cost relatively little and generated a lot more taxes than public housing. The public housing program also created a long-term dependency on federal taxes, since housing authorities needed funds to cover the gap between rents charged and operating expenses. As part of the highly political annual appropriations process, this aspect of public housing proved a major impediment to the program over time. In part, this was because funding often fell short of what was needed, but also because the annual appropriation process perpetually reopened the debate as to whether or not public housing was the best use of taxpayer money.

Evolution

Peter Marcuse has argued that the image of the benevolent state in U.S. housing policy is really a myth and that the federal government has never been very concerned with meeting the housing needs of the poor.[12] Instead, publicly assisted housing has been a means to deal with other problems, such as preventing the spread of disease, jump-starting the economy, accommodating the workers who bolstered U.S. manufacturing efforts during World War II, and dealing with unrest among poor people in cities. Clearly, coalition politics made it necessary for supporters of public housing in the 1930s to pitch it as the solution to multiple problems beyond the immediate need for decent, affordable housing for poor people. The challenge once the Wagner-Steagall Act became law, however, was then sustaining the support of the alliance of the seemingly strange bedfellows—real estate and construction trades, labor unions, settlement house workers, plus an array of other housing activists—needed to pass the act. The wear and tear of coalition politics helps to explain why U.S. policy is more a collection of programs shaped for the most part by ideological differences between Republicans and Democrats and less an "evolution of sophistication and effectiveness in dealing with the problems of bad housing."[13]

The legislative history that brings us to this third turning point is complex, given the many laws and amendments developed over the years to fund, regulate, maintain, and renovate public housing. A few key pieces of legislation, however, highlight the contribution of past policy in the production of concentrated poverty and racial segregation, which is, at least rhetorically, what transformation aims to transform. Table 1.1 outlines several housing acts and amendments that have shaped directly and indirectly the look and location of where poor people's homes—specifically, where public housing was located and what it looked like since first legally conceived in 1937.

Three overarching themes appear in this list: demolition, design, and devolution. Demolition is just that—the razing of buildings and the justification for it—whether slum housing or public housing. Design encompasses the form and scale of replacement buildings and, to a certain extent, goes hand-in-glove with demolition since policy makers are usually try to offer something that is better than what they authorized to be torn down with federal money. Devolution refers to shifting down to a lower level of government the responsibility for implementing policy.[14] While often thought of as a recent phenomenon in federal housing policy for the poor, as already noted, this role of local government has more or less always trumped efforts at setting a national agenda. And even though the 1937 act set a precedent for a national role in housing for the poor, public housing (and subsequent subsidized development in later years) always gave a great deal of power to local government, at least initially, in deciding whether or not to participate.

Demolition

The 1949 Housing Act is remembered as both a high and a low in U.S. housing policy. At the pinnacle was the bold goal of decent housing for everyone, setting an ambitious production target of 810,000 public housing units to be constructed in six years. At the bottom was the slum clearance program that decimated neighborhoods, many of which were occupied by poor African-Americans.[15] Demolition was justified on the basis that the housing (and

Table 1.1

Key Legislation Shaping Public Housing in the United States Since 1937

Legislation and year enacted	Action initiated
Housing Act of 1949	Declared that every American deserves a "decent home and suitable living environment" through urban redevelopment. The act included: • financing for slum clearance (Title I); • increasing FHA mortgage insurance for home buyers (Title II); and • committing federal funds to develop 810,000 new public housing units, primarily on land where slum clearance had taken place, to replace lost units (Title III).
Housing Act of 1954	Introduced urban renewal, which focused on conservation rather than clearance through a "workable program" of rehabilitating and upgrading urban "slum and blight" areas. The act aimed to increase private sector contributions, responsibility of local government, and citizen participation and to use fewer federal dollars to produce more results.
Housing and Community Development Act of 1974	Sought to develop viable urban communities by providing decent housing, suitable living environment, and expanding economic opportunities principally for low- and moderate-income families. Replaced categorical grants with community development block Grant (CDBG) and introduced Section 8 rent supplements for new, existing, and rehabbed rental housing plus funding for development of affordable housing by private sector.
Tax Reform Act of 1986	Eliminated some tax provisions that favored low-income rental housing production and instituted a tax credit system authorizing states to give "tax credit" to property owners to offset taxes on income. Tax credits are generally sold to outside investors, usually syndicated, to raise initial development funds for a project. Projects must have at least 20 percent of units for households at or below 50 percent of median or 40 percent of units for households at or below 60 percent of area median income. Rents are not to exceed 30 percent of income at these thresholds.
Cranston-Gonzales National Affordable Housing Act of 1990	Focused attention on the availability of affordable housing for low- and moderate-income families, and created the HOME program, which provided new resources for nonprofit and public agencies to develop affordable rental and for-sale housing.

businesses too) in many old cities was unsafe due to extreme disrepair. Whole blocks of homes and apartment buildings were deemed unsafe for continued habitation according to different measures of "slum and blight" including overcrowding—a common feature of Chicago's South Side, where thousands of low-income African-Americans, due to vigorously enforced residential segregation, lived in chopped-up "kitchenette" apartments. While over-crowded, the housing stock itself was not always in such bad shape that it warranted demolition. This was the case for the Mecca Flats apartments, a tenement that eventually was torn down following a long struggle that included tenant petitions and other efforts to block the wrecking ball.[16]

While some public housing was built on such land, the amount fell far short of the 810,000-unit goal. In part, federal appropriations were never sufficient to produce that many units. However, even if the funding had existed, there was good reason to believe that local governments and PHAs could not or would not be able to produce such a large number of housing units in such a short period of time. Whether due to lack of political will, racial discrimina-tion, or just sheer refusal to build public housing, new construction never kept up with demolition. Slum clearance meant that land was open for develop-ment, and many cities preferred to replace the low-tax-paying slum dwellers with higher-income families or other users that could help in the revitalization of neighborhoods. For example, rather than replacement housing for the ten-ants at Mecca Flats, the Illinois Institute of Technology expanded and built Crown Hall—a structure designed by Mies van der Rohe—on its site.

Meanwhile, the supply of decent affordable housing continued to fall short of demand in most cities, particularly those with old stock built during rapid industrialization. This was a problem in Chicago, which had an abundance of cold-water flats and overcrowded buildings that really did qualify as blight, but were often the only choice for poor blacks whose housing options were limited by discrimination and a dual housing market. To a certain degree, the 1954 Housing Act was a response to these challenges, shifting attention to the conservation of existing affordable housing units for low-income fami-lies. A "workable program" was required to ensure that local redevelopment plans could be completed. However, having a workable plan did not always mean it was implemented in its entirety, and it did not guarantee that people would not be displaced.[17]

While many communities too deteriorated to redevelop ended up in the slum clearance category anyway, "urban renewal" set a precedent for revitalizing and reusing housing rather than tearing it down. Besides staving off further need for demolition and therefore potentially saving taxpayer money, urban renewal also offered cities a means to preserve poor neighborhoods without forcing the occu-pants out. In other words, not only could urban renewal potentially improve poor housing conditions, it also had the potential to keep poor people from moving into other neighborhoods, thus, as some feared, contributing to decline in those areas. In later years, some critics considered these efforts, especially in black communities, "gilding the ghetto" rather than rebuilding communities, because little was done to deal with the larger systemic issue of racial and economic segregation that had contributed to the decline in many of these neighborhoods in the first place.[18] Still, urban renewal set in motion the idea that communities could be revitalized before they became completely deteriorated.

Design

Public housing design in the United States has always been influenced by modernist architecture, including ideas about form and function and the push to use new materials and building technology. However, this did not initially produce the high-rise buildings associated with public housing today. Initially, "modern" public housing in Chicago and elsewhere was low-rise multifamily buildings and townhouses, often at the same density as housing being produced by private sector developers—but at a larger scale on a single site. Many housing experts consider the 1949 Housing Act the culprit behind the shift to high-rise public housing in the United States. While the act itself did not mandate the form or design of buildings per se, high-rise construction offered a means to meet the very ambitious production goals. The high-rise thus became the only workable solution, especially given limited funding from Congress. Not only presumed to be cost-effective in construction given new technology and the materials used (e.g., poured concrete framing), the high-rise made it possible to build even more units on the same amount of land, which could then accommodate more families being displaced by slum clearance.

Utilizing the Corbusier-inspired "tower in the park" for public housing development was presumed to be a more efficient and effective use of the land. This logic came from both architects and planners. For example, Walter Gropius argued for high-rise buildings in the 1930s on the principle that as height increases so should the space between buildings in order to ensure adequate sunlight for the occupants. As a result, more intense development of a site meant more land could be used for recreation.[19] Similar logic came with the superblock, which was an aggregation of normal urban blocks that allowed more flexibility in configuring buildings but also meant less surface street to pave and less overall infrastructure to develop and maintain. When combined, the high-rise and superblock model resulted in a substantially smaller proportion of the land—as little as 15 percent—being covered by buildings and a great proportion used to provide an open "park-like" space where children could play.[20]

Despite the many good intentions, the high-rise was sharply criticized even before ground was broken. A key concern then, as it is today, was that these buildings were not appropriate for families, especially ones with small children. Supervision of kids playing in the park would require parents to come down from the tower instead of just looking out their window.[21] Critics who considered the buildings themselves to be suitable were concerned that the high-rise did not fit within the design trend for private housing at the time, which was single-family detached homes with individual yards and driveways. As Alexander von Hoffman argues:

> The point here is not that effective child rearing is impossible in high-rise buildings—families live contentedly in the high-rises of Hong Kong and even New York City—but rather that the commitment to tall buildings was unrealistic and out of keeping with American tastes and values. While officials insisted on high-rises, the working and middle-classes were rejecting apartments and flocking en masse to inexpensive single-family homes in the suburbs.[22]

In this regard, the design itself of public housing created not only islands for the poor, but visible beacons of poverty in many cities at a time when cities were losing their middle class. As a result, public housing did not appear to produce the positive results proclaimed by urban renewal policy.

Devolution

The 1954 Housing Act set the stage for a more prominent role for and dependence on the local actors in the private sector to produce and manage affordable housing for poor people. However, it was the 1974 Housing and Community Development Act that effectively ended the public building of public housing. What many housing experts consider a watershed event, the 1974 act came in the middle of scandals, both in the White House and in communities across America. For the latter, the perceived problem was that perhaps the federal government had made a mistake when it began offering money directly to local developers to build low-cost affordable housing. Although bypassing local public housing authorities had some benefits, including bypassing the politics of siting new development, it also had potential pitfalls. Programs in the 1960s, such as Section 235 and 236, for example, had produced thousands of units fairly quickly, but often by fledgling nonprofit organizations that had limited knowledge about affordable housing development. When some projects fell into default on payments, they not only made local headlines but also made federal officials look bad.

The Housing and Community Development Act of 1974 was an attempt to change that image and reality. The sea change came with the Section 8 program, which provided tenant-based assistance (first in the form of certificates, then vouchers) and funding to help the private sector build affordable housing. Involving the private sector was an attempt to bring up to a professional standard the housing product and to minimize investment risk. Tenant-based assistance was a way to respond to demand without building in order to get out of the looming future cost of plans laid by President Richard Nixon's predecessor. Before leaving office, President Lyndon Johnson had set a goal of producing nearly 10 million units of low- and moderate-income housing subsidized by the federal government. Another significant change Nixon made was to consolidate dozens of federal grant programs into the community development block grant (CDBG) program, which would distribute funds annually to urban areas using a needs-based formula. Referred to as "New Federalism," the CDBG program gave local government the responsibility of determining how best to use its allocation of federal funds for housing and community development.

CDBG was significant for community development since it changed the way local nonprofit developers accessed government money. The Section 8 program, however, marked the end of new public housing development since it ostensibly shifted development funds from PHAs to the private sector (both for- and not-for-profit). The Section 8 construction subsidy guaranteed the developer enough money to cover the cost of constructing or rehabbing a building and then to keep rents affordable for low-income renters in at least a portion of the units. These properties were like public housing, because tenants paid a fixed portion of their income for rent (originally 25 percent and now 30 percent) while the federal government paid the rest. To make this system work, a project-based subsidy was guaranteed to the property owner for each unit designated for and occupied by a low-income tenant. In these buildings, tenants are still paying only 30 percent of their income for rent. The monthly rent subsidy remains with the unit, which keeps it affordable for the next low-income family that moves in.

The Section 8 rent subsidy—the most familiar part of the law—was a guarantee to the tenant and the landlord that the federal government would subsidize the rent owed. Unlike the project-based subsidy, a tenant-based voucher "travels with" each family in the form of an official document that says that the government will pay its share of rent as long as the family and the housing unit qualify.[23] A qualified unit is one that meets certain quality standards and has a monthly rent that the government considers reasonable. If the family moves, the voucher (and therefore the rent subsidy) moves with them for as long as they qualify for assistance.

Combined, project-based and tenant-based Section 8 provides assistance to about 3 million households annually, split about equally between both. While this program clearly has the potential advantage of distributing poor people rather than concentrating them as public housing tended to do, it also faces the same problem that public housing did: resistance to both tenants and buildings coming into middle-income neighborhoods. As a result, cities often have higher numbers and proportions of the Section 8 units built under this program and of tenants using vouchers in private rental units than suburbs do. Further, in some cities, the concentration of buildings and tenants has been blamed, just like public housing, for community decline.[24] Whether the cause or not, the Section 8 program came to have an image that was more similar to than different from that of the public housing that preceded it.

A decade later, in 1986, devolution continued with changes in the U.S. tax code that significantly altered the production of private rental housing. First, the law narrowed how depreciation was calculated (among other things), making ownership of rental property less favorable from a tax shelter perspective. Second, the low-income housing tax credit (LIHTC) was introduced as a new tool for generating capital for affordable housing development. The basic premise of the LIHTC is that investors buy tax credits from developers, who then use this capital to develop affordable rental property. There is a formula for determining the credits and proportion of units by income target for each development (either up to 40 percent or up to 60 percent of the area median income). This ensures that units are targeting low- and moderate-income households (often referred to as working poor) and that they stay affordable for at least the life of the tax credit (fifteen years), assuming the building meets specific performance targets each year, if not longer for most developments (up to thirty years).

The limit to the LIHTC program, of course, is that it generally does not target very poor people. Similar criticism has been directed at the HOME program, introduced in 1990. In part this is because the Cranston-Gonzales Act, which created it, focused on a wide range of issues, giving more attention for the first time to people being priced out of the for-sale market. Ratcheting up the targeted income bracket, then, meant that while the act itself brought new funds for affordable housing, it would produce relatively few units to house very poor people. In the meantime, public housing was falling into disrepair, increasingly becoming the stepchild of federal housing policy.

Creating HOPE

Current policy to transform public housing evolved from the HOPE VI program. HOPE stands for Housing Opportunities for People Everywhere.[25]

HOPE VI grew out of the work of the National Commission on Severely Distressed Public Housing, a congressional committee formed in 1989 to "explore the factors contributing to structural, economic, and social distress; identify strategies for remediation; and propose a national action plan to eradicate distressed conditions by the year 2000."[26] This committee concluded that while the majority of the 1.4 million units of public housing were well maintained and managed, a small portion of units—86,000 or about 6 percent —were in "the most distressed and notorious urban developments in the nation, where crime, poverty, unemployment, and dependency were solidly entrenched."[27] In Chicago, this portion included most of the housing, but such developments as Cabrini-Green and the Robert Taylor Homes were cited most often, given their national reputation for crime and extreme poverty.

In 1992, the $5 billion Urban Revitalization Demonstration was officially launched to deal with the estimated 86,000 units in need of revitalization or demolition. Renamed HOPE VI the following year, the program's appropriations and grant-making authority ran to fiscal year 2002.[28] Structured as a competitive grant process, PHAs could get up to $50 million to turn around worst-case developments. These funds could be used to rehabilitate, raze, and rebuild in order to transform "the projects" into lower-density, high-quality public housing communities. Framing the redevelopment strategy was a plan submitted with each PHA's application that would be developed in conjunction with residents.

To a certain extent, the idea for HOPE VI has its roots in the 1972 demolition of the Pruitt-Igoe project in St. Louis, a pivotal moment in U.S. public housing that marked the beginning of a new era in public housing.[29] As the buildings came down, a new vision of public housing was already forming in their place. Fueling an already smoldering debate among architects and planners, demolition of the sprawling Pruitt-Igoe complex made it easy to question the architecture of public housing itself in shaping the destiny of poor families, as did Oscar Newman's work on defensible space.[30] Pruitt-Igoe also introduced the idea that residents could be involved in the management and redevelopment of their housing.[31]

At its core, HOPE VI aimed to transform public housing by changing its physical space (i.e., buildings, site plan, scale), establishing positive incentives for resident self-sufficiency and comprehensive services that empower residents, lessening concentrations of poverty by placing public housing in nonpoverty neighborhoods and promoting mixed-income communities, and forging partnerships with other agencies, local governments, nonprofit organizations, and private businesses to leverage support and resources. Beyond improving housing quality, social services were proposed to help transform the occupants of public housing as well. As former secretary of the Depart-

ment of Housing and Urban Development (HUD) Andrew Cuomo emphasized, HOPE VI had a broad agenda: "This program is about much more than
rebuilding housing. . . . We will give them [residents] the chance to work their
way out of poverty and out of public housing."[32]

Equally important was the aspiration to redevelop how the public viewed
this form of housing in its communities. As Secretary Cuomo told the National Association of Housing Redevelopment Officials at its annual conference in 1998:

> Now, we've been fighting to get support for public housing—and the Ameri-
> can people haven't been with us because they have that picture in their
> mind about public housing—the great high-rise that you built up to the
> sky, and then it sunk so low that it sucked in the surrounding neighbor-
> hood. That is not the story of public housing, and it has been a myth and a
> misperception that has gone on for too long, and has precluded us from
> getting the kind of support that we need.[33]

From this vantage point, the modern high-rise project was a logical target
for redevelopment since it was a visible symbol of long-running but unsuccessful urban housing policy that has negatively impacted communities. HOPE
VI was designed to help PHAs tear down large-scale projects—and the negative image of public housing—so they could be replaced with small-scale,
mixed-income, townhouse developments or suburban apartment complexes
(e.g., Techwood in Atlanta). The success of these redeveloped sites would
depend on getting the private sector to invest in, develop, and then manage
properties, and once completed, non–public housing residents, particularly
middle-income families, to buy into—literally—these new developments and
to support relocated residents moving into their neighborhoods. In order to
do this, HUD reinvented itself.

The need to reinvent public housing can be traced back to the 1980s,
when under the watch of President Ronald Reagan, HUD was engulfed in
controversy over contracts issued to private sector developers and outright cutbacks in budget outlays.[34] By 1993, when President Bill Clinton
took office, public housing was underfunded and under scrutiny, and there
clearly was a need to leverage private sector resources to offset decreased
federal outlays.[35] Even as Clinton increased HUD's budget during his first
two years in office, the "new Democrats" were seeking ways to get more
money into the community development arena without raising taxes.[36]
Borrowing from the Republican playbook, their strategy was to encourage more involvement by nongovernmental actors in funding revitalization activities.

The Clinton administration's support for HUD and public housing ended with the 1994 elections, which shifted Congress to Republican control under the leadership of Speaker of the House Newt Gingrich. In what the National Center for Poverty Law called a preemptive strike, HUD proposed to reinvent itself before the 104th Congress even took office. In December 1994 HUD secretary Henry Cisneros presented *HUD Reinvention: From Blueprint to Action,* which laid out a plan to restructure the agency and streamline its "crazy-quilt programs and hand the funds over to states and cities."[37] The reinvention plan consisted of three components:

1. Public housing: Convert all operating subsidies into tenant-based rental assistance.
2. Block grants: Consolidate sixty programs into three flexible, performance-based funds dealing broadly with housing and community development.
3. Federal housing administration: Transform the FHA into a government-owned corporation, consolidate existing insurance programs into two authorities (single family and multifamily), and restructure current debt on assisted housing.[38]

The last two components, restructuring debt and consolidating programs, were expected to provide fiscal benefits for HUD and all its subsidized housing programs. First, restructuring debt by taking advantage of sharply lower interest rates than those available in the early 1980s when most developments were built reduced the long-term cost of maintaining nonpublic, subsidized housing. This included about 700,000 units developed using the Section 8 rehabilitation or new construction program introduced during the Nixon administration. Second, consolidating programs—another major change initially introduced by Nixon—would further streamline the grant-making process so that HUD could technically spend more on housing production even if it did not see a budget increase. This also could help the Democrats reduce the size of "big government."

The most significant change proposed, however, was converting public housing operating subsidies to rent assistance grants (i.e., vouchers) for tenants. Besides the fiscal benefits that come from improving efficiency, this proposal was expected to have both political and social benefits. The fiscal benefits of shifting to a completely demand-side subsidy meant a reduction in HUD outlays for operating subsidies to PHAs to help cover maintenance costs and debt service. The *Reinvention Blueprint* presented this single payment approach (i.e., rent and operating subsidy combined) as being a more efficient use of funds. It gave PHAs more control in fiscal decisions, since they could exercise more discretion in the use of funds than in the past. HUD officials also claimed that low-income families would greatly benefit, because they would now have the "choice" to stay in public housing or move into the private market.[39] The assumption was that if PHAs had to compete with the private sector, these agencies eventually would have to remove substandard buildings and improve existing units in order to keep operating, which would benefit not only tenants but also the neighborhoods where developments were located.

Local control was a dominant theme in the Clinton administration's reinvention plan for HUD and public housing. Four pieces of national legislation introduced soon after the release of HUD's *Reinvention Blueprint* helped to reinforce the "new, new federalism" of the Clinton administration, which was not unlike prior Republican administrations that assumed that the benefits of concurrently scaling back the federal government's involvement in social welfare programs while significantly increasing local control over policy implementation outweighed the potential costs.[40] Key to increased local control was the 1995 Rescissions Act, which suspended the one-for-one replacement rule previously guiding all public housing redevelopment and modernization efforts. Suspending this requirement opened up the possibility of a whole new approach to redeveloping public housing: PHAs could now tear down projects without having to replace demolished "hard units" with an equivalent number of new public housing units. Whereas in the past any teardown had to be replaced with at least 50 percent of the actual units, the new law allowed PHAs to replace 100 percent with vouchers for use in the private market. Residents who were going to be displaced could now be offered the voucher as a permanent unit.

The next year Congress approved Section 202 of the Omnibus Consolidated Rescissions and Appropriation Act of 1996, requiring all PHAs to assess the "viability" of any property with 300 or more units and a vacancy rate over 10 percent. As a result of this assessment, "nonviable" developments—sites where it would cost more to rehabilitate than it would to demolish and provide residents with vouchers to go into the private sector—were to be removed from the permanent inventory within five years. The viability test was extended in 1998 and mandatory conversion was required of any development with 250 units or more that failed the test. The law also requires that all PHAs conduct a conversion assessment of all of their projects regardless of size. Based on this assessment, a PHA can convert a project if "conversion will not be more expensive than continued operation of the project; conversion will benefit residents and the community; and conversion will not adversely affect the availability of affordable housing in the community."[41]

Finally, Congress signed into law the Quality Housing and Work Responsibility Act of 1998 (QHWRA), with most provisions becoming effective in

October 1999. Marking the official transformation of public housing nation-wide, this act is premised on a belief that more affordable housing is needed; that the government has already invested over $90 billion in rental housing for low-income persons; that public housing is plagued with problems; that the federal method of oversight has aggravated public housing problems; and that public housing reform is in the best interests of low-income persons.[42] The QHWRA makes extensive amendments to the Housing Act of 1937, including:

- Allowing PHAs to establish ceiling rents and to postpone rent increases when a tenant's income goes up (prior to this, rent was determined by income with tenants paying no more than 30 percent of adjusted income; as income went up, so did rent, encouraging higher-income families to move out when the rent exceeded what they would spend for private sector housing);
- Requiring tenants to perform public service or participate in a self-sufficiency program, and requiring PHAs to link tenants to social services;
- Expanding the ability of PHAs to evict tenants and to carry out criminal background checks on prospective public housing tenants and voucher holder;
- Reducing poverty concentrations through "income targeting" to encourage higher-income families to move into public housing while also maintaining minimum thresholds for extremely low-income tenants (i.e., 30 percent of area median income);
- Requiring PHAs to develop five-year strategic plans that for the first time actually link capital, operation, and management and are consistent with local Comprehensive Housing Affordability Strategies and Consolidated Plans within the PHA jurisdiction, which HUD requires jurisdictions to produce in order to receive annual housing funds;
- Streamlining the process of closing buildings through the use of viability testing and tenant-based forms of assistance;
- Making the HOPE VI program permanent in order to provide PHAs with specific public funds that can be used to leverage local resources in order to revitalize "distressed" public housing; and
- Allowing PHAs to own, operate, or assist in the development of mixed-finance projects and to design homeownership programs to sell public housing to tenants.

This series of legislative acts derives from a certain economic common sense that privileges a demand-side approach over a supply-side approach in order to meet the housing needs of low-income households. These acts also give public housing authorities little choice but to reduce the number of permanent public housing units and to minimize the number of low-income tenants in developments by relying more on tenant-based rent assistance grants. While portable, reliance on the Housing Choice vouchers (previously Section 8) pushed on the user the responsibility of finding and securing housing in the private sector. Very specific assumptions about the market need to be in play for vouchers to actually expand choice. These include the availability of units at a fair market rent (i.e., a rent level set by HUD that generally reflects the 40th percentile for a geographic area) in a good neighborhood (i.e., one that is an improvement over the current public housing environment) and, if units are available, the ability of voucher holders to actually use their vouchers (i.e., the landlord is willing to participate and the unit meets housing quality standards set by HUD).

A demand-side approach also means that making transformation work will depend heavily on the housing market, and particularly on private owners of rental property, to maintain a supply of permanent quality housing with reasonable rents that tenants can access. Although shifting the cost of maintaining and producing housing for low-income people to the private sector (both for-profit and not-for-profit developers) may make economic sense in the abstract, it is not necessarily in the best interest of low-income households given the "worsening crisis" in rental housing.[43] Under these circumstances, tenants in communities like Chicago where the housing market has been tight are likely to have less rather than more control over their destiny.[44]

The Future of Public Housing for the Very Poor

At this current juncture, the modern two-tier housing system and the federal government's role in it are simultaneously entrenched and unraveling. On one hand, the United States has reached its highest rate of homeownership, about 69 percent.[45] In 2000, nearly 32 million homeowners were able to take advantage of tax laws that allow writing off the interest paid on mortgage debt, paying property tax, and deferring capital gains on sale of a home for an estimated $103 billion in tax relief.[46] Equally important, most owners also have seen their housing values appreciate, especially during the last decade and in hot markets like Chicago's. The total inventory of "residential fixed investment" in 2004 was worth about $686 billion, nearly 6 percent of the gross domestic product.[47] And this figure is expected to grow since private housing starts—the majority of which are for-sale housing—added at least another 2 million new units of housing by the end of 2004. On the other hand, the supply of public housing, which at its peak was about 1.4 million units, is rapidly shrinking.

While there are about 3 million additional publicly subsidized units produced through various federal, state, and local programs, including the low-income housing tax credit program, and Housing Choice vouchers provide assistance to another 2 million very low-income households, the demand data clearly show that more, not less, affordable housing is needed for the very poor. In 2000, the federal government estimated that nearly 5.4 million families were severely burdened by housing costs (paying more than 50 percent of their income for housing), living in poor housing conditions, or both.[48] The majority are renting housing in the private market and are low-income (earning less than 50 percent of the area median income). Based on income, these families are not likely to qualify for publicly subsidized homeownership programs—the current administration's primary housing policy. However, they would qualify for public housing.

The preceding review of public housing policy in the United States demonstrates that, after all these years, the decision about whether or not government even should be involved in housing the poor is still not determined by demand or need, but rather by the same ideological disputes that shaped the debate nearly seventy years ago. However, this latest turning point in federal policy is different, since it fundamentally and practically reduces the permanent supply of public housing. This means that at least for the near future, one answer to the question "where are poor people to live?" is "most likely not in public housing."

Notes

1. Marie McGuire, Tom Walker, and Terrance Cooper, "50 Years of Housing Legislation," *Journal of Housing* (September/October 1987): 153–155, 158–166.

2. Peter Dreier, "The New Politics of Housing Policy: How to Rebuild the Constituency for a Progressive Federal Housing Policy," *Journal of the American Planning Association* 63 (1997): 6.

3. U.S. Department of Housing and Urban Development, "FHA's Mixed-Income Housing Underwriting Goals," Notice H 97–12, March 7, 1997, p. 1.

4. U.S. Department of Housing and Urban Development, "Public/Private Partnerships for the Mixed-Finance Development of Public Housing Units; Final Rule," *Federal Register* 61, no. 86 (May 2, 1996): 19708–19719 (subpart F to 24 Code of Federal Regulations pt. 941).

5. Alex Schwartz and Kian Tajbakhsh, "Mixed-Income Housing: Unanswered Questions," *Cityscape* 3, no. 2 (1997): 71–92.

6. Lawrence Vale, *From the Puritans to the Projects* (Boston: Harvard University Press, 2000).

7. McGuire, Walker, and Cooper, "50 Years of Housing."

8. Wagner-Steagall Housing Act of 1937 (Wagner-Steagall Housing Act), ch. 896, 560 stat. 888 (September 1, 1937).

9. Gail Radford, *Modern Housing for America: Policy Struggles in the New Deal Era* (Chicago: University of Chicago Press, 1996).

10. See Dennis Judd, "Symbolic Politics and Urban Policies: Why African Americans Got So Little from the Democrats," in *Without Justice for All,* ed. Adolph Reed Jr., pp. 123–150 (Boulder, CO: Westview Press, 1999); and Gregory Squires, *From Redlining to Reinvestment* (Philadelphia: Temple University Press, 1993).

11. See W. Dennis Keating and Janet Smith, "Past Federal Policy for Urban Neighborhoods," in *Revitalizing Urban Neighborhoods,* ed. W. Dennis Keating, Norman Krumholz, and Phil Star (Kansas: University Press of Kansas, 1996); and R. Allen Hays, *The Federal Government and Urban Housing,* 2nd ed. (Albany: SUNY Press, 1995).

12. Peter Marcuse, "Housing Policy and the Myth of the Benevolent State," *Social Policy* 8, no 4 (January–February 1978): 21, 23–26.

13. Marcuse, "Housing Policy," p. 25.

14. Timothy Conlan, *New Federalism: Intergovernmental Reform and Political Change from Nixon to Reagan* (Washington, DC: Brookings Institution, 1988).

15. See Martin Anderson, *The Federal Bulldozer* (Boston: MIT Press, 1964); Scott Greer, *Urban Renewal and American Cities: The Dilemma of Democratic Intervention* (Indianapolis: Bobbs-Merrill, 1965); and Robert Lang and Rebecca R. Sohmer, "Legacy of the Housing Act of 1949: The Past, Present, and Future of Federal Housing and Urban Policy," *Housing Policy Debate* 11, no. 2 (2000).

16. Arnold Hirsch, *Making the Second Ghetto,* 2nd ed. (Chicago: University of Chicago Press, 1998).

17. See Greer, *Urban Renewal;* Hays, *Federal Government.*

18. The phrase "gilding the ghetto" was coined by John Kain and Joseph Persky, "Alternatives to the Gilded Ghetto," *In the Public Interest* (Winter 1969).

19. Walter Gropius, *Scope of Total Architecture* (New York: Harper, 1955).

20. Peter Rowe, *Modernity and Housing* (Cambridge: MIT Press, 1993).

21. See Jane Jacobs, *The Death and Life of Great American Cities* (New York: Random House and Vintage Books, 1961); and Oscar Newman, *Defensible Space* (New York: Macmillan, 1972).

22. Alexander von Hoffman, "Managing Devolution in Public Housing: The New Landscape High Ambitions: The Past and Future of American Low-Income Housing Policy," *Housing Policy Debate* 7, no. 3 (1996): 435.

23. Initially, there were two forms of assistance: vouchers and certificates. Certificates set the limit that tenants would pay for rent at 30 percent of their income and the government would pay the difference up to a "fair market rent." Vouchers set a limit of 40 percent of income. These were eventually merged into the voucher program in 1999 and renamed the Housing Choice vouchers.

24. For example, the development of Section 8 buildings on the far North Side of Chicago in Rogers Park and Edgewater has been blamed for crime and disinvestment due to the concentration of buildings in some parts of these communities.

25. When originally introduced, the H in HOPE stood for Homeownership. HOPE III was a program that allowed local housing authorities to sell public housing to tenants.

26. Government Accountability Office, *HOPE VI: Progress and Problems in Revitalizing Distressed Public Housing* (Washington, DC: GAO/RCED-98–187, 1998), p. 3.

27. U.S. Department of Housing and Urban Development, *HOPE VI: Best Practices and Lessons Learned 1992–2002* (Washington DC: HUD, June 14, 2002).

28. The future of HOPE VI is undetermined at this time. Reauthorization hearings were held in April and May 2003.

29. Von Hoffman, "Managing Devolution."

30. Oscar Newman, *Design Guidelines for Creating Defensible Space* (Washington, DC: U.S. Department of Justice, 1976).

31. The residents at Pruitt-Igoe really launched the whole resident management corporation (RMC) movement in public housing.

32. Andrew Cuomo, "Statement of HUD Secretary, Senate Subcommittee on Housing and Community Opportunity," Washington, DC, April 9, 1997.

33. Andrew Cuomo, "Speech at Annual Meeting of the National Association of Housing Redevelopment Officials," San Antonio, Texas, October 1998.

34. Hays, *Federal Government.*

35. U.S. Department of Housing and Urban Development, "Public/Private Partnerships."

36. Nicholas Lemann, "The Myth of Community Development," *New York Times Magazine,* January 9, 1994.

37. Dreier, "New Politics," p. 7.

38. U.S. Department of Housing and Urban Development, *HUD Reinvention: From Blueprint to Action* (Washington, DC: HUD, 1995).

39. U.S. Department of Housing and Urban Development, *The Transformation of America's Public Housing* (Washington, DC: HUD, 1996).

40. This was the term used to characterize the Clinton administration's devolution of social welfare programs, a position not usually supported by liberal Democrats. It is also in reference to Nixon's "new federalism" and subsequent general revenue sharing and block grants, which laid the foundation for decentralizing and expanding local control over the implementation of national policy. The Reagan-Bush administration further decentralized, giving local government more control over but also greater fiscal responsibility for many programs.

41. U.S. Department of Housing and Urban Development, "Required Conversion of Developments from Public Housing Stock," *Federal Register:* 63, no. 141 (July 23, 1999: 40231-40237, 24 Code of Federal Regulations: 972.

42. *The Quality Housing and Work Responsibility Act of 1998,* (Public Law 105–276, 105th Cong., 2d sess. (1998); see Section 502.

43. U.S. Department of Housing and Urban Development, *Rental Housing Assistance—The Worsening Crisis: A Report to Congress on Worst Case Housing Needs* (Washington, DC: Office of Policy Development and Research, 2000).

44. Janet Smith and Thomas Lenz, *For Rent: Housing Options in the Chicago Region* (Chicago: University of Illinois, Great Cities Institute, 1999).

45. U.S Department of Housing and Urban Development, *U.S. Housing Market Conditions* (Washington, DC: HUD, November 2004).

46. Peter Dreier, "The Truth About Federal Housing Subsidies: Socialism for the Rich, Capitalism for the Poor," in *A Right to Housing: Foundation for a New Social Agenda,* ed. Chester Hartman and Rachel Bratt (Philadelphia: Temple University Press, forthcoming).

47. U.S Department of Housing and Urban Development, *U.S. Housing Market Conditions* (Washington, DC: HUD).

48. U.S. Department of Housing and Urban Development, *A Report on Worst Case Housing Needs in 1999: New Opportunity Amid Continuing Challenges* (Washington, DC: Office of Policy Development and Research, 2001).

2

Public Housing's Cinderella

Policy Dynamics of HOPE VI in the Mid-1990s

Yan Zhang and Gretchen Weismann

Ambivalence toward housing the poor has a long history in America. The HOPE (Housing Opportunities for People Everywhere) VI public housing program was created at a time when national politics veered sharply to the right and the American welfare state came under severe attack. Beginning with a plain-Jane appearance, HOPE VI soon turned into public housing's Cinderella—"the new face of public housing." To date, no one has offered a close account of how HOPE VI evolved and who shaped it over time. This chapter is a first attempt to use John Kingdon's multiple streams framework[1] to reveal the underlying currents driving HOPE VI developments in the mid-1990s when the most fundamental shifts in HOPE VI policy took place.

HOPE VI

Congress created what became known as the HOPE VI public housing program in 1992.[2] Under this competitive grant process, local public housing authorities (PHAs) apply to the U.S. Department of Housing and Urban Development (HUD) for housing revitalization grants. From 1993 to 2002, the HOPE VI program awarded nearly $5 billion in grants that averaged $31 million per housing development, involving over 115,000 distressed public housing units in 114 cities.[3] In the past decade, HOPE VI has constituted the primary vehicle and the most strenuous governmental effort to transform public housing in the United States. As sparkling townhouses replaced long-stigmatized high-rises and barrack-style apartments, HOPE VI generated both praise and controversy. Its wholehearted champions and wholesale critics are easily exemplified:

We are transforming the worst public housing developments in America into outposts of opportunity that will help poor families build better lives and help revitalize America's cities.
—Vice President Al Gore[4]

While it was intended to be a solution to severely distressed public housing, HOPE VI has been the source of new problems as serious as those it was created to address.
—False Hope: A Critical Assessment of the HOPE VI[5]

We are neither boosters for nor naysayers of HOPE VI. Rather, our aim is to explore the "how" and "why" of HOPE VI's drastic shift in policy discourse in the mid-1990s.

From 1994 to 1996, the HOPE VI program took a sharp turn, embarking on a journey from a plain-Jane policy to a Cinderella program. With several regulatory and administrative breakthroughs, HUD quickly fashioned a series of new strategies that encouraged mixed-income developments, the leveraging of private funds, and public-private partnerships. In a very short time, the primary focus of the HOPE VI program moved from a concern about the isolation of families to a concern about the isolation of housing authorities; from a government housing program targeting poor people to a market-driven, mixed-income housing program for the deserving poor and even the well-to-do; and from a modest attempt to cure the ills within the projects to an ambitious plan to revitalize urban communities. HOPE VI was HUD's flagship program—one that would reinvent America's public housing system. It became an icon of the federal agency's competence and its raison d'être.

This chapter shows that the initiation of the HOPE VI program in 1993 offered merely marginal adjustments by refining policy solutions to suit existing problems. The opening of a political window in the mid-1990s—including the arrival of reformist, visionary HUD secretary Henry Cisneros, the "Republican revolution," and the subsequent spillover effects of welfare reform efforts—sent HOPE VI into a substantial departure from its origins. Public housing problems were redefined as part of a larger consideration of government reinvention and devolution in social welfare programs. As Cisneros pushed for doing it over again in HOPE VI, nationally known affordable housing developers like Richard Baron, along with a handful of entrepreneurial public housing authorities, quickly utilized their links to key officials to overcome institutional roadblocks to innovation. Encouraged to think outside the box, local housing authorities emerged as new policy entrepreneurs, supplying their own solutions and driving HOPE VI policy in a new direction.

Understanding Policy Change Through Multiple Streams

In his influential book *Agendas, Alternatives, and Public Policies,* political scientist John Kingdon offers a powerful framework for analyzing policy choice under conditions of ambiguity and within a temporal sequence. Building upon the "garbage can model" of organizational behavior outlined by Cohen, March, and Olsen,[6] Kingdon argues that policy making is a messy process based on the logic of timing and opportunity rather than comprehensive optimization processes. Policy circles, as Kingdon observes, are "organized anarchies" in which members do not understand the full array of processes at work, participants drift in and out of decision making, and members learn from experience and from trial and error.

Kingdon identifies three major streams flowing through the policy-making system—problems, policies, and politics—each of which has its own dynamics and discourse, largely independent of the others. The problem stream addresses why and how particular problems make it onto the policy agenda. Major attributes of this stream include crisis and disasters, feedback from current program operations, and indicator availability. The policy stream is conceptualized as a variety of ideas floating around in a policy "primeval soup," in which solutions are continually combined and reconstituted to yield policy alternatives.[7] The politics stream consists of political events such as national mood change, pressure group campaigns, and administrative or legislative turnover. Issues gain prominence on the policy agenda when three streams—rearticulation of the policy problem, presentation of new, plausible policy alternatives, and changes in the political climate—converge at critical moments in time.

The key to Kingdon's argument is the coupling that must precede major policy change. Coupling takes place when solutions are linked to problems, proposals are linked to political demands, and agenda changes lead to the selection of particular policy alternatives. Policy change is likely to occur when a window of opportunity is opened by compelling problems or by political focusing events.[8] In Kingdon's framework, elected officials and political appointees play a central role in placing an idea on a political agenda. Nonetheless, it is communities of specialists, or networks of relatively "hidden participants," from academics and think tank researchers to career bureaucrats and congressional staffers, who generate policy alternatives. To advocate for policy change, policy communities must do more than simply recognize a policy window through which to push their favored solutions. Policy entrepreneurs are needed, both in and around government, who are willing to invest their resources to promote specific agendas despite uncertain consequences. In order for coupling to succeed, policy entrepreneurs must be poised to take advantage of any opportunity that presents itself. They must prepare arguments to link their solutions to problems, line up political allies, soften up policy communities, and generate favorable sentiment among the public.

In short, policy responses are not necessarily created in a sequential order in which problems are identified and then strategically addressed, as suggested by a stages model based on the logic of rational choice.[9] Rather, the process reflects Kingdon's independently floating streams—complex, serendipitous, and paradoxical—whereby policy outcomes depend on how three streams are joined together, when, and by whom. Applying the multiple streams framework to the policy-making process in one federal housing program, this chapter examines how policy entrepreneurs (at both federal and local levels), working within insitutitional constraints, captured and created windows of opportunity for dramatic policy change.

The Birth of a Plain-Jane Policy

Since the Housing Act of 1937, public housing developments have evolved from places of hope to housing of last resort and from a way station for a temporarily "submerged middle class" to a warehouse for the very poor.[10] By the late 1980s, many troubled public housing projects, particularly in large cities, revealed a high incidence of crime, drug-related activity, poor management, crumbling structures, and social distress. In 1989, as part of the Department of Housing and Urban Development Reform Act, Congress established the National Commission on Severely Distressed Public Housing (NCSDPH) to clarify issues, heighten awareness, and provide solutions to transform the nation's worst public housing. The "crisis" in problem projects, which was confirmed and reinforced in the report issued by NCSDPH in 1992, placed public housing on the political radar screen.[11] HOPE VI was born as the Urban Revitalization Demonstration program when the Senate Authorization Committee and the House Appropriations Committee responded to the report and recognized an opportunity to act.[12]

To craft their argument for reform, policy entrepreneurs who served on the NCSDPH relied on their own research circles outside of Washington to frame the problems and solutions of public housing. By the early 1990s, two sets of prominent solutions rose to the top of the policy primeval soup that served as the intellectual basis for the HOPE VI program. The commonly known one is the National Action Plan proposed by the NCSDP. Based on eighteen months of research including site visits, public hearings, and case studies, the commission concluded that approximately 86,000 units in the nation were in severe distress and that "a new and comprehensive approach" would be required to address the range of problems existing at these developments.[13] Defining the problem of public housing as social and economic, as well as one of bricks and mortar, the commission recommended revitalization in three general areas: physical improvements, management improvements, and social and community services to address resident needs. Many reform-minded members of the commission advocated for the use of low-income housing tax credits (LIHTC), private sector participation, and the creation of mixed-income communities in place of low-income housing. These alternatives were listed in a chapter titled "Non-Conventional Strategies."

A second set of policy solutions, though referenced less often, also served as an intellectual foundation for the HOPE VI program.[14] Known as the Cleveland Report, it drew heavily from a report by Arthur Naparstek, director of the Cleveland Commission on Poverty.[15] Sensing the political opportunities for policy change, Naparstek took advantage of his close access to the chair of the VA-HUD Appropriations Subcommittee, Senator Barbara Mikulski (D-MD), to advocate for community services and civic engagement as a basis for the new public housing program. Mikulski, whose district was affected by dilapidated high-rise public housing, shared Naparstek's idea that public housing revitalization could be achieved through people-based strategies—by "building on community assets, cultivating resident leaderships, and integrating human services."[16]

Meanwhile, Gordon Cavanaugh, then general counsel of the Council of Large Public Housing Authorities (CLPHA), worked with Kevin Kelly of Senator Mikulski's staff to address the issue of turning around the most troubled projects. Emphasizing that certain high-rise developments were not treatable under any available program or approach, Cavanaugh convinced Kelly that to do something meaningful about the problem projects, a significant block grant for one program was needed, which would not be trapped in HUD's existing cumbersome practice of requiring several different approval processes (demolition, disposition, development, etc.).

Informed by the proposals of Arthur Naparstek and Kevin Kelly, as well as the resident energy demonstrated in resident management corporations (RMCs) and the Gateway Initiatives,[17] Senator Mikulski, a Democrat, mustered sufficient support on Capitol Hill to push the new public housing bill through in the twilight of the Bush administration. Though she adopted the language of the NCSDPH's report, Mikulski did not explicitly mention the commission's policy recommendations. Instead, the goal of HOPE VI is described as threefold: (1) shelter, (2) self-sufficiency, and (3) community sweat equity.[18]

Considering the hostile political environment of the time, Mikulski avoided possible opposition from Republican legislators and deliberately gave the Urban Revitalization Demonstration (URD) program a popular name, HOPE VI, appealing to then HUD secretary Jack Kemp, who already supported a public housing homeownership program under the series name HOPE.[19] However, despite the Appropriations Committee's suggestion that HOPE VI was an innovative departure from previous public housing programs, the actual policy changes proposed by HUD were modest. Although Congress gave HUD wide latitude to choose among alternative policy solutions, including those suggested in the NCSDPH report, the agency followed all the old rules and regulations relating to the conventional public housing modernization program. The HOPE VI program design, as demonstrated in the first Notice of Funding Availability (NOFA) published on January 5, 1993, was a continuation of preexisting programs. To a certain degree, it was a redefined version of the Major Reconstruction of the Obsolete Public Housing Program (MROP)[20] with additional community service components administered by the Corporation for National Services.[21]

From Plain Jane to Cinderella

In a spirit of flexibility and entrepreneurship, HUD did not develop HOPE VI–specific regulations. The yearly NOFA, program guidelines, legal opinions, and individual grant agreements substituted for a formally legislated process. At a time when the reform-minded Cisneros was leading HUD to a brave new world, the door of the HOPE VI shop, albeit far from the spotlight, began to open to entrepreneurs who were prepared to push through their visions and solutions, offering their advice about new directions for the program, advocating specific changes in rules and standards, and presenting real-world examples from across the country.

By the early 1990s, a growing acknowledgment of the broad, systematic causes of inner-city poverty and the need for a comprehensive approach to neighborhood revitalization bubbled up in the policy stream. Many housing professionals noted the importance of sociologist William Julius Wilson's work, *The Truly Disadvantaged,* which focuses on structural origins, rather than cultural and behavioral accounts, to explain the emergence of an "urban underclass."[22] Urban deindustrialization and a massive loss of low-skilled jobs from urban centers, Wilson writes, drained neighborhoods of economic means and institutional support. Over the 1970s and 1980s, inner cities became increasingly mired in concentrated poverty as they suffered from the departure of middle- and working-class blacks to the suburbs. The result, Wilson argues, was the rise of impoverished female-headed households, joblessness, and increased "social pathologies." These nonworking families are likely not only to be materially poor, but also to lack the social and human capital that would enable them to climb out of poverty.

In the 1990s, Wilson's intellectual leadership expanded the debate on public housing policies by highlighting the spatial dimension of entrenched societal problems. The former administrator of the Boston Housing Authority published an article in *Housing Policy Debate* on the benefits of economic integration. Responding to the NCSDPH's recommendations of social services and economic development initiatives as "unrealistic optimism," Harry Spence proposed a new social role for public housing—to connect residents to social capital:

> For the past decade, the nation's public housing policy has systematically set about creating public housing neighborhoods that are utterly devoid of social capital. . . . Advocates of a meaningful social role for public housing need to speak forcefully and directly about the public housing experience of the past decade. They need to be clear that there is nothing inherent in public housing ownership that ensures the devastating outcome we are witnessing. They need to argue for a public housing program that provides meaningful access for the homeless and dispossessed to the critical resource of social capital. Such a program would ensure that families of the nonworking poor are integrated with the working poor to foster sinews of connection and trust out of which hope and opportunity grow.[23]

The Boston Housing Authority had been one of the first to receive a HOPE VI grant, and the wholehearted endorsement of the social capital concept by Spence, a well-respected leader in the public housing industry, added substantial weight to the attacks on the "serve the neediest" tenant-selection policies.

Emerging work on a spatially defined "ghetto underclass" and political scientist Robert Putnam's analysis of the role of social capital in economic outcomes suggested both a problem of concentrated poverty and a potential solution. The problems of poor neighborhoods could be "deconcentrated" through the elimination of old ties and the subsequent cultivation of new social networks that support individuals in their efforts to "get by" and "get ahead."[24] Despite limited and contradictory empirical evidence, policy makers soon accepted the theory and linked proposals of deconcentration (operationalized largely through mixed-income housing) to the political demands of the time.

Henry Cisneros—A Visionary Leader in Crisis

In 1993, the forty-six-year-old Cisneros came to HUD as "an advocate of cities, a skeptic of the status quo, and a believer in experimentation, federalism, and the need to provide people with hope."[25] Looking to insert a problem-solving spirit into a regulation-driven bureaucracy, Cisneros envisioned a new role for HUD as enabler, partner, and agent of change.[26] Cisneros quickly introduced the Housing and Community Development Act of 1993 in which he listed "turning around public housing" as the second of his top five priorities. He specifically recommended that HOPE VI be free from statutes and rules governing one-for-one replacement, rent calculations, and site and neighborhood standards—measures that limited the program's flexibility to serve higher-income residents.[27]

A year later, but before the Republican takeover of the 105th Congress, Cisneros pledged to introduce a bold reform of America's public housing system through the Housing Choice and Community Investment Act of 1994.[28] In this bill, Cisneros framed the problem of public housing as the "concentration of very low-income families in dense, high-rise housing" due to federal regulatory restrictions and micromanagement. Highlighting the creation of stable, healthy, mixed-income neighborhoods as the "original goal of public housing," Cisneros presented a solution of "demolishing and replacing" these high-rises with "economically integrated, well-designed, small-scale, affordable housing."[29]

Once again, the issue of whom public housing should serve came up in the congressional debate, putting a spotlight on the fundamental dilemma facing HUD and its reformist secretary. Although public housing required substantial and increasing income streams to overcome shrinking operating subsidies, the secretary was at first reluctant to bring higher-income groups into public housing. Instead, he emphasized working with the residents in public housing and raising their income from within.

> SEN. SARBANES: Now I'm being told that . . . an approach that . . . focused less on the ones that were suffering the most might, in fact, be a better approach.

> SEC. CISNEROS: Sir, let me say this is a difficult call. But my—and it'll be difficult to do. But my belief is that we change income mix not by bringing people of higher incomes to public housing, but by creating opportunities for people who are now in public housing, Section 3 work, jobs in the authorities, jobs with the modernization funds, job training opportunities with which we expect to collaborate with the Labor Department. But this is a harder thing to do than simply, you know, changing income by bringing other people of higher income. But that doesn't solve the problems of the people who are poor who are there now. I think we need to change the dynamic incentive structure for work in public housing as it exists and raise incomes that way.[30]

The moral concerns intrinsic to the rhetoric of serving the poorest of the poor or protecting the social safety net for the poor became much easier to sweep aside after the congressional midterm election in 1994. The Republican congressional leadership, Speaker of the House Newt Gingrich and Senate Majority Leader Robert Dole, used a ten-point "Contract with America" as the party's platform to instigate revolutionary reforms. A balanced budget, welfare reform, tax cuts, term limits, deregulation, devolution, and reinvention became preeminent terms of the new political lexicon. Washington, DC, was caught up in a historic debate over the role, scope, and shape of the federal government. The national mood at the time was Dickensian. Gingrich's political base of support was such that he could recommend orphanages as a solution for struggling single-parent households without much concern for retribution by liberal counterparts in Congress.

In January 1996, President Bill Clinton proudly declared "the era of big government over" in his State of the Union address. Once the easy pick for his campaign message, welfare reform became the compromise of choice as Clinton signaled his willingness to work with an "upside-down" Congress.[31] After a series of highly polemical debates, Clinton signed into law the Republican-oriented Personal Responsibility and Work Opportunity Reconciliation Act of 1996, with a promise to cut welfare spending and impose lifetime limits on its receipt.

Although HUD was one of only seven federal departments that actually enjoyed an increased budget authority during the first year of the Clinton administration, the fate of HUD was reversed in the wake of the congressional shift in 1994. Even Vice President Albert Gore's refrain "to reinvent government" became much more in tune with that of the newly elected Republican majority in Congress. The new principles for reinvention involved termination, privatization, devolution, consolidation, and downsizing the government workforce. Borrowing the best practices from the private sector to support a smaller but more efficient government became the dominant credo.

Groups in favor of reducing spending in social services and those interested in greater privatization of public services gained strength and cohesion from events in Congress and the self-imposed pressure to eliminate the $200 billion plus federal deficit. With conservatives controlling the national dialogue about poverty, HUD—politically "about as popular as smallpox"— was once again placed onto the political chopping block.[32] In 1994, a commission was established by the House of Representatives to explore options for reorganizing HUD out of existence, and fifty-seven representatives signed on to a bill to eliminate the department altogether.

After taking office in 1993, HUD secretary Henry Cisneros attended congressional hearings weekly to lobby for his agency's survival. Realizing that both ends of Pennsylvania Avenue—the White House and Congress—wanted change, Cisneros pledged to reinvent HUD. In his testimony before Congress, he clearly demonstrated the sense of a historic mission on his shoulders: "It comes at a critical moment in HUD's history—a moment when a confluence of events is driving what promises to be the most far-reaching reform of federal housing and urban policy in 60 years."[33]

A few months later, facing the Gingrich-led attack on HUD, the Clinton-Cisneros reinvention proposal envisaged "an orderly and prudent transition to prepare agencies and residents for the shift to a market environment."[34] Hoping to effectively change the poor public perception of HUD, Cisneros stated that it was time to "end public housing as we know it." He asked each of the ten HUD regional administrators for their input on redesigning the public housing program. Immediately after the elections and before the first session of the 104th Congress in 1995, Cisneros released his *HUD Reinvention: From Blueprint to Action,* a proposal that in many respects was far more radical than the legislative proposals of the moderate Republicans.[35] The *Reinvention Blueprint* would have repealed most of the federal housing legislation over the previous sixty years; it suggested consolidation of sixty major HUD programs into three block grants and the conversion of all project-based subsidies into vouchers. The *Reinvention Blueprint* promised to transform HUD from a lumbering bureaucracy into a streamlined partner with state and local governments. Although many of the recommendations in the *Reinvention Blueprint* were not adopted, it set in motion an attempt to craft a bipartisan reform of the nation's public housing over three years.[36] It is debatable whether this action was Cisneros's "preemptive strike" or "terms for surrender." Nonetheless, in the eyes of some housing advocates, Cisneros's strategy succeeded in building support for HUD among moderates in Congress and forestalled the Office of Management and Budget's plans to eliminate the agency.[37]

With substantial budget resources and regulatory flexibilities, HOPE VI became the "first genuine vehicle" for realizing a new vision for public housing. Cisneros's commitment to a dramatic experiment through HOPE VI was evident in his overview given at the HOPE VI conference titled Moving HOPE VI Forward in Changing Times, held on March 27–29, 1995, in Washington, DC:

> Without making drastic improvements, public housing could die a slow death by strangulation, as the American people may gradually cut off its life support systems through Congressional reductions in Federal assistance.
>
> To realize the vision of HOPE VI, HUD must change. We must change our rules and regulations that block innovation, the preference rules and location standards and the many other practices that keep public hous-

ing from becoming a platform for economic lift of individuals, families, and communities.

I will give HUD's new Office of Distressed and Troubled Housing Recovery[38] broad discretion to authorize a wide range of local initiatives and innovations. We will above all else experiment with new concepts and techniques, freeing the grantees from cumbersome restrictions that stifle creativity and imaginative thinking.

Cisneros actively reached out to seek plausible and effective solutions. He brought the best people from the industry together in work groups; he conducted site visits; and he asked a simple question: If you could start public housing all over again, what would you like to see?[39] According to Bruce Katz, then chief of staff of HUD, a site visit to Newark, New Jersey, served as a loud and clear message that "without changing the income composition of the residents, HOPE VI's new development might as well go down the same path as what it has just replaced."[40] This visit decisively marked the end of the plain-Jane era of HOPE VI.

If the *Reinvention Blueprint* provided the compass, the *Final Report of the National Commission on Severely Distressed Public Housing* was the atlas for impending policy changes. Policy entrepreneurs inside and outside of government acted to remove the roadblocks along the way. The section below is an account of how the public housing industry, developers, and other contributors built on the past and skillfully put through their preferred solutions.

PHAs and Housing Trade Organizations— Lobbying for Deregulation

It did not take long after the release of the first NOFA in 1993 and the program's inception for local housing authorities to conclude that HOPE VI was nothing new. At that time they were still constrained by existing regulatory and administrative rules.[41] Almost as soon as HOPE VI implementation began, CLPHA went to Congress to lobby HUD for freedom from "Byzantine-style" regulations for HOPE VI.[42] Andrea Duncan, president of CLPHA, testified before Congress, supporting HUD's proposal (the Housing Act of 1993) to streamline Section 24, thus ensuring broader reforms and deregulations that would expedite "this potentially wonderful program."[43]

The conversation about HOPE VI, however, was only a current amid waves of a broader debate about public housing reforms. As former CLPHA counsel Gordon Cavanaugh stated in his testimony, "the deficiencies of bad developments have a Congressional origin"; thus they demanded congressional solutions, which could in turn position American public housing "in a better light" and "produce real, systemic, responsible budget reduction."[44] Long stymied by federal statutory policies (such as the one-for-one requirement[45] and site and neighborhood standards[46]), large housing authorities and CLPHA actively lobbied for deregulation and the repeal of several key provisions of the Housing Act of 1937.[47] These efforts were supported by HUD's inspector general, Susan Gaffney. In her congressional testimony, Gaffney summarized various studies conducted by housing groups and commissions, academics, public housing officials, and consultants. She listed a set of innovative changes needed in the public housing program—specifically, regulations related to rent, funding, admissions, and replacement housing—to accommodate the problems facing large troubled PHAs.[48]

Outside the congressional floor, in the meeting rooms at HUD, CLPHA's staff and counsel worked with HUD to examine old rules line by line, seeking ways to reduce red tape and streamline prospective innovation.[49] While HUD was confronted with the daunting challenges of making more with less and while local housing administrators were trying to meet HUD's tedious requirements, few noticed that there were other forces at work at the same time. Affordable housing developers, with experience and expertise in large-scale neighborhood revitalization projects and alternative housing finance, stepped in with their solutions.

Richard Baron and the Diaz Opinions

In contrast to HUD and PHA staff, a good number of affordable housing developers were familiar not only with local market conditions but with the particulars of both federal housing regulations and private sector development.[50] Their knowledge and connections gave them an opportunity to capitalize on the reform-minded in government. A handful of developers, including housing expert Richard Baron[51]; Egbert Perry, chair and CEO of the Integral Group LLC; Patrick Clancy, president and CEO of Community Builders Inc.[52]; and Donald Terner, president and CEO of BRIDGE Housing Corporation,[53] went to HUD to enlighten policy makers via the perspectives derived from their direct experience inside and outside the URD program. As Community Builders director Willie Jones explained,

> At that point, URD was essentially $50 million to go fix the worst developments in the country. You can't spend the money on anything except the public housing sites, and you had to use all the other procurement regulations that HUD has. You couldn't mix public housing dollars with private finance dollars on a public housing site. Secondly, it didn't acknowledge

the relationship between a public housing site and the adjacent community. How long do you think it would take a public housing site to fail again? Not very long![51]

One important part of the lobbying effort was to push HOPE VI beyond the boundary of old institutional relationships. With three decades of practical experience in tax-benefit syndication for the nonprofit community, the developers suggested the notion of leveraging private capital into neighborhood development initiatives to fulfill the innovation HUD promised in HOPE VI.

In 1994, Richard Baron (on behalf of the St. Louis Housing Authority) and the Fairfax County, Virginia, PHA requested an opinion from the HUD Office of General Counsel (OGC) about whether they could use funds allocated to them under the public housing program in conjunction with the low-income housing tax credit program. The question required HUD OGC to consider: (1) whether URD, as it read at the time, permitted public housing to be owned and operated by entities other than PHAs, such as limited partnerships receiving tax credits, and (2) whether the act allowed PHAs to provide operating subsidies or capital funds to such entities. In a memorandum dated April 8, 1994, Nelson Diaz, then general counsel of HUD, concluded that the act permitted public housing to be owned by an entity other than a PHA and that private entities could receive operating subsidies and certain capital dollars.[55]

The availability of new construction dollars, coupled with a depressed real estate market in the early 1990s, enabled a discussion about the value of government-subsidized housing, which could not have happened two years before.[56] However, many at HUD were blinded by the real estate downturn and the miserable situation in troubled public housing developments. Even though the HUD general counsel stressed that this change was fundamental and far-reaching, few at HUD would have expected how influential the idea of engaging private industry in the public housing delivery system would turn out to be. The "Diaz opinions," combined with the availability of capital funds under the HOPE VI program, led to significant interest in this method of development and paved the way for public-private partnership and subsequent waves of public housing privatization.[57]

Another part of the lobbying efforts by the residential development industry, which proved to be similarly influential, was to get HUD to look beyond the confines of the physical building of the public housing and thus to treat it as an integral and vital part of the larger neighborhood in which it was located. As a result, the site-and-neighborhood exception policy enabled a "ring" around a development within which PHAs could build replacement housing both on-site and off-site, a profound change in the way public housing and PHAs related to the outside world.

The HOPE VI Office—Reforming Below the Radar Screen

After the first round of grantees was selected in August 1993, the new HUD administration established an Office of Distressed and Troubled Housing Recovery (ODTHR) and began to recruit new people to chart the HOPE VI program. Under the guidance of Secretary Cisneros, HUD chief of staff Bruce Katz, congressional staff (particularly Senator Mikulski's), HUD senior staff, Kevin Marchman (then acting assistant secretary for Public and Indian Housing), and the housing industry all set out to "sell [HOPE VI] as if we were starting from the beginning."[58]

Christopher Hornig took the position of special assistant in charge of drafting and overseeing the NOFAs and individual grant agreements.[59] Hornig's account conveys the rather "accidental" nature of how the program was being shaped at this juncture:

> In the initial days of the HOPE VI program, the mission wasn't that clear to me; it wasn't to anybody. I'd say if there was a policy-making theme when I came in and others came in, it was initially just that—to get HUD out of the business and let the authorities start moving. Eventually, I would say that I, and others in public housing, became aware of this emerging push particularly from McCormack Baron [developers], the push to involve private developers in HOPE VI. That push was originally exerted at a higher level, in conversations between the secretary, Bruce Katz, and others. But at some point, McCormack Baron came to us to start to talk about how they implemented the program in Atlanta, Techwood, and St. Louis Murphy Parks. Then people from Pittsburgh started to come to us. That was the story, until we started drifting into HOPE VI Plus. There was a period where these threads were coming together. Then it was a revolution.[60]

Supplying New Blood from "Upstairs" and the Old UDAG

In early 1994, Mindy Turbov, special assistant to Nicolas Retsinas (then assistant secretary for Housing and Federal Housing Commissioner), was transferred to the HOPE VI office with a mission from "upstairs" where HUD leadership resided.[61] This mission launched the most important transition in the HOPE VI program—the transition to public-private partnerships. Having work experience both in the private sector (as vice president and partner in McCormack Baron & Associates Inc.) and in the public sector (as deputy commissioner for development for the Chicago Department of Housing), Turbov brought a spirit of entrepreneurship to the HOPE VI shop at HUD. In particular, she promoted a new vision of HOPE VI modeled on the Urban

Development Action Grant (UDAG) program of the 1970s and 1980s, which involved engaging private developers in community development. Keeping to the tradition of claiming programmatic turf in government, Turbov fashioned this new direction "URD Plus." A new group of staff who previously worked for the UDAG program was recruited.

In February 1995 Kevin Marchman issued to all URD grantees a memorandum titled URD Plus: A Tool for Neighborhood Revitalization. In this document, PHAs were encouraged to take advantage of the flexibility in the URD program to leverage other funds, including Community Development Block Grant, HOME Investment Partnership Program, state, and private financing, as well as other subsidies and loan funds. The memo also encouraged broader neighborhood revitalization via replacing units in surrounding neighborhoods and the creation of mixed-income development. This URD/HOPE VI Plus initiative became the foundation for what people think of now as HOPE VI.[62]

Selling HOPE VI Plus

The bold idea of involving the private sector met with some resistance from other parts of HUD, from the industry, and from housing advocates. The housing authorities strongly opposed the HOPE VI Plus idea: "It was saying the old guard didn't know how to do things in new ways."[63] The "bunker mentality" of the housing authorities kept them from working with the rest of the real estate world.[64] Not until the Republican landslide in 1994 did everybody understand that things had to change, making the revolution of HOPE VI much easier.[65] Nowhere did the sense of a different political circumstance manifest itself so well as in the 1995 Program Notice:

> [HOPE VI] is a high visibility demonstration program funded with ample Federal resources ($1.6 billion in three years) that is being watched very closely by the Congress, the Administration, and the public.
>
> HUD and the public housing community have been given the opportunity and mandate to revitalize some of the most distressed public housing developments in the Nation and transform them into models of affordable housing for the 21st century . . .
>
> The Secretary's REINVENTION BLUEPRINT places even greater importance on the HOPE VI program. With the prospect that in a few years PHAs will have to rely solely on rental income for their operating revenue, it is even more urgent that they convert their most distressed properties into attractive communities that households with and without rental assistance will want to live in. Developments with units that are too small, poorly

designed, badly maintained or crime-infested will find it difficult to attract certificate holders or market rate renters.[66]

Within weeks, HUD hosted a conference titled Moving HOPE VI Forward in Changing Times on March 27–29, 1995. At a time when the U.S. House of Representatives proposed to substantially reduce FY 1995 low-income housing funding, including HOPE VI, modernization funds, and operation subsidies—with even deeper budget cuts anticipated in FY 1996 and beyond—a wide range of participants including Congress, HUD, PHAs, HOPE VI residents, the Corporation for National Service, and community and supportive services providers were invited to "reconsider" and "reformulate" HOPE VI policies. From that point on, PHAs were encouraged to "think outside the box" and even "go back and substantially revise" their HOPE VI plan in light of these "new realities."[67]

Redefining HOPE VI Through Exemptions and Examples

In the spirit of innovation and reinvention defined by the 1995 NOFA and a series of conferences and executive programs,[68] HUD's HOPE VI staff worked their way through the ambiguity of the HOPE VI statute, trying to find every possible weapon to assist housing authorities in redeveloping distressed public housing. After nearly sixty years on the receiving end of the policy process, public housing authorities were empowered and expected to be active participants in defining policy alternatives. Therefore, the policy direction of HOPE VI was brainstormed and negotiated almost daily through talks between HUD officials and PHAs. Through this process, greater numbers of local housing authorities began assuming new roles as policy entrepreneurs, participating in development consortiums, and compromising in order to secure federal funding. The HOPE VI program, staffed with a group of crusaders for change, actively negotiated within HUD many of the program exceptions and waivers that have eventually come to define the initiative's distinctive innovations.[69]

It was not merely the waivers or exemptions themselves but what the local housing authorities had done and were doing with their flexibility that ultimately created the crucial precedents for HOPE VI as an implemented program. Indeed, HOPE VI staff members at HUD were equally energized by the ideas and efforts springing up in localities across the country. In an effort to assess Turbov's session on "Introduction to HOPE VI Plus" at the 1995 HOPE VI conference in which the Housing Authority of Louisville, Kentucky (HAL) presented its Park DuValle Revitalization Plan,[70] Robert Prescott, deputy director of the HOPE VI division, wrote the following in an e-mail dated April 6, 1995:

I was impressed with vision, scope, and magnitude of the Louisville rede-velopment plan. . . . I doubt that there are more than 10 or 15 PHAs in the country that are thinking in these terms . . . There are the real "movers and shakers," and they need all the reinforcement they can get. IT IS A SMALL NUMBER BUT THEY REPRESENT THE FUTURE. WE ARE TRYING TO NURTURE BUT FRANKLY THE BEST THING WE CAN DO IS GET ONE OF THESE PROJECTS TO CONSTRUCTION SO WE HAVE A REAL MODEL. (Emphasis in original)

One of the "movers and shakers" was the Atlanta Housing Authority (AHA), which worked closely with its developers and HUD to craft a pro-posal for a mixed-finance development that built upon the newly loosened regulatory climate for HOPE VI.[71] The new executive director of AHA, Renée Glover, previously a corporate lawyer, partnered with a joint venture consist-ing of the Integral Group LLC and McCormack Baron & Associates Inc. With the maximum tax credits available from the Georgia Housing and Fi-nance Agency, they pioneered the use of the LIHTC in transforming the Techwood Homes into Centennial Place. Although its original plan focused on renovation, AHA chose to demolish the original structures instead. Cen-tennial Place was turned into a mixed-income community that replaced the original 1,195 units with 900 units (40 percent market rent units, 40 percent public housing, and 20 percent tax credits units). Demonstrating the avail-ability and feasibility of alternative funding sources for public housing rede-velopment, AHA went the furthest in its implementation and soon became the model HOPE VI innovator. Renée Glover was then frequently invited to present and promote her approach at the annual HOPE VI new grantees' orientation conference.[72]

Along with other local examples of mixed-finance approaches, this inno-vation generated interest from other private market developers accustomed to using a combination of subsidies for affordable housing development. Local housing authorities began to partner with others—particularly affordable housing developers—to identify viable strategies, stressing these alliances to inform their negotiations with HUD. The HOPE VI shop actively dissemi-nated local innovations and lessons learned via the Housing Research Foun-dation and encouraged authorities to "see one, do one, and teach one."[73] By 1995, HOPE VI was clearly leading the way toward reform:

It is important for all of us to keep in mind that what we do in HOPE VI will not only affect the 34 developments currently funded, but may offer all housing authorities possible creative solutions to solving similar prob-lems in their own communities. This office has worked from day one under the hope that what we do in HOPE VI will have a profound impact for the rest of the public housing industry.[74]

Jumping on the Bandwagon?

By the end of 1996, the trend toward a new way of doing business was clearly evident to people in public housing circles, both inside and outside the Beltway. The emergent policy consensus in support of mixed-financing and public-private partnerships perfectly illustrates how the politics affects policy choice. Although it was suggested initially by NCSDPH, the idea of incorporating tax credits into public housing as a way to leverage other funds was not part of the first two years of HOPE VI. In a matter of two years, leveraging private funds and public-private partnerships became a primary goal of the HOPE VI program.[75]

At once housing administrators and local developers, facing the most distressed projects in the country, were confronted with the daunting task of integrating two systems that had been almost completely independent over the fifty-eight-year history of public housing. Clearly, the dramatic shift in financial outsourcing demanded both a breadth and a depth of knowledge, drastic change in skill sets and mind-set, and substantial staff capacity on the part of HUD and PHAs. In practice, PHAs took the responsibility for an overwhelming amount of work, including a competitive and fluctuating grant application process, local negotiations with the city and with residents, and complex financing and management operations with private investors and developers. All of this required a steep learning curve for the public sector. Complex financial structures and challenging inner-city sites also deterred most private developers from participating.[76]

As experienced developers of subsidized housing in several major cities applied their knowledge of local market conditions, federal housing regulations, and private sector development, HUD and PHA staff members grappled with Real Estate 101 while trying to fulfill their social responsibilities. Despite huge disparities in knowledge bases, different organizational cultures, and the necessity of negotiating complex and unfamiliar real estate transactions, HOPE VI forced open the door to a new world of leveraging and partnership. In fact, the NCSDPH and the 1993 NOFA had both recognized the limited capacity of local housing authorities as a barrier to innovation. Nearly every policy analysis between 1989 and 1995 noted that public housing authority management and operating systems were often as distressed as the properties they represented.[77] The inability of PHAs to put together a good implementation plan in a timely manner in the first two years cast huge doubt on the feasibility of forging new institutional partnerships. HOPE VI's financial component became a source of confusion and indecision in the first year of leveraging. To many PHAs—especially those on the "troubled" list—this policy choice seemed unexpected and somewhat utopian.

With all the aforementioned obstacles, HUD wholeheartedly promoted the idea of mixed financing and speedily provided a series of workshops and training sessions to HUD headquarter staff and PHAs, hoping to equip them with adequate knowledge to be an equal partner in the federally "arranged marriage."[78] At a time when the public sector was perceived as synonymous with incompetence and as part of the problem, the politically popular choice turned out to be, not surprisingly, the private sector.

In fact, the outline of what would distinctively break HOPE VI away from conventional public housing was foreshadowed in the public dialogue of the early 1990s. In his acceptance speech in 1993, incoming HUD secretary Henry Cisneros emphasized entrepreneurship and the administration's interest in promoting public-private partnerships. Vice President Gore proclaimed that government could not succeed without support from the private sector. Gore actively backed HUD's Empowerment Zone/Enterprise Communities program, in which public-private partnerships served as one of the pillars for community-capacity building. Revisions to the HOPE VI program also capitalized on the spirit of entrepreneurship praised by Congress as the antidote to welfare dependency.

At a time when the administration considered abolishing HUD to balance the budget and co-opt the Republicans' agenda, transformation became the only hope for HUD. Desperate to prove HUD's worth to Congress, Cisneros claimed a new day for the agency in the *Reinvention Blueprint*. More than any other element of reform, HUD emphasized the devolution of control over public housing from the federal government to local housing authorities. Abandoning the conventional claim that poor management was to blame, Cisneros reframed the problem of the severely distressed public housing as the isolation of public housing authorities from the marketplace. Therefore, the solutions offered were for PHAs to go into partnership with developers and to embrace the market and the broader community.

At the local level, in a period when Congress was calling for deep cuts in social programs, interests in support of affordable housing (from the public housing community to the U.S. Conference of Mayors) were eager to support any policy that would bring resources to the inner city.[79] The politically popular model of public-private partnership—however technically adventurous—was advanced by HUD as a key element of reintegrating isolated public housing authorities into the rest of the real estate market.

Between 1993 and 1995 the problems plaguing the most severely distressed public housing remained the same. However, tremendous ferment in the policy stream, made up of academic research about cities, ghettos, poverty, and poor people, provided rationales for the adoption of specific programmatic goals such as deconcentration through mixed-income communities. Local knowledge and experience also contributed to the policy shift. A dramatic development in the political stream—the Republican landslide victory in 1994—and the subsequent spillover effect of welfare reforms further leveraged policy change. Therefore, as part of the larger consideration of government reinvention and devolution in social welfare programs, public housing problems were redefined, not just acknowledged in the midst of the mood of discrediting Washington-driven government. As visionary secretary Henry Cisneros pushed for "doing it over again" in HOPE VI, affordable housing developers like Richard Baron, along with some entrepreneur PHAs, quickly used their effective linkages to key officials to overcome institutional roadblocks to innovation. Encouraged to reconsider both their missions and methods, local housing authorities emerged as new policy entrepreneurs, supplying their own solutions, which in turn drove HOPE VI policy in a new direction.

Notes

We would like to thank Professors Lawrence Vale, Langley Keyes, Xavier Briggs, Martin Rein, Stephen Meyer, Judith Layzer, and our colleagues Laurie Goldman and Kil Huh for their ongoing support and tremendous insights into this research. We would also like to thank the numerous people in the housing industry who shared their HOPE VI experience with us.

1. John W. Kingdon, *Agendas, Alternatives, and Public Policies* (1984; New York: HarperCollins, 2003).

2. HOPE VI, also known as the Urban Revitalization Demonstration (URD) program, was originally created as part of the Department of Veterans Affairs and Housing and Urban Development and Independent Agencies Appropriations Act (H.R. 5679 Public Law 102–389) approved on October 6, 1992. The Quality Housing and Work Responsibility Act (QHWRA) in 1998 rewrote Section 24 of the U.S. Housing Act of 1937 to establish a statutory authorization for the HOPE VI program through September 30, 2002. In the FY 2003 appropriations bill, Congress reauthorized the program through FY 2004.

3. Housing and Urban Development, *HOPE VI: Lessons Learned and Best Practices, 1992–2002* (Washington, DC: U.S. Department of Housing and Urban Development, 2002).

4. Housing and Urban Development, *HOPE VI: Building Communities, Transforming Lives* (Washington, DC: U.S. Department of Housing and Urban Development, 1999), p. 6. In the same publication (p. 4), President Clinton is also quoted as saying: "HUD's HOPE VI grants are a step toward achieving my Administration's goal of helping people help themselves to improve their lives and their communities through hard work. By providing job training and improving the quality, management, and safety of public housing, we are giving hope to communities that have previously known despair."

5. National Housing Law Project et al., "False HOPE: A Critical Assessment of the HOPE VI Public Housing Redevelopment Program," June 2002, I, www.nhlp.org/html/pubhsg/Falseope.pda.

6. Michael D. Cohen, James G. March, and Johan P. Olsen, "A Garbage Can Model of Organizational Choice," *Administrative Science Quarterly* 17, no. 1 (1972): 1–25.

7. The "primeval soup"—the state before life comes into being—which contains the basic ingredients for the beginnings of life. See Kingdon, *Agendas, Alternatives, and Public Policies,* p. 116.

8. Pending retirements, leadership changes, federal and/or provincial elections, and external socioeconomic pressures all foster a political climate that can be conducive to change or retrenchment.

9. The general "stages" model was, for many years, the preeminent theory about policy making. It usually involves agenda setting, decision making, implementation, and evaluation.

10. John Atlas and Peter Dreier, "From 'Projects' to Communities: Redeeming Public Housing," *Journal of Housing* 50, no. 1 (1993): 21–33; Lawrence J. Vale, *Reclaiming Public Housing: A Half Century of Struggle in Three Public Neighborhoods* (Cambridge, MA: Harvard University Press, 2002).

11. In Kingdon, conditions are defined as problems when (1) new indicators are available, (2) dramatic events occur, and (3) existing programs give feedback. Problem definition is bounded by the values and beliefs, comparisons (with other settings), and categories employed by stakeholders.

12. Other legislation, the Housing and Community Development Act of 1992, was in a race with Senator Barbara Mikulski's. It was being developed with the housing authorizers sitting on the Senate Committee on Banking, Housing and Urban Affairs, Subcommittee on Housing and Urban Affairs, which established the NCSDPH in 1989. It would have been natural for this subcommittee to assume the task of creating a new program like HOPE VI, through a traditional authorization process. Besides, the subcommittee was more focused and better positioned to make extensive laws on this subject. However, despite the opposition from the authorizers, Senator Mikulski was reluctant to let another year go by and she pressed for putting the public housing measure into the 1993 appropriations bill. This action was strongly supported by Senator Christopher Bond, a ranking Republican; Representative Louis Stokes (D-OH), an African-American who grew up in public housing; and Representative Bill Green (R-NY), the NCSDPH cochair and, at the time, chair of the House VA-HUD committee. The rationale might have been threefold. First, the appropriations act is subject to yearly renewal; therefore the committee retains the power to confirm subsequent appropriations. Second, the authorization process takes a long time. Finally, the lobbists from trade organizations such as Council of Large Public Housing Authorities pushed for legislative and administrative flexibility.

13. The number was based on an estimate made by Abt Associates Inc. in 1987 of the number of public housing units with high modernization needs. National Commission on Severely Distressed Public Housing, *The Final Report of the National Commission on Severely Distressed Public Housing: A Report to the Congress and the Secretary of Housing and Urban Development* (Washington, DC: U.S. Department of Housing and Urban Development, 1992); National Commission on Severely Distressed Public Housing, *Case Study and Site Examination Reports of the National Commission on Severely Distressed Public Housing* (Washington, DC: U.S. Department of Housing and Urban Development, 1992).

14. This set of solutions was later downplayed by HUD. Bruce Katz, staff director, U.S. Senate Subcommittee on Housing and Urban Affairs (1992–1993); Senior Counsel, Senate Subcommittee on Housing and Urban Affairs (1987–92); and chief of staff, HUD (1993–1996), interview, March 29, 2004.

15. Arthur Naparstek was a professor at the Mandel School of Applied Social Sciences at Case Western Reserve University as well as director of the Cleveland Commission on Poverty at the time. The commission put together a report that proposed an innovative plan to reinvent services for the poor in Cleveland (www.cwru.edu/pubs/cwrumag/fa111998/features/anniversary/sections/s/index.shtml).

16. Arthur Naparstek, interview, March 12, 2004.

17. First started in Boston at the Bromley-Heath development in 1971 and soon thereafter in St. Louis, resident management of public housing emerged as a response to management failures on the part of PHAs. The success of the early efforts sparked the National Tenant Management Demonstration Program (1977–1979) involving seven public housing sites in six cities. However, in an evaluation of the program in 1981, the Manpower Demonstration Research Corporation (MDRC) found that the attempt yielded limited benefits with significant costs and thus recommended against expansion of the program. In the mid- to late 1980s, as vandalism and crime penetrated many public housing communities and public housing authorities failed to respond effectively, some residents began to organize among themselves to take on management and security responsibilities and to uplift living conditions in their developments. Capitalizing on the self-help aspect of RMCs, the Housing and Community Development Act of 1987 promoted a fast-growing movement of resident management and the establishment of an Office of Resident Initiatives within HUD. Despite recognized accomplishments, RMCs were largely considered technically and financially infeasible on a large scale. See William Peterman, "Resident Management: A Good Idea Gone Wrong?" *Journal of Housing* 51, no. 3 (1994): 10–15.

18. Senate Report 102–356, Committee on Appropriations, August 3, 1992, p. 40.

19. Arthur Naparstek, remarks at the Urban Institute's press conference on the Resident Panel Study, July 2002. It is likely that Mikulski, who had a background in social work, aimed to emphasize the people side of transformation and/or support the National Commission of Social Services funded under her committee.

20. In fact, the NOFAs for MROP and HOPE VI in the early 1990s were not very different.

21. Community social services were defined by the Commission on National and Community Service. The appropriations act of 1993 required that a minimum of 80 percent of the HOPE VI grant be allocated for hard construction costs and a maximum of 20 percent for soft costs, although many experts would argue that the degree of socioeconomic need of families in projects demands a higher portion for supportive services and economic development initiatives. The actual funding for soft costs through HOPE VI gradually decreased in the following years.

22. William Julius Wilson, *The Truly Disadvantaged: The Inner City, the Underclass, and Public Policy* (Chicago: University of Chicago Press, 1987).

23. Lewis H. Spence, "Rethinking the Social Role of Public Housing," *Housing Policy Debate* 4, no. 3 (1993): 355, 367.

24. Robert Putnam, *Making Democracy Work: Civic Traditions in Modern Italy* (Princeton, NJ: Princeton University Press, 1993); Robert Putnam, "The Strange Disappearance of Civic America," *American Prospect* 7, no. 24 (1996): 34–48; Xavier Briggs, "Brown Kids in White Suburbs: Housing Mobility and the Many Faces of

Social Capital," *Housing Policy Debate* 9, no. 1 (1998): 177–221. Thanks to Laurie Goldman for pointing out the problem and solution in Wilson and Putnam.

25. It is interesting to see, from his inauguration testimony, that Henry Cisneros was not aware of the HOPE VI program when asked about his take on the 86,000 units of severely distressed housing units. Cisneros responded with his ideas about the troubled authorities instead.

26. Hearing of the Senate Banking, Housing and Urban Affairs Committee, Subject: Confirmation of Henry G. Cisneros as Secretary of Housing and Urban Development, January 12, 1993.

27. The suggested changes in legislative language in Section 24 included deleting the requirement that HOPE VI grantees must be severely distressed projects; increasing the planning grants dollar cap from $200,000 to $500,000 (to help some of the larger housing projects); requiring grant applications to include community service activities in their proposals, such as job training, the opportunity to complete high school requirements, and other programs for disadvantaged youth; deleting the requirement for a national geographic diversity among applicants to allow HUD to put the money where it is needed most; and making changes to demolition or replacement requirements in Section 8. In part because Congress intended to maintain its power over this demonstration program through its yearly appropriation process, rather than setting forth legislative changes, these provisions were not included in the final version of the bill (S. 1299) that was sent to the president (*Cong. Rec.* 139: S. 9698).

28. Note that this was contrary to the conventional wisdom and that Cisneros's reform agenda was merely responding to the hostility of congressional conservatives.

29. Henry Cisneros, testimony before the Senate Banking, Housing, and Urban Affairs Committee, Housing and Urban Affairs Subcommittee: HUD Housing Program Reauthorization, April 28, 1994. Passed in the House but blocked in the Senate, this bill proposed to overhaul the modernization program by enabling funds to be used for demolition and replacement housing. Moreover, PHAs would for the first time be given authority to collectively borrow against future modernization funds and to leverage these borrowed resources with other public and private investments. Many of these reforms would see their final passage four years later in 1998.

30. Cisneros, testimony, April 28, 1994.

31. Randy Weaver, *Ending Welfare As We Know It.* (Washington, DC: Brookings Institution Press, 2000).

32. Guy Gugliotta, "HUD Mans Its Lifeboats," *Washington Post National Weekly Edition,* February 13–19, 1995.

33. Henry Cisneros, testimony before House Appropriations Committee, Subcommittee on VA, HUD and Independent Agencies: Downsizing Government, January 24, 1995.

34. Henry Cisneros, testimony before the Senate Committee on Banking, Housing and Urban Affairs: Public Housing Reform and Empowerment Act, September 28, 2004.

35. The document was released on December 19, 1994. In January 1996, HUD updated it in a new document titled *Renewing America's Communities from the Ground Up—The Plan to Complete the Transformation of HUD.* This second phase of the *Blueprint* revised HUD's original proposal to "voucher-out" all public housing. It suggested improving existing public housing and tenant-based housing assistance delivery through program consolidations and streamlining. Other highlights included getting tough on crime and mismanagement in public and assisted housing, tearing

down and replacing the worst public housing developments, and changing rules to promote self-sufficiency and responsibility.

36. Congress did not agree upon a full vouchering system. In fact, Republicans (including Robert Dole) repeatedly voted to reduce the funding for vouchers. This was in part because it was cost prohibitive and in part because of the NIMBY (not in my backyard) syndrome: many constituencies were afraid that vouchers might lead poor and disproportionately black public housing residents to seek housing in the mostly white suburbs. See Nina Burleigh, "The Suburbs Won't Vouch for This," *Time,* May 13, 1996.

37. Deborah Austin, "Federal Housing Policy: The Road Ahead," *Shelterforce Online,* January/February 1994.

38. The office was later renamed the Office of Public Housing Investments.

39. Milan Ozdinec, interview, March 5, 2004. Milan Ozdinec, currently the deputy assistant secretary for Public Housing Investments, is a career staffer who has worked on HOPE VI since its inception. He served as the division director of the Office of Urban Revitalization in the early years of HOPE VI.

40. Bruce Katz, interview, March 29, 2004.

41. Professor Lawrence Vale, a keen observer and an ardent defender of public housing, also pointed out that the first year's Urban Revitalization Demonstration missed an important window of opportunity for desirable changes in policy, such as occupancy restructuring, to seek a broader clientele for public housing. Familiar with the common strategies espoused in the Comprehensive Improvement Assistance Program in addressing the issue of "problem people," Vale suggested that URD should have taken advantage of the reconstruction period to screen new tenants carefully, introduce higher percentages of working families, and "evict those who are causing problems." See Lawrence Vale, "Beyond the Problem Projects Paradigm: Defining and Revitalizing Severely Distressed Public Housing," *Housing Policy Debate* 4, no. 2 (1993): 147–174. Eleven years later, "with such safeguards," Vale argued, "it would then be possible to re-house a larger percentage of very low-income households in the redeveloped public housing" (personal communication).

42. Wayne Sherwood, interviews, November 2002 and July 25, 2003.

43. Andrea Duncan, testimony before House Banking, Finance and Urban Affairs Committee, Housing and Community Development Subcommittee, March 17, 1994.

44. Gordon Cavanaugh (on behalf of the Council of Large Public Housing Authorities), March 17, 1994. Testimony before the Housing Appropriations Committee Subcommittee for Veterans Affairs, Housing and Urban Development, and Independent Agencies: Restructuring the Federal Government.

45. The one-for-one requirement, which was in place as HUD's regulation from 1979 through 1986, stated that PHAs must replace every housing unit demolished or sold with another unit of public housing. Congress turned it into law in the Housing and Community Development Act of 1987 (Public Law 100–242), which also stipulated that tenants cannot be forced to vacate their existing housing until HUD approves a replacement plan.

46. Site and neighborhood standards, as contained in HUD regulations, require that newly constructed or rehabilitated assisted housing must meet certain criteria for adequacy and suitability. In addition, when a site for this housing is chosen, care must be taken to avoid an undue concentration of persons receiving housing assistance in an area that already contains a high proportion of low-income persons. Further, newly constructed public housing can be built in an area of minority concentration only if (1) sufficient, comparable opportunities exist for housing for minority families, in the

income range to be served by the proposed project, outside areas of minority concentration, or (2) the project is necessary to meet overriding housing needs that cannot be met in that housing market area.

47. In 1994, the House Committee on Banking, Finance and Urban Affairs attempted to give housing authorities more flexibility to trim from their inventories buildings that were no longer viable for providing cost-effective and decent low-income housing. The committee included in its housing reauthorization bill a provision to allow the secretary of HUD to waive the one-for-one replacement law. This bill was not enacted during the 103rd Congress.

48. Susan Gaffney, inspector general of HUD, testimony before the Joint Meeting of the Subcommittees on Employment, Housing and Aviation, and General Oversight, Investigations, and the Resolution of Failed Financial Institutions, March 22, 1994. Gaffney listed the potential benefits of repealing one-for-one as follows: the removal of obsolete or nonviable units from the public housing stock would increase a PHA's cash flow through sale of public housing developments, particularly those on property that has appreciated land value; reduce PHA operating expenses; reduce the need for operating subsidy and modernization funds; and reduce the federal government's debt service obligation incurred when the development was constructed, if the land is not retained for future building. However, oftentimes PHAs do not move forward with replacement because several factors adversely affect the PHAs' efforts to meet the replacement housing requirements, including limited availability of public housing development funds or Section 8 assistance; lack of acceptable sites for new replacement housing developments; and local opposition to the construction of new public housing units.

49. Wayne Sherwood, interview, July 25, 2003.

50. See memorandum from Nelson A. Diaz, HUD general counsel, to Joseph Shuldiner, assistant secretary for Public and Indian Housing, dated March 7, 1994, regarding the relationship of the Urban Revitalization Demonstration to the U.S. Housing Act of 1937; memorandum from Nelson A. Diaz, HUD general counsel, to Joseph Shuldiner, assistant secretary for Public and Indian Housing, dated April 13, 1994, regarding the use of public housing funds to leverage private financing; memorandum from Michael Reardon, HUD assistant general counsel, to Raymond Hamilton, Development Division director, regarding the Fairfax tax credit proposal, dated July 29, 1994.

51. Richard Baron authored or coauthored several studies of public housing, including "The Insider's Guide to Managing Public Housing," coauthored with Robert Kolodny and Raymond J. Struyk and prepared for U.S. Department of Housing and Urban Development, Office of Policy Development and Research, 1983.

52. Currently, Community Builders is one of the most active developers working in the HOPE VI program, with engagements in Louisville (KY), Boston (MA), Cincinnati (OH), Durham (NC), Pittsburgh (PA), Allegheny County (PA), Wheeling (WV), Norfolk (VA), Coatesville (PA), New Brunswick (NJ), and Chicago (IL). Source: www.communitybuilders.org/what_we_do/hopevi_general.htm.

53. A former faculty member at the University of California at Berkeley, Don Turner had also served as the State of California's Director of Housing and Community Development.

54. Willie Jones, executive director of Community Builders, interview October 30, 2003.

55. This was further confirmed by a memorandum dated July 29, 1994, from Michael Reardon, assistant general counsel, on the condition of rule-making (rather than granting waivers).

56. Deborah Goddard, former planning director of the Boston Housing Authority, interview, April 4, 2003.

57. M. FitzPatrick, "A Disaster in Every Generation: An Analysis of HOPE VI: HUD's Newest Big Budget Development Plan," *Georgetown Journal on Poverty Law and Policy* 7 (2000): 421; Megan Glasheen and Julie McGovern, "Mixed-Finance Development: Privatizing Public Housing Through Public/Private Development Partnerships," in *Privatizing Governmental Functions*, ed. Deborah S. Ballati, pp. 9-1–9-69 (New York: Law Journal Press, 2001).

58. Kevin Marchman, interview, August 4, 2004.

59. Hornig later became deputy assistant secretary for Public Housing Investments, an office combining the investment division and the other divisions of ODTHR. Hornig previously had been a partner in the law firm Reno, Cavanaugh and Hornig, representing CLPHA.

60. Christopher Hornig, interview, August 9, 2004.

61. Nicolas Retsinas oversaw the Federal Housing Administration. He is currently the Director of Harvard University's Joint Center for Housing Studies, as well as a Lecturer in Housing Studies at the Harvard Design School and the Kennedy School of Government.

62. It is striking to observe how short the institutional memory is at HUD. Few staff members at the HOPE VI office noticed the history and story of HOPE VI Plus. According to Christopher Hornig, many other initiatives and innovations in HOPE VI got lost once there was administrative turnover, which was partly due to the lack of formal guidebooks and regulations.

63. Hornig, interview.

64. James Stockard, former Commissioner of the Cambridge (Massachusetts) Housing Authority, interview, April 14, 2004.

65. The Office of Distressed and Troubled Housing Recovery was reorganized as the Office of Public Housing Investments in 1995.

66. This document continues:

> Each development has assets and liabilities, and the greatest challenge facing housing authorities is to take a dispassionate and realistic look at each HOPE VI property to determine the following: whether it can be made marketable to people who have other choices of housing assistance; what it would cost and how long it would take to bring the property to a marketable condition; whether the HOPE VI funding will be adequate to make the repairs or revitalization needed; exactly how much rent the units are worth in their current condition and after revitalization; whether the rents the existing vs. revitalized units can command will cover realistic operating costs plus a deposit to a replacement reserve; and finally, whether the rents that can reasonably be expected are so low that the only real alternative is demolition and, possibly, disposition of the site.

U.S. Department of Housing and Urban Development, "HOPE VI-Urban Revitalization Demonstration Program Notice," February 22, 1995, pp. 4–5, www.hudclips.org/sub_nonhud/html/nph-brs.cgi?d=PIHN&s1=95-$[no]&op1=AND&SECT1=TXTHLB&SECT5=PIHN&u=../html/shortcut.htm&p=1&r=50&f=G.

67. Bruce Katz, interview.

68. A conference was held in March 1996, titled Partnerships to Maximize Resources: Privatizing Today's Public Housing—Tools and Opportunities for Housing Authorities *and* the Private Sector—That Increase and Improve the Affordable Hous-

ing Stock (emphasis in original). In November 1996, HUD sponsored the Finance for Public Housing Professionals executive program, aimed at training HUD staff and public housing authorities about real estate fundamentals, principles for lending in the public sector, how to work with lenders, etc.

69. The 1995 NOFA says, "If the Congress should enact legislation that affects HOPE VI, the program may be conformed further to other authorizing legislation. In such event, the PHA may have the opportunity to pursue avenues not currently available under applicable laws. HUD will notify the Field Office and the PHA in writing of any such legislation and will accord the PHA full opportunity (consistent with the progress already made) to amend its HOPE VI Revitalization Plan to take advantage of such opportunities."

70. HAL began planning for the rehabilitation of Cotter Homes through its comprehensive grant program (CGP) in 1993. Taking advantage of the loosened legislative and regulatory environment, HAL conducted market analysis and envisioned the Park DuValle revitalization plan (with input from the public housing residents and the adjacent neighborhoods). The project was financed by a combination of CGP, tax credits, and Community Development Block Grant funds. In 1996, Community Builders Inc. was selected by HAL as the developer for the Park DuValle HOPE VI project.

71. Rod Solomon, HUD assistant secretary for Policy, Program and Legislative Initiatives, lamented that the earlier mixed-finance and mixed-income developments such as Harbor Point did not benefit from the repeal of one-for-one and other waivers of federal regulations. Interview, August 9, 2003.

72. Residents suspected that they would become victims to the powerful corporate interests through the redevelopment process. The citywide resident organization called for Renée Glover's resignation in 1994. See Larry Keating, "Redeveloping Public Housing: Relearning Urban Renewal's Immutable Lessons," *Journal of the American Planning Association* 66, no. 4 (2000): 384–397.

73. Milan Ozdinec, interview, March 25, 2004.

74. Housing Research Foundation, "Ozdinec on the Impact of HOPE VI," *HOPE VI Developments Newsletter* 3 (1995).

75. HUD promulgated an Interim Mixed-finance Rule (Subpart F to 24 *Code of Federal Regulations* pt. 941) in May 1996 to form partnerships with private developers.

76. Peter Smirniotopoulos, "Valuing the Public Sector's Contribution to Public/Private Partnerships: The HOPE VI Experience," *HOPE VI Developments Newsletter* 50 (2002); Urban Land Institute, *Engaging the Private Sector in HOPE VI* (Washington, DC: Urban Institute, 2002).

77. Thomas E. Nutt-Powell, "Public Housing—Dissed and Stressed in a Brave New World," *Cityscape: A Journal of Policy Development and Research* 1, no. 3 (1995): 122–123; Spence, "Rethinking the Social Role of Public Housing," 355–368.

78. Smirniotopoulos, "Valuing the Public Sector's Contribution."

79. Nicholas Lemann, "The Myth of Community Development," *New York Times Magazine,* January 9, 1994.

3

The HOPE VI Program

What Has Happened to the Residents?

Susan J. Popkin

By the end of the 1980s, public housing was widely viewed as a failure, with high-rise projects in many cities having become emblematic of what Rebecca Blank has termed "the most destructive kind of poverty."[1] These communities were characterized by high rates of problems including crime, unemployment, high school dropout, and teen parenthood. Under the new approach embodied in the HOPE VI program, the Department of Housing and Urban Development (HUD) intended to address the concentration of troubled low-income households in public housing by moving away from its reliance on project-based assistance and instead promoting the construction of mixed-income housing and greater reliance on housing subsidies. There was little solid evidence that these new policies would bring about the desired changes[2] but rather a sense that a new, radical approach was the only way to address the problems of severely distressed public housing.[3] Only now is evidence emerging about the impact of the dramatic shift in housing policy on developments, on neighborhoods, and, especially, on residents.[4]

To answer the questions about the outcome of the original residents of HOPE VI developments across the nation, Congress commissioned two systematic, multicity studies in 1999: the "HOPE VI Panel Study" and the "HOPE VI Resident Tracking Study."[5] Both studies were intended to address the question of how public housing transformation has affected the lives of the original residents of HOPE VI developments—those living in the developments prior to the grant award.[6] The panel study focuses on five cities and is tracking the living conditions and well-being of residents from five developments that were first surveyed as revitalization began in mid- to late 2001. The resident tracking study provides a snapshot of the living conditions and well-being of former residents of eight properties in early 2001—between two and seven years after the housing authority received a HOPE VI grant.

The findings from the first phase of this research raise critical questions about whether the transformation of public housing will achieve its potential as a powerful force for improving the lives of low-income families. As developments are destroyed, the residents are being displaced and face an uncertain future. While it appears that most of those who have been relocated have experienced real benefits and are living in better housing in safer neighborhoods, these new neighborhoods are still extremely poor and racially segregated and residents continue to report significant problems with crime and drug trafficking. Further, many of the residents who have received vouchers report struggling to find and keep housing in the private market. Only a small proportion of original residents have been able to move to the new mixed-income housing on the HOPE VI site, while a substantial proportion—about half—have moved to other public housing developments.

Finally, a substantial proportion of tenants awaiting relocation have physical and mental health problems and other serious personal challenges that will make it hard for them to rent in the private sector. Others live in households whose composition—large numbers of children, elderly or disabled heads of household with young children—makes it nearly impossible for them to find suitable units in the private market or the newly transformed housing, for that matter. Without a concerted effort to address their housing needs, these families will be at risk of becoming homeless.

Expectations for Public Housing Transformation

A central premise of HOPE VI is that it is possible to improve the lives of residents of distressed housing developments by either helping them to relocate to better neighborhoods or creating a new, healthier community on-site. This premise is based on a belief among many policy makers and scholars that high concentrations of very low-income households in housing developments lead to negative social and behavioral outcomes. As discussed in the previous chapters, public housing residents may be particularly at risk for experiencing the negative consequences of living in poverty.

The prevalence of crime and disorder in neighborhoods is a key factor. High-crime neighborhoods have particularly adverse consequences for children's well-being. Children growing up in communities marked by crime almost certainly will be exposed to violence and may become victims themselves.[7] Living amid violence negatively affects children's cognitive and emotional development.[8] Further, parents in poor, dangerous neighborhoods are likely to use harsh parenting styles that have negative consequences on children's development.[9] Finally, there appears to be a linkage between high homicide rates and other public health indicators such as low birth weight.[10]

The logic behind public housing transformation is that if neighborhood environments can cause bad outcomes, then policies that reduce concentrations of poverty, such as dispersal and mobility strategies and mixed-income housing, should lead to better ones.[11] However, there is little solid evidence to support the assumption that moving very low-income families from high-poverty communities—or attracting more affluent residents to move to poor neighborhoods—has much effect on low-income residents' life chances, particularly their ability to become self-sufficient. What is clear is that low-income residents benefit in terms of safety and housing quality, which may have longer-term effects on outcomes for families.[12]

Three studies have examined the experiences of very low-income families who moved from distressed public housing communities to lower-poverty neighborhoods: Gautreaux, Moving to Opportunity (MTO), and Yonkers. The Gautreaux research compared outcomes for participants who moved to predominantly white suburbs of Chicago to outcomes for those who moved to revitalizing African-American neighborhoods in the city.[13] A follow-up study indicated that suburban movers were more likely to report having had a job after they moved, although they did not work more hours or earn higher wages than city movers.[14] Findings from a longitudinal study of a small sample of participants indicated that suburban movers' children were more likely to stay in school, to be employed after graduation, and to go on to four-year colleges or universities.[15] While these results have been widely accepted as strong evidence of the benefits of moving public housing families to higher-income neighborhoods, the Gautreaux program had a number of important limitations, particularly the fact that only 20 percent of participants ever moved.[16]

The MTO demonstration program, intended to provide more definitive answers about potential neighborhood effects, involved randomly assigning public housing residents from developments in five different cities to one of three groups: an experimental group that received Section 8 Housing Choice vouchers that could be used only in neighborhoods with less than 10 percent poverty, or one of two control groups (a group that received regular vouchers or a group that remained in public housing).[17] Early findings from small, preliminary studies of the MTO families suggested that the experimental group experienced some significant benefits, especially positive effects on participants' mental and physical health.[18] The full MTO interim evaluation found evidence that movers were living in better housing in safer neighborhoods and that adults experienced substantial improvements in mental health and reduced obesity.[19] Results for youth were mixed, with girls in the experimental group experiencing improved mental health and a lower incidence of behavior problems, but boys showing negative trends in mental health and a higher incidence of risky behaviors. Further, there were no indications as yet of the kinds of employment or educational effects seen in Gautreaux. The Yonkers scattered-site program involved the construction of scattered-site units for minority tenants in predominantly white areas. Xavier de Souza Briggs, comparing outcomes for movers to those for participants who remained in traditional public housing, found that while the participants' new neighborhoods were clearly safer and less stressful, there was relatively little evidence that movers had significant interaction with their new neighbors, gained access to social capital, or experienced socioeconomic benefits.[20]

Effects of HOPE VI

While there is limited evidence on the potential effects of mixed-income and dispersal strategies, we do have some insight into what to expect from public housing transformation and HOPE VI. Based on data collected to date, it seems likely that many former residents will experience improvements in housing and neighborhood quality, which could affect their overall quality of life. It is less clear that involuntary relocation will bring about the same kinds of benefits as experienced by the volunteer participants in the Gautreaux program or even the MTO and Yonkers demonstrations. HOPE VI affects the *entire* population of distressed public housing developments, including people with no desire to move. Lawrence Vale argues that many residents of public housing developments marked by crime and other problems are profoundly ambivalent, fearing leaving as much as they do remaining in place.[21] Long-term residents, many of whom are older or have serious health problems, may not adjust easily to new housing situations. Without special support or assistance, many residents might end up in neighborhoods that are not much different than their original public housing developments.

Although the HOPE VI program began in the early 1990s, we know relatively little about how families have fared as public housing has been transformed. HUD-sponsored research has focused on the physical, social, and economic changes that have occurred at the sites and in the surrounding neighborhoods.[22] This research has documented many positive changes at HOPE VI sites. Other research suggests that by reducing large concentrations of poverty HOPE VI has benefited the neighborhoods around the original developments.[23] Critics of HOPE VI, however, argue that the program has actually made the situation worse for public housing residents.[24] These critics claim that the program has targeted developments that were not truly distressed, that it has substantially reduced the amount of affordable housing in many cities, and that screening criteria have excluded many former residents from new, mixed-income developments. Further, critics note that there is minimal information available to assess accurately how residents have fared during public housing transformation.

Even if better data were available, however, the debate about resident outcomes would be difficult, because there is no consensus about how to define success. Most people would probably agree that it is not defined solely by how many public housing residents return to the redeveloped site. Not returning to the site does not automatically mean that residents are worse off—indeed, they may well have chosen a voucher so they could move to a better neighborhood. Analysis of HUD data suggests that the average census tract poverty rate for HOPE VI residents who received vouchers dropped from 61 percent to 27 percent.[25] While still relatively high, especially when compared to suburban poverty rates, it is an improvement. There is less evidence of improvements in racial segregation, with the majority of households still living in tracts that were predominantly minority. In Chicago nearly all the original residents who moved with vouchers ended up in neighborhoods that were at least 90 percent African-American.[26]

Still, studies of individual HOPE VI sites suggest that many former residents perceive real improvements in their neighborhood conditions, particularly a reduction in crime.[27] The experience varies, obviously, with location and residents. For example, while some former residents in Philadelphia reported less crime, they felt uncertain about their ability to protect themselves and their children in an unfamiliar community.[28] In Minneapolis, relocated residents reported much less crime and greater satisfaction with grocery stores and parks, but less satisfaction with schools, transportation, and health care.[29] Other research raises reason for concern about how original residents have fared. Focus groups with residents from four HOPE VI sites found that relocatees sometimes make choices without having adequate information about Housing Choice vouchers, HOPE VI move-back criteria, and the availability of relocation services.[30] Further, many feared moving to unfamiliar areas, and those who did look elsewhere often reported encountering discrimination or difficulty in finding affordable units.

An early assessment of the revitalization of the Henry Horner Homes in Chicago found that some of the original Horner families living in the new development were having difficulty complying with the terms of their leases.[31] Even more of a concern, few of the original tenants had even tried to return to the development; many had been declared ineligible or left on their own without assistance. Similar problems were found in Atlanta's Techwood Homes.[32] Because of political pressures and housing authority decisions, many of the original tenants were gone by the time the HOPE VI revitalization began. As a result, only about half received the official relocation assistance to which they were entitled. The much-lauded Centennial Place development, which replaced Techwood, includes a smaller number of public housing units; few original residents have been able to benefit from the new housing. More recent findings from Chicago public housing point to problems with the relocation process.[33] During the first phase of relocation, less than half of the residents were able to make successful moves using Housing Choice vouchers. Those who did move reported living in better housing in safer neighborhoods, but most moved to poor, African-American communities not far from their original public housing developments. While the majority of residents faced the kind of barriers that make them particularly hard to house—lack of private market housing experience, large family sizes, physical disabilities, and complex personal problems[34]—the counseling services meant to help residents address these barriers were found to be inadequate.[35] Further, administrative—and political—problems also undermined the relocation effort. Sudhir Venkatesh's study of former Robert Taylor residents in Chicago points to challenges residents might face when leaving public housing.[36] Of particular concern are domestic violence and conflict with off-the-lease household members, often returning offenders who are formally barred from assisted housing. In either case, relocated tenants can be at risk of being evicted and/or losing their voucher.

In sum, the existing single-site research on public housing transformation raises more questions than it answers about how original residents have been and will be affected by the dramatic transformation of public housing. While there are suggestions that residents who have received vouchers are living in better housing in neighborhoods that are at least somewhat better than their original public housing communities, a substantial proportion of former residents appear to be living in neighborhoods that are still very poor and have problems with crime. In particular, evidence from Chicago implies that a subgroup of residents—those with the most complex personal problems or family situations—may have great difficulty making successful transitions to either the private market or revitalized developments, and even more trouble becoming self-sufficient. For these residents, a change in neighborhood environment may not be enough to bring about a meaningful change in life chances.

How Are Original HOPE VI Residents Faring?

As the HOPE VI program neared the end of its original ten-year authorization, advocates began to raise serious concerns about the way the program has been implemented. Compared to the number of public housing units lost, very few units had been rebuilt and very few residents had returned to HOPE VI sites.[37] Furthermore, there was no systematic information available to inform the debate.[38] The "HOPE VI Resident Tracking Study" and the "HOPE VI Panel Study" are the first systematic, multicity examinations of how original residents have been affected by public housing transformation. The tracking study provides a snapshot of the living conditions and well-being of former residents from eight HOPE VI sites where redevelopment activities began between 1994 and 1998—two to six years after the housing authority was awarded a HOPE VI grant.[39] The study involved surveys and in-depth interviews with 818 residents (approximately 100 per site), focusing on the type and quality of housing now occupied by the original HOPE VI residents; their current neighborhood and social environments; and their employment, material hardship, and health.[40] Table 3.1 provides a summary of the status of the eight sites in January 2001.[41]

The panel study builds on the tracking study, focusing on the longer-term location, neighborhood conditions, physical and mental health, and socioeconomic outcomes for 887 original residents of five HOPE VI developments where redevelopment activities began in mid- to late 2001. The five sites are Shore Park/Shore Terrace (Atlantic City, NJ); Ida B. Wells Homes/Wells Extension/Clarence Darrow Homes/Madden Park Homes (Chicago, IL), Few Gardens (Durham, NC); Easter Hill (Richmond, CA), and East Capitol Dwellings/Capitol Plaza (Washington, DC). The study, which looks at housing outcomes, neighborhood outcomes, social integration, health outcomes, child education and behavior outcomes, socioeconomic outcomes, and experiences with relocation and supportive services, involves three waves of surveys and in-depth interviews with residents from the five HOPE VI sites. The discussion that follows is based on data from the first wave, which occurred before redevelopment activities began.[42]

The five panel study sites are quite diverse, as Table 3.2 shows. Wells and East Capitol are very large sites in large central cities, Few Gardens and Easter Hill are midsize sites in moderate-size cities in large metropolitan areas, and Shore Park is a relatively small development in a small city. Wells and East Capitol are both located in cities with historically badly managed housing authorities that had been taken over by outside agencies in 1995 (HUD in Chicago, a federal receiver in Washington); both cities had received multiple numbers of HOPE VI grants by 2000 and were demolishing and replacing most of their family public housing developments. The other three sites were well-managed authorities implementing their first HOPE VI award. With the exception of Shore Park, the sites were in very poor physical condition and all five were considered very high-crime areas.

As Table 3.3 shows, the population in each sample is similar in terms of age, employment, and welfare use. However, two sites have large Hispanic populations—Hayes Valley and Quigg-Newton—so the tracking study sample

Table 3.1

HOPE VI Tracking Study Sites

| Development | Award year | Total original units | Year relocation completed | On-site reoccupancy as of January 2001 | | | Year reoccupancy completed |
				None	Partial	Complete	
Quigg-Newton, Denver, CO	1994	400	1995			✓	2000
Archbishop Walsh, Newark, NJ	1994	630	1996		✓		Litigation—estimate unavailable
John Hay, Springfield, IL	1994	599	1997		✓		2001 (estimated)
Hayes Valley, San Francisco, CA	1995	294	1996			✓	1999
Cotter and Lang, Louisville, KY	1996	1,116	1997		✓		2003 (estimated)
Connie Chambers, Tucson, AZ	1996	200	1999		✓		2002 (estimated)
Christopher Columbus, Paterson, NJ	1997	498	1999	✓			2002 (estimated)
Edwin Corning, Albany, NY	1998	292	1999	✓			2002 (estimated)

Source: Housing authority staff interviews (December 2000 to February 2001).

Table 3.2

HOPE VI Panel Study Sites

	Shore Park/ Shore Terrace Atlantic City, NJ	Wells/Madden[a] Chicago, IL	Few Gardens Durham, NC	Easter Hill Richmond, CA	East Capitol Dwellings/ Capitol Plaza Washington, DC
Year built	1970s	1941, 1955, 1961, 1970	1953	1954	1955, 1971
Original number of units (entire site)	212[c]	3,200	240	273	717[b]
Development type	Family	Family	Family	Family	Family, senior
Building description	Row houses	High-rise, mid-rise, row houses	Row houses	Row houses	Row houses, high-rise

[a]The Wells/Madden site consists of four developments: Ida B. Wells, Wells Extension, Clarence Darrow Homes, and Madden Park Homes.
[b]The East Capitol site also includes a vacant Federal Housing Authority high-rise, which is being demolished, and Capitol View Townhomes, which are being revitalized, bringing the total units to 1,199.
[c]Shore Park also includes a senior high-rise; however, it is not part of the HOPE VI grant and is not included in this study.

Table 3.3

Respondent Characteristics for HOPE VI Tracking Study and Panel Study
(in percent)

	Tracking study	Panel study
Head of household 62 years or older	10	11
Households with children less than 18 years old	57	72
Black	66	89
Hispanic	29	10
In public housing for five years or more	36	72
Head of household employed (full-time or part-time)	49	41
With household income less than $10,000	78	66
Receiving welfare assistance (TANF)	27	32

has a higher proportion of Hispanic respondents. Also, there are fewer households with children overall in the tracking study sample because Newark's Archbishop Walsh and Denver's Quigg-Newton both have a larger older population, and we oversampled households with children at both of the panel study sites with large numbers of older residents. The panel study also has a substantially larger proportion of long-term public housing residents. While this might be due to the particular sites included in the two studies, comparison to HUD administrative data indicates that these respondents are similar to residents of other HOPE VI developments.[43]

Although not shown in the table, analysis from the tracking study indicates that household characteristics play some role in determining the housing option that residents selected. HOPE VI returnees and those who relocated to other public housing units tend to be older and less well educated and to have fewer children than voucher users or households that are unsubsidized. Unsubsidized renters tend to have slightly higher income and are more likely to be employed and to be married than other residents. The panel study will explore in more depth how household and respondent characteristics affect relocation outcomes—in particular, how physical and mental health challenges and other barriers may influence residents' choices.

Housing and Neighborhoods—Before

Baseline data[44] clearly indicate that conditions in many HOPE VI sites prior to redevelopment were terrible—worse than those experienced by other poor renters nationwide. Respondents described problems that clearly placed their health and safety at risk, including units uncomfortably cold (33 percent), water leaks (42 percent), and broken toilets (25 percent). Plumbing problems included hazards such as overflowing toilets, water damage from leaks in neighboring units, stopped-up plumbing, and backed-up sewer systems.[45] About one-third of the respondents reported peeling paint or plaster in their units—problems that can potentially result in lead poisoning. Approximately one-quarter reported cockroach infestations and excessive mold in their units and another 16 percent reported problems with rats and mice. Underscoring the severity of their situations, about one-third reported two or three of these problems and one-fifth report more than three problems.[46] The comments of a grandmother from Chicago's Ida B. Wells development vividly illustrate the costs of living in such substandard housing:

> Now, I have one that's a little slow. That's my baby here, because they had lead, all of them, all of them had lead, and overdoses from living [in another housing development]. . . . [My grandson] will have to go into special education classes. And the little girl, she slobbers all the time. And she's five, and she shouldn't be doing that.

These developments were located in neighborhoods with very high crime rates and with poverty rates that exceeded 40 percent.[47] Overall, about three-quarters of the respondents reported serious problems with drug trafficking and substance abuse in their neighborhoods, and about two-thirds reported equally severe problems with shooting and violence. The high levels of violent crime, drug trafficking, and gang activity meant that residents were at risk for becoming victims or witnesses to the violence that surrounded them. Living with constant fear and anxiety about crime can have negative health and developmental consequences for both adults and children.[48] This strain was evident in the words of two different women who talked about how they managed:

> You mind your business. You try to make it through. If they [drug dealers] come into your little territory, then you kind of have some say. . . . I know my boundaries, I know my limits. Because you know some of these people have guns and they will shoot you, you know? And they are not afraid to shoot you. So you have your boundaries where they know they can go this far with you and you can go this far with them.

> People get killed around here. Like when I first moved around here there was a man over there dead. They've also found bodies over there dead. That's the reason why I don't let my kids go out. If they do go out, we go out of the neighborhood and we'll be back by dark.

A mother from Chicago's Wells described living with constant anxiety: "It's like a lot of times, you be in the house, your kid's outside and you hear gun shots and you drop everything and you run to make sure it's not your child."

The comments from children were particularly poignant, with some recounting harrowing incidents of bullets coming into their rooms or friends who narrowly escaped being shot. Two boys who lived in Durham's Few Gardens described the kinds of incidents that had left them afraid even inside their own homes:

> [One] time I got shocked 'cause there was a man standing by the fence and they was shooting at him, and then the fence was blocking him 'cause they was in a fight and the man got shot in the leg. So that's why I got scared.

> They was shooting one night . . . and they shot into our door and my little brother, he was by the door but he didn't get shot.

Housing and Neighborhoods—After

In contrast, relocated residents[49] indicated that most of them were now living in better housing in neighborhoods that were less poor and had less crime than their original HOPE VI development.[50] Nearly two-thirds of respondents (63 percent) described their current housing as being in good or excellent condition, and most (85 percent) said that their current unit was in the same or better condition as their public housing unit prior to revitalization. Respondents who had moved to revitalized developments reported the best housing conditions, while those who had moved to the private market with vouchers were more likely to report problems.[51]

These residents were also living in neighborhoods that were considerably less poor than their original public housing developments. Strikingly, about 40 percent of those who did *not* return to the original HOPE VI site now live in census tracts with poverty rates of less than 20 percent. A similar number live in neighborhoods that are less poor than their original development but still have poverty rates of over 30 percent. Further, the majority still live in census tracts that are predominantly minority. Tracking study respondents who had been relocated perceived less crime in their communities than those still living in developments awaiting revitalization. While the majority of panel study respondents reported serious problems with crime and drug trafficking, less than half (about 40 percent) of relocated residents reported major problems. Clearly, this number is still high, but represents a substantial improvement over the conditions most lived in prior to relocation.

Looking Ahead: Barriers to New Housing and Self-Sufficiency

Although the evidence shows that a significant proportion of former residents have benefited by relocating from public housing, the research also indicates that many residents will not be as fortunate. Many HOPE VI families waiting to relocate have members with serious physical and mental health problems or histories of domestic violence or substance abuse. These problems create severe barriers to a successful housing transition—or steady employment.

Researchers have documented that living in high-poverty neighborhoods can have serious negative consequences for health, through a process of "weathering," in which the constant stress of living in danger and exposure to the hazards of substandard housing exact a major toll on residents' physical and mental well-being.[52] Rates of low birth weight and infant mortality are high in these communities, as are rates of ailments such as asthma, diabetes, heart disease, and arthritis. Residents of poor neighborhoods are also more likely to be disabled by these illnesses. An assessment of the Jobs-Plus program, targeted at public housing residents, found that these types of health problems were the most consistent barrier to labor market participation.[53]

Many current HOPE VI residents have serious physical health concerns.[54] More than a third of the adults in the panel study reported having a chronic illness or health condition such as high blood pressure, diabetes, or arthritis and more than 20 percent of the adults have asthma. The situation for adults over sixty-five is particularly severe, with few reporting good or excellent health (10 percent) when compared with all adults over sixty-five nationally (39 percent). Further, HOPE VI children are also in worse health than other children their age. One in five children age six to fourteen and one in four younger than that have asthma—more than three times the national average. The high incidence of asthma may be related to the substandard housing in which they live and/or where it is located.[55] Some residents from Richmond's Easter Hill thought there was a connection between their health problems and their environment, which is located near an oil refinery and a major highway. One resident said: "I never had this problem [asthma] before, but once I came here. After two years of being here, they told me that I had asthma. But I've never suffered from that before."

Mental health problems are also common among HOPE VI residents, with nearly one in three reporting poor mental health, a figure almost 50 percent higher than the national average. Nearly one in six adults reported experiencing a major depressive episode in the past twelve months. Respondents talked about the enormous stresses in their lives, stresses that clearly have consequences for their mental health, as these women from Washington's East Capitol and Richmond's Easter Hill attest:

> It's worrying that somebody's going to kick my door through at night. That's the only problem I have. I think about that all [the] time. I wake up sometimes in the middle of the night checking the door three times. Then if you're in the bed asleep and you hear gunshots, you want to jump up and check all the kids and then I lay back down. But that's the only pressure I have right now . . . I don't sleep at all since I moved here.

> I mean, from day to day, you don't never know what's gonna happen. I mean, they up here shootin' and if it's not one thing, it's something else. All the time . . . all that shootin' and stuff. It's got my nerves so bad. I mean you could be sittin' up in here . . . and all of a sudden [somebody] just drives in and starts shootin'. What are you supposed to do? My son, he was scared half to death. He was all down on the floor. That's not good. That part right there is the biggest part that really keeps my nerves on edge all the time.

In addition to living with fear and anxiety because of the dangers that surrounded them, most of these HOPE VI residents face the stresses of being very low income, often with complex personal situations. One woman from Durham's Few Gardens said that she had ended up in the development after fleeing an abusive husband:

> I had just left my children's father and I was going to leave after a short period of time, but after I got the apartment and I began to like it. I didn't go back because I was in a battered situation and the children got so they enjoyed it so I made the best out of it.

Many HOPE VI residents were coping with multiple physical and mental health problems. For example, residents who reported having asthma also reported worse overall health and were more likely to report having a chronic health problem than the general public. Moreover, there was also a strong relationship between depression and reported health status. Among those who scored as depressed, few reported excellent or very good health (21 percent compared with 38 percent of the sample overall). Nearly a quarter of those reporting a chronic health problem were depressed, compared with just 9 percent of residents who had no chronic health problems. The experiences of a family from Chicago's Wells reflect the kinds of extreme challenges reported by respondents from all five sites. The grandmother in this family had custody of her granddaughter. In addition, her adult son was slightly mentally retarded. Although she was only in her early fifties, she had serious health problems and could no longer work.

> My daughter, she got on drugs, so I put her in a drug rehab for like two years . . . the oldest one, you know, she lost everything, like rights and everything. . . . So, now we going to court for her baby. And I don't know, they might let her go back, but, see, my daughter been there, you know, with the drugs and all that, she be having, like, mental, like, let's just say a chemical imbalance, so I don't know if they going to give her back to her. . . . She's staying clean, you know. We went to see her yesterday. She's doing real good, just gaining too much weight. She's 32 . . . I had a stroke about two years ago, so I'm on SSI [Supplemental Security Income] . . . I been back to the hospital. I'm diabetic again.

These situations not only threaten residents' ability to cope with the stress of relocation, but may prevent them from meeting screening criteria for new, mixed-income housing or finding housing in the private market with a voucher. Indeed, as housing authorities increase lease-enforcement and institute new requirements, families like this one may no longer even qualify for traditional public housing.

Impact on Children

Children in these households also faced the stresses from the dangerous environment, substandard housing, and often chaotic family situations. In addition, HOPE VI children attended low-achieving schools that were racially and economically segregated.[56] Both parents and children complained of problems such as inadequate physical environments, ineffective teachers, lack of school supplies, chaotic social environments, threats of violence, and racial conflict. Safety was a particular concern, with many respondents describing fights, gang activity (especially in Chicago and Durham), and shootings. Parental reports about children's behavior suggested that the stresses in the children's lives might be causing health and behavioral problems. About two-thirds of children age six to fourteen had one or more reported behavior problems, and about half had two or more.[57] A mother from Easter Hill described the toll that the dangerous school environment had on her son: "He's been stressed out, having headaches and chest pains, and he started having asthma, having like panic attacks, so we had to take him out of school, and he's seeing a therapist."

While relocating to safer neighborhoods and better and safer schools could lead to improvements in mental health, behavior, and school performance, it could also threaten children's school performance.[58] Other research has shown that frequent school transfers have major implications for children's educational outcomes, with the risk of falling behind increasing with each move.[59] Children in the panel study, many of whom were still in elementary school, were already highly mobile, with one in five having attended three or more schools. Another indication of potential problems is that parents report that even some very young children (five and under) have already been placed in special education for learning problems (11 percent) and for behavior problems (9 percent). The percentage of older children (ages six to fourteen) in special education classes is considerably higher (23 percent for learning problems and 12 percent for behavior problems).[60] Given that many of these children are already at great risk for problems, a very real concern is that, rather than helping them attain self-sufficiency, the stress of relocation may make them even more vulnerable.

Housing After HOPE VI

Where residents ultimately relocate is influenced by a number of variables: their own preferences, the effectiveness of relocation services, local housing options, private market constraints for relocatees searching for housing with vouchers, and trust between relocatees and the housing authority. The majority of residents in the panel study (70 percent) said that their initial preference was to return to the rebuilt HOPE VI site, citing a variety of reasons, including strong social ties to the community and fears about the voucher program. Their comments also indicated widespread confusion about the relocation process and a lack of confidence in the housing authorities.[61]

Many current residents will be unable to meet screening criteria for new mixed-income developments or vouchers—indeed, as discussed earlier, some may no longer even be eligible for traditional public housing. While some residents may opt not to return for positive reasons, a concern is that even successful movers may face risks in the private market. A substantial proportion of families living in the private market was struggling to meet basic needs that had been covered in public housing. Nearly three out of five voucher users said they have had difficulty paying rent or utilities in the past year, as did about half of households that receive no housing assistance. Further, unsubsidized households were more likely than public housing residents or voucher users to report doubling up with other families (13 versus 4 percent) and moving multiple times since relocating. Finally, while many former residents are now living in neighborhoods that are considerably less poor than their original HOPE VI developments, residents have not been as lucky in cities with tight rental markets or sites where demolition has far outpaced the production of new units. About 40 percent have ended up in other distressed, high-poverty communities.

The Future for Residents

The HOPE VI program offers the promise of a better life for residents. At the same time, the program creates the risk that some residents may end up as badly—or even worse—off than they were prior to relocation. Thus far the effects have been mixed, with some former residents clearly better off, others experiencing substantial hardship, and still others at risk for not being able to make a successful transition out of public housing.

The HOPE VI experience thus far illustrates the consequences—whether intended or unintended—of federal policies and programs and of societal reluctance to deal with difficult problems such as racial segregation. In many cities, the poorest and least "desirable" tenants have been warehoused in the worst public housing developments for decades. As the buildings are destroyed, the displaced tenants face an uncertain future. Without serious attention to the issues raised by the research presented here, the transformation of public housing is unlikely to realize its potential as a powerful force for improving the lives of low-income families.

Within the context of the HOPE VI program, the findings from this research highlight the need for interim measures that will bring about better outcomes for families currently affected by HOPE VI. First, supportive services created as part of HOPE VI plans must be comprehensive and include effective case management. Service packages that emphasize only employment will not meet the special needs of residents with physical and mental health problems, disabilities, or such complex problems as domestic violence and substance abuse. Further, housing authorities must pay special attention to older adults during relocation, particularly custodial grandparents or those living in multigeneration households; many of them are frail, disabled, or socially dependent on other residents for their care.

Second, Housing Choice vouchers offer residents choice, but place some at risk of encountering hardship and frequent, disruptive moves. In particular, former residents who have weak credit histories or complex family problems are at a disadvantage in the private market, where landlords' rules may be more restrictive than those in public housing. Housing authorities should help families make replacement housing choices that will work for their households. For example, families with large households are unlikely to find apartments in the private market large enough to meet their needs. These families should be counseled to explore the other available options. Housing authorities should also ensure that there are effective case management and follow-up services for former residents, especially those with multiple risk factors. Further, given the problems residents are encountering with rent and utility payments, residents should all receive realistic premove counseling on the types of costs they are likely to face in private market housing, as well as credit counseling and budget management services. Finally, to prevent former residents from becoming clustered in poor communities, housing authorities—particularly those in tight rental markets—should work with landlords to dispel myths about both the voucher program and its participants. They should also offer clients information about a range of neighborhoods where they can look for housing, as well as support for searches in "nontraditional" areas that may offer greater opportunity.

Third, these findings indicate that rather than offering new opportunities for residents who have suffered the consequences of failed federal programs, public housing transformation may make things worse for at least one subgroup of residents. Residents who face multiple, complex problems may not be able to make a transition to either private market or new, mixed-income housing. Policy makers need to consider more comprehensive approaches, such as supportive or transitional housing, for these hard-to-house families.

Public housing—particularly the dangerous and decayed developments targeted by HOPE VI—has served as the housing of last resort for America's poorest for the past two decades. A substantial proportion of those still living in these distressed developments are literally one step away from becoming homeless—and may become so if relocated to the private market. Without a fundamental refocusing of federal policy and a commitment to addressing the needs of our most vulnerable families, public housing transformation offers these residents little hope for a better life.

Notes

1. Rebecca M. Blank, *It Takes a Nation: A New Agenda for Fighting Poverty* (Princeton: Princeton University Press, 1997).

2. Susan J. Popkin, George Galster, Kenneth Temkin, Carla Herbig, Diane K. Levy, and Elise Richer, "Baseline Assessment of Public Housing Desegregation Cases: Cross-Site Report, Vol. 1" (Washington, DC: U.S. Department of Housing and Urban Development, 2000).

3. Susan J. Popkin, Bruce Katz, Mary K. Cunningham, Karen D. Brown, Jeremy Gustafson, and Margery A. Turner, "A Decade of HOPE VI: Research Findings and Policy Challenges" (Washington, DC: Urban Institute, 2004).

4. National Housing Law Project, Poverty and Race Research Action Council, Sherwood Research Associates, and Everywhere and Now Public Housing Residents Organizing Nationally Together, *False HOPE, A Critical Assessment of the HOPE VI Public Housing Redevelopment Program* (Oakland, CA: National Housing Law Project, 2002).

5. Susan J. Popkin, Diane K. Levy, Laura Harris, Jennifer Comey, Mary K. Cunningham, Larry Buron, with William Woodley, "HOPE VI Panel Study: Baseline Report" (Washington, DC: Urban Institute, 2002); Larry Buron, Susan J. Popkin, Diane K. Levy, Laura Harris, and Jill Khadduri, "The HOPE VI Resident Tracking Study" (Washington, DC: Urban Institute, 2002).

6. The studies were conducted by the Urban Institute and its partner, Abt Associates Inc. The "HOPE VI Resident Tracking Study" was supported entirely from by a grant from the U.S. Department of Housing and Urban Development. The "HOPE VI Panel Study" was supported by a consortium of funders, including the U.S. Department of Housing and Urban Development, the John D. and Catherine T. MacArthur Foundation, the Annie E. Casey Foundation, the Rockefeller Foundation, the Fannie Mae Foundation, the Ford Foundation, the Robert Wood Johnson Foundation, and the Chicago Community Trust.

7. Susan J. Popkin, Victoria E. Gwiasda, Lynn M. Olson, Dennis P. Rosenbaum, and Larry Buron, *The Hidden War: Crime and the Tragedy of Public Housing in Chicago* (New Brunswick, NJ: Rutgers University Press, 2000).

8. James Garbarino, Kathleen Kostelny, and Nancy Dubrow, *No Place to Be a Child: Growing Up in a War Zone* (Lexington, MA: Lexington Books, 1991).

9. Tama Leventhal and Jeanne Brooks-Gunn, "Moving to Opportunity: What About the Kids?" in *Choosing a Better Life: How Public Housing Tenants Selected a HUD Experiment to Improve Their Lives and Those of Their Children: The Moving to Opportunity Demonstration Program,* ed. John Goering (New York: Russell Sage Foundation, 2001); V.C. McLoyd, "The Impact of Economic Hardship on Black Families and Children: Psychological Distress, Parenting, and Socioemotional Development," *Child Development* 61 (1990): 311–346.

10. Jeffrey D. Morenoff, *Place, Race and Health: Neighborhood Sources of Group Disparities in Birthweight*, Report No. 01-482, Population Studies Center at the Institute for Social Research (Ann Arbor: University of Michigan, 2001).

11. Alex Schwartz and Kian Tajbakhsh, "Mixed-Income Housing as Social Policy: The Case for Diminished Expectations" (New York: New School University, 2001); Popkin et al., "Baseline Assessment of Public Housing Desegregation Cases."

12. Susan J. Popkin, Laura Harris, and Mary K. Cunningham, "Families in Transition: A Qualitative Analysis of the MTO Experience, Final Report," Report prepared by the Urban Institute (Washington, DC: U.S. Department of Housing and Urban Development, 2001); Susan J. Popkin and Mary K. Cunningham, "Searching for Rental Housing With Section 8 in Chicago" (Washington, DC: Urban Institute, 2000).

13. James E. Rosenbaum and Susan J. Popkin, "Social Integration of Low-Income Black Adults in Middle-Class White Suburbs," *Social Problems* 38, no. 4 (1991): 448–461; Julie E. Kaufman and James E. Rosenbaum, "The Education and Employment of Low-Income Black Youth in White Suburbs," *Educational Evaluation and Policy Analysis* 14, no. 3 (1992): 229–240; Susan J. Popkin, James E. Rosenbaum, and Patricia M. Meaden, "Labor Market Experiences of Low-Income Black Women in Middle-Class Suburbs: Evidence from a Survey of Gautreaux Program Participants," *Journal of Policy Analysis and Management* 12, no. 3 (1993): 556–573; Leonard S. Rubinowitz and James E. Rosenbaum, *Crossing the Class and Color Lines: Low-Income Black Families in White Suburbs* (Chicago: University of Chicago Press, 2000).

14. Popkin, Rosenbaum, and Meaden, "Labor Market Experiences."

15. Kaufman and Rosenbaum, "Education and Employment of Low-Income Black Youth."

16. Popkin et al., "Baseline Assessment of Public Housing Desegregation Cases."

17. John Goering, Joan Kraft, Judith Feins, Debra McInnis, and Mary Joel Holin, "Moving to Opportunity for Fair Housing Demonstration Program: Current Status and Initial Findings" (Washington, DC: U.S. Department of Housing and Urban Development, Office of Policy Development and Research, 1999); John Goering and Judith Feins, "Choosing a Better Life? Evaluating the Moving to Opportunity Experiment" (Washington, DC: Urban Institute, 2003).

18. For a complete review of MTO research to date, see Goering and Feins, "Choosing a Better Life?" Also, see Lawrence Katz and Jeffrey Kling, *Moving to Opportunity in Boston: Early Results of a Randomized Mobility Experiment,* Princeton University Industrial Relations Section Working Paper 441 (Princeton: Princeton University, 2000); Tama Leventhal and Jeanne Brooks-Gunn, "Changing Neighborhoods: Understanding How Children May Be Affected in the Coming Century," *Advances in Life Course Research* 6 (2001): 263–301.

19. Larry Orr, Judith D. Feins, Robin Jacob, Erik Beecroft, Lisa Sanbonmatsu, Lawrence F. Katz, Jeffrey B. Liebman, and Jeffrey R. Kling, "Moving to Opportunity Interim Impacts Evaluation" (Washington, DC: U.S. Department of Housing and Urban Development, 2002).

20. Xavier de Souza Briggs, ed., *Yonkers Revisited: The Early Impacts of Scattered-Site Public Housing on Families and Neighborhoods*, A Report to the Ford Foundation by the Yonkers Family and Community Project (Teachers College, Columbia University, New York, 1997).

21. Lawrence J. Vale, "Empathological Places: Residents' Ambivalence Toward Remaining in Public Housing," *Journal of Planning Education and Research* 16 (1997): 159–175.

22. Mary J. Holin, Larry Buron, and Michael Baker, *Interim Assessment of the HOPE VI Program: Case Studies,* reports prepared for U.S. Department of Housing and Urban Development, Office of Policy Development and Research (Bethesda, MD: Abt Associates, 2002).

23. Sean Zielenbach, "The Economic Impact of HOPE VI on Neighborhoods," Housing Research Foundation Report (Washington, DC: U.S. Department of Housing and Urban Development, 2002); Popkin et al., "A Decade of HOPE VI."

24. National Housing Law Project et al., *False HOPE.*

25. HUD is currently working on an analysis of the locations of all voucher holders nationwide.

26. Susan Popkin and Mary K. Cunningham, "CHA Relocation Counseling Assessment Final Report," report prepared for the John D. and Catherine T. MacArthur Foundation (Washington, DC: Urban Institute, 2002); Paul Fischer, "Where Are the Public Housing Families Going? An Update," unpublished paper, Lake Forrest College, January 21, 2003.

27. One study of relocation in Chicago documented almost immediate improvements in respondents' mental health, probably a result of living in a safer neighborhood (Popkin and Cunningham, "CHA Relocation Counseling Assessment"). An evaluation of relocation in Seattle also found that residents were generally satisfied with their new situations, particularly the safer neighborhoods, services, and amenities (Rachel G. Kleit and Lynne C. Manzo, "To Move or Not to Move: Determinants of Resident Relocation Choices in HOPE VI," paper prepared for the Joint Meeting of the Association of Collegiate Schools of Planning and the Association of European Schools of Planning, Leuven, Belgium, 2003). Likewise, a study of HOPE VI–like

relocation in Fort Worth found that most former residents felt that their new neighborhoods had less crime, although they were concerned about the lack of access to transportation and about busy traffic on nearby streets (Edith J. Barrett, Paul Geisel, and Jan Johnston, "The Ramona Utti Report: Impacts of the Ripley Arnold Relocation Program Year 1 (2002–2003)" (Arlington: University of Texas, 2003).

28. Susan Clampet-Lundquist, *Hope or Harm? Rebuilding Social Networks After Moving From Public Housing* (Philadelphia: University of Pennsylvania, 2003).

29. Findings from studies of public and assisted housing residents relocated with vouchers find similar results. For example, Orr et al., "MTO Interim Impacts Evaluation" found that residents who moved to lower poverty communities reported less crime, better housing, and better amenities. Likewise, David Varady and Carole Walker find that Alemeda County residents who used vouchers to move to suburban areas reported better conditions than those who remained in traditional neighborhoods (David P. Varady and Carole C. Walker, "Using Housing Vouchers to Move to the Suburbs: How Do Families Fare?" Housing Policy Debate 14, no. 3 (2003): 347–382).

30. Robin E. Smith, "Housing Choice for HOPE VI Relocatees" (Washington, DC: Urban Institute, 2002).

31. Susan J. Popkin and Victoria E. Gwiasda, "Gauging the Effects of Public Housing Redesign: Final Report on the Early Stages of the Horner Revitalization Initiative," report prepared for the U.S. Department of Housing and Urban Development and the John D. and Catherine T. MacArthur Foundation (Chicago: Abt Associates, 1998); Popkin et al., "Baseline Assessment of Public Housing Desegregation Cases."

32. Larry Keating, "Redevelopment Public Housing," *Journal of the American Planning Association* 66, no. 4 (2000).

33. Popkin and Cunningham, "CHA Relocation Counseling Assessment"; Popkin and Cunningham, "Searching for Rental Housing with Section 8 in Chicago"; Susan J. Popkin, Mary Cunningham, and Erin Godfrey, "CHA Relocation and Mobility Counseling Assessment Interim Report," report prepared for the John D. and Catherine T. MacArthur Foundation (Washington, DC: Urban Institute, 2001); Margery Austin Turner, Susan J. Popkin, and Mary Cunningham, "Section 8 Mobility and Neighborhood Health" (Washington, DC: Urban Institute, 2000).

34. Susan J. Popkin, Mary K. Cunningham, and William Woodley, "Residents at Risk: A Profile of Ida B. Wells and Madden Park" (Washington, DC: Urban Institute, 2000).

35. Popkin and Cunningham, "Searching for Rental Housing With Section 8 in Chicago"; Sudhir A. Venkatesh, Isil Celimi, Douglas Miller, Alexandra Murphy, and Beauty Turner, "Chicago Public Housing Transformation: A Research Report," Center for Urban Research and Policy Working Paper (New York: Center for Urban Research and Policy, Columbia University, 2004).

36. Sudhir A. Venkatesh, "Public Housing Transformation: A Long-Term View," unpublished manuscript, 2002.

37. National Housing Law Project et al. *False HOPE*.

38. As of this writing, the future of the HOPE VI program remains in doubt. The Bush administration had proposed eliminating funding for the program in its FY 2004 budget. However, there was still considerable support for the program in Congress and the program was reauthorized, although at a substantially lower level of $50 million. The administration has again eliminated the HOPE VI program in its FY 2005 budget.

39. The Tracking Study has some significant limitations. Because it is retrospective, there is no information on residents' perceptions of their living conditions or economic struggles prior to HOPE VI, so we cannot compare their pre–HOPE VI perceptions to their current reports. Further, because of the retrospective design, the sample underrepresents unsubsidized tenants and others who were difficult to locate. In general, those who are difficult to find are those who move frequently, double up with another family, are homeless, or have moved out of the area; these former residents are likely to have experienced more problems than those we were able to survey.

40. For a full description of the study and research methods, see Buron et al., "HOPE VI Resident Tracking Study."

41. The eight sites included in the study were purposively selected to represent a range of HOPE VI programs, but were not expected to be representative of all 165 sites awarded HOPE VI implementation grants. In selecting the sites, Buron et al., "HOPE VI Resident Tracking Study" sought to include an even distribution of sites across census regions, a mix of developments in midsize and large cities, a range of housing authorities in terms of size and HUD management scores, and a combination of early and more recent awardees. The eight sites were Quigg-Newton Homes (Denver, CO), John Jay Homes (Springfield, IL), Archbishop Walsh Homes (Newark, NJ), Hayes Valley (San Francisco, CA), Edwin Corning Homes (Albany, NY), Christopher Columbus Homes (Paterson, NJ), Cotter and Lang Homes (Louisville, KY), and Connie Chambers Homes (Tucson, AZ).

42. The first wave (baseline) was administered in-person to a sample of 887 heads of households across the five sites during summer 2001. In the two largest sites, Chicago and Washington, DC, a stratified random sample of approximately 200 respondents per site was drawn. At the other three study sites, research staff conducted a census of the entire development. The survey asked specific questions about up to two randomly selected focal children per household, one under age six and one between the ages of six and fourteen. Finally, to complement the surveys, in-depth interviews were conducted with a small sample of parent and child dyads (eight per site) in August and September 2001. Follow-up surveys and interviews will occur at twenty-four and forty-eight months after baseline.

43. G. Thomas Kingsley, Jennifer Johnson, and Kathryn L.S. Pettit, "HOPE VI and Section 8: Spatial Patterns in Relocation" (Washington, DC: Urban Institute, 2001); Buron et al., "HOPE VI Resident Tracking Study;" Popkin et al., "HOPE VI Panel Study."

44. Data in this section come from Popkin et al., "HOPE VI Panel Study."

45. HUD administrative data supported residents' reports—all five of the developments in our study had what HUD called "life-threatening health and safety hazards."

46. The level of reported problems was substantially higher than that reported by poor renters nationwide in the American Housing Survey. See Popkin et al., "HOPE VI Panel Study" for a discussion of these issues.

47. High concentrations of very low-income households in housing developments have been associated with negative social and behavioral outcomes for residents. See, for example, William Julius Wilson, *The Truly Disadvantaged: The Inner-City, the Underclass, and Public Policy* (Chicago: University of Chicago Press, 1987).

48. Garbarino, Kostelny, and Dubrow, *No Place to Be a Child*; Tama Leventhal and Jeanne Brooks-Gunn, "The Neighborhoods They Live In: The Effects of Neighborhood Residence on Child and Adolescent Outcomes," *Psychological Bulletin* 126, no. 2 (2000): 309–337; Morenoff, *Place, Race and Health*.

49. Data in this section come from Buron et al., "HOPE VI Resident Tracking Study."

50. Of the households surveyed, 19 percent were living in a revitalized HOPE VI development, 29 percent were living in other public housing properties, 33 percent were renting units using housing vouchers, and 18 percent had left assisted housing altogether.

51. Buron et al., "HOPE VI Resident Tracking Study."

52. Arline Geronimus, "The Weathering Hypothesis and the Health of African-American Women and Infants," *Ethnicity and Disease* 2 (1992): 207–221; Ingrid Gould Ellen, Tod Mijanovich, and Keri-Nicole Dillman, "Neighborhood Effects on Health: Exploring the Links and Assessing the Evidence," *Journal of Urban Affairs* 23, no. 3 (2001).

53. John M. Martinez, "The Employment Experiences of Public Housing Residents: Findings from the Jobs-Plus Baseline Survey" (New York: Manpower Demonstration Research Corporation, 2002).

54. For a full discussion of health problems and barriers for the *HOPE VI Panel Study* sample, see Popkin et al., "HOPE VI Panel Study"; and Laura E. Harris, Embry M. Howell, and Susan J. Popkin, "Health Problems among Public Housing Residents," unpublished manuscript, 2003.

55. Other factors such as substandard medical care and the higher incidence of smoking among low-income individuals may also exacerbate these problems. See Gary Giovino, M.W. Schooley, B.P. Zhu, J.H. Chrismon, S.L. Tomar, J.P. Peddicord, R.K. Merritt, C.G. Husten, and M.P. Eriksen, "Trends and Recent Patterns in Selected Tobacco-Use Behaviors: United States, 1900–1993," MMWR 43 (SS-3), 1994; C.I. Kiefe, O.D. Williams, C.E. Lewis, J.J. Allison, P. Sekar, and L.E. Wagenknecht, "Ten-Year Changes in Smoking Among Young Adults: Are Racial Differences Explained by Socioeconomic Factors in the CARDIA Study?" *American Journal of Public Health* 91, no. 2 (2001): 213–218.

56. The study incorporated national administrative data to paint a broad picture of the school districts and individual schools that the children in the HOPE VI panel study attend. See Popkin et al., "HOPE VI Panel Study," Chapter 6, for a full discussion.

57. The behavior problems index includes six specific measures: trouble getting along with teachers, being disobedient in school, hanging around with kids who get in trouble, bullying, being restless or overly active, and being unhappy or depressed. Children's mental health is an issue we plan to explore in greater depth in subsequent waves of the panel study.

58. The issue of children's school performance will be explored in much greater detail in subsequent waves of the panel study.

59. Chester Hartmann, "High Classroom Turnover: How Children Get Left Behind," in *Rights at Risk: Equality in an Age of Terrorism,* ed. Dianne M. Piche, William L. Taylor and Robin A. Reed (Washington, DC: Government Accounting Office, 2002).

60. To get a sense of how the panel study children compared to children from other, similar populations, we compared our sample to children in the MTO baseline sample. Like the HOPE VI children, MTO children were also living in public housing in high-poverty neighborhoods at baseline. Our comparison indicates that children in the HOPE VI sample were somewhat more likely to be in special education classes for learning problems than the MTO children (23 percent and 17 percent, respectively,) and slightly more likely than MTO children to be in classes for behavior problems (12 percent and 10 percent, respectively).

61. For a full discussion of relocation preferences, see Popkin et al., "HOPE VI Panel Study," Chapter 8.

_____ Part II

ON THE GROUND IN CHICAGO

RESHAPING PUBLIC HOUSING COMMUNITIES

4

The Chicago Housing Authority's Plan for Transformation

Janet L. Smith

Incremental change is not enough. To reshape public housing in Chicago, a new approach is imperative.[1]

You have a lot at stake. Do not sell yourself short. Think BIG. Think BOLD. Do the RIGHT THING. Seize the DAY.[2]

Transformation: a change in form, appearance or structure.[3]

On February 5, 2000, Secretary of Housing and Urban Development (HUD) Andrew Cuomo went to Chicago to join Mayor Richard Daley, U.S. Congressman Bobby Rush, and members of the Chicago Housing Authority (CHA) board in a ceremony to mark the federal government's approval of the CHA's "Plan for Transformation."[4] This was a momentous occasion since it meant a commitment from HUD to the CHA for $1.5 billion in funding over ten years to implement its plan. The plan, which at the time was estimated to require at least $3 billion to complete, was to reduce the total number of public housing units in the city from about 38,000 to about 25,000.

With fifty-one high-rise buildings slated for demolition, the scale of change was going to be dramatic. Technically there would be about the same number of units at the end (about 25,000) as there were public housing households at the plan's beginning. However, the loss of 13,000 units represented about 2 percent of the total rental housing stock in Chicago and over one-third of the total public housing stock in the city. The low number of replacement units was a serious point of concern for residents, affordable housing advocates, and the CHA, for that matter. In the late 1990s, Chicago was showing signs of its first population growth in several decades. Rents and housing values were rapidly escalating while vacancy rates were going down, especially in high-demand areas on the North Side—this despite an apparent building boom. An immediate concern was the fact that the plan required the demolition of most buildings before new replacement housing was constructed, which meant the relocation of an estimated 6,000 families. While some would move temporarily into existing vacant public housing, many were expected to relocate into the private market with Housing Choice vouchers, either on a permanent or temporary basis.[5]

The potential impact of the Plan for Transformation on the housing market was a concern especially following a HUD-funded study that determined that the rental market in the region was "tight," with a vacancy rate of 4.2 percent.[6] The figure was even lower in low-poverty and predominantly white areas of the city (North and Northwest Side). This meant that most of the available affordable rental housing was located in "softer" markets on the South and West Sides of the city, which were predominantly African-American and relatively poor. Nonetheless, the CHA decided it could go ahead with the plan. Although it was a tight rental market, the research did not say that the market could not absorb relocated households—just that there was a chance residents might end up in highly segregated neighborhoods.[7] HUD then agreed to fund the Plan for Transformation after negotiating many major and fine points, including a legally binding tenants' right to return contract. At the February 5 celebration, Secretary Cuomo offered this reasoning: "CHA has failed . . . CHA must come down. You can no longer put a Band-Aid on a bullet wound. It is a demolition plan, but it is also a tenant-protection plan, and it will do both equally well."[8]

This chapter examines how the plan was developed and how it came to be approved even after residents, local leaders, and elected representatives, including Congressman Rush, raised difficult questions to the CHA and HUD about where poor people were going to live after the buildings came down. I begin with a detailed review of the CHA Plan for Transformation itself, including specific unit counts for each development at the time the plan was approved, and an overview of the context from which the plan came. Following this is an overview of the process that gave specific shape to the plan and to the development of subsequent plans for individual sites since the plan was approved.

The Plan

The CHA "Plan for Transformation" was originally published in draft form for public review and comment on September 30, 1999. The final revised version of the plan was submitted to HUD on January 6, 2000.[9] While not a glossy or highly polished document, it laid out a striking vision of public housing in Chicago that was radically different from what existed at the time. As the CHA described it, the plan

> outlined a fundamentally new approach to public housing in Chicago. The case for change was obvious and urgent, including: a high concentration of extremely poor families; a large stock of physically obsolete family housing plagued with crime and drugs; a new Federal policy environment that includes mandatory building closure rules, affirmative efforts to deconcentrate poverty, and stricter performance standards, especially in the area of physical conditions; limited capital funds to meet needs; excessive overhead costs and a lack of internal management capacity; and resident programs that were duplicative, poorly coordinated, and without substantive performance measure and outcomes.[10]

To address these problems, the CHA's plan focused on several broad areas: property management, human capital development, protective services, admissions, and occupancy policies, Housing Choice vouchers (formerly Section 8), hiring minority- and woman-owned businesses, and an extensive capital program, which was approximately two-thirds the total annual budget. Property management strategies aimed to get the CHA "out of the business of managing real estate, resulting in lower costs and better service."[11] To achieve this goal, property management would be transferred to professional management organizations, which, along with existing resident management corporations, would be given authority, resources, and responsibility "to get the job done."[12] Human capital development meant that residents in CHA property "will be treated as full citizens of the city of Chicago," getting access to city services via development-based outreach workers.[13] Residents would also benefit from a change in protective services, including the transfer of policing functions to the Chicago Police Department and added security coverage at developments for the elderly. Changes in admissions and occupancy policy were significant, with higher lease compliance standards and rent incentives for working families "intended to encourage the development of stable communities and to reward work and responsibility."[14] Housing Choice voucher improvements focused on expanding landlord outreach and mobility counseling, and building on what the CHA labeled "vast improvements in the administration" by the private organization administering the program. Specific funding would be provided to help landlords modify units for nonelderly people with disabilities, using vouchers to move such people out of buildings designated "senior only."[15] Finally, the CHA committed itself to "assuring that this period becomes a real time of opportunity for minority businesses and for other disadvantaged firms and workers."[16] This was in response to Representative Rush's request that the CHA increase the proportion of minority contracts guaranteed.[17] HUD required the CHA to set as a goal (though it did not have to guarantee this goal would be met) awarding 50 percent of redevelopment contracts to minority- and woman-owned businesses—"the highest percentage ever set by HUD."[18] When combined, these changes were to put a new face on the CHA and to show the public what the agency was going to accomplish once more under the authority of the city of Chicago.

A New Image for the CHA

When policy makers signed into law the Quality Housing and Work Responsibility Act in 1998, one goal was to improve the all too often negative image of public housing around the country. This included "transforming" many of the large public housing agencies that, like the CHA, had been in trouble with HUD. Having been run by HUD for nearly four years, the CHA plan was a means to introduce the organization's own transformation, to show the public what the new management could and would do and how it was going to be different from the past.[19] As described in the executive summary, a goal of the CHA's Plan for Transformation was to create a new identity for itself:

> This plan contemplates much more than the physical transformation of public housing. It envisions a new role for the CHA. In the past, the CHA was primarily an owner and manager of public housing. In the future, the CHA will be a facilitator of housing opportunities. It will oversee a range of housing investments and subsidy vehicles. Where appropriate, it will own housing, but it will just as likely provide financial assistance to other private and non-profit development organizations to expand housing opportunities.[20]

The CHA had been the housing of last resort for thousands of poor people for several decades, especially families, seniors, and people with disabilities on fixed income or working at low-wage jobs. Despite its condition, many people called public housing home, having built up a community and network of support and extended family.[21] And many more were trying to get in: CHA had a waiting list of more than 40,000 households. At the same time, the poor quality coupled with a rent system based on paying 30 percent of income meant that the CHA—like many housing authorities—could not attract higher income families to its developments.[22] There were better quality affordable units in the private sector for middle- and upper-income renters, at least until the housing market started heating up in the mid-1990s. As with other PHAs dealing with distressed developments, the CHA's plan was to make its new mixed-income public housing attractive to middle- and high-income families who would pay market prices to rent or buy a unit.

Although CHA's transformation into a "facilitator of housing opportunities" was announced in the plan, its metamorphosis really began in 1995 when HUD took over the CHA after the entire board of directors and the chair, Vincent Lane, resigned. This came after the CHA had failed to deal with severe problems including mismanagement of an estimated $26 million in federal funding.[23] In addition, high vacancy rates in many of its developments coupled with a poor rent collection record had kept the authority on HUD's "troubled list" since 1979.[24] Lane, the man whom former HUD secretary Jack Kemp called "one of the most progressive public housing leaders in the country," had been unable to clean up the CHA. His bold gestures like police sweeps and development lockdowns did not significantly reduce high crime or violence in developments or remedy the many management problems he inherited in 1988. By 1995, Lane's "high hopes" for redeveloping public housing and his earlier political support had been diminished.[25]

Stepping in to run the CHA temporarily was HUD assistant secretary Joseph Shuldiner. Before being made assistant secretary, Shuldiner had been executive director for the Los Angeles Housing Authority (1990–1993) and general manager of the New York City Housing Authority before that, so he was prepared for working in a large PHA. However, the expectations were high. At the takeover, his boss, Secretary Henry Cisneros, said, "The national system of public housing is on trial in Chicago."[26] Shuldiner was later quoted as saying, "Chicago is a symbol of what's wrong with public housing in the United States. If we can turn it around here, we can turn it around anywhere. But if people think HUD is going to come in with a boatload of money, that's not going to happen."[27]

Clearly, the CHA had serious problems—the most immediate being the void in leadership created by the resignation of every one of its board members. Some authority needed to assume responsibility for the day-to-day operations of the CHA and to actually make reforms, including contracting with a private management company to officially operate its 40,000 units of housing. While HUD's takeover was justified by the circumstances and supported by Mayor Daley, it also was an "unprecedented model for intervention," which made members of the Congressional Committee on Government Reform and Oversight uncomfortable.[28] HUD was not intended to run a housing authority that it also was charged with monitoring. Normally, HUD would hire a private management team or even another housing authority or court-appointed receiver to take over a troubled housing authority. The former had been recommended by HUD in 1987 but not acted on; instead, Vincent Lane was brought in. Eight years later the congressional committee's concern was the "immediate impact on the people of Chicago" of HUD stepping in so decisively. Perhaps even more an issue, though, was that eighty-six other troubled PHAs might also need intervention and HUD clearly did not have the capacity or the qualified staff to run several at once.[29]

By late 1995 HUD acknowledged that it could not easily extricate itself from the situation and the committee recommended the following: (1) HUD should promptly secure strong, long-term leadership at the CHA; (2) HUD, and the new CHA management, should develop a long-term strategy for the recovery of the CHA; (3) HUD should maintain a clear distinction between its actions as a federal agency and its actions as CHA manager; (4) HUD's takeover of the CHA should be evaluated as a pilot program to determine the effectiveness of direct HUD intervention at other troubled housing agencies; (5) clear statutory or regulatory standards should be established for HUD intervention at troubled housing agencies; and (6) HUD should do more to support viable resident management corporations (RMCs), particularly those operating in troubled public housing developments.[30] This last point reflected the committee's belief that RMCs can "provide viable private management" that creates opportunity for "resident empowerment and economic uplift."[31] In part, this was based on evidence from Chicago at a building in the Cabrini-Green development, 1230 North Burling, which despite "neglect and abuse" by the CHA had been able to provide quality services and "improved living conditions" for its tenants.[32]

The long-term goal was to clean up and return the CHA to local control under the mayor's leadership. To do this, HUD required wide-sweeping changes in how the CHA was managed. Among the changes Joseph Shuldiner was to advance were privatizing the management of the Section 8 program, reducing the CHA bureaucracy and overall size of the organization, overhauling security and maintenance, and improving the rent collection record. Since HUD was not going to provide any additional money to support this makeover, the job would require ingenuity and cooperation with new partners like the city of Chicago and civic groups such as local foundations and the Metropolitan Planning Council (MPC). A nonprofit civic organization founded in 1934, the MPC was an early proponent of public housing in Chicago. Elizabeth Wood was its first executive director and later head of the CHA. Soon after HUD took over, MPC's housing committee proposed several public housing policy goals for the region that directly targeted the CHA. These included reforming management to enhance efficiency, accountability, and effectiveness at the development level; encouraging public/private linkages to stimulate the production of efficient, high-quality forms of affordable housing; expanding housing options for residents outside of public housing; finding ways to link the need for affordable housing in the Chicago region with the need for increased proximity and accessibility to jobs for residents; and implementing a long-term strategic plan to stabilize and redevelop public housing into mixed-income communities.[33]

Of course, the MPC had no formal or informal oversight relationship with the CHA, so these recommendations were not binding. However, as a long-standing voice for public housing and, in most recent years, public housing reform, the MPC was continuing its role as a watchdog. With HUD's take-over of the CHA as a catalyst, the MPC put the call out for a broader base of support for mixed-income housing in the region. In a series of fact sheets distributed in 1996, an agenda was laid out, showing what could be done based on what *already* was being done at Robert Taylor Homes, Henry Horner Homes, ABLA, and Cabrini-Green.[34] All were being redeveloped, some with HOPE VI grants. All were commended because they used public money to leverage private funding and were being rebuilt as mixed-income communities. Also featured was Harbor Point in Boston and Techwood in Atlanta—two recently redeveloped public housing sites that were considered exemplary mixed-income communities.

Closer to home was Lake Parc Place, which had been developed under Vincent Lane. Lake Parc Place was a pilot project under the Mixed-Income New Communities Strategy (MINCS) demonstration program, which Lane actually had lobbied to include in the 1990 National Affordable Housing Act. The CHA was the only recipient of funding for this pilot project.[35] The MINCS project had two objectives: to renovate and convert existing public housing into mixed-income housing, and to acquire replacement housing in existing low-density, privately owned mixed-income developments. To achieve the first objective, the CHA used HUD funds to renovate two of six sixteen-story buildings in the project.[36] When completed in 1991, each building had twenty-eight one-bedroom units, eighty-five two-bedroom units, and twenty-eight three-bedroom units that cost about $70,000 each to rehab. This cost included a communal play area, childcare center, security desk, and laundry facilities for the development. The combination of low rents and location (near Lake Michigan and not far from downtown and the University of Chicago) made Lake Parc Place attractive to moderate-income families (median income about $24,000) who moved into about half the units. Residents that had been relocated in 1988 or their children filled the rest.[37] Each group was evenly distributed by floor throughout each building.

Early research suggested that the mixed-income experiment was working: higher-income families seemed willing to live side by side with public housing residents. A survey of residents found that nearly 80 percent of all tenants was satisfied or very satisfied with the development.[38] Public housing families especially appreciated the higher public safety and lower rates of violence. Despite these early positive results, the plans for the remaining buildings and the proposed replacement housing proved to be controversial and by the mid-1990s nothing had been done on either.[39]

As the Metropolitan Planning Council worked to build a larger base of support for affordable housing in the region, the CHA was making some significant changes to decrease bureaucracy and improve its service. At the end of 1995 the Section 8 program was privatized when the Quadel Consulting Corporation was hired to manage the CHA's approximately 14,000 certificates and vouchers. Quadel, based in Washington, DC, specializes in providing training, consulting, and management for subsidized housing programs. The company formed a subsidiary, CHAC, Inc., to manage the Chicago Housing Choice Voucher Program. CHAC inherited a waiting list that was unorganized and not computerized. After about a year and a half of cleaning, CHAC opened up its list to add new families.[40] In only a few weeks, about 100,000 households registered to be put into a lottery and then about 35,000 were picked to be on the list. Before CHAC could get to people on this list, it had to begin remedying a lawsuit against CHA and HUD claiming that Latinos were not receiving equal access to public housing resources. The settlement required CHAC to give Section 8 vouchers to approximately 500 low-income Latino families.[41]

A challenge for CHAC was the barriers that made it difficult for families to actually use their vouchers in the time period they had to search and secure a unit. A 68 percent success rate in summer 1998 prompted CHAC to have the Urban Institute do a series of focus groups to better understand what families faced when searching for housing.[42] Based on the experiences of people who failed to find housing between 1996 and 1998, the barriers included having a limited search time (up to ninety days was allowed at the time), especially when working; finding units large enough and landlords willing to accommodate large families; having enough money to cover transportation to search and to pay for credit checks and security deposits; personal problems; physical disabilities; and discrimination.[43]

At the end of 1998, the CHA had been taken off HUD's "troubled list." Several changes had helped the organization get to this point: privatizing the Section 8 voucher program, increasing rent collections, evicting noncompliant tenants, privatizing management at some developments, and straightening up CHA's books. Most of these changes occurred behind the scenes, visible to HUD and its regulatory review but not so evident to residents. For the people of Chicago, evidence that CHA was changing came when four public housing buildings on the South Side were imploded in less than five minutes on December 12, 1998. Weeks of preparation and stories in local papers explaining the logistics and cost-savings of imploding buildings drew a crowd of thousands to a closed section of Lake Shore Drive. The press coverage following the event featured Toni Preckwinkle, the alderman for the area, describing the new mixed-income community that would help her to improve the ward.

A few months later, in February 1999, a consortium known as the Chicago Futures Forum heard a presentation by Bruce Katz from the Brookings Institute that reiterated the presumed benefits of mixed-income public housing. Katz had been at HUD with Joseph Shuldiner and had been counsel and staff director to the Senate Subcommittee on Housing and Urban Affairs. His talk, entitled "The Transformation of Chicago's Public Housing: Challenges and Opportunities," encouraged—even challenged—the CHA and the region to think larger than simply rehabbing buildings.[44] In Katz's view, the task should be to look at public housing in the broader context of the region and the need for deconcentrating poverty to help the poor as well as the city. Citing research about how costly it was for cities to provide services to neighborhoods with high concentrations of poverty—a logical assumption even without data—Katz argued that mixed-income public housing could lower municipal expenses.[45]

During the spring of 1999, a bigger vision for the CHA was developing as the city of Chicago negotiated with HUD to take back the CHA, which it did on May 27, 1999. Mayor Daley announced "the beginning of a new era in public housing in Chicago" and the end of HUD control and Joseph Shuldiner as CHA chief. Key to CHA's turnaround, according to the mayor, was the agreement with HUD that "gives us the flexibility to begin transforming public housing in Chicago. It reduces red tape and enables us to design creative solutions specifically for our situation here in Chicago."[46] A long-term plan submitted for HUD's approval would guide the city and the CHA. The plan would be completed by the end of the year under the leadership of CHA's new CEO, Phillip Jackson. Jackson, who had been chief of staff at the Chicago public schools, grew up in Robert Taylor Homes. Despite growing up in the projects, he had made a success of himself first as vice president of Kroch's and Brentano's, a well-known local bookstore, and then as Chicago's deputy budget director before going to work at the school district.[47] With the CHA directly under the rule of the mayor, Daley proclaimed that "residents of public housing are—first and foremost—residents of Chicago. We are one city and one people. And I am confident that by working together, we can recast public housing for the next century, built around a common vision of a better quality of life for all Chicagoans."[48]

Reducing the Stock

Of course, what made the CHA's plan and approach "fundamentally new" was the massive and widespread demolition that was to take place. In the executive summary, the CHA explained its bold vision:

> The Agency will demolish upwards of 18,000 obsolete housing units, mostly open gallery style high-rises. By removing these units from the inventory, the Agency will be able to concentrate its capital resources to rehabilitate/redevelop about 25,000 units. While the overall loss of project-based housing is concerning (a net loss of approximately 13,000 units), there is no alternative.[49]

Then and now, housing advocates and CHA residents considered the loss of project-based assisted units the major flaw of the Plan for Transformation. However, this was not because they wanted to retain the buildings "as is" or even rehab them unless structurally it made sense, but rather because more than 25,000 units of public housing units were needed in the city. As the CHA described in its accompanying Five-Year PHA Plan, an estimated 140,685 extremely low-income families were severely impacted by the short supply of affordable housing in Chicago. While the CHA acknowledged this predicament, it also claimed "there is no alternative" to this outcome. Despite the need, it was clear that HUD and Congress were not likely to build new public housing in the near future except for what was needed to replace "obsolete" units, and even then, the preference was to give relocating residents vouchers rather than hard units.[50] So on the production side was a funding problem—the maximum funding CHA could expect from HUD was $1.5 billion. This meant that the CHA had to raise at least another $1.5 billion from the private sector and other public resources to complete the plan just so it could provide enough housing for all the occupants. Building any additional public housing meant raising even more capital.

On the demolition side, the CHA had no choice since the units and the buildings had failed the so-called viability test in 1996.[51] As described in Chapter 1, Rescissions and Congress required under Section 202 of the Omnibus Consolidated Appropriations Act all PHAs to determine which would cost more: to repair and bring up to code "distressed" units or to provide tenants of those units vouchers to live in a private market unit for twenty years and demolish the building.[52] The viability test, which was applied to all developments with 300 or more units and at least a 10 percent vacancy, initially failed about 18,500 units in fourteen developments.[53] This represented 62 percent of the family housing stock, and with 11,000 units of these units occupied, it meant relocating about 34,000 people.[54] Any building that failed had to be "removed from CHA's inventory in five to ten years."[55] And with one-for-one replacement rescinded the previous year, there was no requirement to replace these units other than to give families a voucher and appropriate relocation support.[56]

At the time it was completed, many public housing supporters thought that the viability test had overstated the problem in Chicago, which represented the greatest number of failed buildings in the nation and more than one-sixth of total units that HUD required be demolished.[57] A report from the Metropolitan Planning Council suggested the number was inflated because the per-unit operating expenses were calculated using the cost for the entire building including vacant units—of which there were many—instead of only the cost of operating those occupied.[58] Also, the number of units failing the test would decrease if the calculation included either the potential revenue stream of vacant units that could be rehabbed and occupied, or the cost of operating only the occupied units. Another expense not accounted for was the per-unit cost of board-up and demolition. When this was taken into consideration, the number of units that failed decreased to about 11,000, since several buildings had units with monthly costs (rent assistance, utilities, management, and renovation) that were only a few dollars different from the average cost of the voucher.[59] The most consistent critique of the test, however, was that rental market conditions and the replacement cost of housing were ignored; in other words, the cost of building each development anew—a standard appraisal technique—was not even in the equation.

The viability test appeared to be better suited for assessing HUD's liability than it was for gauging the viability of rehabilitating and retaining public housing in Chicago. However, after some adjustments, the number of failed units was lowered to about 11,000. Even so, the CHA told HUD that it planned to construct only about 4,300 replacement units on-site, although it did plan to renovate about 6,300 units at other sites.[60] While this would be equivalent to the total number of occupied units to be demolished, it still meant a real loss of about 7,000 units of permanent public housing.

When HUD allowed the CHA to retest its units and lower the number of units to be demolished, it also required the CHA and any housing authority in the same situation to identify and secure public and private resources to jump-start the new replacement units, which were to be developed in mixed-income communities.[61] Two questions came from housing advocates: what proportion of the income mix would be for public housing residents and how secure would be the private funding? In considering how the CHA might be able to produce the results HUD required, Wardell Yotaghan, a resident of Rockwell Gardens and cofounder of the newly formed Coalition to Protect

Public Housing, said: "Over the years the mind-set has moved from solving problems to shifting them somewhere else. . . . If there's a tremendous economic problem in public housing, they're going to be the same disadvantaged people wherever they go."[62] At the time CHA's executive director, Joseph Shuldiner, was reported to say that he "understands those concerns. But he has faith that HUD will give Chicago enough room to slowly transform public housing and will not use the new test to undermine the Authority's plans."[63] Yet only two years later, the CHA's Plan for Transformation" outlined a more aggressive schedule for demolition that included all 18,000 units that had failed the first test while providing very little information on what additional funding specifically would be utilized or whether it was even secured.

Regarding the scale of demolition, the plan was blunt: "Given these fiscal and legislative parameters, and given the untenable conditions under which many residents live, the Agency will demolish upwards of 18,000 units, primarily high-rise family properties for which there is no reasonable potential for renovation."[64] However, while the plan was precise about the number of units to be razed, the plan was imprecise about the exact number of public housing units that would be included in each redeveloped site and the sources of funding that would ensure that the units could be built. The plan's only firm commitment was to have an approximate total of 25,000 units of public housing when the plan was completed. As Table 4.1 shows, sites that had firm plans were those that had been engaged in redevelopment planning or had already received HOPE VI grants (Category 1). Henry Horner Homes, which had a HOPE VI grant but also was covered by a consent decree that determined the number of replacement housing units, will be discussed in more detail in Chapter 8. Cabrini-Green is the subject of Chapter 6 and ABLA of Chapter 7. In addition to the previously obtained funding that was committed to these developments, the CHA was going to spend $149 million out of the plan's budget to complete them. Figure 4.1 shows the location of these developments and others to be redeveloped or rehabbed.

The capital plan did provide a total number of public units after revitalization for each of the other categories of housing. The number of senior units (Category 2) would stay the same while the number of scattered-site units (Category 3) would decrease by 8 percent. Funding for both would come from HUD, with $350 million allocated to renovate senior housing, including adding air conditioning and making required accessibility improvements, and $77 million to renovate all but 236 scattered-site units that "did not warrant further investment" and would be demolished.[65] Units included in Category 4, non-202 family properties, were in developments that had not been subject to the viability test. The capital program allocated $107 million to rehab these developments. The Lawndale Complex was to be demolished

Table 4.1

Occupancy and Demolition Plans for CHA Housing by Category, 1999

	Before			After	
	Existing units 10/01/99	Occupied units 10/01/99	Demol-ished units	Total units	Public housing
Category 1: Existing redevelopment commitments					
Governor Henry Horner Homes	1,743	682	1,201	1,136	1,086
Frances Cabrini Extension North	926	152	926	2,300	700
ABLA	3,235	1,079	2,776	3,278	1,463
Ida B. Wells/Madden/Darrow/ Homes	2,891	1,426	2,821	2,530	1,008
Robert Taylor Homes B	—	—	—	251	251
Raymond Hilliard Center	710	307	—	710	390
Washington Park Homes	56	13	—	56	14
Lakefront properties	—	—	—	964	441
Category total	9,561	3,659	7,724	11,225	5,353
Category 2: Senior developments					
Total units	9,480	8,044	—	9,480	9,480
Category 3: Scattered sites					
Total units	2,922	2,400	236	N/A	2,254
Category 4: Non-202 family properties					
Cabrini Extension Lincoln	18	18	?	?	?
Lake Parc Place	300	235	?	?	?
LeClaire Courts	300	270	?	?	?
Washington Park Homes low-rises	488	226	?	?	?
Lawndale Complex	187	1	?	?	?
Lawndale Gardens	128	120	?	?	?
Lathrop Homes	925	747	?	?	?
Bridgeport Homes	155	136	?	?	?
Wentworth Gardens	422	386	?	?	?
Lowden Homes	128	115	?	?	?
Category total	3,051	2,254	797	NA	2,254
Category 5: 202 Family properties Mid-rises and Low-rises					
Cabrini Rowhouses	586	466	?	?	?
Trumbull Park Homes	486	382	?	?	?
Harold L. Ickes Homes	1,006	823	?	?	?
Dearborn Homes	800	603	?	?	?
Altgeld Gardens	1,998	1,713	?	?	?
Subtotal	4,876	3,987	889	NA	NA
Gallery High-rises					
1230 N. Burling	134	106	134	?	?
Cabrini Extension South	597	474	597	?	?
William Green Homes	968	550	968	?	?
Rockwell Gardens	1,136	439	1,136	?	?
Stateway Gardens	1,644	689	1,644	?	?
Robert Taylor A	1,734	785	1,734	?	?
Robert Taylor B	2,050	774	2,050	?	?
Washington Park high-rises	468	192	468	?	?

(continued)

Table 4.1 *(continued)*

	Before			After	
	Existing units 10/01/99	Occupied units 10/01/99	Demol-ished units	Total units	Public housing
Randolph towers	155	137	155	?	?
Subtotal	8,886	4,146	8,886	NA	NA
Category total	13,762	8,133	9,775	TBD	5,000
Grand total	38,776	24,490	18,532	TBD	24,773

Source: Chicago Housing Authority, "Plan for Transformation," January 6, 2000.
NA = Not available; TBD = To be determined; ? = Unknown.

(and was in 2001). At Washington Park an in-place plan would tear down about half of its low-rise buildings. For the remaining developments, the CHA assumed that "because of their age and design, modest density reduction is also anticipated" and that "in order to maximize funds" available and to ensure that all 2,254 of the current occupants would have a replacement unit, the CHA would have to seek development partners.[66]

Category 5 developments, which had been subject to the viability test, included 13,762 units in high-rise, mid-rise, and low-rise buildings.[67] All of the high-rise buildings—8,886 units—were slated for demolition. The commitment for replacement units was a "minimum" of 5,000 units for all, with the distribution to be determined in the planning process for each development, which would begin soon after the plan was approved. This category, obviously, contained the largest set of questions for which CHA could not provide definite answers. In part, the vagueness about the outcome for these developments was deliberate and made sense, since the CHA assumed that specific plans would be developed for each after the Plan for Transformation was approved and specific waivers requested by CHA were granted. These waivers included "augmenting the Section 202 cost test with the market-driven program, which would allow rehabilitation of some or all buildings in a development if they can be viable in the Chicago market place" for five properties that were primarily mid- and low-rise developments.[68] The eight remaining properties would be demolished since these all were gallery-style high-rise buildings. Assuming this waiver was granted, CHA explained, "Resident representatives and community partners will be involved in both establishing the criteria for selecting developers and in the actual selection process. Additionally, the Agency will provide the residents at each site with technical assistance funds to help in shaping the development program and/or re-use plans for each property."[69]

Obviously, the fate of these buildings was uncertain until the plan was approved and only if HUD granted that particular waiver. However, once HUD's

Figure 4.1   Public Housing Sites to be Redeveloped or Rehabbed

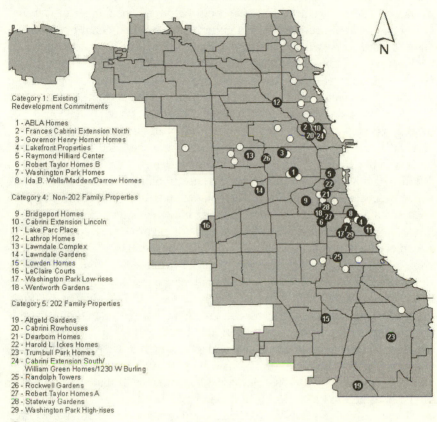

Category 1: Existing
Redevelopment Commitments

1 - ABLA Homes
2 - Frances Cabrini Extension North
3 - Governor Henry Horner Homes
4 - Lakefront Properties
5 - Raymond Hilliard Center
6 - Robert Taylor Homes B
7 - Washington Park Homes
8 - Ida B. Wells/Madden/Darrow Homes

Category 4: Non-202 Family Properties

9 - Bridgeport Homes
10 - Cabrini Extension Lincoln
11 - Lake Parc Place
12 - Lathrop Homes
13 - Lawndale Complex
14 - Lawndale Gardens
15 - Lowden Homes
16 - LeClaire Courts
17 - Washington Park Low-rises
18 - Wentworth Gardens

Category 5: 202 Family Properties

19 - Altgeld Gardens
20 - Cabrini Rowhouses
21 - Dearborn Homes
22 - Harold L. Ickes Homes
23 - Trumbull Park Homes
24 - Cabrini Extension South/
       William Green Homes/1230 W Burling
25 - Randolph Towers
26 - Rockwell Gardens
27 - Robert Taylor Homes A
28 - Stateway Gardens
29 - Washington Park High-rises

○ Senior Housing

expected approval was forthcoming, the CHA would turn to the marketplace to determine the true viability of these developments as mixed-income public housing. If the rehabbed buildings could be expected to attract market-rate tenants, either because of location or quality or both, then most likely the buildings would not be demolished. Some tenants, however, feared that location would actually be the key factor driving the decision whether to demolish and how much public housing—if any—to build back on-site. This fear was based on the perception that location near a strong market increased the likelihood that a developer would be interested in the profit that could be made from the market portion of the units in a mixed-income public housing development. This also might mean fewer public housing units and more tenants vouchered out of the site. Of the five Section 202 properties, the market was strongest around the Cabrini Rowhouses at the south end of the Cabrini-Green development site. These rowhouses had been built before the remainder of Cabrini-Green and had not been included in either the demolition count or HOPE VI plans for the site. As will be discussed in detail in Chapter 6, the development's leadership was embroiled in a lawsuit at the time with the CHA, the city, and HUD to get control of the redevelopment process, so there was speculation that these units would not be razed if residents won the lawsuit.

Conditions were very different at Altgeld Gardens, which had about 1,700 of its 2,000 units occupied. Public housing advocates assumed that this development would not be demolished but instead rehabbed and retained as 100 percent public housing with the only income mixing occurring by bringing in families with incomes between 30 and 80 percent of the area median. Not only was this development geographically isolated on the far South Side, in a very economically depressed section of the city, but tenants had recently sued the CHA on the premise that due to the presence of environmental toxins, the site would need a thorough cleanup before it could be habitable.[70] While this situation might seem to dictate demolition, the Environmental Protection Agency found no conclusive evidence that contaminants caused the health problems that residents identified in their suit. Phillip Jackson, CHA's chief at that time, promised the residents further tests and pledged that "If we find out that this housing is not safe, we have an obligation to take care of you."[71] To date, there has been no discussion of demolition and a "comprehensive rehab" of Altgeld Gardens has begun. There are no firm plans to make this a mixed-income community other than for the full range of income levels that are eligible for public housing (up to 80 percent of the area median income).[72]

The potential marketability of the remaining three developments without demolition and new construction continues to be unclear. Trumbull Park Homes, located on the South Side, is undergoing substantial rehabilitation. Like other developments built before World War II, these buildings are two-story row houses that already meet many of the design goals for redeveloped public housing—low density with each unit having its own entrance and yard space. As of 2004, it was unclear if and how market-rate units will be included in the development. Near the fast-growing South Loop and west of the newly expanded McCormick Place convention and exposition center, both Harold Ickes Homes and Dearborn Homes were potentially attractive locations for market-rate developers. However, at the time the plan was developed, there was relatively little residential development activity near them. Subsequently, new private development has increased. Currently both developments are occupied, serving as what CHA labels "relocation resources" and "providing capacity for residents who have moved from other developments undergoing redevelopment or rehabilitation."[73] The future of these developments is unknown.

When considering the Plan for Transformation as a complete package, the overall loss of public housing units for families was significant. Technically, the combined number of public housing family units to be developed or rehabbed in Category 1 (5,353), Category 4 (2,254), and Category 5 (5,000) was only about 1,400 fewer units than the actual number of family households (compare 12,607 units to 14,046 families). However, the absolute loss of what had been family units—even if not occupied—was ten times that, 14,000, the majority of units that the CHA planned to demolish. Another source of unit reduction, though not technically through demolition, was the request by the CHA to be allowed to designate any building "senior only." By HUD granting this waiver, CHA was able to segregate its senior buildings by moving out all nonsenior tenants, which meant relocating all disabled tenants under the age of fifty-five into private market units.[74] Typically, this population consisted of single men and women who were either physically or mentally disabled, including those with substance addiction and HIV/AIDS. Regardless of the particular disability, advocates pointed out that even with a voucher, the private market was not very accommodating to this population and that some of the relocatees would probably end up homeless.[75] Still, funds were made available to help landlords that were willing to modify housing for access, and eventually, the city of Chicago committed to build about 750 units of supportive housing primarily for individuals with disabilities in order to support the city's plan to end homelessness and the CHA Plan for Transformation concurrently.[76]

Residents and advocates also raised questions about two important aspects of the plan that were not being addressed directly by the CHA: the fact that there were fewer tenants when the plan was developed than there had been when the viability test was completed, and the fact that there was no firm commitment of funding to develop the replacement units beyond what the CHA would get from HUD—assuming it would get all the funding it had requested over the ten-year period. On the first point, the CHA's commitment to providing the same number of units as there were households would have yielded many more units had the CHA been required to rehouse everyone in the developments as of 1997. While firm data are hard to pin down, in 1995 there had been 14,687 families living in the thirteen developments that were slated for demolition. By August 1998, there were only 9,073. About 1,000 families had been evicted and another 1,300 had taken vouchers to relocate. The whereabouts of the other 3,300 families were unknown as of December 1998.[77]

While there is no proof that the CHA began evicting tenants simply to empty buildings, especially at the family high-rise developments that had failed the viability test, an article in the *Chicago Reporter* suggested this might be the case. Comparing the lower eviction rates and overall decline in residents in family housing not slated for redevelopment to those in developments that were, the conclusion drawn was that "the CHA is stepping up evictions in buildings it has targeted for redevelopment—a move that reduces the number of public housing tenants the agency must provide with replacement housing."[78] While there were not that many evictions annually (less than 5 percent of the occupied units), there was an increase in the rate of evictions over time. However, it was debatable if evictions actually "surged" because of the CHA's intent to clean buildings out in order to reduce its responsibility to tenants. Offering an explanation, Shuldiner claimed that evictions were up because the agency was finally managing its properties responsibly. The CHA finally was evicting people who should not be allowed to stay in public housing because they were delinquent in paying their rent even after efforts to "cure" the problem. Advocates expressed concern that since public housing usually was the last resort for poor people, those being evicted were likely to become homeless. Of course, this point was hard to prove, since as Ed Shurna from the Coalition for the Homeless noted, "People don't always say where they are going. . . . That is not something you can get your hands on. It's frustrating."[79] Perhaps even more frustrating and more important were the stories about people leaving voluntarily. The *Chicago Reporter* article included interviews with residents who were afraid to relocate to other public housing sites or into the private market for fear of gangs. And still others, fearing they would be evicted because of violations, just left.[80]

On the issue of firm funding for redevelopment, two interrelated concerns emerged at this point—both prospective problems but deducible from past behavior of developers and the CHA. The first was based on a fear of the unknown. Many housing advocates and residents thought that once buildings were demolished, the CHA would run out of money to rebuild—especially if Congress in the future decided not to keep its end of the agreement. The CHA would then have no practical means to meet its obligation unless other sources of funding were found. Following the patterns of the existing redeveloped family sites, the expectation was that in these circumstances relatively few new public housing units would be built. Based on what was already happening at Category 1 developments, it was becoming evident that the nonpublic housing was dominating the mix in many of the mixed-income developments. For example, Wells/Madden Park, which had what many considered a successful resident participation process, had a proportionally large percentage of public housing units—1,000 out of the total 2,500 units (40 percent)—developed back on-site. This figure was nearly 500 units short of the number of families in the development at the time and represented a total loss of over 1,800 permanent units. At nearly 44 percent public housing,

ABLA had about the highest proportion *at the time,* with 1,463 public housing units out of a total of 3,278. However, as described in Chapter 7, the
market in the area was clearly changing and the loss of nearly 1,600 units of
low-cost, permanent, affordable rental housing in this community meant that
the many former CHA residents would most likely need to move to another
neighborhood. Finally, there was Cabrini-Green. Construction was beginning off-site on the first phase of redevelopment, offering no more than 30
percent public housing, while 50 percent of the units were market rate—and
some selling for more than $400,000. As with ABLA, the surrounding area
was clearly becoming a strong housing market.

Driving the mix at all three developments was the market-rate housing,
which in effect squeezed out public housing. Despite the proportion of public housing in the mix being equal to (or, in some cases, higher than) the
proportion of market rate and affordable units, the total number of public
housing units was still less than what had initially existed at the site. In the
context of the surrounding area, public housing was a very small proportion
of the total amount of development taking place. Observing this, residents
had good reason to believe that the sites with question marks in Table 4.1—
developments CHA had not determined a final count for—would have fewer
replacement public housing units.

The Planning Process

The Plan for Transformation emerged from a set of circumstances that restricted the process for developing the plan itself, some imposed by formal
guidelines affecting all PHAs and some unique to the Chicago experience.
This section examines four factors specified in the Plan for Transformation
introduction in order to show how each affected the plan: (1) the 1998 Quality Housing and Work Responsibility Act (QHWRA) requirement that public
housing authorities undertake annual and five-year plans beginning January
1, 2000; (2) the return of the CHA to local control on June 1, 1999; (3) the
memorandum of understanding between Chicago and HUD upon the return
of local control, requiring the city to "establish an action plan and identify
the regulatory flexibility, legislative flexibility, and resources necessary to
achieve performance benchmarks on which we will mutually agree"; and (4)
HUD's mandating that 18,000 units of CHA housing should be demolished
based on failure of the viability test. Each of these conditions came with its
own set of stakeholders and rules for engagement, and all affected how the
Plan for Transformation was developed. Of the four, the QHWRA requirement was the only one that provided an explicit protocol for developing a
plan. The other three created a context in which CHA and others worked to

shape the plan, both through traditional public processes such as hearings and presentations and through the kinds of traditional behind-the-scenes negotiation and consultation that generally shape all planning activities.[81] Although it is not easy to disentangle the effects of these different forces acting on the Plan for Transformation's development, it is important to look at the role each played in the plan's development and final approval by HUD. I begin with a quick overview of what is required by the QHWRA, then lay out how the other factors—return to local control, the memorandum of understanding, and the viability test—shaped the planning process, specifically the ability of residents and the public to change the plan.

Quality Housing and Work Responsibility Act

QHWRA guidelines for public housing authorities to develop five-year plans described the process and the expectation that participation should involve both consultation and collaboration with public housing residents, social service providers, the community, and the PHA.[82] Engaging the array of players needed to make the development happen was assumed to ensure that services would be delivered. It also was a means to get stakeholders—especially residents—to buy into the plan and become active participants in the future of their development. Procedurally, each PHA was to develop its plan with residents "who adequately reflect and represent the residents assisted by the PHA," using "reasonable outreach activities to encourage broad public participation" and public comment prior to submittal to HUD. The involvement of residents was to occur early with formation of a resident advisory board (RAB), either a newly formed group for the purpose of making recommendations in the development of the plan or an existing group such as a jurisdiction-wide resident council that complied with tenant participation regulations. (In Chicago, the Central Advisory Council is the RAB equivalent, with an elected representative from each development.) The RAB was to provide input on the plan's contents. The public, to be involved later and in a more traditional manner, was expected to provide feedback for the PHA to take under advisement.

HUD stated that "In order to facilitate collaboration, PHAs should encourage the RAB's participation from the inception of the planning process."[83] However, HUD also recognized that "securing participation by residents during the planning process may pose a challenge for some PHAs" so HUD suggested several strategies to engage residents, such as making personal invitations and providing child care, refreshments, and/or a stipend. Serving on the RAB also fulfilled community service hours required under the QHWRA.[84] HUD considered all these important "selling features" that can entice resident involvement and encouraged PHAs to "make clear" that:

the partnership between the residents and the PHA is of benefit to both parties. The residents are provided with an opportunity to voice their concerns so that their needs are addressed and they can become involved in the planning process. The PHA also gains essential information from the residents about the improvements that need to be made at the agency's developments and residents' self-sufficiency needs.[85]

Although the RAB was required, its role was inconsequential since "PHAs are required to consider the RAB's recommendations to the Plan but are not required to agree with them."[86] PHAs were required to submit for review to HUD all written recommendations and any other public comments with the transformation plan. If some discrepancy or disconnect was found between the plan and what residents and/or the community wanted, then HUD could ask for reconciliation before giving its approval of the plan. As the next section illustrates, there were several points along the way where this was possible.

Return of CHA to Local Control and the Memorandum of Understanding With HUD

The requirement that the city of Chicago should reclaim control over the CHA from HUD was a critical factor affecting the plan since it put the city and Mayor Daley in a powerful, but also potentially vulnerable position. As the CHA was being turned over, HUD released more demanding performance criteria that threatened the agency's "improved status" and potentially could have returned it to the "troubled list." While HUD later agreed to work with the city to help it comply, this was not a good "new start" for the CHA. In response, the first priority for the new CHA chief, Phillip Jackson, was to clean house and eliminate waste. Jackson let go many long-term and new employees, eventually reducing the CHA staff from about 2,300 to less than 1,000. This step included firing the CHA police and returning the sites to Chicago Police Department district responsibility. While this move clearly angered many members of the security force, the mayor saw it as part of the process of reconnecting CHA residents as citizens of Chicago.[87]

In an equally bold move, Jackson did a Geraldo Rivera–type exposé on local news to show the amount of waste that he had inherited from HUD's leadership: expensive vehicles; computers and other equipment sitting in a warehouse unused, providing no apparent benefit to residents or the organization. This public shaming of HUD infuriated officials in Washington, DC, as evidenced by a series of faxes sent from HUD's legal counsel, Howard Glaser, later revealed when the city was trying to get HUD to approve its plan. A *Chicago Tribune* account quoted the first fax from Glaser: "What kind of bull—— is this?" The second, referring to the cooperation agreement with the city that Glaser had just signed on behalf of HUD, read "Consider the deal cancelled."[88]

What transpired during the months following release of the draft "Plan for Transformation" suggested that HUD was not going to support the CHA's request for waivers or commit to the full $1.6 billion needed to implement the plan. Soon after the draft plan was released, a letter was sent to the mayor's chief of staff, Julia Stasch, suggesting that HUD had been blindsided by what the CHA proposed. HUD assistant secretary Harold Lucas called for public hearings in Chicago within the next thirty to forty-five days. In response, a couple of days before the arrival of federal officials to hold their hearing, Mayor Daley made a public request to HUD: "I ask the U.S. Department of Housing and Urban Development to play a constructive role in the process by supporting our local effort to solve a problem previous HUD administrations helped to create over the past 30 years."[89] More pointedly, Daley said, "What we need from Washington is flexibility and a steady source of funding for public housing,"[90] referring to the waivers requested by the CHA that were to make it easier to tap into current market activity and to borrow against future funding from HUD. The same day, nearly 1,000 protesters at City Hall asked for a moratorium on the demolition of all public housing. Two days later, Jackson asked why HUD was even in Chicago reviewing a plan that the CHA had not yet officially submitted to HUD. Lucas responded, "We want to make sure that the temperature in this matter doesn't get to the point where it burns the house down."[91]

At the hearing, HUD took a firm position on what it expected of the CHA in return for approval of the plan—if HUD would approve it at all. First, Lucas said that before HUD would approve razing CHA high-rises the CHA would have to identify replacement housing for displaced residents in advance. Second, Lucas said that an annual market study should be used to pace demolition in order to ensure that tenants would be able to find housing. Third, he said that CHA relocatees should have the right to refuse replacement housing in the suburbs, reflecting a concern among some tenants that this would be their only choice for replacement housing.[92] In response, the *Tribune* described Mayor Daley as having "angrily denounced Lucas and another top HUD official last week for meddling."[93]

The Viability Test and Demolition

HUD's requirement of an annual rental market study stemmed from a concern that there might not be sufficient housing in the private sector to absorb so many people moving out of public housing. When the viability test results required the CHA to displace a large number of families, the Coalition to Protect Public Housing (CPPH) had asked HUD to determine if indeed there would be sufficient housing options for relocated tenants. HUD had agreed to fund a study to gauge rental vacancy rates and prices in the region. While HUD supplied most of this money, complete funding came from a consortium that included the CHA, the Chicago Department of Housing, the Illinois Housing Development Authority, which funds affordable housing development throughout the state, and several foundations, including the MacArthur Foundation. In November 1998 the consortium, which was managed by the Metropolitan Planning Council, issued a request for proposals to provide a comprehensive analysis of the region's rental market.

Beyond providing answers to basic questions about the supply and demand for rental housing by location, size, quality, and accessibility, the study was to determine where growth and change were most likely to occur and what impact moving families out of CHA housing would have on the private sector rental housing market. The study also had to consider other trends, such as future revitalization of neighborhoods, voucher holders' recent experiences in finding and securing housing in the market, welfare reform, and expiring Section 8 project-based contracts—all of which would likely change the supply of and demand for affordable rental housing in the coming years. The project required a quick turnaround if the CHA was to use it to develop its plan and to allow public input based on the findings. The team hired was led by researchers at the University of Illinois at Chicago working in collaboration with the Urban Institute, which had recently completed a research study of Section 8 recipients' experience with using vouchers in the private market.

The research, which included a survey of rental properties in the region, was not completed until late August 1999.[94] As a result, the CHA had little time to incorporate the findings in the draft of the plan. More important, there was about a three-month gap between when the data were produced and when the summary report containing the findings was made available to the public. This meant that the public did not have the market study results until after the CHA began its public hearings on the plan in early November. As time passed, there was growing suspicion among advocacy groups that the data were being withheld for a reason. Publicly undisclosed at the time was the scrutiny by HUD's legal counsel of the findings, particularly the 4.2 percent vacancy rate, since this would affect the ability of the market to absorb CHA families. The research showed that technically there were enough units for relocatees to move into, although it was likely that they would be concentrated in the relatively soft and segregated housing markets on the city's South and West Sides and in southern Cook County. When the regional rental market report was finally released on November 23, 1999, the reaction was mixed.[95] The CHA viewed the results as a green light to move the plan forward. Reading the same data, the CPPH and others asked HUD to stop the plan from moving forward, since a 4.2 percent vacancy rate proved that a tight rental market would make it difficult for so many public housing residents to relocate. Despite these findings, the CHA submitted its final "Plan for Transformation" with the same level of demolition and the same number of replacement units as in the draft. HUD's response was a public promise to "undertake annual market studies to ensure that the number of displaced families does not exceed the number of units available to holders of Section 8 vouchers."[96] To date, three so-called market studies have been conducted; however, none have been made available to the public.

The Limits to Public Participation

On its face the CHA appeared to follow HUD's plan development and review protocol outlined in the QHWRA. The plan lists the many meetings held at different developments and citywide, plus the various means used to disseminate the document for review: on the Internet, through the mail, and by directly delivering copies to residents. The Central Advisory Council (CAC), which is an elected body and the equivalent of an RAB for the entire CHA, reviewed the draft document after its release. However, in statements made in early October, the CAC claimed that it had not been formally involved in the process to develop the plan.[97] As one CAC member said, "From the beginning, we should have been there at the table."[98] Similar reactions came from people who attended public hearings. Still, many community-based groups, housing advocates, and religious leaders did come out to speak to the issue of relocation, the lack of replacement housing, and the plan's ambitious pace.

In the end, while the process can be criticized because it did not include residents early enough, the process was also flawed because from the start it was not designed to engage all residents—just the elected leadership and "officially recognized" representatives of CHA residents. At the CHA board meeting where the plan was approved, the CAC came out in support of the plan.[99] During the meeting, members of the Coalition to Protect Public Housing held up signs that said "CHA always lies" and "Build First" in protest. A member of the CAC explained later, "With or without us, they were going to submit anyway . . . at least this way, we are able to include our comments."[100]

However, it would be misleading to assume that involving more residents might have changed the outcome. The CHA did not have to respond to the complaints and concerns raised by anyone participating in hearings, including elected officials. As Joseph Shuldiner later said, the CHA had "to show they have taken them [public and residents] into account, but doesn't have to do what they say."[101] While officials from HUD and Congress actually did hear from many residents during special hearings preceding release of the final "Plan for Transformation" and even appeared to respond by publicly questioning the CHA's ability to relocate so many families and rebuild so many units in such a short period of time, the CHA appeared to ignore their concerns when submitting its plan. Of course, these same HUD officials approved the plan and many of the same elected representatives endorsed it despite there being no change in the number of units to be demolished or developed. Needless to say, many public housing residents and advocates were both perplexed and outraged.

Status of the Plan for Transformation in Early 2005

Only a few high-rise buildings are still standing on the South Side and they are slated for demolition soon. As of the fall of 2005, nearly 90 percent of the CHA senior housing units had been rehabilitated, and 1,639 units of mixed-income housing had been produced. By the end of 2005, the CHA planned to pass the halfway mark by completing development or renovation of 14,450 public housing units out of the total 25,000 unit commitment.[102] This will include 1,914 family units in redeveloped sites, 1,187 family units in rehabbed buildings, 8,806 senior-only units in rehabbed buildings, and 2,543 scattered-site housing units for families.

Some progress has been made in planning for the Category 4 and 5 sites, in which the CHA had not determined the number of replacement units. As Table 4.2 illustrates, five of the nine non-202 sites (Category 4) have plans for redevelopment. These sites will be rehabilitated and generally retain a similar unit count as before the Plan for Transformation. The CHA has not determined if it will rehabilitate or redevelop the Lathrop Homes site, which has more than 900 units and is in a prime location. It is also strategic in the city's larger planning agenda since it is along the North Branch of the Chicago River, where efforts are under way to connect the waterway to the downtown by making it more pedestrian- and bike-friendly.

The status of Category 5 family sites is less certain. The original commitment for these developments was to demolish 9,775 and rebuild or rehabilitate a total of 5,000 units. As of FY 2005, only five of the thirteen developments have plans. Still, this accounts for 4,010 units. Assuming the CHA sticks with its original 25,000-unit count at completion of the Plan for Transformation, this means that the remaining sites, containing a total of 4,717 units, will need to be reduced to less than 1,000 units. While the two sites that

Table 4.2

Status of Redevelopment in Family Properties Undetermined in the Original Plan for Transformation (PFT), 2004

	Total public housing units pre-PFT	Total units when PFT completed	Units delivered through FY 2004	Units under construction to deliver FY 2005	Planned FY 2006	Planned FY 2007	Planned FY 2008	Planned FY 2009
Category 4: Non-202 family properties								
Lake Parc Place	300	300	150	150	0	0	0	0
LeClaire Courts[1]	300	TBD	NA	NA	NA	NA	NA	NA
Washington Park Homes low-rises[1]	488	TBD	NA	NA	NA	NA	NA	NA
Lawndale Complex[2]	187	TBD	NA	NA	NA	0	0	NA
Lawndale Gardens	128	128	28	100	0	0	0	0
Lathrop Homes[3]	925	TBD	NA	NA	NA	NA	NA	NA
Bridgeport Homes	155	107	81	26	0	0	0	0
Wentworth Gardens	422	344	94	150	100	0	0	0
Lowden Homes[4]	128	126	126	0	0	0	0	0
Category 5: 202 family properties								
Frances Cabrini Rowhouses[1]	586	TBD	NA	NA	NA	NA	NA	NA
Trumball Park homes	486	458	150	150	158	0	0	0
Harold L. Ickes Homes[1]	1,006	TBD	NA	NA	NA	NA	NA	NA
Dearborn Homes[1]	800	TBD	NA	NA	NA	NA	NA	NA
Altgeld Gardens	1,998	1,998	425	425	425	575	458	0
1230 N. Burling[2]	134	TBD	NA	NA	NA	NA	NA	NA
Cabrini Extension South[2]	597	TBD	NA	NA	NA	NA	NA	NA
William Green Homes[2]	968	TBD	NA	NA	NA	NA	NA	NA
Rockwell Gardens	1,136	264	18	59	0	34	119	34
Stateway Gardens	1,644	439	0	95	35	83	60	166
Robert Taylor A & B[5]	3,784	851	74	91	136	183	183	184
Washington Park high-rises[2]	468	TBD	NA	NA	NA	NA	NA	NA
Randolph Towers[2]	155	TBD	NA	NA	NA	NA	NA	NA

Source: Chicago Housing Authority, "FY 2005 Annual Plan–Plan for Transformation Year 6," September 2004; accessed May 18, 2005.
[1]Rehabilitation property; [2]Redevelopment property; [3]Redevelopment or rehabilitation property; [4]Includes rehabbed units (total units = rehab [54] + new construction [72]); [5]"Units delivered through 2004" includes units developed in 2002.
TBD = to be determined; NA = not available.

function as relocation resources, Harold Ickes and Dearborn Homes, are designated as "rehabilitation sites," advocates sense that their location near the hot South Loop market favors demolition, especially if the CHA is not going to have more than 25,000 units in its portfolio.

In addition to making progress on its capital program, the CHA in its plan for year 6 also boasts of the "considerable investment in the areas surrounding CHA properties—such as upgrading public infrastructure, adding new public amenities, and increasing private residential and commercial investment."[103] While the actual amount of investment is unknown, it is evident that the city is spending a lot of money in nearly every community where public housing has been demolished. New streets and sidewalks are being cut through the old superblocks on the South Side where Robert Taylor Homes and Stateway Gardens once stood. Even more noticeable is the new private sector market-rate housing being built in nearby areas that for decades had seen little or no real estate activity. With prices typically starting at a quarter of a million dollars for a three-bedroom condominium, the area is clearly changing.[104] These changes appear to contradict what the U.S. General Accounting Office (U.S. GAO) had expected in 1996, which was that "some severely distressed properties in severely distressed neighborhoods, such as Robert Taylor Homes B in Chicago . . . may not be able to attract investment partners or leverage the funds needed to transform neighborhoods."[105] However, these improvements are supported by data in a more recent U.S. GAO report that suggests that overall improvements are taking place in many neighborhoods surrounding several redeveloped or redeveloping HOPE VI sites.[106] Whether or not the market will sustain this level of development is still unknown.

As laid out in the original "Plan for Transformation," the CHA no longer positions itself as a housing provider, but rather is now a "facilitator" of housing. On one hand, this means that the CHA in conjunction with the city's Department of Housing now functions like other state and local agencies that help to develop affordable housing by distributing public funds to qualified for-profit and nonprofit entities. On the other hand, the stream of money for public housing available to the CHA is limited to what HUD has committed to the CHA. Any additional units will require the city to dip into its own affordable housing development sources, including other federal housing production dollars—low-income housing tax credits, community development block grant money and HOME Investment Partnership Program funds—and the private sector. While the city and the CHA apparently have been successful in pooling of resources so far, the funding climate for affordable housing development has changed in the last few years and it is unclear how this change has or will affect the CHA's ability to fulfill its outstanding obligations. The CHA is competing with other affordable housing developers for support from the same limited pot of funding, which may present a significant challenge in the coming years not only for the CHA but for other affordable housing developers—many of whom have been working in Chicago communities for decades. Of course, the CHA and its plan are also getting support that no other housing developer would or could get, with the issuance of bonds its greatest potential source of funds. In addition, given the long list of "collaborators" in the year 6 plan, the CHA clearly has developed a broad base of support among investors.[107] Noticeably absent from the list is the Coalition to Protect Public Housing.

Notes

1. Chicago Housing Authority, "Plan for Transformation Draft for Public Comment," September 30, 1999, p. 2.

2. Bruce Katz, "The Transformation of Chicago's Public Housing: Challenges and Opportunities," speech at the Chicago Futures Forum sponsored by the MacArthur Foundation, February 26, 1999, (emphasis in original).

3. Webster's Dictionary, 1996.

4. Melita Marie Garza, "CHA to Be Torn Up, Rebuilt; $1.5 Billion Plan Razes 51 High-Rises, Boosts Minority Firms," Chicago Tribune, February 6, 2000.

5. Chicago Housing Authority, "Plan for Transformation," January 6, 2000.

6. See Janet L. Smith and Thomas Lenz, For Rent: Housing Options in the Chicago Region, (Chicago: University of Illinois, Great Cities Institute, 1999). While there is no single threshold to determine if a rental market is tight, at the time HUD was using a vacancy rate of 6 percent.

7. Smith and Lenz, For Rent.

8. Garza, "CHA to Be Torn Up."

9. The CHA asked for a total of thirty-nine waivers dealing with funding, development regulation, occupancy, modernization, procurement, Section 8, and administration. See Chicago Housing Authority, "List of Waivers and Requests," September 30, 1999.

10. CHA, "Plan for Transformation," p. 7.

11. CHA, "Plan for Transformation," p. 2.

12. CHA, "Plan for Transformation," p. 2.

13. CHA, "Plan for Transformation," p. 3.

14. CHA, "Plan for Transformation," p. 3.

15. CHA requested "authority to designate any or all senior buildings as 'senior only.'" See CHA, "List of Waivers and Requests," September 30, 1999.

16. CHA, "Plan for Transformation," p. 3.

17. Noreen Ahmed, "HUD to Review CHA Overhaul Plan: Federal Scrutiny Coming This Week," Chicago Tribune, January 24, 2000.

18. Garza, "CHA to be Torn Up."

19. CHA, "Plan for Transformation," p. 4.

20. CHA, "Plan for Transformation," p. 4.

21. Larry Bennett and Adolph Reed, "The New Face of Urban Renewal: The Near North Redevelopment Initiative and the Cabrini-Green Neighborhood," in Without Justice for All, ed. Adolph Reed Jr. (Boulder, CO: Westview Press, 1999), pp. 175–211.

22. Michael Schill, "Chicago's Mixed-Income New Communities Strategy: The Future Face of Public Housing?" in *Affordable Housing and Urban Redevelopment in the United States,* ed. Willem Van Vliet (Thousand Oaks, CA: Sage, 1997).

23. This amount included $15.3 million in misappropriated CHA pension assets and $4.3 million in misappropriated health insurance payments, and "millions of dollars lost through fraudulent actions by outside vendors and CHA personnel." See Committee on Government Reform and Oversight, "The Federal Takeover of the Chicago Housing Authority—HUD Needs to Determine Long-Term Implications," fifth report, 104th Congress, H. Rept. 104–437, December 21, 1995, p. 4.

24. The Public Housing Management Assessment Program (PHMAP), introduced as a method of evaluating performance of PHAs in the 1990 Affordable Housing Act, used twelve criteria, including vacancy rates and operating expenses. In 1995, eighty-three PHAs were on the "troubled list" and most were small (less than 100 units). While this number had decreased substantially since PHMAP was first introduced (130 in 1992), the U.S. General Accounting Office still had concerns that the criteria were not actually accurately assessing management performance and were actually misjudging small authorities. See "HUD Should Improve the Usefulness and Accuracy of Its Management Assessment Program," GAO-RCED 97–27, January 1997.

25. For a good account of Vincent Lane's early support but also controversial ideas to clean up public housing, see Jorge Casusa, "High Hopes: Many Think Public Housing Is a Lost Cause: Vince Lane Doesn't Agree," *Chicago Tribune Magazine,* July 22, 1990.

26. *Patrick Reardon, "Older Leader Leaves: Lane Tries to Be Diplomatic," Chicago Tribune,* June 1, 1995.

27. "Profile of Joesph Shuldiner," *Chicago Reporter,* March 1998.

28. Committee on Government Reform and Oversight, "Federal Takeover," p. 1.

29. Committee on Government Reform and Oversight, "Federal Takeover," p. 10.

30. Committee on Government Reform and Oversight, "Federal Takeover," pp. 2–3.

31. Committee on Government Reform and Oversight, "Federal Takeover," p. 6.

32. Committee on Government Reform and Oversight, "Federal Takeover," p. 14.

33. Metropolitan Planning Council, "Fact Sheet # 1: Early Reforms and Organization at CHA Public Housing," March 1996.

34. Metropolitan Planning Council, "Fact Sheet # 2: Redevelopment and Rehabilitation of Public Housing," October 1996.

35. Schill, "Chicago's Mixed-Income New Communities Strategy."

36. Before being redeveloped, Lake Parc Place was known as the Olander Homes.

37. Schill, "Chicago's Mixed-Income New Communities Strategy."

38. James Rosenbaum and Nancy Fishman, "The Early Reactions of Lake Parc Place Residents," 1994, unpublished paper cited in Schill, "Chicago's Mixed-Income New Communities Strategy."

39. Two things happened in the early 1990s that prevented further development. First, local leaders opposed more low-income housing being built in the community. Second, control over development, including conveyance of land, was transferred to the hands of the community via the establishment of a "conservation area" by the city. This meant that the CHA could not get land from the city without approval from this group, which did not want more public housing either. See Schill, "Chicago's Mixed-Income New Communities Strategy."

40. Susan J. Popkin and Mary Cunningham, "CHAC Section 8 Program: Barriers to Successful Leasing Up" (Washington, DC: Urban Institute, 1999).

41. *Latinos United et al. v. Chicago Housing Authority and United States Department of Housing and Urban Development,* 1996.

42. Popkin and Cunningham, "CHAC Section 8 Program." At the time the report was issued, the authors noted that the success rate had already gone up.

43. To address these barriers, CHAC instituted strategies including a mobility program to help interested participants move into less poor and less segregated areas of the city and region. Also, CHAC offered security deposit loans and grants for qualified families plus a resource center and outreach to get landlords more interested in the program. The time limit was eventually eliminated for relocatees.

44. Katz, "Transformation of Chicago's Public Housing."

45. Katz, "Transformation of Chicago's Public Housing."

46. "Statement of Mayor Richard M. Daley—CHA Transformation Announcement," Office of the Mayor, City of Chicago, May 27, 1999.

47. "Statement of Mayor Richard M. Daley."

48. "Statement of Mayor Richard M. Daley."

49. CHA, "Plan for Transformation," p. 2.

50. Congress cut back the overall HUD budget by about $7 billion in 1995 but supported full funding of HOPE VI. In 1998, Congress added funding for 50,000 vouchers with passage of the Quality Work and Housing Responsibilities Act (QWHRA).

51. The cost of demolition was not included in the budget since another source of HUD funding would be used.

52. Also known as "202" requirements, referring to the section of the law that outlines the test.

53. The test was two-pronged: First came the cost comparison; failure, required the second test. The second test, entitled "reasonable revitalization," required the CHA to demonstrate that the revitalization could (1) be accomplished within reasonable cost limits, (2) be realistically funded, (3) sustain full occupancy and structural soundness for at least twenty years, (4) meet standards for density and concentration of extremely low-income families, (5) be continued as public housing because its site was not impaired in any way that would disqualify it. For discussion and critique of the test results, see Robin Snyderman, "CHA Units Fail Viability Test," Metropolitan Planning Council, 1997.

54. Snyderman, "CHA Units Fail Viability Test."

55. Snyderman, "CHA Units Fail Viability Test."

56. The Uniform Relocation Act of 1970 "assures people uniform and equitable treatment of persons displaced from their homes, businesses, or farms by Federal and federally assisted programs," including assisting with the cost for moving and other related relocation expenses.

57. Snyderman, "CHA Units Fail Viability Test."

58. Snyderman, "CHA Units Fail Viability Test."

59. Snyderman, "CHA Units Fail Viability Test."

60. Snyderman, "CHA Units Fail Viability Test."

61. Robert O'Neil, "Condemned," *Chicago Reporter,* October 1997.

62. O'Neil, "Condemned."

63. O'Neil, "Condemned."

64. CHA, "Plan for Transformation," p.13.

65. CHA, "Plan for Transformation," pp. 15–16.

66. CHA, "Plan for Transformation," p. 16.

67. Randolph Towers was not subject to 202 requirements even though it is a high-rise development. However, CHA included it in Category 5.

68. CHA, "List of Waivers and Requests," p. 2.

69. CHA, "Plan for Transformation," p. 13.

70. See Jennifer Peltz, "Living at CHA Site Called Health Hazard: Suit Cites Sicknesses at Altgeld Gardens," *Chicago Tribune,* October 24, 1999. In the lawsuit, residents claimed higher than expected rates of cancer and other disease.

71. Peltz, "Living at CHA Site Called Health Hazard."

72. Chicago Housing Authority, www.thecha.org/housingdev/family_sites.html, accessed December 5, 2004.

73. Chicago Housing Authority, www.thecha.org/housingdev/family_sites.html, accessed December 5, 2004.

74. The actual number of disabled people to be relocated was not determined; however, based on HUD data on occupants in Ida B. Wells, Cabrini-Green, Dearborn Homes, ABLA, Stateway Gardens, Washington Park, Henry Horner, and Rockwell Gardens, there were at least 1,700 disabled people under the age of sixty-two living in these developments in 1998 (see "1998 Picture of Subsidized Households").

75. A key opponent was and still is Access Living, a disability rights advocacy group and Center for Independent Living serving Chicago area.

76. City of Chicago Department of Housing, "Build. Preserve. Lead. Affordable Housing Plan 2004–2008," November 2003, p. 10.

77. Brian Rogal, "CHA Tenant Evictions Jump as Buildings Fall," *Chicago Reporter,* December 1998, p. 1.

78. Rogal, "CHA Tenant Evictions Jump," p. 1.

79. Rogal, "CHA Tenant Evictions Jump," p. 3.

80. Rogal, "CHA Tenant Evictions Jump," p. 6.

81. See, for example, John Forester, *Planning in the Face of Power* (Berkeley: University of California Press, 1989).

82. U.S. Department of Housing and Urban Development, "Public Housing Agency Plan Desk Guide," www.hud.gov/, accessed September 21, 2001.

83. This requirement in the QWHRA excluded people who were not expected to work due to either age or disability.

84. HUD, "Public Housing Agency Plan Desk Guide," p. 93.

85. HUD, "Public Housing Agency Plan Desk Guide," p. 96.

86. HUD, "Public Housing Agency Plan Desk Guide," p. 98.

87. *Melita Marie Garza,* "CHA Dumps Cop Force in Revamp: City Police Viewed as Better Security," *Chicago Tribune,* October 13, 1999.

88. Melita Marie Garza, "Daley Lashes Out at HUD for Public Housing Troubles Remarks at Kick-Off Event for Hospital's Housing Project," *Chicago Tribune,* October 29, 1999.

89. Garza, "Daley Lashes Out."

90. James Janega, "CHA Chief Questions HUD Officials," *Chicago Tribune,* October 31, 1999.

91. Gary Washburn and Matt O'Connor, "HUD Tacks If's to CHA Rehab Plan; Daley Told to Honor Residents' Wishes," *Chicago Tribune,* November 16, 1999.

92. Washburn and O'Connor, "HUD Tacks If's to CHA Rehab Plan."

93. Melita Marie Garza, "CHA Again Holds Off on Pan for Overhaul," *Chicago Tribune,* December 10, 1999.

94. The research team had asked and was given permission to extend its time in the field to boost the response rate to its survey.

95. Smith and Lenz, *For Rent*.

96. Melita Marie Garza and Gary Washburn, "Study Plots Effect of CHA Housing Rehab Plan: Tight Market Still Likely to Have Affordable Units," *Chicago Tribune,* November 23, 1999.

97. Melita Marie Garza, "Tenant Leaders Decry Major Makeover," *Chicago Tribune,* October 5, 1999.

98. Garza, "Tenant Leaders Decry Major Makeover," quoting Theresa Ricks, president of the Dearborn Homes Local Advisory Council.

99. Melita Marie Garza, "CHA Gives Go Ahead to $1.5 Billion Overhaul of Public Housing, *Chicago Tribune,* January 7, 1999.

100. Garza, "CHA Gives Go Ahead," quoting Francine Washington, president of Stateway Gardens Local Advisory Council.

101. Cory Oldweiler, "Residents Lack Role in Revamped Public Housing," *Chicago Reporter,* April 2002.

102. Chicago Housing Authority, "FY 2005 Annual Plan—Plan for Transformation Year 6," September 2004.

103. CHA, "FY 2005 Annual Plan," p. i.

104. While still below the median sales price for the region, the Grand Boulevard community saw a 132 percent increase in median values of single-family homes between 1998 and 2002 compared to the city of Chicago overall, which increased less than 50 percent in the same time period.

105. U.S. General Accounting Office, "HOPE VI: Progress and Problems in Revitalizing Distressed Public Housing," Washington, DC, GAO-98–187, 1998.

106. U.S. General Accounting Office, "Public Housing: HOPE VI Resident Issues and Changes in Neighborhoods Surrounding Grant Sites," report to ranking minority member, Subcommittee on Housing and Transportation, Committee on Banking, Housing and Urban Affairs, U.S. Senate, Washington, DC, GAO-04–109, November 2003.

107. CHA, "FY 2005 Annual Plan."

5

Community Resistance to CHA Transformation

The History, Evolution, Struggles, and Accomplishments of the Coalition to Protect Public Housing

Patricia A. Wright

The organizing efforts of Chicago's public housing residents to save public housing were a surprise to many observers and critics because Chicago had a reputation for having some of the worst public housing in the nation. In 1996, when Congress required public housing authorities across the country to assess whether their housing units should be saved or turned into housing vouchers, Chicago had twice as many "distressed" units as any other city in the country.[1] Despite Chicago's public housing stock being the worst in the country, many public housing residents wanted to fight for their chance to rebuild their communities. They did not want to be thrown into a private housing market that did not want them or did not have enough units to accommodate them.

In 1996, Wardell Yotaghan, a public housing resident who was president of the Chicago Association of Resident Management Corporations (CARMC), started having discussions with other public housing leaders about how the federal changes would affect the future of public housing in Chicago. CARMC included all the resident management corporations (RMCs) operating in the Chicago Housing Authority (CHA) developments. The RMC organizations had been initiated and encouraged by Jack Kemp, the secretary of the Department of Housing and Urban Development (HUD) in the Reagan administration. The 1987 Housing and Community Development Act contained a provision to provide grants and pay for technical assistance to support public housing authorities and tenant groups interested in resident management. Chicago public housing residents embraced this concept and more public housing RMCs were formed in

Chicago than in any other city in the country. The residents of individual build-ings, groups of buildings, or entire public housing developments had to organize and have a referendum to set up the RMC. If the referendum passed, elections were held for the RMC board of directors. Once elected, the RMC board had to go through extensive training before receiving a contract from the CHA to take over the management. So it took a lot of organizing and commitment for resi-dents to comply and establish a resident management program.

Up until 1996, federal law prohibited public housing authorities from de-molishing any public housing units unless they could be replaced. In 1996, the Congress suspended this one-for-one replacement rule. Through CARMC, Wardell Yotaghan had good relationships with the RMC board presidents throughout the city. He began to talk to them about these federal policy changes. Yotaghan approached Regina McGraw at the Wieboldt Foundation and Bruce Orenstein at the Chicago Video Project for their assistance to fund an organizing campaign to educate public housing residents about these changes. The Wieboldt Foundation had funded several of the public housing resident management corporations in the city. McGraw and Orenstein put Yotaghan in touch with the Chicago Coalition for the Homeless and other religious and advocacy organizations in the city. It was the staff of the Chi-cago Coalition for the Homeless that Yotaghan talked to first about the pro-posed legislative changes and, particularly, the threatened demolitions and elimination of one-for-one replacement of public housing units. Wardell thought that the elimination of one-for-one replacement in public housing units would increase homelessness in Chicago and elsewhere. According to Lydia Taylor, who worked with Yotaghan at the Rockwell Gardens RMC, "It is one thing to say that dilapidated housing needs to be torn down and new housing needs to be built. But it is another thing to read the fine lines and find out that there really was not a plan to replace every unit."

The public housing residents sought the advice of the Chicago Coalition for the Homeless staff in forming a new organization to protect the rights of public housing residents and to ensure the continued existence of public hous-ing in Chicago. According to Edward Shurna, lead organizer at the Chicago Coalition for the Homeless:

> It was September 1996 when Wardell Yotaghan of Rockwell Gardens, Carol Steele and Cora Moore of Cabrini-Green came to our offices to meet with us. Basically, they said that they were not getting their voice or message out as residents. They needed a broader group of people who were not public hous-ing residents that would help get the message out. They were looking to form a coalition and they asked us to organize a coalition of public housing residents and nonpublic housing residents to fight for the future of public housing.

The Coalition to Protect Public Housing (CPPH) was formed two years before the introduction of the 1998 Quality Housing and Work Responsibility Act (QHWRA). The act's subsequent passage with bipartisan support demonstrates that the public housing tenants' concerns in 1996 were well founded. Many provisions of the 1998 QHWRA had originally been in the 1996 HUD appropriations bill. For example, the 1998 QHWRA ended the one-for-one replacement requirement. After 1998, the local public housing authority had only to demonstrate to HUD that the units were obsolete and not cost-effective in order to demolish them. One provision of the 1996 HUD appropriations bill also required a viability study for half of the 40,000 public housing units in Chicago. The viability study was to compare the costs of maintaining the existing public housing units to the costs of replacing those units with a Section 8 (now called Housing Choice) voucher for an apartment in the private market. This viability study and the fight to keep the one-for-one replacement requirement was the main impetus for the formation of the CPPH. CPPH included public housing residents and seventy supporting community, civic, and religious organizations. It was the goal of the CPPH to (1) understand the impact that the federal legislative public housing changes would have in Chicago and (2) intervene in the decision-making process so that public housing residents would not be unduly harmed by the proposed changes.

This chapter discusses the accomplishments and the obstacles faced by the Coalition to Protect Public Housing as it organized local resistance to the plans of the CHA and joined other coalitions nationally to oppose the plans of the federal government to privatize and eliminate public housing. First I will lay out the events between 1996 and 2004 that form the history of this resistance. Then I will discuss the accomplishments and major obstacles that the members of the coalition faced in getting their message out to the general public and the policy makers in Chicago and Washington, DC.

The Early Years of CPPH: 1996 to 1999

In its early years, fall 1996 to June 1999, CPPH organized and sponsored a number of activities to broaden the policy debate and bring attention to the changes in public housing and how they affected the residents. The CPPH decided to work on numerous fronts. Its activities included workshops called Saturday Schools, similar to the educational workshops of the civil rights movement. These workshops informed residents about their rights as tenants and the impact of federal legislative changes on public housing in Chicago. In the first two years of the coalition's work, Saturday Schools were held at Cabrini-Green on the North Side, Rockwell Gardens and Jane Addams Houses on the West Side. The coalition members also organized more than thirty meetings at different public housing developments beyond the three Saturday School sites. These included LeClaire Courts on the far West Side, Robert Taylor Homes, Dearborn Homes, and Ida B. Wells and Washington Park on the South Side. At these meetings, residents were asked to join the coalition and attend its meetings and public actions.

Every week public housing residents and other supporters attended what became known as the Wednesday meeting. This forum was open to all, public housing residents and anyone interested in the issue, to discuss what was happening in the different developments and to plan future activities. Wardell Yotaghan and Carol Steele chaired these meetings. The Wednesday meetings became the forum where public housing residents could be heard and where supporters could get firsthand information on what was happening in the public housing developments across the city. As part of the meeting's agenda, Yotaghan would include an item titled "News from the Developments." At these meetings, residents shared their experiences. Pamela Alfonso from the Metropolitan Tenants Organization, a tenants' rights organization, recalls, "These meetings were unruly, loud, and passionate. It was a real reminder of what was happening to the residents. The Wednesday meeting was the table that had a lot of faces and the best ideas for action really came from."

Contributions of Coalition Member Organizations: Organizing and Research

In addition to the Chicago Coalition for the Homeless, several other citywide religious, academic, and community organizations contributed to organizing and research to build the outreach and educational agenda of CPPH. Early in 1997, the Community Renewal Society (CRS) became actively involved in the CPPH organizing effort. The CRS, founded in 1882 by the Congregational Church (predecessor of the United Church of Christ), is a metropolitan Chicago social justice organization. The CRS assisted CPPH in organizing prayer vigils at different public housing developments. As part of this effort, the CRS staff organized an Interfaith Network, which brought together public housing residents, clergy, and laity.

The Jewish Council on Urban Affairs (JCUA) also helped organize the Interfaith Network and the vigils, bringing progressive rabbis and synagogue members to the vigils. The JCUA, founded in 1964, works with grassroots organizations on issues such as job creation, affordable housing, community reinvestment, and neighborhood stability. The CRS and JCUA brought an insistent moral voice to the work of the coalition.

In early 1997, the CPPH leaders asked us at the Nathalie P. Voorhees Center for Neighborhood and Community Improvement (VNC) at the University of Illinois at Chicago to do research for them on two issues. The VNC is a university center that works with community groups on affordable housing research. The research was, first, to assess the reliability of the Section 8 voucher program to provide affordable housing for public housing residents and, second, to do a financial analysis of the redevelopment plans for the Cabrini-Green public housing development.[2] This Cabrini-Green analysis was included because the CPPH, as part of its agenda, supported the Cabrini-Green Local Advisory Council in its federal civil rights lawsuit against the Chicago Housing Authority and the city of Chicago. This lawsuit, filed in October 1996, claimed that the residents' rights were violated because the residents were excluded from the redevelopment planning process and the plans would adversely affect African-American women and children who are the majority residents of Cabrini-Green.

In its report, released in May 1997, the Voorhees Center found that public housing families using Section 8 vouchers were locating in areas of the city that were occupied by over 90 percent black households. Thirty percent of the families had to return their vouchers because they could not find a suitable housing unit. This was happening because black public housing households were entering into a tight housing market in which there were, in effect, two low-income households looking for every affordable unit in the Chicago metropolitan area.

The report's analysis of the proposed Cabrini-Green redevelopment found that despite the tight housing situation, Cabrini-Green would lose 974 units for very low-income tenants. Private developers had been acquiring land around Cabrini-Green and a burst of luxury housing development was already driving up real estate prices in the area. Despite this boom in development, the city of Chicago was offering $281 million in public subsidies for the redevelopment in the area. The report did a preliminary estimate of the proposed residential redevelopment, including the public housing land and some adjacent city- and privately owned property. Based on the proposals in the plan, the report estimated that at least $100 million in profits would be generated to private developers.

The release of the report yielded a great deal of press coverage for the coalition. The report's authors and the coalition leadership were on several talk radio shows. For several months after the release of the report, the coalition presented the report's findings and a video prepared by the Chicago Video Project called *Mixed-In, Not Mixed-Out* to public housing developments and church and other social groups for discussions of the public housing policies and issues. This video, shown to hundreds of groups over the next few months, presented some of the findings of the report and included interviews with public housing leaders and residents on how the current legislation and the vouchering-out process would adversely affect them.

These organizing and research efforts culminated in the first Juneteenth event, a march on the Chicago Housing Authority offices and city hall. It was Wardell Yotaghan who suggested that every year the coalition should stage an event on June 19. June 19, or Juneteenth, is the oldest known celebration of the ending of slavery.[3] This first Juneteenth march and rally was one of the most successful events that the coalition planned in terms of numbers of people who attended. It included public housing residents from across the city along with supporters from churches and other advocacy groups. Its success was due in large part to Yotaghan's leadership. Lydia Taylor, who helped organize the first Juneteenth event, recalled his role in the buildup to the event:

> Wardell had a vision that we could really change things and his articulation of that really kept people motivated. For example, when we were planning the first rally and the question was asked, well, how many people are we going to have at this march? Wardell would say 10,000 and it would blow people's mind. I do believe some people felt that we couldn't disappoint this man. We have got to get 10,000 people out here.

Although the coalition did not achieve the goal of 10,000 attending the rally, some estimated that close to 2,000 people did attend. The event's organizers felt this was a good turnout for the coalition's first big event. Ethan Michaeli, the editor of *Resident Journal,* a newspaper for public housing residents, remembers covering the first Juneteenth rally:

> That was a very interesting scene because a lot of the Local Advisory Council [elected public housing leaders] presidents came to that event. I remember I saw Deverra Beverly—she is one of the most successful presidents. She is probably as powerful as an alderman. . . . I talked to Deverra and she brought 200 people. You probably could have brought more people, I told her, and she said yes—she could have but I am holding back a little bit. And I asked her why. Well, I wanted to bring enough to show I am bringing support but I really don't know what this organization is and what it is intending to do. . . . If they are going to work collaboratively with us, then we will work with them.

The elected public housing leaders, the local advisory council (LAC) members, did help organize residents to attend the first Juneteenth rally and march. But the issue of whether the LAC leaders would continue to work collaboratively with the CPPH turned out to be one of the key conflicts that the coalition faced in its organizing efforts.

Leadership and Conflict: CPPH and the Local
Advisory Councils

In each public housing development, every three years, the residents elect a local advisory council. The president of each LAC is then a member of the Central Advisory Council, the CAC, which is the citywide elected body of public housing residents. The LACs and the CAC are the officially recognized elected public housing representatives who negotiate with the Chicago Housing Authority and the federal Department of Housing and Urban Development. With the changes in public housing legislation, the LACs and the CAC represent the tenants' views on redevelopment plans and other major decisions affecting the future of public housing.

Besides the CHA and HUD officials, politicians also worked closely with the LACs in their districts or wards during elections to bring out the public housing residents to vote. The LACs and the CAC are considered by many public housing residents to be a political arm of the local politicians in the city. Some of the CPPH members were concerned that political favors and payoffs influenced the LACs' willingness to take an independent stand on public housing redevelopment issues. As Deidre Matthews, a coalition activist said, "It is hard to put all the CAC and LAC members into one bag because maybe some took money, maybe some didn't. Maybe some just don't understand what they're reading, maybe some do. Some have contracts [with CHA], some don't."

Ethan Michaeli, the editor of *Resident Journal,* felt that it was a mistake to form the CPPH and compete with the LACs and CAC to represent the interests of public housing residents:

> I thought to form an outside group of people was going to be a big mistake. . . . It was undermining LAC leadership. The LACs are not perfect and they are as problematic as any political office in the city. I often call them half alderman without pay. But a lot of them do a lot of good stuff for their residents and the residents really like and respect them.

The coalition had some meetings with politicians, particularly on the West Side of the city, but the politicians were ambivalent about how to work with the coalition versus continuing to work with the LACs and CAC. According to Lydia Taylor, one-time executive director of the resident management corporation in Rockwell Gardens:

> I think the elected officials were really kind of up in the air [about CPPH]. In the early years of the coalition, I think our credibility was growing with the elected officials and they began to see what we were talking about. But

maybe for political reasons they continued to stay on the side of the fence that the CAC was on. The bottom line was that the CAC is who [they] have been working with and that is who [they] will work with.

Edward Shurna, the Coalition for the Homeless organizer, recalls that Wardell Yotaghan did not want CPPH to be seen as a threat to the LACs:

> Wardell had a vision which I thought was good, but I had to grow to see that it was good. Initially, I did not agree with it. But [Yotaghan thought] we did not want to be against the LAC. These were not the people who were ultimately going to change the policy. They were not the power brokers. I was in the school that said that they were the legitimately elected people so why shouldn't we challenge them. But Wardell's point was that would have been in-fighting and we were not going to get anywhere with that. And I think he was right. Because ultimately they do not hold that power.

How to work with or around the LACs and CAC would continue to be a point of discussion and conflict in the coalition's organizing work.

Aftermath of the CPPH Report

In the fall of 1997, the city's corporation counsel and the CHA lawyers subpoenaed the notes and raw data of the Voorhees Center staff's report that had been sponsored by CPPH. In addition, the Wieboldt Foundation, which had partially funded the report; John Donahue, the executive director of the Coalition for the Homeless, who had been acknowledged as a reviewer in the report; Bruce Orenstein of the Chicago Video Project, who had used some of the report's findings to do a video on Cabrini-Green; and Jane Ramsey of the Jewish Council on Urban Affairs were all subpoenaed by the city and CHA as part of the Cabrini-Green lawsuit. When the Voorhees Center staff resisted turning over their interview notes, the city's corporation counsel threatened court action. Most of those who received subpoenas were subjected to long depositions (four to twelve hours each) that questioned their involvement with the coalition and the results of the report's findings. The substance of the subpoenas and the atmosphere in the depositions were clearly hostile. The unusually harsh response of the city and the CHA to the report's findings was probably because the Cabrini-Green lawsuit was threatening the viability of the proposed Near North Development Plan and its public and private financing. Also evident was the lack of tolerance by the city, CHA, HUD, and some of the local media for public housing residents having a say in the future of the redevelopment process. A local *Chicago Tribune* columnist, John McCarron, in his discussion of the Cabrini lawsuit demonstrates this point of view:

> The remaking of CHA has triggered one nasty headline after another. The tenants' organizations at Cabrini-Green, Henry Horner Homes and other projects undergoing redevelopment seem always to be challenging CHA in federal court. Activist tenants and their tax-funded lawyers have been quick to shout "genocide" or "ethnic cleansing" or some other hysterical accusation.[4]

HUD Takeover of CHA: 1995 to 1999

During this early period of CPPH activity, the federal government was running the day-to-day operations of the CHA. In 1995, HUD had taken over the CHA due to poor management and scandal. HUD secretary Henry Cisneros appointed Joseph Shuldiner to put the agency back in good financial and management standing so it would be taken off the HUD list of troubled housing authorities. Before taking over the CHA, Shuldiner had been the general manager of the New York public housing authority and executive director of the Los Angeles public housing authority. Beginning in 1993 and until he was assigned by HUD to manage the CHA, Shuldiner had had the position of HUD assistant secretary of public housing and Indian housing. In this position, Shuldiner was responsible for the management, planning, direction, and policy formulation of all federal activities relating to the operations of public and Indian housing and the tenant-based Section 8 Program. Shuldiner was considered one of the nation's leading experts and practitioners of public housing management. The combination of having Shuldiner in Chicago and the CHA having the most units threatened by the HUD viability test, put Chicago in the spotlight as the "poster city" for the new federal approach to the privatization of the public housing program.

HUD Sit-In Brings Results

The CPPH continued to organize demonstrations to call attention to the lack of information and planning regarding the HUD viability study to move public housing residents into the private housing market and eliminate nearly half of the city's public housing units. One of the most successful demonstrations was a March 1998 sit-in at the regional HUD offices in Chicago. The sit-in led to a meeting with HUD secretary Andrew Cuomo in the summer of 1998. At this meeting, the coalition secured a commitment from Cuomo that HUD would not approve redevelopment plans for Chicago public housing until a regional rental market study determined the availability of affordable units in the private sector. HUD, CHA, the city of Chicago, the state of Illinois, and several local foundations commissioned the study in February 1999.[5]

Another result of the discussions with Secretary Cuomo was the formation of an oversight committee of public officials from the HUD regional office, CHA, and the city of Chicago, community and civic organizations, and coalition members. The coalition wanted to use this committee to review and adopt a relocation contract to guarantee the rights of public housing residents.

Relocation Contract

One of CPPH's main goals called for a relocation contract that contained guarantees to public housing residents including the choice to remain in their redeveloped community. The CPPH contract proposal included the description of four relocation choices for public housing residents and a list of eight guarantees.[6] All residents would have four choices: (1) to remain in an existing, rehabilitated public housing unit; (2) to move into a new public housing unit on-site or in an adjacent community; (3) to move into a public housing scattered-site unit outside of the existing community; or (4) to receive a Housing Choice voucher that guaranteed preidentified units that were acceptable to the tenant, and had a life span of fifteen to twenty years. The eight guarantees included the following: (1) residents would participate in the planning process; (2) no residents would be forced to move out of their existing community; (3) residents would not have to move unless there were guaranteed apartments available to them; (4) no occupied units would be demolished until replacement units had been built or identified; (5) residents would not have to make more than one move; (6) residents would not have to pay for moving costs; (7) legal remedies would be available if civil rights are violated during redevelopment; and (8) reasonable schedules would be established for rehabilitation and/or production of replacement housing. Lawyers at the Sargent Shriver National Center on Poverty Law assisted CPPH in drafting what became known as the CHA Leaseholder Relocation Contract. William Wilen, the lead attorney on the Henry Horner court case, worked on the CPPH proposal, patterning the contract choices and guarantees after the settlement Henry Horner residents had previously negotiated for their redevelopment (see Chapter 8). This document was first presented and discussed at several of the CPPH Wednesday meetings and Saturday School sessions. It was also one of the main topics discussed at the oversight committee meetings. The CHA staff, at the direction of Joseph Shuldiner, negotiated with the coalition concerning the content of the relocation contract. CPPH pushed for the contract to be an addendum to the CHA standard lease.

Shuldiner Is Ousted

In June 1999 HUD returned CHA to local control. In practice, this meant that Chicago's mayor, Richard M. Daley, was back in charge since he made the appointments to the CHA board. The mayor also ended the CHA contract with Joseph Shuldiner. Under the leadership of Shuldiner, the coalition had its greatest impact on CHA policies. The main accomplishments were the commencement of the negotiations of the relocation contract as an addendum to the CHA tenant lease agreement, the HUD agreement to do a regional rental housing analysis, and the formation of the oversight committee. At the end of his tenure as executive director of CHA, Carol Steele observed that Shuldiner "began to realize and respected us for what we were doing."

When the city took over and fired most of the CHA staff working during Shuldiner's tenure, the CPPH had no written commitment from the CHA that the relocation agreement would go forward as planned. Coalition members tried to continue the negotiation with the new Daley-appointed CHA executive director, Phillip Jackson, and his staff, but without success. This new CHA administration, appointed by the mayor, stopped coming to the oversight committee meetings and did not continue the negotiations on the contract. According to Edward Shurna:

> We started the oversight committee to see if we could make some policy changes. We stayed with the oversight committee for a good year. But that was when Shuldiner was still in power. Once he left, the new administration [under the mayor] never wanted to take part in the oversight committee.

Richard Wheelock of the Legal Assistance Foundation had been appointed by the CAC as one of its legal counsels. In this position, Wheelock worked with the CAC to include the relocation contract in the agreements being negotiated with HUD for the CHA redevelopment. Consequently, some aspects of the relocation contract were included as an addendum to the standard CHA lease. At a CHA hearing on the draft "Plan for Transformation" on November 16, 1999, Jackson made a public announcement that gave credit to the coalition for its original work on the relocation contract and its push to make it an addendum to the CHA lease. While CPPH members were proud that they had stood up for public housing tenants' rights, they also knew that the relocation contract ended up being a mere shadow of what they had hoped for to protect the rights of public housing residents.

Regional Rental Housing Market Study

The oversight committee met regularly until the city took over the CHA, at which time another committee was formed to oversee the rental market study. This committee was named the Technical Advisors Panel and was overseen by a civic community group, the Metropolitan Planning Council (MPC). Although the coalition had been the driving force to procure the commitment from HUD secretary Cuomo to do the rental market study, it was the MPC that was designated the overseer of the rental study and that received the funding and fiscal responsibility for the study. Coalition members viewed this turn of events as the work of the mayor's office, which was unwilling to give credit to organizing groups like the CPPH. Instead, the credit and contract were given to another group that was "friendlier" to the mayor and his administration. In this case, for example, the Metropolitan Planning Council's executive director, Mary Sue Barrett, had previously served in the mayor's Office of Intergovernmental Affairs.

CPPH was given one seat on the Technical Advisors Panel. The rest of the committee was composed of representatives of the government funders of the study: HUD, the city of Chicago, the Illinois Housing Development Authority, the CHA, an expert in marketing from the private sector, and an expert in survey research from the University of Chicago. This Technical Advisors Panel met for six months until the report was released in November 1999. On the recommendation of this Technical Advisors Panel, the Metropolitan Planning Council contracted with researchers from the University of Illinois at Chicago, the Urban Institute, and Applied Real Estate Analysis Inc. to do the study.

When the regional market rental study, titled *For Rent: Housing Options in the Chicago Region,* was released, it included a number of "sobering findings."[7] The estimated overall rental vacancy rate in the region was 4.2 percent. This is a very tight rental market. HUD considered the threshold of 6 percent as a tight housing market.[8] The report concluded the following:

> Demand for affordable rental housing is great in both the city and the suburbs, among both the general population and groups like the homeless and those leaving welfare. The region is characterized by high levels of racial segregation and poverty concentration that in turn influence the attitudes, practices and choices of property developers, managers and tenants.[9]

Despite these sobering findings, the CHA ignored the results of the report. In fact, the CHA preempted its official release by the Metropolitan Planning Council. Despite an agreement among all the sponsors and advisers to wait until the report was officially released by MPC, the CHA leaked the report to one of the major newspapers in the city and spun the contents in such a way to deflect attention from the report's implications for the CHA's plan to locate thousands of public housing residents into the private rental market over the next five years.

The Coalition's Work Continues Despite the Loss of a Key Leader

In June 1999, Wardell Yotaghan, the coalition's key leader and one of its founders, passed away. Yotaghan had become ill in the spring and had spent a number of months recuperating from an acute asthma condition. Then, suddenly, just a few days before the 1999 Juneteenth event, he was rushed to Cook County Hospital and died of a heart attack. The loss of Wardell Yotaghan was deeply mourned by all the coalition members. According to John LeFlore of the Metropolitan Tenants Organization:

> He knew how to keep balance within the coalition between the different [support] groups and the residents. In my twelve years of organizing, Wardell was the best at his strategic role of leader. He knew where the pressure points were and he did not lose focus on his leadership role.

Reverend Calvin Morris of the Community Renewal Society commented:

> Part of the challenge of the coalition since I have been here has been Wardell's death, which was a very serious jolt to us . . . I think that the coalition in a very classic way went into a momentary nosedive after Wardell's death. It happens when people grieve and they don't always acknowledge it or are aware of it.

Yotaghan's leadership was clearly missed. For the remainder of 1999, the momentum of the coalition's ongoing agenda, planned under his leadership, kept things moving ahead. The 1999 Juneteenth event went on as planned and became a tribute to Yotaghan's leadership and commitment to public housing. This event was a people's tribunal attended by the HUD regional director, CHA and city officials, and public housing residents to discuss the future of public housing. It was held at the Teamster's Auditorium building on Chicago's West Side.

For the remainder of that summer, organizing efforts concentrated on bringing people out to a march on city hall in October 1999. The march turned out to be a response to the release on September 30, 1999, of the CHA draft

"Plan for Transformation." This march was attended by close to 1,000 people, including many union groups mobilized by the organizing efforts of a new coalition ally, the Chicago Jobs with Justice organization. Jobs with Justice is a national network of coalitions, connecting labor, faith-based, community, and student organizations to work together on workplace and community social justice campaigns. The unions were concerned that the draft plan called for laying off 636 employees or 26 percent of the CHA workforce. According to Sarita Gupta, the Chicago Jobs with Justice organizer:

> After talking to Wardell, I realized that there needed to be a bigger and more powerful base of people around this [public housing] issue and if there was some role that I could play through Jobs with Justice in helping create that base or figure out ways to better support it, then that would be the way to go.

The release of the CHA draft "Plan for Transformation" and the regional rental market study intensified the efforts of the coalition to use the rental market study information to evaluate and offer modifications to the CHA draft plan before it was finalized and sent to HUD for final approval. Through the end of 1999, the coalition members were still hopeful that their organizing efforts would influence the final draft of the CHA plan that would be sent to HUD.

The CHA Draft "Plan for Transformation"

The CHA draft "Plan for Transformation" contained an ambitious demolition and development schedule that aimed to reduce the 1999 stock of public housing from 38,000 to 25,000 units in less than ten years. To do this, the CHA proposed a $1.5 billion ten-year plan. It also called for laying off 636 CHA employees.[10] The Plan for Transformation eliminated CHA on-site social services and proposed instead that public housing residents be referred to existing city and community social services. Property management of all developments would be contracted out to private vendors. (See Chapter 4 for more details on the CHA Plan for Transformation.)

Reactions to the CHA Draft Plan

The coalition members called for HUD to hold local hearings regarding the CHA's draft "Plan for Transformation." It was hoped that HUD officials would be more receptive than city and CHA officials to the input of public housing residents and coalition members and would pressure the CHA to make needed adjustments in its proposed plan. The coalition's main objection to the proposed plan was the reduction of public housing units when the need for public housing was increasing. The coalition also thought that the plan's reliance on having public housing residents take Section 8 vouchers to find housing in the private rental market was unrealistic. This criticism was based on the regional rental market study's documentation of the tight rental market. The regional rental market study also demonstrated that there was continuing racial discrimination in the housing market. Consequently, many relocated CHA families were using the vouchers to move to areas that were as segregated as the CHA communities they were leaving.[11]

The Central Advisory Council (CAC) wrote a letter to HUD outlining its objections to the draft CHA "Plan for Transformation." The CAC letter, dated October 30, 1999, said that the plan "fails to address the city's worsening affordable housing crisis." The letter requested that the CHA withdraw its plan and "sit down with the residents to develop a strategy that better addresses their needs."[12] The CAC's strong objections to the CHA draft plan was encouraging news to many of the coalition members.

In addition to the objections voiced by the coalition and the CAC, a disagreement had developed between the city and CHA officials and HUD officials. This rift derived from a July 1999 news conference at which Mayor Daley's recently appointed CHA chief, Phillip Jackson, had put on display some wasteful CHA spending items, such as bicycles and computers, purchased while Joseph Shuldiner was the CHA executive director. This enraged HUD officials in Washington, DC.[13] In addition, a few HUD officials had serious misgivings about the impact of the proposed transformation plan. According to columnist Robert Novak, "A high-ranking HUD official told me he considers public housing 'a blunder of historic proportions' but questioned what Chicago plans."[14]

HUD staged its own public hearings on the transformation plan. These public hearings were held in addition to hearings held by the CHA to receive public comments. A HUD representative attended one of the coalition's Wednesday meetings to ask for the coalition's input on the HUD hearings and to ask coalition members to testify at the hearings. According to Carol Steele, Wardell Yotaghan's successor as CPPH chair, "I think the coalition played a major part in the [HUD] hearings. We met with Congressman Danny Davis, and we met with HUD individuals to discuss the need for these hearings." The HUD hearings were well attended. Steele recalled that Harold Lucas, HUD's assistant secretary for public housing, stated that the days in which federal officials in Washington work behind closed doors with city hall to decide what's best for local neighborhoods are over.

Congressman Danny Davis chaired the HUD hearing on the West Side, and Congressman Bobby Rush chaired the HUD hearing on the South Side. Rush had recently run an unsuccessful campaign for mayor against Mayor Daley. So these events were some evidence of conflicts within the Democratic Party in Chicago. The coalition members viewed these divisions as opportunities to bring some changes to the draft "Plan for Transformation." Several conversations with HUD officials had led coalition members to believe that HUD had some misgivings about the CHA draft plan and would ask for some modifications.

Eventually, the Central Advisory Council (CAC) signed on to the draft CHA "Plan for Transformation," even though its chair, Mamie Bone, asserted that the CAC had "no meaningful participation in formulating this plan" and that the plan "does not meet the mark of excellence that is needed to make the CHA communities viable or improve the quality of life for its residents."[15] The CAC went ahead and approved the plan with hopes that, in Bone's words "Additional discussions with CHA will result in a plan that will ease any resident fears of business as usual and it's all about the contracts."[16] Unfortunately, once the plan was approved, these discussions did not happen. Ethan Michaeli, editor of the *Resident Journal,* described the backdrop of the CAC's failure to use its power to make meaningful changes in the plan:

> When the city came in [to take back control of the CHA] they really came in like storm troopers. People were fired. People were fired in ridiculous ways. You would go to the bathroom and come back and police officers were at your desk and told you to take only your personal belongings and not come back. Hundreds of people were fired in this way. This was the pattern from the city and how it interacted with the [CHA] staff and the [CHA] residents. They dictated to the residents and everyone else what was going to happen. They presented a plan that was significantly a half of the barest price tag of what Shuldiner had offered. . . . The CAC started to organize. They went to their congressional reps that were behind them like Bobby Rush and Danny Davis—and Jesse Jackson Jr. This was still during the Clinton administration so HUD was interested. They put together a HUD hearing on the West Side. So, somehow, before the HUD hearings were over, the CAC signed off on the plan. I don't know why . . . I can imagine it was irritating to the congressional reps and others interested in working with the CAC. Here was their big chance to renegotiate the plan before it went into effect and they blew it.

The CAC signing onto the draft "Plan for Transformation" was a tremendous setback. For a short period of time, the CAC and the coalition had been raising similar objections to the way CHA was preceding without resident input and without taking into account the larger picture of the shortage of affordable housing in the Chicago region. Although the CAC and the coalition did not talk to each other officially or coordinate their objections to the draft plan, they were raising the same concerns and asking for similar remedies and changes.

On February 6, 2000, the CHA, the city and HUD held a press conference to announce HUD's approval of the Plan for Transformation. Although some HUD officials, particularly Harold Lucas, had concerns about the CHA's plan, HUD secretary Andrew Cuomo characterized the Plan for Transformation as "one of the highlights of his administration."[17]

The CPPH Is Isolated

For a few weeks after the plan's approval, there was a back-and-forth of editorials in the *Chicago Tribune* between the CHA and its supporters and the coalition and its supporters. Coalition members, however, began to feel isolated in their opposition to the CHA and its plan. As Edward Shurna recollected:

> In 2000, we were the only ones that said that the transformation plan was a sham. We were the lone wolves in the city of Chicago. I can remember the foundation people saying that the train is out of the station and you guys are left behind. My response was that the train was probably going to be derailed because the transformation plan is not going to do what the nice glossy pictures say it is going to do. We were saying back then how are they going to do all of this? This was before we started saying—Where is the money, where is the land and where are the people going? But I think that we did fumble awhile as we sought for ways to have an impact once they passed the plan. Once it got passed, what position do you take when everyone else is saying this is the new ball game?

In 2000, CPPH lost all its direct funding. The coalition had operated on a very meager budget, which financed three staff persons, two of them public housing residents. But over the course of 2000, each of the foundations that had contributed to the work of the coalition terminated its contributions. Once the foundations pulled back, the coalition was totally dependent on member organizations to donate staff and other resources to keep the coalition going. As James Field, the lead Community Renewal Society organizer put it, "When HUD approved the CHA plan that was a turning point in the eyes of many of the foundations. And I think there was a feeling too, we were not going to where they wanted us to go."

At this same time, the largest foundation in Chicago, the John D. and

Catherine T. MacArthur Foundation, underwent a leadership change, which produced a major shift in its approach to funding community development. Jonathan F. Fanton became its president and hired Julia Stasch, who had been Mayor Daley's chief of staff and city commissioner of housing, as the foundation's vice president. When in the mayor's office, Stasch had been the mayor's point person on the CHA Plan for Transformation. Soon after these personnel changes, the MacArthur Foundation took a very aggressive approach to support the efforts of the CHA in its implementation of the Plan for Transformation. From 1999 to 2002, the MacArthur Foundation gave $17 million in grants in support of the plan.[18] The coalition only once, in 1999, submitted a proposal to the MacArthur Foundation to request funds to support its organizing efforts with the residents. The foundation did not fund this proposal. After the CHA Plan for Transformation was passed, according to Edward Shurna of the Chicago Coalition for the Homeless, "Every organization that has been a part of the coalition has been criticized, taken flak and probably lost funding as a result . . . so it has not been a stand without some risks involved."

The Later Years: Keeping the Coalition Together After 2000

Once HUD approved the transformation plan, the coalition members began an internal debate on the way forward. According to Shurna:

> We started to look around and say—where do we go from here? Some wanted to fight on the grounds we had before, and others were saying that we need to recognize that it is a new day. It was part of the confusion. One group was saying that nothing has changed, and others said we had to deal with the new reality. It took us awhile. This was a period too when we did not have an organizing presence on the ground. . . . We would make plans but they would not go anyplace because there was no one there to carry it out. No one could be held accountable to follow through on things. I think it was also a questioning time. Do we continue to fight on this? How do we continue to fight?

In 2000, there were fewer coalition meetings, and the Wednesday meetings stopped altogether. Fewer meetings meant less of the internal discipline and accountability that are needed for effective coalition work. During this period, one of the coalition member groups, the Revolutionary Communist Youth Brigade (RCYB), which is affiliated with the Revolutionary Communist Party, USA, attained a much higher profile in the organizing effort. The RCYB is part of a twenty-five-year-old Maoist organization. This was a cause for concern among some other coalition members because the RCYB had on several occasions taken actions contrary to the overall purpose and agreed-upon strategies of the coalition.

In February 1999 the coalition had established an executive committee to oversee the coalition policies and organizing work. Wardell Yotaghan chaired the executive committee; after his death, Carol Steele became the chair. One-half of the seats were to be held by public housing residents. The following groups were to hold nonpublic housing resident seats on the executive committee: Jewish Council on Urban Affairs, Chicago Coalition for the Homeless, Community Renewal Society, Metropolitan Tenants Organization, Access Living, the University of Illinois at Chicago Voorhees Neighborhood Center, National Center on Poverty Law, and the Revolutionary Communist Youth Brigade. There was much discussion about including the RCYB. According to the minutes of the February 1999 meeting:

> Rev. Morris stated that the involvement of the RCYB on the Executive Committee was problematic because of how the Coalition would be viewed. Wardell replied that the RCYB had fulfilled the description of a board member that we approved and that to exclude them would be discrimination.[19]

All the public housing residents voted to include the RCYB on the executive committee even as the non–public housing groups voted against or abstained from including it. Consequently, the RCYB was a member of the executive committee. According to John LeFlore of the Metropolitan Tenants Organization:

> It has been annoying to people that in the course of an event there might be RCYB literature that may have not been appropriate. When checked on this issue, and specifically asked or told that they should not have the literature at this or that forum, they adhered to that. I think that despite these challenges, overall I think the coalition benefited much more from the RCYB than they had a negative impact on the coalition. I think a lot of the negative impact came from funders. . . . Bottom line, they were there when a lot of the other coalition members were not. To give them credit, they never hid who they were. A lot of leftists groups do. I do not agree with them, but I respect them.

During the aftermath of the Plan for Transformation approval in 2000, Yotaghan's leadership on the executive committee was greatly missed. He had been the one to keep all the different groups together, despite their differences, focused on the fight for public housing. According to Calvin Morris:

After Wardell's death, not unlike when Dr. King was assassinated, when all the lieutenants went their separate ways and did their own thing, there was a time for a while when the coalition would have a demonstration some place, not well attended or put together, but it was a way for some of the coalition to express themselves but it was not a unified expression. It was an expression of a segment of the coalition. I think we have gotten through that period with the reemergence of the executive committee. But there was a bumpy period there for sure.

This "bumpy" period lasted through most of 2000 while the coalition tried to decide on a new agenda. Beauty Turner, a Robert Taylor Homes resident, agreed that this was a difficult time for the coalition:

I stepped away from the coalition for a while after Wardell passed away. I was there to protect public housing and protect the people in it—not to continue to debate every little trivial situation that was occurring within the coalition.

Also contributing to this "bumpy" period was Carol Steele's engagement with the Cabrini-Green lawsuit and consent decree negotiations with the city, CHA, and the Habitat Company (see Chapter 6). These time-consuming negotiations, which continued until the spring of 2000, kept her from being more involved on the executive committee and the work of the coalition. After much deliberation, the executive committee decided on a new strategy. Ed Shurna described this shift in strategy as follows:

I think the coalition started to get back more credibility when we started holding the CHA accountable to their own plan instead of saying we are opposed to the plan. We are opposed to the plan, but they cannot even do what they say they are going to do. So we started looking at what they said and started showing the inconsistencies of what they said. We started to ask questions about whether they could actually do the 25,000 units or not.

2001: Focus on the CHA Board Meetings

In 2001, with a new strategy in hand, the executive committee members decided to focus the coalition's organizing activities around attending the monthly CHA board meetings. At each CHA board meeting coalition members would raise questions about the progress of the Plan for Transformation. Public housing residents who were allied with the coalition were encouraged to give testimony about what was happening at their public housing developments.

Since 1997 the coalition had had its major annual organizing event on the African-American Independence Day, Juneteenth (June 19). By coincidence, the CHA board meeting was scheduled for June 19, 2001, at the Charles Hayes Family Center near the Robert Taylor Homes and Stateway Gardens developments. The coalition decided to take advantage of this coincidence by bringing out public housing residents and coalition supporters to attend this meeting as its annual Juneteenth event.

A few days before the planned demonstration on June 19, Calvin Morris, Community Renewal Society executive director, received a call from the president of the CHA board, Sharon Gist-Gilliam, requesting a meeting to discuss the demands of the coalition. This meeting was held at the CRS offices on June 14, 2001. Gist-Gilliam came to this meeting with Terry Petersen, the CHA executive director, and several other CHA staff persons. Several of the CPPH Executive Committee members laid out the coalition's concerns and demands. The meeting began with Reverend Morris giving a history of the coalition and presenting its concerns about demolishing so many units before rebuilding new ones. Reverend Morris said that the public housing residents were bearing the burden of the CHA's lack of planning for replacement units and the poor maintenance of the housing while families waited to be relocated. John Donahue of the Chicago Coalition for the Homeless emphasized the need to stop demolitions until on-site construction began in each development. Carol Steele added that twenty-five Cabrini row houses were vacant and available for occupancy by families that were being displaced. William Wilen of the National Center on Poverty Law asked about the status of the bond financing and referred to a Chicago Rehab Network study that found that the CHA would be $1 billion short in meeting its goal of 25,000 units of renovated or new public housing units. Jane Ramsey of the Jewish Council on Urban Affairs, Patricia Wright of the UIC Voorhees Center, and John LeFlore of the Metropolitan Tenants Organization raised other issues related to the accountability of the CHA board, the need for additional land to build all the promised units, and residents' need for better information about what it meant to be lease compliant and eligible for relocation benefits. The meeting was cordial. However, none of the questions raised by the coalition members was answered. CHA board president Sharon Gist-Gilliam listened politely but said that the CHA plan would proceed without delay.

Consequently, the coalition proceeded with its plans to bring out as many ministers as possible to disrupt the Juneteenth board meeting. The Community Renewal Society's Interfaith Network made a special commitment to bring ministers to "bear witness." On June 19 the coalition and its supporters, numbering close to 250, took over the CHA board meeting for several minutes. Thirteen ministers agreed to do civil disobedience and be arrested if necessary. According to the *Chicago Sun-Times,* "Protesters turned Tuesday's Chicago Housing Authority Board meeting into a combination of spiritual sing-along, spirited speechmaking and a teach-in on the best way to rebuild public housing."[20] Although the coalition and its supporters disrupted the meeting's official business, there were no arrests. The organizers felt that the event was a success and that it brought new energy to the efforts of the coalition. Throughout 2001, the coalition members continued to attend, raise questions, and testify at the monthly CHA board meetings.

Local Advisory Council Elections

In fall 2001, the coalition decided to work on ensuring fairness in the upcoming local advisory council elections in each development. The contract to conduct the elections was awarded to the Citizens Information Service (CIS), a citywide civic organization, at the October 2001 CHA board meeting. The elections were scheduled for December 11, 2001. This gave CIS a limited amount of time to do the necessary preparations for the elections. But CIS had experience running the past LAC elections and had also overseen the elections for the public schools' local school councils. The coalition set up a committee to discuss how the coalition could work to ensure fair LAC elections. According to Daniel Romero, the CRS organizer working with the coalition:

> We began talking with CIS very early on to try to just develop some kind of a rapport with them and try to develop some kind of an ad hoc oversight group through the coalition. Initially I think things went pretty well. We weren't happy with everything that happened initially, but in terms of the relationship, CIS was pretty open with us.

What made the elections important to the coalition was that Carol Steele had decided to run for the LAC presidency at Cabrini-Green. Steele had been the LAC vice president and the president of the Cabrini-Green row house development. But only the president of the LAC for all the Cabrini developments held a seat on the CAC, which directly advised and had a voice in the larger CHA public housing policies and decisions related to the Plan for Transformation.

In November 2001, the coalition held a press conference at Cabrini-Green because critical information needed to make the elections successful was being withheld. "CIS is not the problem," stated Rene Maxwell, a Cabrini-Green resident and member of the coalition's executive committee:

> CIS has not received the list of development boundaries, and they have not
> received the list of absentee/homebound voters from CHA. Without these
> lists CIS cannot properly inform residents about the election process, and
> candidates don't know how many signatures are needed for petitions. This
> looks like the elections that happened three years ago.[21]

Indeed, the coalition had made involvement in the LAC elections a priority because the previous LAC elections in 1998 had been so poorly conducted that the coalition had called for another round of elections at every
development. The CHA refused to conduct new elections citywide but did
agree to hold a second round of elections at forty-one out of the total 123
polling sites.[22] The validity of these 1998 LAC elections was a sore point
with the coalition because the LAC presidents elected at that time, as members of the CAC had signed off on the Plan for Transformation.

At the November 2001 press conference, the coalition demanded that
the elections be postponed to give CIS more time to make sure that the
elections would be fair and properly organized. The coalition ended up
playing a major role in having the elections postponed until January 22,
2002. On LAC Election Day, the coalition organizations acted as poll watch-
ers at a number of public housing developments, including Cabrini-Green,
Robert Taylor Homes, ABLA, Rockwell Gardens, and Washington Park
Homes.

Controversial Victory at Cabrini-Green

The key victory that day was at Cabrini-Green. Carol Steele won the LAC
election in a close race with the incumbent candidate, Cora Moore. However, Steele's victory was not without controversy. Two events became
the center of the controversy, which landed the election in court. The first
event was that after the votes were counted and tallied at the Cabrini
Rowhouses, the ballots disappeared. The CIS coordinator lost the ballots
somewhere between leaving the Cabrini Rowhouses polling place and
arriving at the downtown CIS office. The other event occurred at the
Cabrini building at 1230 Burling Street, where the election judges did
not initial the ballots before they were given to voters. After the polling
place closed, when the mistake was discovered, one of the election judges
dumped the ballot box and initialed all the ballots. This was done in front
of numerous witnesses.

Illinois election law is very clear on both of these events. In the case of the
missing ballots, the tally sheet is counted as valid even without the ballots; in
the Burling Street case, ballots must be initialized to be valid. The votes at

the Rowhouses were valid, and the votes at 1230 Burling Street were not. On January 14, the CIS declared Carol Steele the winner.

Cora Moore filed a lawsuit in early February to challenge the election results. Moore's lawsuit attempted to enjoin CIS from declaring Steele the winner of the election. Kate Walz and William Wilen of the National Center on Poverty Law took on Carol Steele's case. According to Walz, "We knew that the law was in Carol's favor. It was an airtight case because of the Illinois election law." Michael Lavelle, an election law expert who had been head of the Cook County Board of Elections, also worked on Steele's case pro bono. The case was assigned to Judge Raymond Jagielski, who hears election law disputes in Cook County. Moore hired attorney Richard Means, an accomplished Illinois election law lawyer, who had the active support of the CHA. In mid-February, Means and CHA's attorney, George Brown, went to court and asked for arbitration to be invoked to decide the case. The CHA lawyer argued that the election should be decided by federal HUD rules instead of Illinois election law. In addition, the CHA argued that the arbitration should be between the CHA and CIS, and not the candidates. Judge Jagielski rejected this approach but nevertheless decided to send the dispute to an arbitrator.

Early on in this process, Judge Jagielski ruled that Carol Steele should take the LAC president's seat at Cabrini and also the seat on the CAC until the ruling was decided via the arbitration process. The arbitration process took from February to July (posttrial briefs), and the ruling came in August 2002. The arbitrator ruled in Steele's favor. It was an important victory for the coalition to have Steele take a seat on the Central Advisory Council. She would be an independent and critical voice on the CAC.

LAC Voter Turnout

At Robert Taylor Homes, Barbara Moore (not related to Cora Moore), who was active in the coalition, was reelected as the vice president of Robert Taylor Section B. In fact, Barbara Moore won 30 percent more votes than the candidate who ran and won for President. In other races where coalition supporters or allies ran for office, they did well but not well enough to win. What was apparent, however, was that where coalition supporters or allies ran for office, the voter turnout was larger than in other public housing developments. Overall, the voter turnout was very low citywide, approximately 10 percent. For example, at the Robert Taylor Homes, only 182 out of 3,400 eligible leaseholders voted. According to Armando Santana of CIS, the residents did not think there was any point in voting when many candidates ran unopposed; when LAC seats were contested, residents expected the incumbents to win.[23]

April Briefing 2002

Beginning in 2000, the coalition sponsored an annual event called the April Briefing. This event was a platform that brought together many of the public housing residents whom the coalition had worked with over the years with other housing and advocacy groups to discuss new information and public housing research that the coalition and other organizations had sponsored related to the CHA transformation plan. In 2002, the April Briefing was especially well-attended due to growing concerns about the relocation of public housing residents into the private housing market. In addition, the demolition of many of the public housing units was proceeding rapidly even though very few replacement-housing units were under construction.

On April 23, 2002, the April Briefing was held at Grace's Place in Chicago's South Loop. Over 150 people attended. William Wilen, attorney for the Sargent Shriver National Center on Poverty Law, was the keynote speaker. Wilen updated everyone on the latest CHA numbers related to the demolition, rehabilitation, and construction of new units.

> As of the end of 2001, demolition had far outpaced new construction and rehabilitation. According to CHA's 2002 (Moving to Work) Annual Plan, dated October 16, 2001, CHA demolished 3,426 units in 2000 and prior years, and another 3,901 in 2001, for a grand total of 7,327. During this time, CHA constructed only 624 units in 2000 or prior years, and only 75 in 2001, for a grand total of 699 new units. However, 643 of these new units were required to be constructed under the Horner (461) and Cabrini (76) consent decrees and the Memorandum of Agreement (106) in the Lakefront case, regardless of the Plan for Transformation. So actually, CHA has constructed only 56 new public housing units (at Robert Taylor) under the Plan for Transformation as of the end of 2001. In addition, CHA has rehabilitated 2,195 units (90 at Horner, 329 at ABLA, 1,026 senior units and 750 scattered site units).[24]

Wilen also commented on the low numbers of public housing units being built back on-site, the resegregation of public housing families under the Section 8 program, and the shortfall of CHA funding and land to build all the units promised.

On this same panel, Kathleen Clark, attorney and executive director of the Lawyers' Committee for Better Housing Inc., followed up with a recent study completed by her organization, which revealed that landlords denied housing to tenants with Housing Choice vouchers in up to 70 percent of the encounters they tested.[25] Gene Moreno, another panelist, reported on a study completed by the Chicago Rehab Network that estimated that the CHA might fall short $1.3 billion to complete its promised 25,000 public housing units.

A second panel was composed of public housing residents, including Barbara Moore of Robert Taylor Homes. She raised these important questions: "America the beautiful, but beautiful for whom? Is it just beautiful for the politicians, the rich and the famous? Do poor people really have a place in America?"[26] The April Briefing, which attracted a substantial number of public housing residents and others interested in housing issues, was covered in the local newspapers. This media coverage earned the attention of the CAC.

Reaction and Change at the CAC

Since the January LAC elections, Carol Steele had taken her place on the CAC representing the Cabrini-Green development. Mary Wiggins, the president of Washington Park, became the new CAC president. In addition, the CAC was provided funds to hire an executive director, Olamenji O'Connor, to work on administrative and policy issues. After the April Briefing, O'Connor called Edward Shurna to discuss the coalition's activities. Several of the CAC members did not like the organizing tactics that coalition members had been using at the CHA board meetings. However, the April Briefing had received positive press and raised important questions about the relocation of public housing residents into the private market, the rapid pace of demolitions, and the lack of new construction.

In early June several members of the coalition's executive committee met with Wiggins and other CAC members to share their concerns about the CHA transformation plan. The coalition and the CAC agreed to meet again to continue this discussion.

Juneteenth 2002—Tent City

Coalition members, led by staff at the JCUA, had been doing extensive organizing at the Ida B. Wells public housing development on the South Side. Consequently, it was decided to hold the Juneteenth 2002 event there. A tent city was constructed on an abandoned lot adjacent to the Ida B. Wells development. According to Daniel Romero, the CRS organizer who worked on the tent city:

> this was one of the most widely covered events that the coalition ever had, in terms of media exposure and coverage. Several radio and TV stations, both of the two major dailies, print media, Channel 7 and Channel 5 did remote feeds from the site itself. It was really a tremendous success from a

media exposure standpoint. Whether that translates into real victories on the ground, of course we just have to wait and see.

Several of the Wells residents had decided to challenge the CHA grievance procedure because they were not satisfied with where they were being relocated. One of the purposes of the tent city was to give support to these residents in their fight to stop the demolition of their buildings until the CHA began building new replacement units on the Wells site.

Independent Monitoring of CHA Progress

During the summer of 2002 the CHA and the CAC hired a former U.S. attorney, Thomas Sullivan, to do an independent monitoring report on the relocation process for CHA residents. In addition, the CAC sent a letter on August 27, 2002, to HUD deputy secretary Alphonso Jackson requesting an update of the rental market study completed in 1999. According to this letter:

> The need for such a study is becoming more and more apparent. The Urban Institute, the same group that issued the 2001 market study under contract to HUD, recently released its study of 190 CHA families who chose a Section 8 voucher as their first choice for replacement housing. . . . The success rate for these voucher users was disturbingly low. The study found that after one year only 38% of these families had moved into a private market unit with a Section 8 voucher, while the rest remained in a public housing unit.[27]

The coalition also sent a letter to the HUD deputy secretary in support of the CAC request for a new market study.

The Coalition Evaluates Its Progress

On October 4, 2002, CPPH held a retreat to evaluate its work and plan for the upcoming year. For the most part, the coalition members thought it had been a good year. Despite having no outside funding, the coalition had persisted. The April Briefing and the Juneteenth tent city had received good press coverage. As Ed Shurna of the Coalition for the Homeless commented at the retreat, "We are still here." The coalition is seen as a "force that won't go away," said another participant at the retreat.[28]

At the retreat, William Wilen and Kate Walz of the Sargent Shriver National Center on Poverty Law updated the coalition members on a possible lawsuit related to the failure of the CHA to provide needed assistance to families affected by the Plan for Transformation. Particularly troubling to the lawyers was the resegregation of many CHA families into high-poverty, predominantly African-American neighborhoods when they were displaced from public housing and opted to use the Housing Choice voucher program. In addition, the lawyers thought that the social services offered to the displaced public housing residents needed improvement. The Poverty Law Center was in discussion with the Business and Professional People for the Public Interest (BPI) and the Chicago Lawyers' Committee for Civil Rights Under the Law to jointly file suit against the CHA regarding these issues. In January 2004, talks were still being held with the CHA in order to remedy these issues and avoid litigation.

The coalition held its last 2002 event by demonstrating at city hall in front of the mayor's office. The coalition called for a halt on all demolitions until the CHA built or rehabilitated additional units in its developments throughout the city. The demonstration was held at the mayor's office in anticipation of the upcoming mayoral election in February 2003 and as an expression of the coalition's view that Mayor Daley was the key promoter of the Plan for Transformation.

Release of the CHA Monitoring Report

The "Independent Monitor's Report No. 5 to the Chicago Housing Authority and the Central Advisory Council," known as the Sullivan report after its author, Thomas Sullivan, was completed and given to the CHA and CAC in January 2003. Initially, the CHA refused requests to release the report to the public. Then, the CHA gave the report exclusively to the *Chicago Sun-Times.* According to the *Sun-Times,* the Sullivan report demonstrated that, "As the CHA relocates thousands of families out of public housing, it is converting its 'vertical ghettos' into horizontal ones and is failing to provide promised help to down-and-out families."[29]

In his report, Sullivan made fifty-four recommendations to improve the social services and the relocation counseling that public housing residents were receiving. According to the *Chicago Sun-Times,* "Top CHA officials embraced many of Sullivan's recommendations and planned to meet . . . with resident leaders to mull them over." But CHA chair Sharon Gist-Gilliam expressed her misgivings on some of the report's findings: "We can have Jane Addams herself helping these folks, but if you won't pay your rent, no counseling in the world is going to help."[30] According to the Sullivan report, the CHA board and officials generally overstated the success of the relocation process, "inevitably call[ing] into question the reliability of the CHA as to all its other claims of success for the Plan for Transformation."[31] After the release of the report, the

CHA extended Thomas Sullivan's contract as independent monitor for one more year.[32] Many housing activists saw this as a good sign.

Class Action Suit Filed

On January 23, 2003, a few weeks after the Sullivan report was given to the CAC and the CHA board, a class action lawsuit was filed against the CHA. The Sargent Shriver National Center on Poverty Law, the Chicago Lawyers' Committee for Civil Rights, and BPI filed the suit on behalf of current and former CHA residents who had moved from CHA developments to poor, segregated communities. According to a *Sun-Times* article:

> The suit accuses the CHA of failing to live up to legal agreements promising to help families move into racially and economically mixed areas. The plaintiffs want the court to enter an injunction forcing the CHA to develop a program that would integrate residents into racially integrated communities and to comply with other agreements between the agency and its residents.[33]

For several years different coalition members had raised the possibility of a class action lawsuit to stop the Plan for Transformation. As early as 1998, Wardell Yotaghan had convened a meeting to explore legal strategies to stop the CHA from emptying out and demolishing public housing buildings. At the time, the lawyers who attended the meeting concluded that not enough had happened to prove malfeasance or bad faith in the public housing redevelopment process. It would take four years of families being systematically resegregated in the private housing market, with many other families left homeless, before a case could be made to improve the process. But, as William Wilen of the National Poverty Law Center pointed out, the 2003 litigation was not as extensive or as critical of the public housing redevelopment process as what Wardell Yotaghan had been proposing in 1998. Yotaghan had wanted to stop the demolition altogether and reinstate the one-for-one replacement.

Housing as a Human Right

A major setback in 2003 was the loss of two more of the coalition's leaders. Rene Maxwell, a Cabrini-Green resident and poet who had been an organizer for the coalition, and John Donahue, the executive director of the Chicago Coalition for the Homeless, died. Both these men had been profiled in Studs Terkel's most recent book, *Hope Dies Last: Keeping the Faith in Troubled Times*.[34]

In November 2003, the coalition sponsored a public hearing regarding the federal HOPE VI program and the low-income housing crisis in Chicago. The hearing, held at the Metcalfe Federal Building in downtown Chicago, consisted of four panels of twenty testifing experts. The hearing was attended by over 150 persons including most of Chicago's congressional representatives: Janice Schakowsky, Bobby Rush, Jesse Jackson Jr., and Danny Davis. The public hearing examined the performance of the HOPE VI program in Chicago and made recommendations to the congressional representatives on continuing and improving HOPE VI.

Two months later, on January 31, 2004, CPPH started discussing housing as a human right by presenting a workshop for the Chicago Social Forum. The Chicago Social Forum was a local effort to connect to the World Social Forum.[35] The workshop described the coalition's work in Chicago and how it relates to international efforts to fight for housing as a human right. Before this, members of the coalition had attended the fiftieth anniversary of the Universal Declaration of Human Rights in New York City in 1998 and had testified at the United Nations. The Chicago Social Forum gave the coalition an important and timely opportunity to build on these earlier efforts and to further explore how its public housing work could be connected to broader human rights standards and principles.

CPPH's participation in the Chicago Social Forum generated an interest and enthusiasm both within the coalition and in the general public to articulate the concept that housing is a human right. Consequently, at the coalition's annual retreat in early February 2004, CPPH members decided to more aggressively develop a human rights campaign. In part, the human rights approach was adopted because of the coalition members' frustration with their inability to effect change at the local and national level through the actions and remedies they had tried in the past eight years. However, it was also an appeal to build an alternative social vision based on the dignity of human life and to resist current policies that are eroding the long-fought-for social programs such as public housing.

Thus far, one of the coalition's biggest accomplishments has been a visit with Miloon Kothari, the United Nations Special Rapporteur on Adequate Housing. Kothari flew to Chicago on April 25, 2004, specifically to meet with public housing residents at Cabrini-Green. Kothari is the international community's highest-ranking expert on housing issues, and he reports directly to the UN High Commissioner for Human Rights in Geneva, Switzerland. CPPH had invited Kothari to learn about CHA's massive demolition of public housing units. In his discussions with Cabrini-Green residents, Kothari acknowledged that there indeed seems to be a human rights crisis in the forced evictions of public housing tenants from their units. It is important to note that Kothari has never undertaken work in the United States before, so his Cabrini-Green visit was all the more significant. CPPH continues to work closely with Special Rapporteur Kothari to advise him about conditions in Chicago and help him prepare correspondence regarding the national public housing crisis. The coalition also organized a forum on April 28 that focused on the right to housing in international law and the human rights violations that are occurring as a result of the demolition of public housing in Chicago. More than 250 people attended this event, which was well covered in the media.

In May 2004, the coalition invited two internationally renowned experts with extensive experience in using the human rights framework to conduct a training session for coalition members. Bret Thiele, the legal director of the Centre on Housing Rights and Evictions (COHRE) in Geneva, Switzerland, and Bruce Porter, the director of the Social Rights Advocacy Centre in Canada, discussed several topics: an overview of the international human right to adequate housing; the successful use of human rights strategy in Canada and elsewhere; how to document human rights violations and gather personal testimonies; how to do a shadow report; and petitioning the Inter-American human rights system.

In the relatively short time since the coalition launched this effort, it has attracted national and international attention. One CPPH member spoke at the National Low Income Housing Coalition's annual meeting on a panel about housing and human rights. Other coalition members have been invited to participate in several national networks of U.S. groups that are using a human rights framework to fight for social justice in their communities. CPPH has also been invited to be a lead agency in the Poor People's Economic Human Rights Campaign, the most significant national initiative to fight for justice using economic rights strategies.

Obstacles Facing the CPPH

The Coalition to Protect Public Housing has faced numerous obstacles yet has achieved some success in its efforts to organize public housing residents with their allies in churches, housing groups, and other advocacy organizations. The coalition's main purpose was to bring these voices together to critically evaluate and influence how the changes in federal and local public housing policy would affect the lives of public housing residents. Beauty Turner, of Robert Taylor Homes, put it succinctly, "It [CPPH] was really about being there with the people and letting them know they had someone other than themselves." In this next section, I will examine the main obstacles that the coalition faced in its organizing work and, as Turner put it, "being there with the people."

There have been two main obstacles to the work of the coalition. The first obstacle is the political environment, nationally and locally, related to public housing policy. The second obstacle is the difficulties of organizing public housing residents, particularly within the Chicago political context.

National and Local Political Environment

In the 1990s, federal public housing policy, not unlike welfare policy, was under attack by a broad bipartisan consensus. This attack is best characterized by Senator Robert Dole's comment during his 1996 bid for the presidency that public housing is "one of the last bastions of socialism in the world."[36] Senator Dole was not quite right about the world context, but he was right in suggesting that the public housing program was the closest that the United States had gotten to the socialist idea of making housing a human right or entitlement. Many coalition members thought that this view of public housing was worth protecting and fighting for. The coalition members were reacting to the political shift in Washington, DC, to privatize public housing and reduce the federal commitment to public housing. This shift aims to minimize the role of government in providing or protecting its citizens' basic human needs—like housing. In this view, housing is not considered a social or government responsibility. It is the personal responsibility of each person or family to compete for housing in the private market.

During the last decade the policy shift to privatize the public housing program was played out in several pieces of legislation passed by Congress. Most notably, a provision of the 1996 annual spending bill for the federal Department of Housing and Urban Development (HUD) mandated public housing authorities to hire private consultants to do "viability studies" for all the housing developments that had a vacancy rate of 10 percent and more than 300 units. The viability test compared the cost of maintaining the existing public housing units to the cost of using Section 8 vouchers for units in the private market. This mandated viability test was the beginning of the end of public housing, as we know it, nationally and in Chicago. It turned the discussion away from maintaining public housing developments to relocating public housing families into the private sector as quickly as possible. It was this legislation that CPPH was initially formed in 1996 to oppose. In 1998, the Quality Housing and Work Responsibility Act, the new public housing law, incorporated the provisions of the 1996 annual spending bill, which meant the permanent elimination of the one-for-one replacement principle for public housing units. Once this happened, it was difficult for CPPH to keep the one-for-one replacement principle at the center of its agenda. Some coalition members thought that when the coalition dropped the fight for one-for-one replacement it lost the main thing it was fighting for. According to Lydia Taylor:

> [F]or the coalition not to still be talking about one-for-one replacement means that they have accepted a mindset of let's approach what is winnable . . . and when that [one-for-one replacement] got lost then that really changed things.

From 1996 until 2000, two years after the 1998 public housing legislation passed, the coalition members continued to attend national gatherings to protest the privatization of the public housing program. The Center for Community Change, a national community development advocacy group, organized some of these meetings. However, the arguments, protests, and actions regarding privatization and the elimination of one-for-one replacement were ignored. The prevailing ideology of both the Republican and Democratic Parties supported privatization of public housing and scaling back the existing public housing stock operated as a separate housing sector. Despite the numerous documented problems with the Section 8 housing voucher program, both Democrats and Republicans supported this program as a replacement for the public housing program. Meanwhile, back at home in Chicago, the coalition lost its fight to modify the CHA Plan for Transformation in 2000. One of the major obstacles to the coalition's efforts was the local political environment.

The CHA Plan for Transformation received HUD approval in 2000, which was a presidential election year. The influence of the Daley family in the Democratic Party, nationally and in Chicago, is legendary. Richard M. Daley has been mayor of Chicago since 1989. His father, Richard J. Daley, was mayor of the city from 1955 to 1976. The current Mayor Daley's brother, William Daley, served as the secretary of commerce during the administration of President Clinton before resigning in order to chair Albert Gore's presidential campaign in 2000. The Democrats in Washington, anticipating the upcoming presidential election and mindful of Illinois's status as a swing state in presidential contests, wanted to strengthen their alliance with Mayor Daley. One direct way of sealing this alliance was by approving the CHA Plan for Transformation.

Independent Voices Extinguished

Three times in the 1970s and 1980s independent Democrats won the Chicago mayoralty, but this period ended abruptly when Harold Washington, who served as mayor from 1983 through 1987, died in office. Following Richard M. Daley's election as mayor in 1989, the local independent movement slowly deflated. Since 1989, the mayor has developed a sophisticated method of controlling many of the activists who in the past were part of the independent community development movement. This has been accomplished through city contracts and funding to many of these groups. Reverend Calvin Morris observed this change in the Chicago political landscape:

> We have a Daley in office who is as powerful as his father and perhaps more so—and not because the [Democratic Party] machine is stronger today but because the voices outside of what was then the machine, the voices outside his political structure, are weak, weak to nonexistent.

Since taking office, Mayor Daley has consolidated his support in neighborhoods throughout the city. Consequently, it is difficult for independent voices to be heard or have an impact on city or public housing policy. James Field, the CRS organizer, made the following observation on the local political environment that the coalition was operating in:

> The longer Daley is in power the more power he has and the less likely people are going to speak out against anything. You are fighting against very large odds. So the progress is not going to be as great with a mayor who has almost dictatorial powers.

While the mayor has few critics, he has many supporters. For example, many of the downtown civic groups were very supportive of Mayor Daley taking back local control of the CHA. According to Regina McGraw of the Wieboldt Foundation:

> When Daley took it [CHA] over, the civics were saying, "Oh, good!" I think he was able to get the civic organizations to believe that with the city in charge, things would go as well as they had with school reform . . . I am now in charge! We know I take care of the city well. I will take care of this problem.

In taking back local control of the CHA, it was telling that Daley moved quickly to remove Joseph Shuldiner as the CHA executive director, although Shuldiner was one of the most experienced public housing administrators in the country. But Shuldiner was far too independent for the mayor's taste. According to Ethan Michaeli of the *Resident Journal,* "Joe Shuldiner never had the support of the mayor, city council, or anybody else in Chicago. He was just out there on his own." Mayor Daley did not want someone "out there on his own" and not beholden to the local political establishment. Once Daley took control of the CHA, he wanted people in place at the CHA whom he could trust to follow through on the mandates coming out of the mayor's office.

Middle-Class Support for the CHA Plan for Transformation

Middle-class people, of all colors, who are moving back to the city, are the constituency that the mayor is trying to appease in the demolition of the public housing developments. As James Field of CRS observes:

> Things are rapidly changing, and the middle and upper classes are being drawn back into the city. Poor people are being pushed out of the city. Who is the city being rebuilt for? It is clear that poor people are not a high priority on the list.

As Edward Shurna of the Coalition for the Homeless questioned, "Don't you wonder why there is no big outcry from the black or white middle-class community about public housing? There is certain agreement by both communities that this is a good thing."

Reverend Morris of CRS reached out to many of the civil rights and other community organizations in Chicago to find out why they did not support or join the coalition's efforts:

> As I have talked with people in the city and some of the nonprofit organization advocacy people, [they said] we wish you well but we do not think it is a winnable issue and we are going to focus on efforts we think we can win.

Why did many nonprofit organizations and civil rights groups not get involved in the coalition or view its fight as nonwinnable? One reason, as discussed above, is the political environment in Chicago, where the power of the mayor's office has made dissent and the questioning of mayor-endorsed policies difficult. Since Richard M. Daley threw so much of his political weight behind winning HUD approval of the CHA Plan for Transformation, most felt that going against this plan was "nonwinnable."

More important, many of the civic organizations and policy and foundation people agreed with the CHA's premise that public housing developments had created pockets of concentrated poverty in the city and needed to be demolished. While many were concerned about how the plan was being implemented, they still pulled their support for the coalition's work. Alexander Polikoff, the senior staff counsel of Business and Professional People for the Public Interest (BPI), one of the downtown policy groups in Chicago, best presents this point of view:

> For me the case made by Harvard's William Julius Wilson is entirely persuasive. . . . Wilson speaks of the "social pathologies" of ghetto communities, and adds that, if he had to use one term to capture the differences in

the experiences of the ghetto poor from the poor who live outside, it would be "concentration effects"—meaning social pathologies generated when a neighborhood is composed exclusively of ghetto poor . . . so persuaded am I of the life-blighting consequences of Wilson's concentrated poverty circumstances, that I do not view even homelessness as clearly a greater evil.

And Polikoff goes on to say:

Painful though it is—we should stick with our present course. Even if we don't get more money, and even if efforts to improve relocation don't succeed, society should continue to tear down its public housing high-rises.[37]

This statement represents the prevailing view of local and national policy makers and much of the middle class. The coalition struggled against this view in its efforts to redevelop, not displace, public housing and its residents. It was the position of the coalition that public housing residents should have a choice to either stay in redeveloped public housing units or move to private sector housing with a voucher. No residents should be forced to move out of their existing community. The coalition's position was that the CHA Plan for Transformation was bound to worsen the local affordable housing crisis and increase the number of homeless families. Unlike Alexander Polikoff, the coalition members insisted that public housing is often the difference between a worse place to live and homelessness, and the coalition saw homelessness as clearly a greater evil. At a presentation Carol Steele gave at a 1999 community forum, she explicitly laid out this position:

As we got into this fight I began to see what they [CHA and city officials] were proposing for my people. They were proposing for my people to be evicted and become homeless . . . that is why I am in this fight; because I have been at the homeless shelters and I have seen people waiting to get in.[38]

As outlined in the themes for this book, policy makers represented by Alexander Polikoff's statement continue to make the same major mistake of the urban renewal plan in the 1950s and 1960s—the presumption that experts know what is best for public housing residents. Refusing to take the concerns of public housing residents seriously, policy makers take the cavalier attitude that they know what is best for the poor, even if it means homelessness.

Public Housing and Coalition Organizing

Another obstacle that the CPPH faced was the difficulty of organizing a coalition of public housing residents with religious and other housing advocacy organizations. From the beginning, the public housing residents who founded CPPH wanted this mix of residents and outside support groups. But as much as this combination of membership had its strengths, it also caused suspicion among some public housing residents. According to Ethan Michaeli:

> There have been many people coming in to organize the residents and then profiting from it themselves. Either they are affiliated with some developer or social service agency or something else, and they have gotten the people all excited and then leave them high and dry.

A history of residents feeling ripped off by outsiders made organizing public housing residents difficult for the coalition. It was made even more difficult because many of the residents had a hard time believing that the redevelopment changes would be so dramatic. In addition, many of the duly elected public housing leaders were reluctant to join in the coalition's efforts.

The Conflict With the Local Advisory Councils

It was the elected leaders of the local advisory councils in the public housing developments who generated much of the suspicion about the CPPH. According to Lydia Taylor, these suspicions prevented the coalition from being more effective in organizing residents:

> I would say the propaganda about CPPH prevented some folks from getting involved. Propaganda like the coalition is not a coalition of residents but what do they call us, do-gooders. The LAC and CAC saw the CPPH as competition versus a partner in trying to improve the quality of life for residents.

The LACs felt threatened by the coalition because the public housing leaders in the coalition—particularly, Wardell Yotaghan, Rene Maxwell, and Carol Steele—did speak out on the issues, and their positions appealed to a significant number of public housing residents. Several coalition members also thought that LAC leaders were threatened by CPPH activism because of what many of them had to lose personally. As Edward Shurna commented:

> They are threatened by anybody who says anything different than what they say. And some of them do have jobs or money from the CHA. [For] some of them, we might be hurting their own little nest egg.

Most of the elected public housing leaders supported the mayor and his CHA policies. As Reverend Calvin Morris stated:

There are many public housing residents aligned to the Daley political order who are supported and funded and who receive perks because of these relationships and who find the transformation plan wonderful and are presented as people who trust the plan, trust Terry Petersen [CHA executive director], Sharon Gist-Gilliam [CHA board president] and . . . whose role is to counter the role of the coalition and to call into question the legitimacy of the coalition.

Although in the early days of the coalition there were attempts to work with the elected LAC leaders, these efforts were thwarted. Once the CAC signed on to the Plan for Transformation, LAC presidents became more defensive about their complicity with the CHA. Increasingly, after 2000, they generally saw the coalition as a nuisance. This was unfortunate because if there ever was a need to have resident solidarity it was during this period of rapid demolitions and haphazard resident relocation efforts.

Resident Fear and Intimidation

Several of the coalition organizers who had worked in different settings and with a variety of groups felt that collaboration with public housing residents presented them with a difficult challenge. According to Morris:

I think one of the weaknesses of the coalition has been our inability to organize the public housing residents. I think there are all kinds of reasons for that. I think, first of all, public housing residents living as they do under that kind of system are vulnerable to threats and intimidations and the fear of retaliation, vulnerable to being bought out because there are many residents in fairly . . . precarious circumstances.

Edward Shurna of the Coalition for the Homeless also commented on this climate of fear:

You cannot have organizing when people are afraid to be evicted from their house, if they are afraid something is going to happen to their kids from the gangs if they get involved. . . . Organizing requires some trust and connections. Overcoming the fear has not happened. Only Wardell, Carol, Beauty, Miss [Barbara] Moore, Rene Maxwell, and a few others have stood up. I blame the system, not the people, for making this happen.

Through intimidation, favors, or other perks, the CHA had residents looking out for themselves and not acting in solidarity as a community. Without adequate resources to hire more organizers, the coalition found it difficult to reach a critical mass of residents that could counteract these CHA tactics. Rene Maxwell described a conversation with an elected building president about his responsibility to represent the best interests of the residents who elected him: "I spoke out and said, 'Well, aren't you supposed to be looking out for the residents?' He said, 'No, I'm looking out for my family, man. I don't know where you came from.'"

Inadequate Financial Resources

Many coalition members felt frustrated that the coalition has not been able to build or sustain a large base of public housing residents. Besides the obstacles of suspicion of outsiders, resentment from the elected leadership, and the fear of intimidation and reprisals if a resident joined the coalition, an underlying obstacle that the coalition could not overcome was fiscal. According to Reverend Morris:

> I think we could do a much better job if we had the resources, if we had the money to fund and sustain organizing efforts in the developments. In the last couple of years, there is a reluctance and outright refusal on the part of some of our funders to provide the kind of resources that would allow us to do that. So that part of the inability to build more of a resident base for resident empowerment, to allow the coalition to recede and the residents to move to the fore, I think that has been because we have not had the resources to put organizers in the various housing developments.

Not having adequate resources to hire organizers made it difficult to follow up with residents and bring enough residents to public action in order to influence the mayor and the CHA officials to make changes. Without a critical mass of involved residents, the few residents who do step forward are isolated and easy targets for reprisals. According to Sarita Gupta of Jobs with Justice:

> We can't expect residents to risk themselves politically and personally. I think if we don't figure out how to engage more residents in this process then we really are losing a major opportunity to create a longer term movement around public housing in the city and ongoing community issues.

The coalition's efforts highlight the serious constraints upon political mobilization by poor people in contemporary cities. The coalition's demonstrations, workshops, prayer vigils, and public hearings brought out hundreds and sometimes a few thousand people. But these efforts received limited attention from the mainstream media and were generally ignored by the CHA policy makers.

The Achievements of the CPPH

Despite these obstacles, the coalition has had some success in its organizing. Most of the coalition members agree that its main successes have been
the relocation contract as an addendum to the CHA lease, the meeting with
HUD secretary Cuomo that led to the commissioning of the 1999 Chicago
regional rental market study, the 2002 election of Carol Steele to the CHA
Central Advisory Council, the support that the coalition has given to the
legal action and consent decree at Cabrini-Green, and the November 2003
coalition-sponsored public hearing on the HOPE VI program.

In addition, the coalition has been effective at reaching out to the general
public about the public housing issue. According to Ethan Michaeli of the
Resident Journal:

> I think it has been effective at getting the message out to the people who do
> not live in public housing. That has been its strength. It really does offer an
> alternative view of what is going on in public housing to the general public.

For example, the video *Mixed-In, Not Mixed-Out* by the Chicago Video Project
was one of the outreach tools used by the coalition. This video was shown to
hundreds of groups throughout the Chicago region.

Another strength of the coalition has been the mix of public housing residents and the support organizations working together on the issues. Both
Pam Alfonso of the Metropolitan Tenants Organization and Sarita Gupta of
Jobs with Justice commented that the strength of the coalition was the diversity of the support groups and the fact that so many of the groups had stayed
"at the table" for as long as they had. Edward Shurna of the Coalition for the
Homeless reiterated the importance of the coalition's staying power when he
commented, "The strength is that we have been a consistent voice since the
first Juneteenth until now to call into question the CHA's policies."

And lastly, strong public housing residents have led the coalition. Although
CPPH has struggled to increase the numbers of public housing residents in
the coalition, a core of resident leaders has stuck with the coalition through
the years. As James Field commented, "They are about the issues, not about
themselves." John LeFlore of the Metropolitan Tenants Organization also
felt that the resident leadership made the difference in the success and effectiveness of the coalition:

> The coalition had outstanding resident leadership, particularly in Wardell
> [Yotaghan]. He had an uncanny ability to see strategies, see them from a
> leadership perspective. He had an exciting spirit, which he brought to the

coalition . . . this has continued through Carol Steele. The coalition has stepped up with resident leaders who have done a good job.

As the work of the coalition continues, Beauty Turner, former resident of Robert Taylor Homes, writer, and housing advocate, speaks for all the coalition members and supporters when she says:

> My work with the coalition was a good thing because it gave me organizing skills. It gave me a chance to vent and a chance to learn and be informed. I would not change it for the world. Because of the people I met who were smart, intelligent people from all over. Excellent people from every walk of life and every race and I learned from every person who was there.

The Coalition to Protect Public Housing and its members have led a campaign to raise questions, educate, and organize public housing residents and the general public on what is at stake in this dramatic shift in public housing policy. The coalition experienced many ups and downs in the participation of public housing residents and other support groups since it first came together in 1996. But, as Beauty Turner noted, it has been a diverse group who welcomed everyone willing to discuss and work together. The coalition operates in a political environment, locally and nationally, that is dismissive of organizing that promotes open, democratic policy deliberation. An underlying assumption of the coalition's work is that if the redevelopment process includes the residents in the decision making, it will be a more equitable, accountable, and humane process.

According to the popular and influential policy makers of our day, poverty is a behavioral problem. In this way of thinking, the emphasis is on developing social services to help the public housing residents deal with their behavior problems. Its underlying assumption is that residents are not capable or prepared to be active participants in the redevelopment plan in Chicago. Policy should be left to experts. The coalition challenged these assumptions and organized public housing residents to take an active part in the decision-making process. In this effort, the coalition was, according to Ed Shurna, "swimming upstream" and "fighting the current" of the prevailing ideology. Yet the hypocrisy of the mainstream view and its use to house the rich at the expense of the poor is evident from the experience of CPPH. Nowhere is this clearer than in the case of Cabrini-Green, which is the subject of the next chapter.

Notes

Sixteen personal interviews for this chapter were conducted between June 2002 and June 2003 according to the University of Illinois at Chicago Institutional Research

Board Protocol Number #2002–0135. The interviews were audio taped and transcribed to ensure accuracy.

1. "Chicago Housing Authority: Condemned," *Chicago Reporter,* October 1997.

2. Patricia A. Wright, Yittayih Zelalem, Julie deGraaf, and Linda Roman, "The Plan to Voucher Out Public Housing: An Analysis of the Chicago Experience and a Case Study of the Proposal to Redevelop the Cabrini-Green Public Housing Area," Publication #V-155, Nathalie P. Voorhees Center for Neighborhood and Community Improvement, University of Illinois, Chicago, May 1997.

3. On June 19, 1865, Union soldiers, led by Major General Gordon Granger, landed at Galveston, Texas, with news that the Civil War had ended and that all slaves were free. This was two and a half years after President Lincoln's Emancipation Proclamation, which had been become official on January 1, 1863. Source: www.elecvillage.com/juneteen.htm.

4. John McCarron, "Here Today, Gone Tomorrow: Getting Rid of Some of Chicago's Worst-of-the-Worst Eyesores—Finally," *Chicago Tribune,* June 6, 1997.

5. Janet Smith and Thomas Lenz, *For Rent: Housing Options in the Chicago Region* (Chicago: University of Illinois, Great Cities Institute, 1999).

6. "If Not Here . . . Where?" Coalition to Protect Public Housing brochure, April 15, 1997.

7. Smith and Lenz, *For Rent.*

8. M2M Program Operating Procedures Guide, April 1999, pp. 3–9.

9. Smith and Lenz, *For Rent.*

10. Melita Marie Garza, and Flynn McRoberts, "Leaner, Cleaner CHA Envisioned in Overhaul," *Chicago Tribune,* October 1, 1999.

11. Joel Simon, "Issues Related to the New CHA Plan for Transformation," internal discussion document of the Coalition to Protect Public Housing, November 3, 1999.

12. "Comments and Objections Regarding CHA's Plan for Transformation by the CHA Central Advisory Council," letter, October 30, 1999.

13. "Knock Off This CHA Ego Flap," *Chicago Tribune* editorial, November 8, 1999.

14. Robert Novak, "Infighting Stymies Housing Reforms," *Sun Times,* November 4, 1999.

15. Mamie Bone, Chair of Central Advisory Committee, statement at Department of Housing and Urban Development hearing, October 30, 1999.

16. Bone, statement.

17. Alex Kotlowitz, "Where Is Everyone Going?" *Chicago Tribune Magazine,* March 20, 2002.

18. "MacArthur Foundation Announces Nearly $3 Million in Support of Chicago's Plan for Public Housing Transformation," press release, July 18, 2002, www.macfound.org.

19. Coalition to Protect Public Housing, executive committee meeting minutes, February 18, 1999.

20. Curtis Lawrence, "CHA Activists Raise the Roof," *Chicago Sun-Times,* June 20, 2001.

21. Coalition to Protect Public Housing, press release, November 1, 2001.

22. John Chase, "CHA's Election Woes Persist," *Chicago Tribune,* December 23, 1998.

23. Liam Ford, "Turnout Low; Most Re-elected at CHA," *Chicago Tribune,* January 29, 2002.

24. William P. Wilen, attorney, National Center on Poverty Law, draft remarks CPPH April Briefing, April 23, 2002.

25. Kathleen Clark, "Locked Out: Barriers to Choice for Chicago Housing Voucher Holders: A Report Based on Voucher Testing of Chicago Landlords," Lawyers' Committee for Better Housing Inc., April 2002, www.lcbh.org.

26. Barbara Moore, testimony on panel, CPPH April briefing, April 23, 2002.

27. Richard M. Wheelock, on behalf of the Central Advisory Council, letter to Alphonso R. Jackson, deputy secretary, U.S. Department of Housing and Urban Development, August 27, 2002.

28. Coalition to Protect Public Housing, annual retreat minutes, October 4, 2002.

29. Kate N. Grossman, "CHA's Big Gamble," *Chicago Sun-Times,* January 13, 2003.

30. Grossman, "CHA's Big Gamble."

31. Brian Rogal, "Watchdog Criticizes CHA Plan," *Chicago Reporter,* March 2003.

32. Rudolph Bush, "CHA Stays with Its Relocation Monitor," *Chicago Tribune,* March 21, 2003.

33. Curtis Lawrence, "CHA Failing to Help Families, Suit Alleges," *Chicago Sun-Times,* January 23, 2003.

34. Studs Terkel, *Hope Dies Last: Keeping the Faith in Difficult Times* (New York: New Press, 2003).

35. The World Social Forum is organized as an alternative to the economic summit of government leaders in Davos, Switzerland. The World Social Forum brings together many people's organizations concerned about human rights around the world.

36. Peter Dreier, "The GOP's Cynical Attack on Public Housing," National Housing Institute, www.nhi.org.

37. Alexander Polikoff, "Public Housing," *For the Public Interest: The BPI Newsletter,* February 2003.

38. Carol Steele, presentation remarks, Committee for New Priorities Forum, November 1999.

6

The Case of Cabrini-Green

Patricia A. Wright, with Richard M. Wheelock and Carol Steele

The Cabrini-Green public housing development, located close to the beaches of Lake Michigan, is adjacent to two of the most affluent and desirable neighborhoods in Chicago, the Gold Coast and Lincoln Park. For this reason, many Cabrini-Green residents have been anticipating a "land grab" for as long as they can remember. One milestone in this thinking was only eleven years after the last high-rise was built on the Cabrini-Green site. In 1973, the city of Chicago and a group of downtown corporations unveiled the "Chicago 21" plan, which called for the redevelopment of the Chicago Central Area. The central area included the central business district along with the first ring of neighborhoods around it. This included the Near North community where Cabrini-Green is situated, the Near West area where Addams, Brooks, Loomis, and Abbott (ABLA) public housing is located, and the Pilsen and Chinatown areas on the South Side of the downtown business district.

"Chicago 21" was a response to the changing economic base of the city from industrial to service sector. As the economy of the city shifted from blue-collar to white-collar jobs, "Chicago 21" promoted policies to redevelop the land near the central business district to accommodate this new class of higher-paid, more educated workers. The plan was also in response to the so-called white flight to the suburbs of many of these workers in the 1950s and 1960s. The plan promoted rehabilitating and building new housing in the central area and its surrounding neighborhoods, converting underutilized industrial land and buildings to living spaces, and mimicking the commercial malls of the suburbs in the city. For many of the low-income, blue-collar Latino, black, and white ethnic residents of the neighborhoods affected, "Chicago 21" meant displacing them for higher-income people who could pay higher taxes.

After World War II, much of the public housing in Chicago had been built in this then undesirable inner-city ring, close to the industrial and transportation networks of highways and rivers. "Chicago 21" was thus one of the first signals from city hall and its developer and corporate supporters that the future of Cabrini-Green, ABLA, and other public housing near the central business district was uncertain. Cabrini-Green residents joined with residents of ABLA, Pilsen, and others in the Coalition of Central Area Communities to protest the intent and assumptions in this plan. This coalition was one of the first citywide neighborhood coalitions that brought together Latinos, blacks, and ethnic whites to question the priorities of city redevelopment policies. Since the 1970s, Cabrini-Green residents have continuously fended off other city plans and developers who tried to plan for their area without their participation.

In this case study, we will discuss how Cabrini-Green residents and their leaders have responded to this constant pressure for redevelopment and why they are determined to take the mandate of resident participation in the HOPE VI legislation seriously and be partners in the redevelopment of their community.

The Cabrini-Green Development

Cabrini-Green is a complex of three developments built over a period of twenty years. The first development, the Cabrini Rowhouses, was built in 1942. It consists of two- and three-story buildings with 586 units on a sixteen-acre site. Cabrini Extension, North and South, built in 1958, contained 1,925 units in fifteen buildings that are seven, ten, and nineteen stories. In 1976, the top four floors of three of the nineteen-story buildings were closed off.[1] By 2004, Cabrini North buildings with 957 units were torn down as part of the HOPE VI redevelopment plans. The last part of the complex, Green Homes, was built in 1962. It consisted of eight buildings with 1,096 units. These buildings were fifteen and sixteen stories. The entire Cabrini-Green development covers seventy acres. In 1977, the Cabrini-Green development housed 14,088 people.[2] By 2004, the development had dwindled to a population of 4,525 residents thanks to units being taken out of service due to the closing of the top floors in some of the buildings, units converted to other uses such as tenant social services, the demolition of units, and the increasing vacancy rate due to lack of maintenance.

The residents of Cabrini-Green are 99 percent African-American, and this has been the case for almost the entirety of the development's history. In 2004, the average income for families living in the Rowhouses and Cabrini South was $8,479; for families in the Green Homes, it was $7,166. Meanwhile, the median family income of their neighbors in Lincoln Park and the

Table 6.1

Cabrini-Green Developments, 2004

Development name	Total units	Occupied units	Total number of residents
Cabrini Rowhouses	586	406	1,077
Cabrini North	402	86	243
Cabrini South	597	363	1,050
Green Homes	1,102	571	2,155
Total	2,687	1,426	4,525

Source: Chicago Housing Authority, "Moving to Work Annual Plan for Transformation, FY 2004."

Gold Coast is among the highest in the city: Lincoln Park median income is $137,030 and Gold Coast median income is $113,083, compared to the city of Chicago median family income of $42,724.[3]

The resident leadership of Cabrini-Green is keenly aware of the development pressures because of these wealthy neighbors. Over the years, the resident leaders have volunteered for any and all programs to improve the conditions at Cabrini-Green in an effort to ensure its continued existence.[4] In the 1970s they formed a local advisory council (LAC), which was elected to represent tenants to the Chicago Housing Authority (CHA) Central Advisory Council. Since then they have formed four resident management corporations, published newsletters and a community paper, and created at least eight other tenant-run organizations that include a job training center, business enterprises, and tenant services (security and substance abuse).

As in other communities facing unemployment and disinvestment by public and private interests and despite the best efforts of the majority of community residents, gangs formed, and their sporadic violent criminal activities are what make the news. In 1992, a young resident of Cabrini-Green, Dantrell Davis, was shot on his way to school. This tragic incident made national news, and many considered it the turning point when the CHA began serious discussions with the federal Department of Housing and Urban Affairs (HUD), about the redevelopment of the area.[5]

HOPE VI and Redevelopment Plans

In 1993, Vincent Lane, CHA executive director, worked with the Cabrini-Green LAC members to develop a redevelopment plan for the Cabrini-Green development. This plan was then turned into an application for the federal HOPE VI Urban Revitalization Demonstration to finance the improvements in the plan.[6] On May 23, 1993, the CHA and the Cabrini-Green LAC entered into a redevelopment agreement for a portion of Cabrini-Green utilizing these federal HOPE VI resources. A total of $50 million in federal HOPE VI funding was requested, with $40 million going to the new construction of 303 public housing replacement units on-site and the other $10 million earmarked for social services. In addition, the CHA secured public housing development funding for another 190 replacement units.

This plan called for the demolition of three high-rise buildings containing 660 units. The plan was completed before Congress suspended the one-for-one replacement requirement. Thus, under the plan the 660 units lost to demolition would be replaced with 493 newly constructed units and 167 Section 8 vouchers. Unfortunately, the plan was not implemented before Lane was forced to resign in June 1995. At this time, the federal government stepped in and took over the CHA.

In October 1995, Joseph Shuldiner, the new CHA executive director appointed by HUD, issued a new request for proposals for the Cabrini-Green redevelopment. The original plan described above, which the Cabrini-Green LAC had negotiated with Lane, was included in the new request for proposals. In addition, the request for proposals required additional market units to be developed and financed separately to create a mixed-income development.[7] A screening committee was formed in January 1996 to review the submitted proposals and to make recommendations to the CHA. The Cabrini-Green LAC was represented on this screening committee along with representatives from the city, CHA, and a private developer, the Habitat Company. The Habitat Company was represented on the committee because it was the court-appointed receiver for the CHA's scattered-site program under the terms of the *Gautreaux v. Chicago Housing Authority* order. After several months of review, all the proposals were rejected for failing to meet the requirements of the request for proposal (RFP), and the screening committee meetings ended.

At this time, the city of Chicago and the CHA organized their own private meetings to discuss an alternative strategy for the Cabrini-Green area. The representatives from the Cabrini-Green LAC were excluded from this new round of meetings. When the residents became aware of these meetings, they requested that their representatives attend and participate. The city representatives refused to include the residents and the CHA representatives refused to require that the city include them.[8] This new round of meetings resulted in the Near North Redevelopment Plan, which was announced by the city and CHA at a June 1996 press conference.

The Near North Redevelopment Plan is a comprehensive initiative, which encompasses ninety acres of land for redevelopment. The Near North Redevelopment Plan includes the construction of 2,300 units of housing, a new library, a police station, a new school, parks, and commercial facilities. The redevelopment is to be undertaken by private investors assisted by significant public funds and land. The bulk of the public funds, $281 million, was to be raised by the designation of the area as a tax increment financing district.[9]

In this plan, a total of eight Cabrini-Green buildings were to be demolished instead of the three that had been targeted under HOPE VI. The additional demolition expanded the CHA land available for development from 9.3 acres to twenty acres. In 1995, two Cabrini buildings with 398 units were demolished. With the proposed demolition of an additional six buildings with 921 units, the existing housing units at Cabrini would be reduced to 2,284 units or by 36.6 percent. Out of the proposed 2,000+ new units in this plan, 1,000 would be built on CHA land. The proposed breakdown of replacement units included only 650 units or 30 percent of the total development designated as units eligible for public housing (only half of which would be available for very low-income families). As part of the plan, these 650 units would be acquired by the CHA, which would then rent the units. The CHA would use $40 million of the earlier HOPE VI funding and an additional public housing development grant to buy 493 units.

The plan called for the demolition of 1,324 very low-income Cabrini-Green units with only 325 units reserved for very low-income families. This represented a loss of 969 very low-income units. Due to the income restriction in this plan, over 80 percent of the proposed units would be unaffordable to current Cabrini-Green residents or other very low-income households. Most of the units would be built for middle- and upper-income households making more than $44,000 a year. It was estimated that the market-rate, for-sale units would cost as much as $400,000. The proposed plan had 1,150 market units, the source of most of the developer's profits. Research conducted by the University of Illinois at Chicago (UIC) Nathalie P. Voorhees Center for Neighborhood and Community Improvement (Voorhees Center) estimated that the developer of the proposed development would make between $100 to $136 million profit.[10]

Cabrini-Green Residents File Federal Fair Housing and Civil Rights Lawsuit

In response to this plan, the Cabrini-Green LAC decided that the residents' rights as residents and citizens had been violated and they sought legal redress. Richard M. Wheelock, an attorney at the Legal Assistance Foundation of Chicago, had been working with the LAC on its HOPE VI planning and negotiations since 1994. The LAC asked the Legal Assistance Foundation to assist it in filing a lawsuit. Consequently, on October 24, 1996, the Cabrini-Green LAC filed suit in federal court (*Cabrini-Green Local Advisory Council v. Chicago Housing Authority*) to stop the plans by the CHA to "demolish over 1,300 units of public housing as part of its strategy to 'revitalize' the development."[11] The suit charged violation of the federal Fair Housing Act and Title VI of the Civil Rights Act of 1964. Specifically, the suit charged that the redevelopment plans would adversely affect African-American women and children because they are disproportionately eligible for public housing compared to the general population. In addition, the redevelopment plans broke the CHA commitment not to demolish buildings before replacement units were built, and buildings that were to be rehabilitated were now being scheduled for demolition. The suit also claimed injury to the Cabrini-Green LAC because it was denied participation in the planning process, thereby effectively denying resident consultation, which is required by HOPE VI, Section 18 of the federal act and the memorandum of agreement signed by Vincent Lane when he represented the CHA.[12]

The suit contended:

> [I]n their closed door meetings, the defendants (CHA and The City of Chicago) developed a plan which changes the Cabrini-Green area from a low-income public housing area to a "mixed income community" which they believe will revitalize the area. This plan will result in a community that will drastically reduce the presence of low-income African American households by substantially supplanting the current population with households making more than 50% of the median income, the majority of which will be non–African-American and non–Cabrini-Green residents. . . . The defendants have been aware of the fact that the adverse impact of their decision to permanently eliminate approximately 1,000 units of housing for families of very low income, would fall predominantly upon African-American families with children.[13]

The suit was first filed in October 1996; a preliminary injunction hearing was held in December. At this hearing, the federal judge enjoined the planned demolition of 1150–1160 N. Sedgwick until further order of the court. In January 1997, the court denied CHA's motion to dismiss the lawsuit. Beginning in fall 1997, the Corporation Counsel for the city of Chicago subpoenaed notes and raw data of researchers whose work was part of the basis for the lawsuit. Potential witnesses for Cabrini-Green tenants were also served subpoenas demanding personal information, and they were subjected to long depositions (four to twelve hours each). The substance of the subpoenas and the atmosphere in the depositions was hostile and purposely intimidating. The unusually harsh response of the city and the CHA to the lawsuit was probably due to the fact that the suit was threatening the viability and time-table of the proposed Near North Redevelopment Plan.

First Settlement Reached

During the discovery period of the trial, the LAC, the CHA, and city officials began meeting to try to negotiate an out-of-court settlement. The initial court date was postponed as negotiations continued. After two full years of nego-tiation, a settlement was reached. In the consent decree, the LAC, the CHA, and the city of Chicago agreed to a final settlement of all claims alleged in the case by the LAC and by the residents who are members of or are repre-sented by the LAC.[14] The LAC agreed to the demolition of the six buildings and the CHA agreed to provide the funding and construction of at least 895 public housing eligible units on the HOPE VI site. Of these, 700 were public housing units designated for families earning at or below 30 percent of the Chicago area median income, while the remaining 195 units were to be low-income housing tax credit units, affordable to families with incomes at or below 40 percent.

The demolition of the buildings had to occur in two phases. Three buildings could be demolished as soon as the consent decree was signed and approved by HUD. Under the terms of the consent decree, no further demolitions could occur until 300 units of public housing were under construction; CHA had identified the funds for an additional 400 units in the HOPE VI planning area; the sites for these units had been identified; and the request for proposal for the construction of these units had been issued. The CHA further agreed to main-tain the three additional buildings scheduled for demolition in decent and safe condition until the replacement units were built and the families relocated.

The consent decree also provided for the Cabrini-Green LAC to be a part-ner in the development of the new public housing units. The Cabrini-Green LAC would have a 51 percent stake in the ownership of the general partnership for the development of these sites. The RFP for these development sites would include language to this effect and give extra points to developers who maxi-mize LAC participation. The consent decree that included the above provi-sions plus a number of others were reviewed and approved by the Cabrini-Green LAC on July 28, 1998, twenty-one months after the filing of the lawsuit. Resi-dents considered it an important victory. But the victory was short-lived.

In late summer 1998, just as all three parties were going to sign the con-sent decree, the Habitat Company, the private developer that had been desig-nated as receiver for the CHA scattered-site program, filed an emergency motion before the *Gautreaux* court judge, Marvin Aspen, to enjoin CHA from signing the proposed consent decree. Judge Aspen ruled that Habitat was first entitled to an opportunity to review the proposed consent decree. The Habitat Company objected to the income-targeting for the low-income housing tax credit units, stating that restricting these units to families making less than 40 percent of the area median income would threaten the ultimate success of the project. It also objected to the provision that the Cabrini-Green LAC would have a 51 percent interest, claiming that no qualified developers would bid for a project subject to this requirement.

The debate over the terms of the consent decree now resumed with the participation of the Habitat Company. The sudden entry of Habitat into the process after two years of negotiation was highly suspicious. Residents contended that Habitat was entering on behalf of developers with an interest in the project and maybe even the city, which had been prepared to offer developers major profits through land subsidies. But Habitat stood to gain substantial profits itself. Habitat's status as *Gautreaux* receiver awards it 3 percent of the dollars spent on new family housing construction plus overhead costs. HUD had budgeted $21.9 million for Habitat's services but had paid only out $17.3 million.[15]

Habitat's objections had as their basis the ruling in the *Gautreaux v. Chicago Housing Authority* lawsuit of 1966. That ruling placed substantial restrictions on the construction of additional public housing in predominantly African-American areas. The Cabrini-Green LAC, through its Legal Assistance Foundation attorneys, requested a waiver of this ruling and sought to have "the Cabrini-Green public housing development (designated as) a 'revitalizing area,' which would allow for the construction of low income and public housing in the area."[16] The Cabrini-Green LAC based its waiver request upon the consent decree terms originally agreed to by the LAC, the city, and the CHA, and it urged the court to disregard Habitat's objections. On September 28, 1999, Judge Aspen denied the waiver motion of the Cabrini-Green LAC, citing Habitat's objections as the basis of his ruling.

Negotiations with Habitat continued until spring 2000, when a second settlement was reached. This settlement retained the requirement that the LAC have an ownership interest in the project, although this interest was limited to no more than 50 percent. In addition, the number of affordable rental units, funded through the low-income housing tax credit program, was increased to 270.

Final settlement was memorialized in a consent decree, approved by Judge David H. Coar, the judge presiding over the *Cabrini-Green Local Advisory Council* case, and Judge Aspen, the judge presiding over the *Gautreaux* cases. In addition, Aspen granted Habitat's motion requesting a waiver of the *Gautreaux* order and a declaration that the Cabrini development was a "revitalization area" based on the provisions of the consent decree.

Consent Decree Provisions Enacted

Pursuant to the terms of the consent decree, the CHA proceeded to form a working group to provide ongoing direction and oversight of the Near North Redevelopment Plan. Under the consent decree, the following are represented in the working group: the Cabrini-Green LAC, a community representative from the Near North area, the CHA, the city, counsel for *Gautreaux* plaintiffs, and the receiver, the Habitat Company. The consent decree further states:

> Under the Gautreaux Receivership Order, and other applicable law, CHA or its successor, the Receiver, and the City will have final decision-making authority in their respective areas of responsibility. A representative of the City shall chair the Working Group. A HUD staff member may attend the Working Group meetings as a non-member observer.[17]

On October 11, 2000, the Cabrini working group had its first meeting and subsequently has met on the second Tuesday of every month.

In addition to the creation of the working group, the consent decree provided, among other things, for the following:

- Approximately 1,000 housing units would be built on-site and in the immediate community to serve very-low-income families, including 700 public housing units and 270 affordable units, within the overall context of a mixed-income community.
- The LAC would partner with a private developer, including a sharing of fees and profits, to codevelop units on the Cabrini Extension North site.
- Families displaced from the eight Cabrini Extension North buildings slated for demolition (unless evicted or convicted for certain criminal behavior) would have the right to return to a newly constructed unit in the neighborhood. Second preference would be given to families living in the remainder of Cabrini who expressed an interest in being included on the waiting list.

During 2001, the LAC worked with the CHA to create a lottery, as provided for in the decree, that would give first preference to families displaced from the eight Cabrini Extension North Buildings who wished to return to one of the new units to be built in the area. The working group also worked with the Chicago's Department of Housing to draft and issue a request for proposals for the Cabrini-Green Extension North site, which required that the LAC be included as partner in the development team to be selected for the site. The LAC drafted and executed with the CHA a memorandum of agreement, which allowed the LAC to issue its own requests for proposals to hire technical assistance consultants with the $400,000 awarded to it under the consent decree. In addition, the LAC completed the following tasks in 2001:

- Negotiated a consolidation plan for the three buildings on Larrabee Street where the CHA has agreed to make up to $1.5 million in repairs to two buildings in exchange for the vacating of the third.
- Drafted a request for proposals for a city-owned site just north of the development.
- Negotiated issues surrounding the development of new units at North Town Village, including the screening procedures for selection of residents on the waiting list, the model lease to be used for the public housing families, and mechanisms for reaching out to displaced families to apply for units at North Town Village.
- Negotiated with the CHA so that the CHA is required to notify the LAC of its intent to evict residents in the Larrabee buildings and to meet with the LAC regarding the proposed evictions.
- Submitted a formal complaint to the CHA regarding the failure of the CHA's demolition contractor to hire residents as required under Section 3.
- Conducted a social services needs survey of the residents with the assistance of Loyola University.

Near North Redevelopment Continues

By 2003, there were eleven private mixed-income projects, in various stages of development, in and around the Cabrini-Green area. These developments will have 1,244 units of which 254 are designated public housing units (see Table 6.2). This means that the CHA has agreements with these developers to lease these units for public housing residents.[18] Most of these units are one- and two-bedroom apartments. The displaced families from the eight demolished buildings are in a lottery for these units. The families are prioritized depending on when their buildings were demolished or they vacated their apartments. Of course, the families' needs related to bedroom size also come into play in the assignment of apartments. There is a second waiting list for Cabrini families who want to move into these developments but are not the displaced families from the eight demolished buildings. The president of the Cabrini-Green LAC and the Legal Assistance Foundation attorney, Richard Wheelock, monitor this process to see which families are being housed according to the waiting lists. The CHA Relocation Department does the tenant screening and assignment from the waiting lists.

Table 6.2

Public Housing in Private, Mixed-Income Developments Near Cabrini-Green, 2003

Development	Total units	Public housing units
North Town Village I	116	39
North Town Village II	145	40
Orchard Park	54	13
Old Town Square	113	16
Old Town Village East	140	28
Old Town Village West	134	38
Mohawk North	80	16
Mohawk Partners	15	5
Montgomery Ward	288	16
River Village	180	25
Renaissance North	59	18
Total	1,324	254

Cabrini Extension North Site Negotiations

In fall 2001, the Cabrini-Green LAC representatives and their lawyer assisted in the drafting and editing of the request for proposals issued by the City Department of Housing for the eighteen-acre Cabrini Extension North site. This is the original HOPE VI site first funded in 1994. In 1994 it was a 9.3-acre site but was later expanded by the CHA.

There were four developers who responded. Over the course of several months the proposals were evaluated and three out of the four developers were interviewed. In the end, the developer team of Holsten and Kenard was selected as the finalists to codevelop with the Cabrini-Green LAC the Cabrini Extension North site. Holsten and Kenard are the developers of the North Town Village development, which is part of the Near North redevelopment area and is located on city-owned land directly west of the Cabrini-Green Homes on Halsted Street. Negotiations on the terms of the partnership between Holsten and Kenard and the Cabrini-Green Local Advisory Council began in December 2002.

Creation of Cabrini-Green New Beginnings

Once negotiations began between the LAC and Holsten and Kenard, the LAC began to work on forming its development entity to partner on the development. The LAC had hired the UIC Voorhees Center and the UIC City Design Center to be its real estate development consultants. In addition, in fall of 2002, Jeff Leslie of the University of Chicago Law School

Edwin F. Mandel Legal Aid Clinic offered his services and his interns to assist in transactional legal work. This work involved the term agreement negotiations with Holsten and Kenard that laid out the responsibilities of all the partners in the development and also the by-laws and incorporation of the Cabrini-Green development entity.

A series of special LAC workshop meetings was held in 2003 at which the Voorhees Center staff and Mandel Legal Clinic staff discussed the various options for the structure of the development entity, its by-laws, and the name of the newly formed community development corporation. The LAC voted to name the corporation Cabrini-Green New Beginnings (CGNB). The directors of CGNB will be appointed by the LAC. The corporation was registered with the state of Illinois in January 2004, and the papers for tax-exempt status—501(c)(3)—were filed in spring 2004.

Protracted Negotiations to Forge a Partnership Agreement

The negotiations between CGNB on one side and Holsten and Kenard on the other to redevelop the Cabrini Extension North site took longer than expected due to a number of setbacks and disagreements related to the terms of the partnership agreement. The negotiations were delayed due to disagreements about several issues, particularly, the provision of the community and supportive services to the public housing residents who would move into the new development. In addition, Kenard withdrew from the project in May 2003. Kenard was to be the managing member in charge of the market-rate, for-sale component of the development. This delayed the negotiations until Holsten found another partner. In November 2003, Holsten introduced Kimball Hill Homes to CGNB as the new partner to replace Kenard. Kimball Hill Homes was founded in 1939 and builds 40,000 homes a year. Kimball Hill is also a partner with Allison Davis, a Chicago developer, in the Stateway Gardens public housing redevelopment on Chicago's South Side.

The Cabrini consent decree determined that the LAC would administer and contract out all community and supportive services (CSS). It further determined that funds for such service delivery would come from the HOPE VI CSS budget ($10 million) and the project budgets from development on CHA land. In this regard, the LAC would be the managing partner for the CSS and budget for the development.

During the negotiations, Holsten and the LAC had discussed a joint venture for both the property management and the CSS. Both the LAC and Holsten were compromising on sharing control in these two areas. Holsten was not required by the consent decree and had not agreed in its development bid proposal to share the property management responsibilities with the LAC.

The LAC, via the consent decree, had administrative and contractual control over the CSS. Joint venture descriptions were drafted for discussion at the negotiation meetings held in the early months of 2003. However, in May 2003, Peter Holsten changed his position and withdrew his offer to joint venture on the property management, announcing that he could no longer agree to the ultimate decision-making authority on the CSS resting with the LAC. This was a direct challenge to the consent decree. The negotiations came to a standstill.

In June 2003, the lawyers for the LAC consulted with the CHA and provided an update on the stalled negotiations. On June 4, 2003, the LAC lawyers sent a letter to Peter Holsten, stating that the CHA general counsel, Gail Neimann, had asked "that all parties continue negotiating in order to reach a mutually acceptable agreement."[19] Meanwhile, Peter Holsten's search for a new private development partner ensued. Once Kimball Hill Homes was on board, another wave of negotiations on the partnership took place until the end of the year. The management of the CSS by the Cabrini-Green partners continued to be a stumbling block for both Holsten and its new partner.

In January 2004, the CHA and the city of Chicago filed a joint motion in federal court to modify the consent decree. They asked for a modification regarding the LAC management of the community and supportive services program. The federal judge, David Coar, allowed some legal discovery on the issue and then personally assisted a negotiated agreement among the city, the CHA, and the LAC. Judge Coar then approved an "agreed order modifying consent decree" that added language to the consent decree that the Cabrini-Green LAC would jointly develop the CSS program with the Holsten Development Corporation. Judge Coar also added in this order that all the remaining provisions of the consent decree shall remain "in full force and effect."[20]

The Cabrini-Green LAC agreed to this compromise by accepting the joint development of the CSS program with the Holsten Development Corporation. The president of the Cabrini-Green LAC, Carol Steele, was reassured by Judge Coar's statement that a lot of blood, sweat, and tears had gone into the consent decree and so any changes to it would not be taken lightly. This was important because Richard Wheelock was concerned that the CHA's motion to modify the consent decree would be the first step in dismantling it, and particularly the role of the LAC as partner in the development. According to Carol Steele, it was clear that Judge Coar was not inclined to do so, particularly when he added, "all the remaining provisions of the Consent Decree shall remain in full force and effect." Once the negotiations were agreed upon and Judge Coar signed the order modifying the consent decree in March 2004, the Cabrini-Green LAC and Peter Holsten and his partner resumed meeting in order to move toward breaking ground for the new development. In the spring of 2005, the LAC renamed its development arm the Cabrini-Green LAC Community Development Corporation (CDC). That same spring, the CDC, Holsten, and Kimball Hill finally signed a partnership agreement. The partnership is currently in the process of negotiating a master development agreement with the CHA for the Cabrini Extension North site.

Recent Redevelopment Conflicts

Cabrini-Green North is only one part of the Cabrini-Green development complex. It is the only part that is being developed under the consent decree. According to the CHA's latest edition of the "Plan for Transformation," the Cabrini-Green Rowhouses are to be rehabilitated and the CHA's plans for the rest of the complex, the William Green Homes and Cabrini Extension South, are still undetermined.

However, in late spring 2004, the residents of the Green Homes and Cabrini South received 180-day notices, requiring 350 families living in those building to move out by October 20, 2004. The CHA issued these notices without having consulted with the Cabrini-Green LAC. The CHA is required to inform the LAC before taking such drastic action. What surprised the LAC was that the notices were issued and the CHA slated nine addresses for demolition while at the same time hiring a planning consultant to propose a plan for the redevelopment of the Green Homes and Cabrini South. The planning process was still under way and needed to be presented to the LAC and the larger Cabrini-Green working group for approval.

The LAC tried but was unable to engage the CHA in negotiations to find an orderly process for vacating the targeted buildings, consolidating residents who want to remain on-site in buildings that will be maintained until new housing is available, and allowing families who want to move off-site to do so in an orderly fashion. Since the entire site will not be developed at once, there is no justification for depopulating the site in this way. The LAC wanted a relocation process that is phased, as the redevelopment will be, and, as such, consistent with federal regulations.

Consequently, the LAC filed a complaint for declaratory and injunctive relief on June 3, 2004. This complaint sought an order declaring the CHA's 180-day notices unlawful and injunctive relief staying their implementation so that a phased relocation plan could be developed, including consolidation of buildings and an option for families who wish to remain on-site, pursuant to the redevelopment planning process that the LAC has already agreed upon. The case was assigned to federal judge William J. Hibbler, who held several sessions in late June 2004 to hear the CHA and LAC arguments before granting a temporary restraining order on the notices. The judge ordered a door-to-door survey in all the affected buildings in order to find out whether the families preferred staying at Cabrini, taking a Housing Choice voucher, or moving to another public housing development in the city. The door-to-door survey had to be done by one CHA representative accompanied by a LAC representative. This door-to-door survey was completed in July.

According to the numbers in the 2004 CHA transformation plan, 350 families lived in the seven targeted buildings. However, The CHA served only 266 families with 180-day notices in April 2004. The CHA contended that its resident rosters for these buildings had to be "cleansed" before it issued the 180-day notices because the rosters contained families that were no longer in residence. This meant families that had transferred to other developments, vacated units, or been evicted.

In late September and early October 2004, the CHA reported that only 173 families were served with 90-day notices to vacate. During the months between the 180-day notices and the 90-day notices, the CHA stated that seventy families had moved, vacated, transferred, or been evicted from the affected buildings. In addition, during this time, the CHA agreed to keep the buildings at 364 W. Oak and 365 W. Oak (originally targeted to be emptied) open. This meant that an additional twenty-five families from these buildings that received 180-day notices did not receive 90-day notices because their buildings were not closing. Two families that had not previously received 180-day notices received 90-day notices.

Of the 173 families served 90-day relocation notices, the CHA reported that 120 chose to move with a Housing Choice voucher. The remaining fifty-three families asked to be temporarily relocated to public housing units in the Cabrini community. Of the 120 families who chose a Housing Choice voucher, only seventy-four actually used the voucher and moved to the private market. The remaining forty-four families ended up moving to a public housing unit.

The CHA has refused to agree to maintain any buildings before new units are built. It plans to demolish all the buildings before any units will come back on-site. This has made many families opt for the Housing Choice vouchers because they have little hope that they will get new units, or they do not know how long they will have to wait and where they will live before they get the new units.

Initially, the CHA targeted seven buildings to be emptied and demolished in 2005. Then, CHA took two buildings off the list. These two buildings will be demolished in 2006. In early 2005, the CHA moved families out of the five buildings under the court's supervision. The court ensured that the CHA provided every resident who wanted to stay in the community a rehabilitated public housing unit elsewhere in the Cabrini development.

The CHA also had filed a motion to dismiss the 2004 complaint. On January 11, 2005, Judge Hibbler denied the CHA's motion to dismiss. The court found that the plaintiffs (Cabrini LAC) "have shown by a preponderance of the evidence that Defendants' (CHA) decision to issue 180 day relocation notices to over 300 families without a redevelopment plan in place has caused actual and threatened harm." Further, the judge stated that although the parties have made some progress in developing and implementing a relocation plan, they have only done so with the court's involvement. Therefore, the court cannot say with absolute certainty that the "alleged unlawful behavior" of the CHA will not recur if the complaint is dismissed.[21] Judge Hibbler plans to continue to monitor the relocation process.

As noted earlier, the residents of Cabrini-Green have a tradition of community involvement and participation that goes back to the earliest days of Cabrini-Green's existence as a public housing complex. The most recent efforts of the Cabrini-Green residents and their elected leadership to be partners in the planning decisions and redevelopment of Cabrini-Green are merely following this strong tradition. The Cabrini-Green residents have demonstrated great resiliency and resolve in their determination to be active participants in the improvement of Cabrini-Green. Unfortunately, despite this resolve, this case study chronicles how the CHA, city officials, and the *Gautreaux* receiver have thrown up barriers all along the road to the redevelopment of Cabrini-Green to diminish and thwart the participation of residents in this process.

Notes

1. Devereux Bowly Jr., *The Poorhouse: Subsidized Housing in Chicago 1895–1976* (Carbondale: Southern Illinois University Press, 1978).

2. Robert Lefley and Harry Shaffner, *CHA Statistical Report, 1977* (Chicago: Chicago Housing Authority Executive Office, Information and Statistics Division, 1978).

3. U.S. Census Bureau, Census 2000 Summary File (SF3), Table P77. The family median income for the Gold Coast is for the census tracts in the Near North Community Area east of Wells Street.

4. Larry Bennett and Adolph Reed, "The New Face of Urban Renewal: The Near North Redevelopment Initiative and the Cabrini-Green Neighborhood," in *Without Justice for All,* ed. Adolph Reed Jr., pp. 175–211 (Boulder, CO: Westview Press, 1999).

5. Bennett and Reed, "New Face of Urban Renewal."

6. Patricia A. Wright, Yittayih Zelalem, Julie deGraaf, and Linda Roman, "The Plan to Voucher Out Public Housing: An Analysis of the Chicago Experience and a Case Study of the Proposal to Redevelop the Cabrini-Green Public Housing Area," Nathalie P. Voorhees Center for Neighborhood and Community Improvement Publication, V-155, University of Illinois, Chicago, May 1997. All the facts and details related to the HOPE VI process and Near North Plan were first researched and discussed in this technical report.

7. Wright and Zelalem, "Plan to Voucher Out Public Housing."

8. *Cabrini-Green Local Advisory Council v. Chicago Housing Authority.* Defendants include City of Chicago, an Illinois Municipal Corporation, and Joseph Shuldiner, in his official capacity as Executive Director of CHA: Complaint for Declaratory and Injunctive Relief, in the United States District Court for the Northern District of Illinois, Eastern Division, No. 96C 6949, p. 20.

9. A tax increment financing district allows the city to sell bonds to redevelop an area and use the extra property taxes generated by the development to pay off the bonds.

10. Wright and Zelalem, "Plan to Voucher Out Public Housing."

11. Legal Assistance Foundation of Chicago, "Tenants File Suit to Have Voice in Cabrini-Green Revitalization," press release, October 24, 1996.

12. *Cabrini-Green Local Advisory Council v. Chicago Housing Authority.*

13. *Cabrini-Green Local Advisory Council v. Chicago Housing Authority.*

14. Consent Decree, *Cabrini-Green Local Advisory Council v. Chicago Housing Authority et al.* The following paragraphs summarize the main points from the consent decree.

15. Brian Rogal, "Private Firm Keeps Tight Grip on Public Housing," *Chicago Reporter,* November 1999.

16. Order, *Gautreaux v. CHA,* 66C1459, September 28, 1999.

17. Consent Decree, *Cabrini-Green Local Advisory Council v. Chicago Housing Authority et al.*

18. Chicago Housing Authority, "Plan for Transformation Year 3 Moving to Work (MTW) Draft Annual Plan FY 2002," released for public comment, September 1, 2001.

19. Richard Wheelock, attorney at law representing the Cabrini-Green Local Advisory Council, letter to Peter Holsten, Holsten Development Corporation, June 4, 2003.

20. "Agreed Order Modifying Consent Decree," *Cabrini-Green Local Advisory Council v. Chicago Housing Authority et al.,* March 17, 2004.

21. Judge William J. Hibbler, "Memorandum Opinion and Order," *Cabrini-Green Local Advisory Council, Louise Gates, Yvonne Campbell, Veronica Campbell, Sarah Haynes, Anthony Commons, Ramona Lee, and Veronica Marshall v. Chicago Housing Authority*, No. 04 C3792.

22. Hibbler, "Memorandum Opinion and Order."

7

A Critical Analysis of the ABLA Redevelopment Plan

Larry Bennett, Nancy Hudspeth, and Patricia A. Wright

On January 14, 2004, the Chicago City Council approved the LR Development consortium's plan to thoroughly reconstruct the Addams, Brooks, Loomis, Abbott (ABLA) Homes on Chicago's Near West Side.[1] The city council's decision concluded a planning process that began in the mid-1990s. Nevertheless, during this near-decade of redevelopment "planning," several of ABLA's high-rise buildings were demolished, and the oldest portion of the development, the Jane Addams Houses, was emptied of its residents. In the late 1990s there was also a substantial rehabilitation project conducted in the Robert Brooks Homes section of ABLA, a rehabilitation that entailed the demolition of several hundred units of housing. As we write this chapter, project reconstruction in the wake of the city council's approval of the Roosevelt Square mixed-income development has just begun, with the Chicago Housing Authority (CHA) anticipating the completion of Roosevelt Square toward the end of this decade.

Our critical analysis of the ABLA demolition and Roosevelt Square development process follows four main lines of inquiry. In the next section of this chapter we tell the story of ABLA in the context of the post–World War II history of its neighborhood, the Near West Side. Our point is both to reveal the complex processes that contributed to the decline of ABLA after the 1970s and also to note the ABLA residents' efforts, running back to the 1970s, to preserving the quality of life in their public housing community. Our second focus is on the logic of mixed-income community development and public housing resident dispersal revealed by the ABLA redevelopment process. In the late 1990s the city of Chicago published a pamphlet entitled "Holistic Urban Redevelopment: The ABLA Homes Model," which asserted that the

ABLA redevelopment "represents a new public policy standard for the City of Chicago and sets a new course for creatively redeveloping and revitalizing public housing complexes here and, perhaps, across the U.S."[2] Taking this claim seriously, we explore the sources of this "new public policy standard" while also examining its implications for the on-the-street reshaping of life in the soon-to-be-built Roosevelt Square community. Our third line of inquiry looks at planning and project implementation processes characterizing the ABLA redevelopment, noting in particular the substantial disregard for public housing resident concerns evidenced by these processes. Finally, we look at ABLA, Roosevelt Square, and the gentrifying Near West Side of the late 1990s and early 2000s. It is our contention that a core irony associated with the redevelopment process at ABLA is the CHA and city of Chicago's determination to remove public housing residents from a neighborhood that had become increasingly mixed-income in the years preceding the demolition of the ABLA homes.

The Evolution of the ABLA Housing Development

The Chicago Housing Authority's (CHA) ABLA development is, in fact, a compound group of residential communities that were built over a quarter-century spanning the late 1930s through the early 1960s. The oldest section of the ABLA complex is the Jane Addams Houses, initially 1,027 residential units located in thirty-two two-, three-, and four-floor buildings. Built by the New Deal's Public Works Administration, the Addams Houses opened in 1938. Just to the south of the Addams Houses, a second low-rise development of 834 apartments, the Robert Brooks Homes, was completed by the CHA in 1943. Apartments in the Brooks Homes were initially reserved for workers in war-related industries. Although sharing the Addams Houses' low-rise profile, the Brooks Homes—each structure two floors in height and arranged in a rigidly geometrical pattern on what had been eight city blocks—from the outset had a more barracks-like character than its companion project north of Roosevelt Road.[3]

The next component of the ABLA development was Loomis Courts, housing 126 families in two seven-story, gallery-style buildings, that is, structures employing exterior walkways to connect stairwells and elevators with individual units. Upon its completion in 1951, the Loomis Courts project was recognized for its architectural merit ("one of the ten best new publicly financed housing projects in the nation") by the National Association of Housing Officials.[4] In 1955 ABLA was substantially enlarged with the completion of the Grace Abbott Homes on the western flank of the Brooks Homes. Most of the Abbott Homes' 1,200 apartments were located in seven fifteen-floor high-rise buildings, though edging the Abbott grounds were a number of low-rise structures holding a few dozen residential units. The final significant additions to the ABLA area were the three Brooks Extension buildings, sixteen-floor high-rise structures holding 449 apartments. The Brooks Extension buildings, located just east of the original Brooks Homes, accepted their first tenants in 1961.[5]

Before building demolitions began in the 1990s, the various components of the ABLA development totaled 3,600 apartments. Curiously, only in the 1970s or 1980s were the Addams, Brooks, Brooks Extension, Loomis, and Abbott developments routinely viewed as a single project. For example, Devereux Bowly Jr., in his authoritative history of subsidized housing development in Chicago, *The Poorhouse,* notes that with the construction of the Abbott Homes, this area was the city's "largest slum clearance site at that time."[6] However, Bowly never uses the term *ABLA*, and he discusses the Addams, Brooks, Brooks Extension, Loomis, and Abbott developments as separate residential complexes. The term *ABLA* first appears in press accounts of neighborhood affairs in the early 1970s, but it refers not to the housing development, but rather to a residents' group representing tenants of the various CHA developments in this section of Chicago's Near West Side.

Indeed, the popular image of ABLA as a single development (as well as the CHA's administrative treatment of these rather distinctive, though very proximate residential complexes as a single residential community) may be a function of the radical physical restructuring of Chicago's Near West Side in the quarter-century following World War II. An approximately four-square-mile quadrangle just to the west of Chicago's downtown core, the Near West Side in the early decades of the twentieth century was one of the city's principal ports of entry for European immigrants.[7] Beginning in the 1940s the Near West Side was substantially reconfigured by a series of major development and public works projects, including the hospital expansions associated with the formation of the Illinois Medical Center, the construction of the Eisenhower (Interstate 290) and Dan Ryan (Interstate 90/94) Expressways, and the development of the University of Illinois at Chicago (UIC) campus. The UIC proposal generated considerable local opposition, which for a time linked ethnic Italian, African-American, and Puerto Rican immigrant activists.[8] In addition to demolishing structures that housed nearly 2,000 families and over 600 businesses, the UIC project, according to its historian, George Rosen, had this ancillary effect: "the further movement of blacks into the area from Roosevelt Road to the Eisenhower Expressway between Ashland and Halsted was stopped and contained. It was stopped in the sense that no additional blacks entered the area, and it was contained in the sense that all blacks living in the area were confined to the Jane Addams projects."[9]

In effect, by the late 1960s the CHA developments constituting ABLA were separated from the remainder of the Near West Side by the medical center complex to the northwest and on the northeast by UIC, which was described by one local observer as a "huge fortress."[10] Directly north of ABLA remained a remnant residential community undergoing rapid real estate development and politically dominated by a planning committee "composed almost entirely of Italian residents."[11] Finally, in the spring of 1968, the Near West Side's Madison Street commercial corridor (north of the Eisenhower Expressway) was devastated by rioting in the days following the assassination of Martin Luther King Jr. The impact of these projects and events was staggering: between 1950 and 1980 the Near West Side's population declined from 160,000 to 57,000; during the same thirty years the Near West Side lost half its housing units.[12]

By the 1990s the forces that had physically scarred and driven thousands of residents from the Near West Side during the previous four decades collided with a powerful wave of countervailing trends: private investment patterns and public policies aimed at expanding Chicago's downtown core. During the 1990s the Near West Side's population and housing unit figures remained constant, in spite of the demolition of several hundred public housing units at the ABLA and Henry Horner Homes.[13] In the heart of the Near West Side, a new sporting facility, the United Center, housed the Chicago Bulls and Blackhawks professional sports franchises and hosted a variety of special events, such as the Democratic Party presidential nominating convention in 1996. The city of Chicago funded infrastructure improvements along the Greek Town commercial corridor at the eastern end of the Near West Side, upgraded the gateway streets leading from the Loop to the United Center, and assisted UIC campus expansion south of Roosevelt Road.[14] The most visible physical change in the Near West Side was the rush of residential development—both new construction and loft conversions—that sprouted between Halsted Street and Ashland Avenue. Nevertheless, new residential development occurred throughout the Near West Side, even on the fringes of the Henry Horner and ABLA CHA developments. The scale of the recent development boom on the Near West Side is demonstrated by the growth of private residential lending during the 1990s, as indicated by Table 7.1.

In its 1997 application for HOPE VI funding to advance the redevelopment of ABLA, the CHA described this area as "plagued with thousands of City building code violations" and, as such, subject to "serious physical and social distress."[15] This was not always the case. As late as the early 1970s, local journalist Jack Mabley described the Addams Houses as "the first and still one of the best public housing projects in Chicago."[16] The story of the

Table 7.1

Near West Side Residential Lending

Year	Number of loans	Dollar value
1990	233	$26,405,000
1992	380	$67,909,000
1994	387	$57,404,000
1996	647	$89,023,000
1998	1,309	$202,583,000
2000	1,809	$348,477,000

Source: The Woodstock Institute, *Community Lending Fact Books*, 1990–2000.

ABLA development's decline is complicated, and it is important to review its main components in order to underline the degree to which current redevelopment plans ignore crucial aspects of this public housing neighborhood's history as well as some of its significant contemporary assets.

By the early 1970s there were at least two organizations advocating improvements in the ABLA development, the ABLA Complex and the Community of United People (COUP). The concerns of activists in the ABLA development were twofold: (1) "slowness of repairs, poor security, and lack of other services," and (2) anxiety over the prospect that they might be pushed out of their neighborhood.[17] The latter perception was amplified by the release in 1973 of "Chicago 21," a plan issued by the city of Chicago in collaboration with the Chicago Central Area Committee (CCAC), a prominent downtown business organization. The underlying vision of "Chicago 21" was the postindustrial transformation of central Chicago, by virtue of which the manufacturing and transportation land uses, as well as the working-class and low-income residential areas to the north, west, and south of the Loop, would give way to new office, commercial, and upscale residential development.[18]

The prospect of this kind of neighborhood transformation struck a particularly powerful chord on the Near West Side, which had already witnessed the development of the Illinois Medical Center district and the UIC campus and which had been further segmented by the two expressway corridors. One of COUP's leaders, Willie Baker, described his neighborhood's situation in the following way:

> It's already evident that the City plans to make the West Side one of the most desirable neighborhoods in which to live. . . . You know and I know that to accomplish this, the City and the big money people will have to provide housing in the area for middle and upper middle-income people.

It's inconceivable to me that they will allow low-income families to remain in the neighborhood.[19]

COUP's practical response to this scenario was to propose that the CHA offer Addams Houses tenants forty-year leases and support a tenant management program. Although the Addams Houses residents did not achieve their ultimate aim of project self-management, by autumn of 1976 the CHA did commit to bring the development "up to building code standards."[20] In short, signs of physical decline in the ABLA area were evident by the early 1970s, but at that time a committed cadre of project residents sought to improve their living conditions and fend off prospective initiatives that threatened to push them out of the Near West Side.

In spite of the limited improvements won by ABLA-based activists in the 1970s, for much of the subsequent two decades their community shared in the neighborhood decline that was sweeping the Near West Side. The physical condition of the ABLA development declined precipitously. A notable low point was reached in the 1980s when the ABLA heating system regularly broke down during the winter months.[21] Like other CHA developments, ABLA was also subject to periodic outbursts of violent criminal activity.[22] During this period one strand of continuity with the past was nonetheless unwelcome: the persistent speculation by residents and outsiders alike that public housing on the Near West Side was threatened by impending neighborhood change. Situated just west of the UIC campus and configured in a manner that might allow rehabilitation as dormitory space, the Addams Houses, in particular, were assumed by many observers to be the next beachhead for UIC campus expansion.[23]

The most recent phase of ABLA's history began in 1995, when the development's local advisory council (LAC) won a $200,000 HOPE VI planning grant from the U.S. Department of Housing and Urban Development (HUD). The initial focus of ABLA redevelopment was the three Brooks Extension high-rise buildings, which subsequently have been demolished. In 1996, 1997, and 1998 the CHA applied for HOPE VI revitalization grants. Although its 1997 proposal was rejected, the CHA received just under $60 million in HUD support via its 1996 and 1998 proposals. Between 1998 and 2000 the Brooks Homes section of ABLA was completely revamped. The number of residential units was reduced from 834 to 329, with the remaining structures reconfigured as town houses grouped around a series of courtyards. In 1999 the city of Chicago released the "Holistic Urban Redevelopment" booklet, which envisioned a new ABLA neighborhood designed in keeping with "new urbanist" precepts (low-rise buildings, "traditional" architecture, reintroduction of a within-development street grid) and including a mix of rental and for-sale properties. The distribution of unit types reported in "Holistic Urban Redevelopment" is noteworthy: 1,084 public housing units for very low-income residents (and an additional 383 very low-income public housing units off-site), 845 affordable rental and for-sale units (intended for families earning between 35 percent and 120 percent of the area median income), and 966 market-rate units.[24] This distribution of housing unit types had previously appeared in the CHA's 1998 HOPE VI revitalization grant application.[25]

On the ground, the relationship between the planning and implementation of ABLA's redevelopment has seemed at best haphazard. For example, in October 1996 the CHA began efforts to close the Jane Addams Houses but provided one group of tenants with only six days' notice that they were to vacate their dwellings.[26] Over the next several years, as portions of the Brooks and Abbott developments and all three Brooks Extension high-rises were demolished, residents regularly complained about the conditions of the temporary housing provided in the remaining ABLA buildings. In the spring of 2001, following a visit to the Abbott high-rise at 1324 S. Loomis Street, CHA CEO Terry Peterson ordered the building's property manager, H.J. Russell, to perform emergency repairs.[27] In the spring of 2002, planning consultant Thomas Finerty, who has worked with the ABLA LAC since the mid-1990s, described conditions in the 1510 W. 13th Street Abbott building in this fashion: "People have been getting stuck in the elevator and waiting hours to get out; people who lived on the 14th floor were coming home with groceries and finding the elevator completely out . . . it will be weeks and weeks before the major elevator repairs will be done."[28]

Another curious feature of the ABLA planning process has been the sequencing of activities. Formal, resident-centered discussions of how to rebuild the development began with the awarding of the initial HOPE VI planning grant in 1995, and during the next several years planning consultation extended throughout the Near West Side. According to the CHA's 1997 HOPE VI proposal: "The Local Advisory Council (LAC) and ABLA residents have been involved in planning for the future of their development for several years." And following these within-development discussions, "accompanied by representatives of the City of Chicago and/or the LAC leadership, the CHA has met with representatives of the University of Illinois; the Illinois Medical District; St. Ignatius College Prep; the West Side Consortium . . . the University Village Association; the West Side Community Conservation Council as well as private individuals."[29] By 1999, when the "Holistic Urban Redevelopment" booklet was issued, the city of Chicago seemed to characterize the plan to redevelop ABLA as a fait accompli. Not only were specific target figures set for the distribution of housing unit types, but the introduction to this document (quoted previously) contended that the

planning of and overall vision reflected in the ABLA redevelopment represented benchmarks meriting emulation by the implementers of future public
housing makeovers.

In fact, at approximately the same time the city of Chicago issued an
RFP for a development manager "to plan and implement a mixed income
residential development on the site of the CHA's ABLA Homes and certain
adjacent parcels."[30] And although this RFP carried over the housing-type
target figures and new urbanist neighborhood vision found in the "Holistic
Urban Development" booklet, the earlier document's "four principles of
holistic urban redevelopment"—"common goal," "collaboration," "community participation," and "continuity"—had been replaced by a new set
of "four basic principles": "create diverse, mixed-income communities,"
"establish collaborative partnerships among public and private interests,"
"give public housing families a choice," and "help public housing families
become self-sufficient."[31] Evidently, the "new public policy standard" represented by the ABLA development was not quite fixed in the minds of the
project's planners.

In the spring of 2001, Telesis Corporation, which had won the development manager contract, conducted neighborhood hearings on the ABLA redevelopment. The result of this exercise was a document entitled "ABLA
HOPE VI Redevelopment: Amended and Restated Revitalization Plan," which
deviated in no significant way from previous ABLA planning and grant application materials: "The plan is grounded in the principles of the 'New Urbanism' (really, the 'old urbanism')—the street grid is restored—houses will
be street facing, a pedestrian scale street front, creating a 'walkable' neighborhood, with major streets—including Taylor and Roosevelt restored." Indeed, the same distribution of very low-income, affordable, and market-rate
housing types (1,084,846—an increase of one, and 966, respectively) presented in previous planning documents was carried over in the "Amended
Plan."[32] Later in 2001 the CHA, city of Chicago, and Habitat Corporation
(receiver for the CHA's new family housing developments) issued an RFP to
develop the Brooks Extension triangle at the eastern end of the ABLA site.
In the following spring this RFP was withdrawn due to a lack of interest by
private developers.

The final phase of planning for the ABLA redevelopment ensued with the
issuing of another RFP, in November 2001, for the entire ABLA area. A year
later, although the ABLA working group (representing the LAC, public agencies, and private participants with an interest in the redevelopment effort) was
divided in its assessment of two competing proposals, the CHA selected LR
Development as "master developer" for ABLA. The CHA, according to a press
account, was impressed by the LR consortium's previous experience in public

housing development, as well as its proposal to earmark $4 million for social services, job training, and other resident-directed programs.[33] Substantively, LR committed itself to the new urbanist design principles articulated in previous ABLA planning documents and a rigorous follow-through on the housing-type projections first articulated in the 1998 HOPE VI application. Regarding the latter, LR planned to rebuild ABLA in several phases, and its phase-by-phase projection of unit mixes was numerically consistent throughout.[34] In effect, apart from the completed Brooks Extension units and the rehabilitation of the Loomis Courts (as affordable for-sale units), each subsection of the new ABLA—to be renamed Roosevelt Square—will include very similar proportions of very low-income, affordable, and market-rate units.

The Intellectual Roots of the ABLA Redevelopment Plan

LR Development's plan for the refashioning of the ABLA complex culminates a sequence of consultations, decisions, and intermediate initiatives running back to the mid-1990s. From the standpoints of physical design and unit mix, there is indeed little that is new in the LR vision of Roosevelt Square. For example, the distribution of very low-income, affordable, and market-rate units at Roosevelt Square is nearly identical to housing-type target figures that appeared in ABLA planning documents as early as 1998. More generally, the vision of a redeveloped ABLA neighborhood as presented by LR Development is consistent with the vision of public housing redevelopment that has swept the nation's cities since the mid-1990s.

The physical designs and public policy aims that are transforming ABLA and other public housing developments in Chicago are characteristic of the federal government's HOPE VI program and its approach to correcting the defects of severely distressed public housing developments. The intellectual roots of HOPE VI are derived from a cluster of notions ranging from questionable hypotheses about the workings of economically diverse communities to a new version of architectural determinism. The acknowledged twin pillars of the HOPE VI public housing redevelopment program are the mixed-income community concept and new urbanist physical design. Another unacknowledged line of thinking that drives the ABLA/Roosevelt Square redevelopment is what political scientist Edward Goetz has called the "new community development" model of neighborhood revitalization.[35]

Mixed-Income Communities

One of the key principles anchoring the Roosevelt Square proposal, and HOPE VI more generally, is the concept of the mixed-income community, derived from the work of sociologist William Julius Wilson. Wilson and others have argued that the social problems in inner-city poverty neighborhoods are largely the result of the geographical concentration of poor families.[36] Bruce Katz of the Brookings Institution cites "a direct correlation between these neighborhoods of high poverty and such key social indicators as declining school performance and relatively high rates of criminal activity, family fragmentation, substance abuse and teenage pregnancy."[37] As a particularly identifiable type of high-poverty, African-American neighborhood, public housing has been "singled out as the most egregious example of how spatial concentration of poverty leads to welfare dependency, sexual promiscuity, and crime."[38] This notion has provided the rationale both for the dispersal of public housing residents with vouchers (the Moving to Opportunity program) and the demolition of public housing structures. In the effort to "end public housing as we know it," the Clinton administration and a conservative Congress successfully used deconcentration of the poor as the rationale for repealing the federal statute requiring the one-for-one replacement of demolished public housing units.[39]

As stated in the HOPE VI program's objectives, redevelopment will "provide housing that will avoid or decrease the concentration of very low-income families."[40] To achieve this goal, two redevelopment strategies have evolved under HOPE VI: relocating public housing residents, presumably to low-poverty neighborhoods, and, at the same time, allowing others to remain in newly created mixed-income communities on the sites of the original developments.[41]

Coincidentally with the emergence of the HOPE VI program in the early 1990s, CHA chair Vincent Lane began to promote the idea that the public housing population in Chicago was too uniformly poor and, as a result, had become disconnected from mainstream social and economic institutions. Accordingly, public housing areas had evolved into breeding grounds for criminality, family breakup, and other social pathologies—that is, environments in which even upward-striving individuals could be trapped. Nationally, the HOPE VI mixed-income strategy has aimed to reduce the concentration effects produced by packing too many poor people into areas bereft of stabilizing populations or institutions. Or, as Vincent Lane phrased the point in 1994, "We need socioeconomic diversity or we will never solve the problems of the inner city."[42]

Wilson's research has been challenged by a variety of scholars, some observing that he has exaggerated the geographical separation of contemporary African-American middle-class from working- and lower-class urbanites, others suggesting that, historically speaking, his portrayal of internally harmonious African-American communities before the civil rights era is dubious.[43] Though this element of Wilson's interpretation of African-American communal relations before and after the civil rights era seems not to have been addressed in the social science literature, there is a further striking anomaly in Wilson's description of the decline of African-American inner-city communities. In effect, Wilson argues that once civil rights initiatives, in combination with the relaxation of previously segregative real estate practices, permitted the African-American middle class to flee residential areas such as Chicago's South Side "Black Belt," large numbers of prosperous African-Americans did not hesitate to move into outlying city or even suburban neighborhoods. Yet this very same group is presumed by Wilson to have been the "glue" holding together the mixed-class ghettos of the pre–civil rights era. This is a curiously truncated characterization of how communal harmony had been maintained in African-American neighborhoods, seemingly orchestrated by a group that, once the opportunity was provided, felt weakly enough rooted in the old areas of settlement to depart in very short order.

In spite of the various uncertainties associated with Wilson's account of inner-city African-American neighborhood deterioration in the 1970s and 1980s, the remedy for turning around such areas—socioeconomic diversity, linked to role modeling by more affluent, incoming neighborhood residents— has become an ironclad precept for CHA officials and the various developers and consultants working with the public housing agency. Many proponents of mixed-income housing assume that role modeling will be a largely passive process, that public housing residents will benefit from merely observing some of their neighbors departing for work in the morning. A perspective on social class mixing that is less condescending to the character of low-income people construes another kind of benefit growing out of interactions between lower-class and middle-class people. In this view, middle-class neighborhood residents—holding jobs, with ties to people and institutions across the city—can become intermediaries linking isolated poor people to resources and economic opportunities that they would not otherwise encounter or even know exist). In the following statement, the authors of a 1996 Metropolitan Planning Council report joined these two points:

> [O]ne of public housing's greatest obstacles is its isolated concentration of poor people, a phenomenon that destroys the norms of everyday life and perpetuates social and economic deprivation. Many argue that economic integration through the presence of higher-income tenants can contribute to a more stable environment by exposing public housing residents to role models and the linkages they bring to the broader community.[44]

Finally, what might be the most baldly instrumental of the mixed-income community's presumed virtues is the expectation that in such a social environment, middle-class people will be inclined to monitor the actions of their less affluent neighbors, intervene to sustain a modicum of local civility, and, if necessary, call on formal authorities to control the actions of the lawless.[45]

Though the belief that poverty should be deconcentrated has become an article of faith for many policy analysts and is also endorsed by a variety of advocacy groups, there is in fact only a smattering of evidence confirming that mixed-income developments actually improve the life chances of the poor residing in them or reduce negative behavior such as crime and drug use.[46] Although dramatic decreases in crime have been observed in some developments that were converted from public housing to mixed-income, this may merely indicate that, due to strict screening policies, criminals have been turned away.[47] In his 2002 overview of mixed-income housing developments, Alastair Smith noted that the most extensive study at that time, a comparison of seven mixed-income developments, found low or very low levels of neighboring and that few market-rate tenants attended building activities. Conversely, racial homogeneity, similar household composition (families with children versus childless households), and similar economic circumstances were positively associated with interaction among neighbors, a finding that certainly undercuts the logic of the social benefit of mixed-income housing.[48] In general, most improvements in mixed-income developments appear to be due to stricter management policies and screening procedures. Could improved management practices and better physical housing quality achieve the same success with a population of all low-income tenants? According to housing specialist Rachel Bratt, "If you provide very low-income people with good management, a good living environment, good maintenance, and housing that blends in, mixed income may not be necessary."[49]

This is an especially relevant observation when considered in the context of the physical revitalization that adjoins the ABLA development. In an analysis of thirty-two HOPE VI sites across the country, Edward Goetz found that the income levels of ABLA development neighbors made this a unique site. According to the U.S. census, 20 percent of families in the one-mile square area surrounding and including ABLA earned more than $100,000 in 1999. That is more than three times the average across the thirty-two examined HOPE VI sites.[50] Considering this larger neighborhood context, ABLA residents do not live in concentrated poverty. By the time of the 2000 census, middle-class and wealthy homeowners had become a significant component of the ABLA neighborhood. While some critics have charged that HOPE VI leads to gentrification, it could be argued that, in the case of ABLA, gentrification led to HOPE VI.[51]

New Urbanism

The second key principle anchoring the Roosevelt Square redevelopment plan is "new urbanism," a design philosophy that has been promoted by leading contemporary architects such as Andres Duany and Elizabeth Plater-Zyberk and employed, most notably, in the construction of the Disney Corporation's "new town" in central Florida, Celebration.[52] For many architects and planners, new urbanism is—just as characterized in the Telesis Corporation's amended ABLA plan—the "old urbanism": traditionalist architecture, low-rise construction, residential and commercial structures directly abutting sidewalks, and "walkability" between residential, commercial, and public space uses. Or, to reverse the formulation, new urbanism rejects the basic modernist design vocabulary—tall residential buildings, expansive open spaces, strict separation of residential from commercial uses—that came to define CHA high-rise public housing developments such as Robert Taylor Homes and the post–World War II additions to the Cabrini-Green and ABLA complexes.

In Chapter 10 of this volume, Janet Smith discusses at some length the use of new urbanist design techniques in contemporary mixed-income residential developments. In reference to Roosevelt Square, we limit our comments to noting two interesting design departures from new urbanist doctrine and in particular from the design principles articulated by Jane Jacobs, the intellectual source of much new urbanist writing and practice.[53] LR Development's proposal for Roosevelt Square sets the density at twenty-seven units per acre. This is far lower than Jacobs's threshold of approximately a hundred units per acre as the base density that will yield substantial resident use of local facilities as well as informal on-the-street interaction.[54] Similarly, although LR Development scatters a handful of commercial storefronts around the edges of Roosevelt Square, it is only nominally a mixed-use project. In practice, if not in accordance with either their planning documents or some of the principal tenets of new urbanism, the designers of Roosevelt Square appear to be catering to the expectations of the middle- to high-income purchasers of their market-rate residential units. For this purchaser population, relatively low residential densities and land use separation—rather than high densities, busy commercial streets, and frequent sidewalk encounters with neighbors and strangers alike—typically are the physical features defining a desirable neighborhood environment. In effect, although LR Development has talked the new urbanist talk in marketing its Roosevelt Square plan, it has walked a much more conservative design program onto the streets of the Near West Side. Given these considerations, it seems extremely unlikely that the design of Roosevelt Square will contribute much, if anything, to the sort of street vitality and social mixing so prized by the advocates of new urbanism.

The New Community Development

CHA documents seeking to advance the redevelopment of the ABLA area are filled with direct references to mixed-income development and new urbanism. The broader content of these documents, without making any such explicit references, reflects a third trend in recent neighborhood regeneration efforts, what Edward Goetz of the University of Minnesota terms the "new community development" model.[55] Unlike the old community development —emphasizing incumbent neighborhood resident initiatives, especially with the aim of shoring up the affordable, rental housing stock—the new community development typically seeks to weed out undesirable residents, deemphasizes rental housing preservation, and presumes that the importation of more affluent homeowners will yield overall neighborhood improvement. Although Goetz's description of new community development practices focuses on the Minneapolis/St. Paul region, among his examples of new community development practice is the Vincent Lane–era Operation Clean Sweep initiative at Robert Taylor Homes.[56]

In many respects, the new community development model reflects a set of widely held assumptions about renters, homeowners, and, more generally, desirable neighborhood conditions. The problem with this constellation of assumptions is that they are little more than a widely circulated (and often internally contradictory) set of prejudices, as evidenced by the following statement—which represents a characteristic "homeowner" view of renters— reported by anthropologist Constance Perin in her study of popular attitudes toward housing and land use in the United States, *Everything in Its Place:* "The renters tend to be more transient. They're a lower class of people. They haven't been able to raise the down payment and decide what they want to do with their lives, they haven't grown up, they're not mature and so forth."[57]

From the standpoint of neighborhood redevelopment initiatives, the new community development gives priority to the interests of incoming, more affluent residents: "Community plans beg[i]n to reflect the interests of these residents, interests . . . more likely to focus on supporting ownership and reducing emphasis on services to renters and low-income residents."[58] As such, although city and public housing agency officials may construe the new community development as a time-tested method of achieving neighborhood improvement, given the demographic complexity of many inner-city neighborhoods (including, by the way, the ABLA area), what the new community development also accomplishes is a tilting of the political scales in favor of the neighborhood expectations of affluent residents. If neighborhood improvement is defined narrowly as the enhancement of local property values, the new community development probably does play a direct and predictable role in achieving this end. If, however, neighborhood development is defined more broadly as an inclusive process involving the wide range of local interests, new community development does not offer an equitable distribution of benefits across the neighborhood income and social class spectrum in areas such as the ABLA neighborhood.

The Flawed ABLA Redevelopment Process

Apart from the shaky intellectual foundations that have animated city of Chicago and CHA plans to redevelop the ABLA area, the practical approach to handling redevelopment in this section of Chicago's Near West Side also reveals a series of glaring shortcomings. Indeed, the city of Chicago and CHA seem to have learned nothing from the difficulties associated with redeveloping other CHA complexes in the last decade and have also managed to violate some fundamental and widely accepted principles of effective redevelopment planning. In the next several pages we address these issues via the following topics: (1) the ABLA plan's relocation imperative, (2) planning and consultation breakdowns, (3) the protracted time line for demolition, relocation, and new construction, and (4) the deficiencies of the Roosevelt Square mixed-income community strategy.

The Relocation Imperative

At minimum, since the CHA's filing of its HOPE VI application in 1998, the planners of ABLA's redevelopment have assumed that the new ABLA area community will contain far fewer units of public housing than in the past (1,084 units on-site as opposed to approximately 3,600, with the former figure increasing to 1,467 if one assumes that 383 off-site units will be built). Moreover, a comparable citywide reduction in family public housing units was built into the CHA's Plan for Transformation adopted in early 2000.[59]

In part, the resulting relocation imperative—the assumption that neighborhood improvement will be effected by removing a large share of the public housing population—is a direct outgrowth of new community development thinking: only by reducing the density of the low-income population can a viable neighborhood be achieved. But relatedly, the CHA proposes that through the use of Housing Choice vouchers, former public housing residents will be able to find better, private-sector housing in integrated neighborhoods not subject to concentrated poverty. The deficiency of this scenario turns on the overall tightness of the local rental housing market, combined with the unwillingness of many landlords to accept large family groups as tenants.[60] Over the last several years of building teardowns and tenant relocation, various researchers have documented that the CHA's deconcentration efforts have produced, at best, marginal neighborhood improvements for relocatees.[61] In a recent updating of research that Paul Fischer of Lake Forest College has conducted over the last decade on the residential choices of Chicago Section 8/Housing Choice voucher (HCV) users and, in particular, former CHA residents, he writes:

> The high-rise developments have been historically characterized as some of the most racially isolated in the city, but moving with an HCV has not reduced racial isolation significantly. HCV relocatees are moving to Census Tracts that are almost as racially segregated as the areas they are relocating from. HCV relocatees move to areas that are, in general, less poor with higher median incomes than the sending high-rise development Census Tracts. But in the larger citywide context, most relocatees are still moving to areas of economic despair having low median incomes and high poverty rates.[62]

The barriers confronting public housing relocatees, furthermore, have been magnified by the CHA's hasty efforts to move residents out of public housing. In January 2003 the independent monitor retained by the CHA to evaluate its relocation efforts noted:

> In July, August and September 2002, the large number of HCV-eligible families still in CHA buildings, coupled with imminent building-empty dates, and the relatively small number of relocation counselors, caused a rush to place families in rental units. This in turn led inevitably to placing families hurriedly, and to relocating families into racially segregated areas already overwhelmingly populated by low-income families. We were told . . . residents were moved to HCV units without having had any real opportunities to make thorough and thoughtful surveys of available private rental units.[63]

In effect, the CHA's overriding commitment to remove residents from its developments that it has failed to maintain properly—before and during the planning and redevelopment process—has exacerbated relocation problems that are intrinsic to the low-cost rental housing market in Chicago.

There is, finally, a telling irony associated with the ABLA relocation imperative. Like several other CHA developments, such as the Cabrini-Green complex and the Henry Horner Homes, ABLA is located at the edge of the city's geographically expanding, economically vital central area.[64] In the years to come, as more affluent residents and new enterprises press into the Near West Side and other neighborhoods once viewed as undesirably distant from either the Loop or the lakefront, a myriad of job and entrepreneurial opportunities can be expected to materialize. The city of Chicago and the CHA are removing large numbers of public housing residents from neighborhoods such as the Near West Side just at the point when new private investment and, very likely as well, ancillary public investment in infrastructure and schools promise to greatly improve both economic opportunity within the neighborhood and the local quality of life.

Planning and Consultation Issues

From a strictly procedural standpoint, the production of the Roosevelt Square plan has observed the characteristic protocols of neighborhood planning. Certainly, the redevelopment of ABLA has not been rushed into the implementation phase, and there has been a sequence of formal consultations with a group of local residents. Nevertheless, there is much evidence to suggest that, substantively, the discussions and planning exercises that have yielded Roosevelt Square have failed to tap the wide array of ABLA resident interests and, more generally, have subordinated public housing residents' concerns to the neighborhood vision of major local institutions and middle-class neighborhood residents.

Within ABLA, resident representation has been monopolized by a local advisory council leadership dominated by its president, Deverra Beverly. A *Chicago Tribune* profile of Beverly not only characterized her as "an ideal tenant leader for the CHA" (due to her willingness to accept massive scaling back of the ABLA development) but further observed, "Many tenants say they feel personally obligated to her for both their apartments and for something entirely new for many in the neighborhood—employment."[65] This sense of indebtedness to Deverra Beverly may also be attributable to a considerable degree of official reputational boosting. Beverly, for example, has been the recipient of public congratulation from none other than Mayor Richard M. Daley.[66] Just south of Roosevelt Road, the city of Chicago has designated a section of Loomis Street "Honorary Deverra Beverly Way."

In the mid-1990s, a group of residents unwilling to accept the city and CHA approach to project redevelopment plans formed the Concerned Residents of ABLA (CRA) and attempted—without much success—to influence the planning effort. Eventually, in May 2004, working with attorneys from the Sargent Shriver National Center on Poverty Law, the Chicago Lawyers' Committee for Civil Rights Under Law, and pro bono attorneys from Sonnenschein, Nath, and Rosenthal LLP, CRA filed suit against the CHA and the Habitat Company (the *Gautreaux* receiver in charge of developing off-site public housing) to "redress the harm to current, former and potential future residents of the Addams,

Brooks, Loomis, and Abbott (ABLA) public housing development." According to the CRA's filing, the CHA and Habitat, "mandated to use public money to reduce racial segregation, have conceived a plan which fails to alleviate the blight of segregation for these very poor, African-American, female headed households and in fact reinforces and perpetuates segregation through the Redevelopment Plan."[67] In July 2004, the federal district court denied the plaintiff's motion. Judge Marvin Aspen, who oversees the *Gautreaux* receivership, ruled that it was too late for the plaintiffs to intervene in the ABLA redevelopment process. Though convinced of its strong case, CRA and its attorneys decided that it would be fruitless to file an appeal.

In light of the broader impacts likely to result from the rebuilding of ABLA, the city and CHA's attention to soliciting beyond-the-development opinions on this project, again, conforms to good planning practice. However, press accounts suggest that the last three to four years of community discussion about ABLA redevelopment have been dominated by local institutional representatives and the University Village Association (UVA), a group representing middle-class and wealthy local homeowners. The concerns of the UVA—which has been in the past a bitter opponent of affordable housing development on the Near West Side—have mainly turned on questions of architectural detailing, public space landscaping, and residential "de-densification."[68] In December 2003, the city council's approval of LR Development's proposal for Roosevelt Square was held up by continued objections attributed to the UVA and some of its neighborhood allies.[69]

In short, contrary to the line adopted in city- and CHA-sponsored documents, the planning of Roosevelt Square has been a contentious process. Given the clear lack of unanimity among ABLA residents about the future of their development, the city and the CHA's unwavering commitment to Deverra Beverly and the ABLA LAC is noteworthy. In the mid-1990s, when the Cabrini-Green LAC took a position contrary to CHA plans for that development (see Chapter 6), city officials broke off discussions with the LAC, claiming, in effect, that the LAC was unrepresentative of the broader Cabrini-Green population. In the words of then-CHA executive director Joseph Shuldiner, "Why should one set of residents dictate how everybody's going to live for the next 100 years?"[70] This was in spite of the fact that there was no mobilized, resident opposition to the Cabrini-Green LAC. Conversely, at ABLA there has been a vocal opposition, but city and CHA representatives have never retreated from their support of the Beverly faction nor sought out the opposition to hear its concerns. From the standpoint of the city and the CHA, effective dialogue with public housing residents appears to be consultation in which the residents, at the outset and throughout the process, agree to the premises advanced by city and public housing agency officials.

The Protracted Process of Demolition, Relocation, and Construction

The CHA began to move residents out of ABLA buildings in the mid-1990s and initiated demolitions by the late 1990s, several years in advance of formalizing the neighborhood redevelopment plan from which Roosevelt Square has emerged. In the case of the Addams Houses, residents were relocated when the public housing agency had no firm sense of what the future of that portion of the ABLA development would be. The temporary housing provided to these relocatees has typically not been a good fit. Older residents of the Addams Houses have found high-rise accommodations in the remaining portions of the Abbott development to be, at the least, inconvenient. As we have noted previously, even CHA CEO Terry Peterson found the quality of maintenance in the Abbott buildings to be unsatisfactory.

Among the long-standing protocols of federal government redevelopment policies has been the provision of relocation assistance (financial and advisory). Effective redevelopment planning is presumed to include a substantial commitment to advance provision of relocation housing for individuals and families who must move due to redevelopment activities. In fact, local governments and redevelopment agencies have often been lax in meeting these obligations. Local officials frequently carried out federal government-sponsored urban renewal demolition in an overly aggressive way, paying little attention to the housing needs of families to be removed from urban renewal areas.[71] There is also a long and, indeed, international history of escalating neighborhood deterioration preceding redevelopment, with holdover residents suffering from deteriorated accommodations, increased vandalism as buildings are stripped of piping and other salvageable materials, and even personal physical attack.[72] All of this is well known in the architecture, city planning, and housing professions, yet the city of Chicago and the CHA have persisted in a haphazard process of planning, demolition, and temporary relocation that has reproduced all these ills.

Mixed-Income Redevelopment, In Practice

Assuming that project implementation follows through on the targets set by project planning, Roosevelt Square's ultimate unit mix will be 37 percent very low-income public housing, 30 percent moderate-income housing, and 33 percent market-rate housing. The percentage of very low-income public housing units is characteristic of the mixed-income redevelopment proposals that the city and the CHA have advanced since the mid-1990s. For example, the Near North Redevelopment Plan, announced in mid-1996, anticipated that 30 percent of the housing in the new neighborhood would be very low-income public housing.[73] Previously, CHA chair Vincent Lane had proposed mixed-income developments of a rather different character. Notably, the Lake Parc Place redevelopment on the mid-South Side was a 100 percent public housing initiative, with a fifty-fifty split between very low-income tenants and "working poor" residents.[74]

It was at the point in the mid-1990s when the city of Chicago and CHA discovered substantial interest among private developers in collaborating on public housing redevelopment plans that the income spectrum for mixed-income housing was stretched (to extend from the very poor to the decidedly prosperous) and the approximately one-third very low-income public housing ceiling emerged. The precise source of this numerical threshold is unclear, though there is a fairly extensive real estate and sociological literature on neighborhood racial "tipping points," and in this literature the one-third proportion often figures as the maximum minority population percentage at which a local racial equilibrium can be achieved.[75] However, in summarizing research on tipping points and, in particular, the role that white residents' racial prejudice plays in neighborhood transition, sociologist John Yinger notes, "for the most prejudiced neighborhoods, tipping will occur as soon as the first black moves in, but in the least prejudiced neighborhoods integration might be sustained at a composition of 50 percent black or more."[76] More generally, Yinger argues that a variety of factors—many having to do with the practices of local institutions—influence neighborhood racial stability or instability:

> In some cases, the actions of real estate brokers, lenders, and government officials magnify the forces that cause racial or ethnic transition. In other cases, community groups, real estate brokers, and public agencies have acted together to break the vicious cycle and maintain integration. The underlying process that promotes racial or ethnic transition is strong, but . . . institutional factors can boost the speed with which this transition takes place or, under some circumstances, prevent it from happening at all.[77]

There is, in fact, no numerical formula that will guarantee either racial balance or a high degree of supportive neighborly interaction in either existing communities or new developments such as Roosevelt Square. Much depends on individual residents, whether or not an inclusive pattern of neighboring and neighborhood organizations emerges, and the support of institutional agents such as realtors and city government. It is quite unlikely that the putative benefits of mixed-income development will be realized in developments such as Orchard Park, a mixed-income community adjoining

Cabrini-Green in which a fence has been erected to separate the market-rate and public housing sections.[78] For mixed-income development to work—according to its own presuppositions—neither fencing nor a particular proportioning of units will be the causal element. Rather, as John Yinger suggests, it will be a complex array of interpersonal and organizational practices.

Mixed-income communities have been advocated as a universal solution to the problem of concentrated poverty. Given that, historically, public housing was often constructed in inner-city areas that had been previously abandoned by the middle class, the notion of economically integrating concentrated poverty neighborhoods would appear to have merit. However, this is a "one size fits all" approach that overlooks the fact that many public housing developments today are located in areas that are decreasingly isolated and economically disadvantaged. In fact, many public housing developments, like ABLA, are located in neighborhoods where increasing numbers of middle- and upper-income people wish to live: situated close to central business districts, with convenient access to public transportation and expressways, and adjacent to employers and other institutions. Today, ABLA's location is not in the least "isolated," and its residents would benefit from remaining in their community.

Thanks to the local gentrification that occurred during the 1990s, the real estate market in the area immediately surrounding the ABLA development is actually quite high-priced compared to the rest of Chicago. In 2000, according to the U.S. census, 38 percent of the owner-occupied housing in the one square mile surrounding and including ABLA was worth more than $300,000. Only 9 percent of the owner-occupied housing in the city of Chicago was valued at this level.[79] New luxury residential projects that are currently under construction adjacent to ABLA will only increase local housing values and the number of upper-middle- and upper-income households in the area. Considering the volume of high-priced luxury housing that is already being produced by private developers, it would appear that the CHA—by committing one-third of the Roosevelt Square development to market-rate housing—has lost sight of its mission to provide shelter for those who are not served by the private housing market. CHA residents and affordable housing advocates are voicing a valid concern when they propose that the promotion of mixed-income developments in gentrifying areas is little more than a justification for the removal of poor families from neighborhoods in which the value of local property is shooting skyward. In Chicago, this is occurring not just at ABLA, but also is under way at Cabrini-Green and the Henry Horner Homes. In several other public housing developments, such as Jazz on the Boulevard on Chicago's South Side, this type of "transformation" is likely to follow.

Figure 7.1   **ABLA Neighborhood Area**

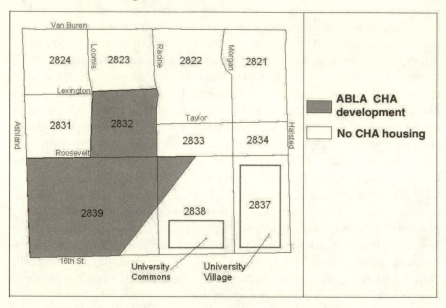

The Likely Neighborhood Impacts of Roosevelt Square

LR Development's program of construction and its siting targets (that is, phase-by-phase distribution of public, affordable, and market-rate units) are clear enough for us to anticipate how this development, as well as ongoing private residential projects in the vicinity, will affect the racial and income profile of the ABLA area. For this purpose, we have examined the CHA's construction phasing plans and U.S. census figures for the eleven-tract, one square mile–area surrounding the ABLA development.

The planning area of analysis that we have designated as the "ABLA neighborhood area" (see Figure 7.1) is approximately one square mile and includes all the ABLA development components. The boundaries of this territory correspond to expressways, major arterial roads with nonresidential land uses on either side, and railroad tracks. These are natural physical demarcations that with proper planning could create an identifiable neighborhood.[80] By closely examining this area, we will demonstrate that it is unnecessary to remove ABLA families, if—as the CHA asserts—the aim of the Roosevelt Square project is to create an economically diverse neighborhood. Indeed, as of 2000, the one square mile–area portrayed in our map was already economically diverse. And when all the current housing that is under construction in these census tracts is completed, we conservatively estimate that the ABLA area will contain a majority of households earning over $100,000 per year. The vast majority of the market-

Table 7.2

Race and Ethnic Composition in ABLA Area, 1990 and 2000

	1990		2000		Change 1990–2000	
	Number of people	Percent of population	Number of people	Percent of population	Number of people	Percent of population
ABLA area total	18,808		14,513		−4,295	−22.8
White non-Latino	4,697	25.0	4,189	28.9	−508	−10.8
Black non-Latino	11,601	61.7	7,131	49.1	−4,470	−38.5
Asian non-Latino	1,193	6.3	1,868	12.9	675	56.6
Latino all races	1,274	6.8	994	6.8	−280	−22.0
Other	43	0.2	331	2.3		
North of Roosevelt	10,947		9,338		−1,609	−14.7
White non-Latino	4,671	42.7	4,157	44.5	−514	−11.0
Black non-Latino	3,839	35.1	2,111	22.6	−1,728	−45.0
Asian non-Latino	1,193	10.9	1,865	20.0	672	56.3
Latino all races	1,204	11.0	931	10.0	−273	−22.7
Other	40	0.4	274	2.9		
South of Roosevelt	7,861		5,175		−2,686	−34.2
White non-Latino	26	0.3	32	0.6	6	23.1
Black non-Latino	7,762	98.7	5,020	97.0	−2,742	−35.3
Asian non-Latino	0	0.0	3	0.1	3	na
Latino all races	70	0.9	63	1.2	−7	−10.0
Other	3	0.0	57	1.1		
City of Chicago						
White non-Latino		37.9		31.3		
Black non-Latino		38.6		36.4		
Asian non-Latino		3.5		4.3		
Latino all races		19.6		26.0		
Other		0.4		2.0		

Sources: 1990 U.S. Census Table P010, STF1; 2000 U.S. Census Table P4, SF1.

rate housing currently under construction in these census tracts is affordable only to households whose annual earnings exceed $80,000.

In Table 7.2 we present the racial and ethnic breakdown for the ABLA area in 1990 and 2000. The area south of Roosevelt Road (specifically, tracts 2838 and 2839) remained an African-American enclave during the 1990s even as the population north of Roosevelt Road diversified, notably via an increase in Asian residents.

Indicative of the gentrification occurring in the area north of Roosevelt Road, the census data reveal that white (non-Latino) and Asian households moved into the area north of Roosevelt at an increasing rate during the 1990s. Nearly as many or more white households moved into the four north-of-Roosevelt census tracts (2822, 2823, 2824, 2831) tracts in the fifteen-month period from January 1999 to March 2000 than had moved into these tracts in

Table 7.3

ABLA Area Families and Population Below Poverty Level, 1989 and 1999

	North of Roosevelt	South of Roosevelt	ABLA area level	Chicago
2000	total	total	total	total
Total families (all income levels)	1,874	1,193	3,067	
Percent below poverty level				
(all family types)	17.7	52.8	31.4	16.6
Total population	9,609	5,292	14,901	
Percent below poverty level	30.6	60.5	41.2	19.6
1990				
Total families (all income levels)	689	1,361	2,050	
Percent below poverty level				
(all family types)	30.0	79.0	51.0	18.3
Total population	10,076	6,051	16,127	
Percent below poverty	36.3	79.1	54.7	21.6

Sources: 1990 U.S. Census Table P117, P123 STF3; 2000 U.S. Census Table P87, P90 SF3.

the entire four-year period 1995–1998. At the same time, relatively few African-American and Latino households moved into the area north of Roosevelt. The census also shows that the only householders who moved into the area south of Roosevelt Road were black, and these households only moved into the ABLA public housing tracts 2838 and 2839.

Also noteworthy is the replacement of family households by nonfamily households in the area north of Roosevelt Road during the 1990s. Typically, families with children are the households that move out of gentrifying areas even as nonfamily households, such as singles or unmarried adults, replace them. For this reason, gentrification often coincides with an area's loss of population—smaller households tending to replace larger ones. Between 1990 and 2000, the loss of family households exceeded the total decline in households by 136 (371 compared to 235). In effect, this means that at least 136 nonfamily households replaced family households. In combination with the recent spurt in white households settling in this area, we are observing two clear signs of gentrification. And in contrast, the south-of-Roosevelt Road census tracts experienced a decline both in family households (647) and nonfamily households (109).

The Local Income Profile: Poverty and Affluence

In Table 7.3 we present census-derived, incidence-of-poverty figures for the north-of-Roosevelt (census tracts 2821–2824 and 2831–2834) and south-of-

Table 7.4

Family Income Percent Distribution in 1999: ABLA Neighborhood Area and Chicago (percent of total families)

Family income in 1999	North of Roosevelt	South of Roosevelt	ABLA area	Chicago city
Less than $10,000	14.2	33.2	16.2	10.7
$10,000 to $19,999	10.2	27.4	14.6	11.6
$20,000 to $49,999	22.1	32.2	25.1	34.8
$50,000 to $74,999	17.9	4.5	15.2	19.3
$75,000 to $99,999	10.9	1.1	8.8	10.4
$100,000 or more	24.7	1.6	20.0	13.2
Total	100.0	100.0	100.0	100.0

Source: 2000 U.S. Census Table P76, SF3.

Roosevelt areas (census tracts 2837–2839). Of these tracts, tracts 2834 and 2837 had very limited populations in both 1990 and 2000. However, since 2000, two large private developments—which will hold nearly 1,800 units of housing—have been under way in tract 2837 (and to the west in tract 2838). Table 7.3 reveals quite clearly that the concentration of residential poverty, both in the 1990 and 2000 census, was substantially greater south of Roosevelt Road.

Nevertheless, by 2000 the eleven-tract ABLA area was becoming an economically diverse neighborhood, though also a neighborhood of sharp economic disparities. There were both a higher rate of poverty than the city as a whole and a higher rate of affluence, with 20 percent of the families in the area earning $100,000 or more in 1999. For the city as a whole, only 13 percent of the families reported earnings this high. The total income distribution of the ABLA area compared to the city is presented in Table 7.4.

The preceding demographic analysis demonstrates that—contrary to the CHA's assertions that it must undertake special measures to attract affluent residents to its mixed-income developments—the ABLA area has for some time been attracting affluent residents. In 2000, the one square mile ABLA neighborhood area was already wealthier than Chicago as a whole, despite also having a higher poverty rate. Since the census was recorded, nearly 2,000 new market-rate housing units have been built or are under construction in this area, and these units are being marketed, to a great extent, to very prosperous home-purchasers. Given the sale prices of units in these new developments, as well as the absence of rental housing within them, we conservatively predict that the affluence of the ABLA neighborhood will only increase in the coming years.

Table 7.5

Number, Type, and Location of Units in ABLA Redevelopment Plan

Type of unit	Number north of Roosevelt	Number south of Roosevelt	Total
Brooks Homes (existing public housing)	NA	329	329
CHA rental (new public housing)	213	542	755
Subtotal: public housing	213	871	1,084
Loomis Courts (existing, affordable)	NA	126	126
Rental—affordable (new)	86	249	335
For sale CHA (new)	14	36	50
For sale—affordable (new)	90	245	335
Subtotal: affordable housing	190	656	846
For sale market rate (new)	276	690	966
Total	679	2,217	2,896

Source: Chicago Housing Authority.

Roosevelt Square and the New ABLA Neighborhood

The LR consortium's Roosevelt Square plan specifies a six-phase development sequence, and in each phase just over 30 percent of the units will be public housing. However, the far larger portion of the Roosevelt Square development will be south of Roosevelt Road, and as a result, over 70 percent of the new public housing units will be built in the section of the ABLA area that has persisted as an African-American, largely low-income enclave (again, specifically tract 2839). However, this assessment of the new development's tendency to sustain the relative isolation of the neighborhood's public housing population understates the situation, given that 329 units of public housing have already been renovated south of Roosevelt Road. Table 7.5 presents the distribution of unit types within the completed Roosevelt Square development. It should be noted that preceding the approval of the LR proposal, the CHA had also committed to rehabilitating the 126 Loomis Courts apartments (south of Roosevelt Road), which will be marketed as for-sale, affordable units.

The effect of the Roosevelt Square redevelopment of the ABLA site, combined with the preceding, small-scale CHA activities at ABLA, will be to sustain the racial and income tilt of the ABLA area's social geography. The largest share of the market-rate construction will be north of Roosevelt Road, where there have been clear signs of gentrification for more than a decade. Most of the affordable and public housing units will be built south of Roosevelt Road.

Yet the reshaping of the ABLA area will be nearly as much a product of the two new developments rising on its eastern blocks as of the Roosevelt Square development. Nearing completion south of Roosevelt Road to the east of the ABLA/Roosevelt Square site (in census tract 2837) is University Village, a 930-unit development.[81] Assuming the currently advertised distribution of units and the projected market prices in University Village, 613 of 930 units, or 66 percent, will be priced at more than $300,000—a price that we conservatively assume is affordable only to families earning more than $100,000 annually. Still under construction, and also to the east of ABLA/ Roosevelt Square (in census tract 2838) is University Commons, a residential development (850 units) whose unit and price composition will also be overwhelmingly market-rate. Our estimate based on existing price data is that only 4 percent of the units will be priced below $250,000 and thus affordable to moderate-income families earning $50,000 to 80,000 per year.

In short, in an area of eleven census tracts in which market-rate residential development has boomed for a number of years, 80 percent of the new public housing to be produced in conjunction with the redevelopment of the ABLA project will be concentrated in two census tracts (2839 and a narrow slice of adjoining 2838). As in the past, local public housing units will be largely segregated, but, with the passage of time, within an increasingly prosperous neighborhood. The plan to replace ABLA with Roosevelt Square is, in fact, a model to create a parcelized neighborhood of haves and have-nots. If, indeed, mixed-income development is thought to be a concept that applies to street-by-street and neighborhood-wide integration of housing types, and thereby residents, the ABLA/Roosevelt Square plan falls far short of achieving the aims that have been so aggressively proclaimed by its sponsors.

Notes

1. Fran Spielman, "D'Angelo Overshadows CHA Deal," *Chicago Sun-Times,* January 15, 2004.

2. City of Chicago, "Holistic Urban Redevelopment: The ABLA Homes Model," n.d.

3. Devereux Bowly Jr., *The Poorhouse: Subsidized Housing in Chicago, 1895–1976* (Carbondale: Southern Illinois University Press, 1978), pp. 19–21, 34–35, 40–42.

4. Bowly, *Poorhouse,* pp. 72–73.

5. Bowly, *Poorhouse,* pp. 90–93, 121.

6. Bowly, *Poorhouse,* p. 91.

7. Chicago Fact Book Consortium, *Local Community Fact Book Chicago Metropolitan Area 1990* (Chicago: Academy Chicago Publishers, 1995), p. 103.

8. Jeannye Thornton, "Italians, Blacks, and Latins Join Together in Demands," *Chicago Tribune,* June 8, 1972.

9. George Rosen, *Decision-Making Chicago-Style: The Genesis of a University of Illinois Campus* (Urbana: University of Illinois Press, 1980), p. 139.

10. Anthony Sorrentino, *Organizing Against Crime: Redeveloping the Neighborhood* (New York: Human Sciences Press, 1977), p. 225.

11. Clarence Page, "Near West Side Revamp Sparks Hope, Skepticism," *Chicago Tribune,* March 30, 1972.

12. Chicago Fact Book Consortium, *Local Community Fact Book Chicago Metropolitan Area* (Chicago: Chicago Review Press, 1984), p. 76.

13. Chicago Fact Book Consortium, *Local Community Fact Book 1990,* p. 104; Northeastern Illinois Planning Commission, "Profiles of General Population Characteristics, 2000 Census," May 2001; City of Chicago, "Graphic Profiles of the City and the Community Areas, Chicago 2000," n.d.

14. Blair Kamin, "The Big Fix," *Chicago Tribune Magazine,* August 4, 1996; Linda Lutton, "Will Development Bury the Barrio?" *Chicago Reader*, April 24, 1998.

15. Chicago Housing Authority, "ABLA 1997 HOPE VI Revitalization Application," July 17, 1997, p. 2.

16. Jack Mabley, "Little Italy Refuses to Die," *Chicago Today,* April 12, 1971.

17. "Tenants Seek Takeover," *Chicago Defender,* March 27, 1973; Robert McClory, "COUP Fights for Addams Project," *Chicago Defender,* September 17, 1974.

18. Chicago Central Area Committee, "Chicago 21: A Plan for the Central Area Communities," September 1973; Joel Rast, *Remaking Chicago: The Political Origins of Urban Industrial Change* (DeKalb: Northern Illinois University Press, 1999), p. 32.

19. Stanley Ziemba, "Fear CHA Will Sell Their Home," *Chicago Tribune,* December 26, 1974.

20. "Addams Tenants Win Victories," *Chicago Defender,* October 28, 1976.

21. Jorge Casuso, "Long, Cold Wait Enhances the Beauty of a New Boiler," *Chicago Tribune,* November 30, 1989.

22. Scott Burnham, "4 CHA Residents Shot by Angered Gunman," *Chicago Defender,* March 2, 1992; Lee Bey, "48 Arrested, 9 Handguns Seized in ABLA Sweep," *Chicago Sun-Times,* December 23, 1992.

23. Michelle L. Landis, "UIC Seeks Public Housing," *Chicago Flame,* October 15, 1991.

24. City of Chicago, "Holistic Urban Redevelopment, p. 13.

25. Chicago Housing Authority, "1998 HOPE VI Application—ABLA Homes," July 26, 1998, p. 22.

26. Cathleen Falsani, "CHA Residents Given 6 Days to Pack Up and Move," *Chicago Tribune,* October 15, 1996.

27. Cam Simpson, "Top CHA High-Rise Written Up," *Chicago Tribune,* April 23, 2001.

28. Gail Mansfield, "Addams, Brooks Developments Behind Schedule as CHA Plans to Issue New RFP for All of ABLA," *Chicago Near West/South Gazette,* May 3, 2002.

29. Chicago Housing Authority, "ABLA 1997 HOPE VI," pp. 53, 55.

30. City of Chicago, Department of Housing, "Request for Proposals: Development Management Services for the Mixed-Income Redevelopment of ABLA Homes," n.d., p. 1.

31. City of Chicago, "Holistic Urban Redevelopment," p. 3; City of Chicago, Department of Housing, "Request for Proposals," pp. 2–3.

32. Telesis Corporation, "ABLA HOPE VI Redevelopment: Amended and Restated Revitalization Plan," June 30, 2001, p. 10.

33. Kate Grossman, "Development Team Picked for Mixed-Income Housing," *Chicago Sun-Times,* December 18, 2002.

34. Thomas O. Weeks and Stephen M. Porras, letter to Dan Rockafield (Habitat Corporation), August 30, 2002; "ABLA Phasing Unit Count and Mix Proposed Distribution," October 1, 2003.

35. Edward G. Goetz, *Clearing the Way: Deconcentrating the Poor in Urban America* (Washington, DC: Urban Institute Press, 2003).

36. William Julius Wilson, *The Truly Disadvantaged: The Inner City, The Underclass, and Public Policy* (Chicago: University of Chicago Press, 1987); *When Work Disappears: The World of the New Urban Poor* (New York: Knopf, 1996). See also Christopher Jencks, *Rethinking Social Policy: Race, Poverty, and the Underclass* (Cambridge, MA: Harvard University Press, 1992) and Christopher Jencks and Paul E. Peterson, eds., *The Urban Underclass* (Washington, DC: Brookings Institution, 1991).

37. "The Transformation of Chicago's Public Housing: Challenges and Opportunities," Speech to the Chicago Futures Forum, February 26, 1999. This quotation appears in Alastair Smith, "Mixed-Income Housing Developments: Promise and Reality," Cambridge, MA: Joint Center for Housing Studies of Harvard University, Neighborhood Reinvestment Corporation, October 2002.

38. Jeff Crump, "Deconcentration by Demolition: Public Housing, Poverty, and Urban Policy," *Environmental and Planning D: Society and Space* 20 (2002): 581.

39. Jeff Crump, "Deconcentration by Demolition." See also Susan J. Popkin, Bruce Katz, Mary K. Cunningham, Karen D. Brown, Jeremy Gustafson, and Margery A. Turner, "A Decade of HOPE VI: Research Findings and Policy Challenges," Washington, DC: Urban Institute and Brookings Institution, May 2004.

40. Section 24 of the United States Housing Act of 1937 as amended by Section 535 of the Quality Housing and Work Responsibility Act of 1998 (P.L. 105–276), quoted in Popkin et al., "A Decade of HOPE VI," p. 2.

41. Popkin et al., "A Decade of HOPE VI."

42. Barry Pearce, "Cabrini Plans Spark Near North Contest," *Apartments and Homes* (Chicago), May 6, 1994.

43. Douglas S. Massey and Nancy A. Denton, "Trends in the Residential Segregation of Blacks, Hispanics, and Asians," *American Sociological Review* 52, no. 6 (1987): 802–805; Nancy A. Denton and Douglas S. Massey, "Residential Segregation of Blacks, Hispanics, and Asians for Socio-Economic Status and Generation," *Social Science Quarterly* 69, no. 4 (1988): 797–817; Norman Fainstein, "Race, Class, and Segregation: Discourses About African-Americans," *International Journal of Urban and Regional Research* 17, no. 3 (1993): 384–403. For an analysis challenging "concentration effects" as the source of many inner-city social problems, see David Reingold, Gregg G. Van Ryzin, and Michelle Ronda, "Does Urban Public Housing Diminish the Social Capital and Labor Force Activity of Its Tenants?" *Journal of Policy Analysis and Management* 20, no. 3 (2001): 485–504.

44. Metropolitan Planning Council, "Changing the Paradigm: A Call for New Approaches to Public Housing in the Chicago Metropolitan Area," October 1996, p. 15.

45. James E. Rosenbaum, Linda K. Stroh, and Cathy A. Flynn, "Lake Park Place: A Study of Mixed-Income Housing," *Housing Policy Debate* 9, no. 4 (1998), 734–735.

46. Crump, "Deconcentration by Demolition."

47. During a visit to the redeveloped, mixed-income Orchard Gardens (formerly Orchard Park) development in Boston in March 2002, a police officer observed, "the drug dealers had not been converted into good citizens, but had moved onto a different part of the neighborhood." See Smith, "Mixed-Income Housing Developments," p. 22.

48. Smith, "Mixed-Income Housing Developments." For other research on HOPE VI mixed-income strategy, see Susan Clampet-Lundquist, "HOPE VI Relocation: Moving to New Neighborhoods and Building New Ties," *Housing Policy Debate* 15, no. 2 (2004): 415–447; Popkin et al., "A Decade of HOPE VI"; Susan J. Popkin, Diane K. Levy, Laura E. Harris, Jennifer Comey, Mary K. Cunningham, and Larry F. Burton, "The HOPE VI Program: What About the Residents?" *Housing Policy Debate* 15, no. 2 (2004): 385–414; and Jerry J. Salama, "The Redevelopment of Distressed Public Housing: Early Results from HOPE VI Projects in Atlanta, Chicago, and San Antonio," *Housing Policy Debate* 10, no. 1 (1999): 95–142.

49. Smith, "Mixed-Income Housing Developments," p. 21.

50. *Concerned Residents of ABLA* ("CRA"), *Carolyn Nance, Wandra Stimage, LaTonya Willett, and Lorree Brown, et al., Intevenor-Plaintiffs v. Chicago Housing Authority,* Intervenor-Defendants, in the United States District Court for the Northern District of Illinois Eastern Division, No. 66C1459, filed May 14, 2004. First Amended Intervenors' Complaint, Statement by Edward G. Goetz.

51. Larry Keating, "Redeveloping Public Housing," *Journal of the American Planning Association* 66, no. 4 (2000): 384–398; Christopher Swope, "Rehab Refugee," *Governing,* May 2001, p. 40.

52. Andres Duany, Elizabeth Plater-Zyberk, and Jeff Speck, *Suburban Nation* (New York: North Point Press, 2000); Michael Pollan, "Town-Building Is No Mickey Mouse Proposition," *New York Times Magazine,* December 14, 1997; Douglas Frantz and Catherine Collins, *Celebration, U.S.A.* (New York: Henry Holt, 1999); Andrew Ross, *The Celebration Chronicles* (New York: Ballantine Books, 1999). In reference to new urbanism and public housing, see Blair Kamin, "Can Public Housing Be Reinvented?" *Architectural Record,* February 1999, pp. 84–89.

53. Jane Jacobs, *The Death and Life of Great American Cities* (New York: Vintage Books, 1961).

54. LR Development Company LLC, "Request for Proposals for Master Developer for the Mixed Income Redevelopment of ABLA Homes," August 30, 2002, p. C. 1–3; Jacobs, *Death and Life,* p. 212.

55. Goetz, *Clearing the Way,* pp. 117–125.

56. Goetz, *Clearing the Way,* p. 118.

57. Constance Perin, *Everything in Its Place: Social Order and Land Use in America* (Princeton, NJ: Princeton University Press, 1977), p. 42.

58. Goetz, *Clearing the Way,* p. 123.

59. Chicago Housing Authority, "Plan for Transformation," January 6, 2000, p. 2.

60. Metropolitan Planning Council, "For Rent: Housing Options in the Chicago Region," Prepared for MPC by the University of Illinois at Chicago, November 1999, p. 36.

61. Paul B. Fischer, "Section 8 and the Public Housing Revolution: Where Will the Families Go?" Chicago: Woods Fund, September 4, 2001; Susan J. Popkin and Mary K. Cunningham, "CHA Relocation Counseling Assessment," Washington, DC: Urban Institute, 2002; "Robert Taylor Homes Relocation Study," A Research Report from the Center for Urban Research and Policy, Columbia University, September 2002, p. 6.

62. Paul B. Fischer, "Where Are the Public Housing Families Going? An Update," September 9, 2004.

63. Thomas P. Sullivan, "Independent Monitor's Report No. 5 to the Chicago Housing Authority and the Central Advisory Committee," Chicago, January 8, 2003.

64. City of Chicago, "The Chicago Central Area Plan: Preparing the Central City for the 21st Century," Draft Final Report to the Chicago Plan Commission, May 2003. See also Chapter 11 of this volume.

65. Flynn McRoberts, "Home Is Where the Problem Is," *Chicago Tribune,* October 25, 1998.

66. McRoberts, "Home Is Where the Problem Is."

67. *Concerned Residents of ABLA v. Chicago Housing Authority,* First Amended Intervenors' Complaint.

68. In reference to the University Village Association's past opposition to affordable housing on the Near West Side, see Peggy Constantine, "Academy Square Is Stalled, But the Battle Is Still Running," *Chicago Sun-Times,* April 15, 1983; Gail Mansfield, "UVA Position Paper Promotes Dialogue on ABLA Revitalization," *Chicago Near West/South Gazette,* January 5, 2001.

69. Gary Washburn, "ABLA Vote is Delayed, Deplored," *Chicago Tribune,* December 18, 2003.

70. Blair Kamin and John Kass, "Daley's Cabrini Dream," *Chicago Tribune,* June 28, 1996.

71. Chester Hartman, "The Housing of Relocated Families," in *Urban Renewal: The Record and the Controversy,* ed. James Q. Wilson, pp. 293–335 (Cambridge, MA: M.I.T. Press, 1966); Robert Fogelson, *Downtown: Its Rise and Fall, 1880–1950* (New Haven, CT: Yale University Press, 2001), p. 378.

72. Robert Caro, *The Power Broker: Robert Moses and the Fall of New York* (New York: Vintage Books, 1975), pp. 961–983; Larry Bennett, *Neighborhood Politics: Chicago and Sheffield* (New York: Garland, 1997), pp. 129–142.

73. Office of the Mayor, "Mayor Daley Announces Near North Redevelopment Plan," news release, June 27, 1996.

74. Michael H. Schill, "Chicago's Mixed-Income New Communities Strategy: The Future Face of Public Housing," in *Affordable Housing and Urban Redevelopment in the United States,* ed. Willem van Vliet, pp. 135–157 (Thousand Oaks, CA: Sage, 1997). The mix of one-third market-rate units, one-third affordable units, and one-third public housing units is one of a variety of market-rate/affordable/public housing compositions that has been used at mixed-income developments around the United States, with the public housing proportion running as high as 80 percent. See Smith, "Mixed Income Housing Developments."

75. Richard P. Taub, D. Garth Taylor, and Jan D. Duncan, *Paths of Neighborhood Change* (Chicago: University of Chicago Press, 1984), p. 142.

76. John Yinger, *Closed Doors, Opportunities Lost: The Continuing Costs of Housing Discrimination* (New York: Russell Sage Foundation, 1995), pp. 119–120.

77. Yinger, *Closed Doors,* p. 122.

78. Ray Quintalla, "New Neighbors Draw the Line at Cabrini," *Chicago Tribune,* July 31, 2003.

79. 2000 U.S. Census Table H74, "Value for Specified Owner Occupied Housing Units," SF3 (Sample Data), *American Factfinder.*

80. A recent article in the *Chicago Tribune*'s real estate section uses these same boundaries in its accompanying map and discusses "the creation of a new neighborhood that will swell the area's population." See John Handley, "To Market We Go," *Chicago Tribune,* February 22, 2004.

81. John Handley, "New Village on Campus: A College Town Rises from the Dust of Maxwell Street," *Chicago Tribune,* April 28, 2002.

8

Relocated Public Housing Residents Have Little Hope of Returning

Work Requirements for Mixed-Income Public Housing Developments

William P. Wilen and Rajesh D. Nayak

Public housing residents and advocates have long worried that redevelopment projects funded by the federal HOPE VI program fail to provide sufficient replacement units for very low-income families displaced in the process.[1] Indeed, some public housing advocates have even filed litigation focused on the loss of affordable housing units.[2] But displaced families now face another looming obstacle to their return to public housing: public housing authorities around the country are adopting stringent tenant screening criteria that promise to prevent many displaced families from returning to the few public housing units that are rebuilt in their historic communities.[3]

As we write this chapter, the Chicago Housing Authority (CHA) is entering the sixth year of its ten-year redevelopment plan, the Plan for Transformation, funded in part by the HOPE VI program. The plan calls for the CHA to demolish its entire inventory of high-rise public housing while rebuilding or rehabilitating 25 thousand very low-income housing units over a ten-year period.[4] Of these 25,000 units, only 6,205 public housing units will be rebuilt on the sites of former public housing developments, as part of redeveloped mixed-income communities.[5] But for families who seek to return to these few units, the CHA has adopted an especially stringent, arbitrary, and in part impermissible set of tenant screening criteria, including minimum work requirements.[6] Judging by the lessons of welfare reform, many displaced families have little hope returning to the limited number of units being rebuilt. In contrast, at one CHA development in particular—the Henry

Horner Homes—many families have remained and have already moved into their new apartments thanks to the reasonable tenant screening process in place there, in large part due to the resident's strong participation in the Horner redevelopment process.

In this chapter, we first provide context for the work requirements by recounting the progress of CHA's Plan for Transformation thus far.[7] Next, we explore the particularly troubling work requirements adopted by CHA generally. We also propose potential litigation strategies to challenge these criteria in hopes of allowing more displaced residents to benefit from HOPE VI by returning to their historic communities. Finally, we describe an alternative tenant screening process, currently in place at the Henry Horner Homes.

Background

The negative consequences of the CHA's tenant screening criteria are especially troubling in the context of the overall Plan for Transformation, which originally promised significant protection for families displaced by its massive demolition and relocation programs. This section recounts the history of the Plan for Transformation and its status now, just after its halfway point.

History of the Plan for Transformation

The history of the Plan for Transformation demonstrates that it is dependent on certain important resident protections. While the CHA did not officially implement the Plan for Transformation until 2000, the plan's genesis dates back to 1996, during which time the U.S. Department of Housing and Urban Development (HUD) had taken control of the CHA from the city of Chicago.[8] In that year, Congress passed the Omnibus Consolidated Rescissions and Appropriations Act of 1996 (OCRA), Section 202 of which required public housing authorities to conduct a "viability assessment" of certain distressed public housing developments.[9] Under an interim rule published by HUD, public housing authorities had to conduct a "cost test" for developments with characteristics specified in Section 202. For these developments, if the revitalization costs were more than the cost of providing tenants therein a Section 8 voucher, the housing authority had to "voucher out" the development —that is, to provide tenants Section 8 tenant-based or project-based assistance or relocate them to other public housing units. Once the building was vacated, it would be demolished and thus removed from the public housing inventory. In 1998, the CHA submitted its proposal to HUD, finding that seven developments or subdevelopments were subject to the vouchering out requirement and that ten developments or subdevelopments were not.[10]

CHA proposed demolishing 11,176 units of the 18,999 affected units and providing between 10,594 and 10,644 total replacement units.[11]

In May 1999, HUD and CHA entered into a memorandum of understanding that required CHA to submit a plan for the return of control of CHA to the city of Chicago. To this end, CHA submitted its Plan for Transformation to HUD in January 2000. Under the plan, almost 22,000 units were to be demolished, including all of CHA's high-rises, and CHA was to construct or rehabilitate 25,000 units over a ten-year period to accommodate the approximately 25,000 families in CHA occupancy as of October 1, 1999.[12] In February 2000, HUD approved CHA's Plan for Transformation.

In order to facilitate the Plan for Transformation, HUD approved the CHA's application to be a participant in the Moving to Work Demonstration Project in 2000.[13] Because of this designation, HUD waived numerous restrictions on the CHA's funding and numerous regulatory requirements, all of which gave the CHA more flexibility to implement the Plan for Transformation.[14] HUD also agreed to provide CHA with approximately $1.56 billion over ten years (2000–2009), which purportedly was enough money to enable CHA to demolish and replace or to rehabilitate 25,000 public housing units.

As a condition of the Moving to Work Agreement, though, HUD required CHA to adopt a "legally enforceable lease amendment containing other protections regarding tenant rights."[15] Pursuant to this requirement, CHA and the tenants' elected Central Advisory Council negotiated a relocation rights contract providing that all families who were CHA residents as of October 1, 1999, had a conditional right to return to public housing.[16]

Status of the Plan for Transformation

So far, the Plan for Transformation has presented two particularly troubling trends. First, the CHA's demolition has vastly outpaced its rebuilding efforts, with the rebuilding schedule regularly delayed. Second, families displaced into the private market with Housing Choice vouchers have been routinely resegregated into very low-income, predominantly African-American communities.

The pace of demolition and rebuilding has been especially troubling. As noted, the ultimate goal of the Plan for Transformation is to provide CHA tenants with 25,000 new or rehabbed units between 2000 to 2009, even though this figure is substantially below the low-income housing need.[17] There were about 39,000 units when the plan began; CHA has demolished or will demolish almost 22,000 of these units, including all of CHA's high-rises and many of its mid-rises and low-rises, which altogether constituted approximately 56 percent of CHA's total housing stock in 1995. Approximately 67 percent of the 25,000 units (16,772) will be rehabilitated for seniors, families and scattered-site residents. Only about 25 percent of the units (6,219) are to be newly constructed or rehabilitated public housing units built in large, mixed-income communities.[18] Another 8 percent of the units (2,009) will be either rehabbed or replaced by new construction.

As of September 2005, demolition has far outpaced new construction and rehabilitation. CHA has demolished 18,997 units, which is 88 percent of the total of 21,647 units to be demolished under the Plan for Transformation. Most of this demolition occurred in developments slated to be mixed-income communities: Cabrini-Green, Horner, Rockwell Gardens, ABLA, Stateway Gardens, Robert Taylor Homes, Madden-Wells, and Washington Park.

In contrast, through September 2005, CHA constructed or rehabilitated only 1,937 units in mixed-income communities, which is only 31 percent of the 6,219 units scheduled.[19] However, 1,171 of these 1,937 new units (60 percent) were required to be constructed or rehabilitated under the Horner (640) and Cabrini (332) consent decrees and the memorandum of agreement in the Lakefront case (199), regardless of the Plan for Transformation. So actually, CHA has constructed or rehabilitated only 766 public housing units in mixed-income communities in six years under the Plan for Transformation as of September 2005. In addition, the construction of new mixed-income units is really backloaded, with 51 percent of the total or 3,165 units slated for completion in 2008 and 2009, the last two years of the plan.

Equally troubling, because of the massive demolition, many families have been resegregated with Housing Choice vouchers into very low-income, predominantly African-American neighborhoods. Many residents were forced to temporarily relocate into the private market with Housing Choice vouchers (formerly Section 8) or to other public housing units in areas not slated for mixed-income development. Researchers and CHA data show that between 1995 and 2005, approximately 4,851 families were relocated from CHA housing with vouchers.[20]

Paul Fischer of Lake Forest College noted in a January 2003 study that most families relocated from CHA housing are resegregated into other very low-income, majority African-American neighborhoods where housing conditions are not appreciably better than those they left. Fischer found that 82.4 percent of the families that the CHA moved with Housing Choice vouchers between 1995 and August 2002 were relocated to high-poverty areas that were between 90 percent and 100 percent African-American.[21]

In February 2004, Sudhir Venkatesh of Columbia University and others (including CHA resident activist Beauty Turner and We the People Media) completed a report titled "Chicago Public Housing Transformation: A Research Report." This analysis noted, "From Jan.–May 2003, the CHA responded not only to the critical feedback from advocates and researchers, but also ongoing litigation by reorganizing relocation and social service delivery to families."[22] Venkatesh described changes including integrating the delivery of social services with the relocation of families, providing contractual incentives to relocation counseling agencies to locate families outside poor African-American areas, giving families greater exposure to "opportunity areas," reorganizing the certification process to help families become lease compliant, and restructuring the service delivery apparatus of the Chicago Department of Human Services. Unfortunately, the preliminary results were not encouraging: in 2003, 97 percent of all CHA families moved into "non-opportunity areas" that did not meet either the "low-poverty" (under 24 percent) or racial integration (under 30 percent African-American) requirements set out in the relocation rights contract. Compounding the problem, 62 percent of the families moved after August 1, giving them at most a month to prepare for the school year—though 50 percent moved after the school year began. Venkatesh wrote that, "based on these findings, we conclude that in the aggregate, the 2003 relocation did not yield a marked improvement over past years."[23]

Also in February 2004, CHA's independent monitor, Thomas P. Sullivan, issued his report discussing relocation in 2003. Although the report documented several improvements made by CHA during 2003, there were still very serious problems relating to mobility. According to Sullivan, CHA's laudable contractual efforts to induce Plan for Transformation Phase III residents to move to opportunity areas were not successful. The data for Phase III-2003 show that 97 percent of residents with Housing Choice vouchers moved to highly segregated, high-poverty areas of Chicago; only 3 percent moved to opportunity areas. Further, Sullivan found a direct correlation between the area's poverty rate and the poor quality of the units to which residents moved. If poverty is greater than 24 percent, 71.4 percent of the units will fail Housing Quality Standards inspections.[24] Considering the difficult path that residents face in the private market, returning to the public housing rebuilt in mixed-income developments might provide them with their best chance at living in a truly integrated community.

Work Requirements Serve as a Barrier to Return

Although displaced families have a contractual right to return to public housing under the relocation rights contract, the contract stipulates that families applying for units in the mixed-income developments must meet certain property-specific tenant screening criteria.[25] CHA families protected by the relocation rights contract may be conditionally admitted to public housing for a minimum of one year if they are considered to be "working to meet" the criteria, which is defined as being engaged in activities through which they will meet the tenant screening criteria within one year of occupancy.[26] CHA cites its Moving to Work status as the authority for implementing many of these tenant screening criteria, including stringent work requirements.[27] But many families will probably find work requirements especially difficult to meet in such a short period of time and thus may not be allowed to return to the public housing units rebuilt in mixed-income developments.[28]

The Work Requirements

All families who apply to live in rental units in the CHA's mixed-income public housing are subject to two sets of tenant screening criteria: the authority-wide Minimum Tenant Selection Plan (MTSP) and local tenant selection plans adopted at each development.[29] The CHA unilaterally designed and adopted the MTSP to apply to all CHA mixed-income developments.[30] Pursuant to the relocation rights contract, each new development has adopted or will adopt an additional set of property-specific tenant screening criteria, each known as a local tenant selection plan, developed by the working group engaged in the planning process at each property.[31]

Perhaps most troubling, the CHA has instituted remarkably inflexible minimum employment requirements in both the MTSP and the local tenant selection plans governing many of its mixed-income communities.[32] The authority-wide MTSP and many site-specific tenant selection plans share a common basic employment requirement keyed to the number of hours worked: nonexempt heads of household (primary leaseholders) must work a minimum of thirty hours per week (hereinafter classified as an hours-based work requirement).[33] In the MTSP and these hours-based tenant selection plans, all other nonexempt family members between the ages of eighteen and sixty-one must also work thirty hours each week or be engaged for that time in any combination of enumerated alternative activities: enrollment and regular attendance in an economic self-sufficiency program; verified job search and/or employment counseling; basic skills training; or enrollment and consistent attendance in a regular program of education, including General Educational Development classes, secondary or postsecondary education, or English proficiency and literacy classes.[34]

The MTSP and all hours-based tenant selection plans provide some exceptions. If a family has two adults, the MTSP and some—but not all—site-specific tenant selection plans exempt one of them from this hours-based work requirement to facilitate the care of "young children," so long as the other is working.[35] All of the hours-based plans exempt the following individuals from the work requirements: those over the age of sixty-two, those with public or private retirement pension income, and some disabled individuals and their primary caretakers.[36] Only one tenant selection plan provides an additional important exemption for individuals who cannot meet the requirement "temporarily (for a period of less than 12 months)" due to a "serious medical impairment."[37]

At least one tenant selection plan in particular employs an entirely different model for employment screening criteria than the hours-based approach. This tenant selection plan considers the head of household's employment history and current work status (a work-history model): "A CHA family who is a working family shall have a requirement of one year of verifiable work history, or being engaged in training, apprenticeships, or other similar programs that lead to employment opportunities prior to lease-up."[38] While this work-history model promises to make reasonable accommodations for persons with disabilities, it contains none of the enumerated exceptions found in the hours-based tenant selection plans.[39]

The wide disparities between these two versions of the employment criteria suggest that the MTSP and the various site-specific tenant selection plans are potentially incompatible. The MTSP purports to present the minimum or floor requirements for applicants to each development: "each private developer may supplement the criteria . . . to include more rigorous screening requirements."[40] We cannot determine, however, whether the hours-based MTSP or the work-history tenant selection plan provides the controlling "more rigorous" criteria. Worse, the CHA may attempt to overlay the MTSP hours-based approach atop the work-history tenant selection plan, in which case displaced families must meet both high standards.

For displaced families who hope to return, the hours-based approach alone is troubling in light of existing research on the work requirements established through the Temporary Assistance for Needy Families (TANF) program. As just one example, a recent report sponsored by and submitted to the Illinois Department of Health and Human Services by Mathematica Policy Research Inc. studied a group consisting of single-parent TANF recipients in Illinois in November 2001. Mathematica found that only 39 percent of TANF recipients surveyed were working at all, with only thirty percent working more than 30 hours per week.[41] Further, the Mathematica study comports with the findings of similar studies of TANF-mandated work requirements throughout the nation.[42] Though families in public housing are certainly not completely interchangeable with the TANF population, these findings are nonetheless instructive. As in the analogous case of TANF-induced work requirements, families living in public housing face tangible barriers to meeting these requirements, especially within the one-year time frame they are given (as opposed to five years in TANF).

When the CHA released the Minimum Tenant Selection Plan for public comment, numerous advocates submitted critiques of this hours-based work requirement.[43] Fundamentally, these advocates agreed that any employment requirements must be flexible enough to reflect the individual obstacles that families face when they are moving into the workforce. Beyond that, the advocates offered numerous concrete suggestions for implementing more attainable hours-based employment criteria.

Statutory and Contractual Authority for Legal Challenges

Despite numerous legitimate objections, the CHA nonetheless adopted strict, inflexible work requirements. Public housing authorities around the country will probably look to the CHA as a model for redevelopment. Advocates may be forced to pursue litigation in order to blunt the ill effects of such work requirements. In this section, we very briefly highlight some potential claims for advocates challenging these requirements.

Fair Housing Act Claims

Most broadly, advocates may argue that the work requirements in general constitute familial status discrimination under the Fair Housing Act.[44] The work requirements will have a greater adverse impact on single mothers with children than on childless adults, since these single mothers cannot fulfill the work requirements without sufficient access to child care.[45] In light of the high unemployment rate among African-American men, advocates can argue that the work requirements have an adverse disparate impact on black men as well.[46] Strict work requirements would thus tend to exclude both underemployed persons with children and unemployed African-American men, both in violation of the Fair Housing Act.

Source-of-Income Discrimination

Jurisdictions that have source-of-income antidiscrimination laws have another potential tool for battling the employment requirements in general. These laws generally prohibit discrimination on the basis of a person's lawful source of income.[47] Most public housing residents pay a flat 30 percent of their adjusted income toward rent.[48] A family that has significant nonwage income—for example, from child support payments or public benefits—could effectively pay the same rent as a family that derived all its income from wages. Yet the first family would nonetheless be forced to work thirty hours per week in order to meet public housing work requirements—that is, it would be forced to earn wage income in order to maintain its housing. In effect, by instituting inflexible work requirements, a public housing authority is requiring families to provide income earned from wages and rejecting the equivalent in nonwage income. Advocates can argue that this requirement thus constitutes source-of-income discrimination.[49]

Americans with Disabilities Act

If public housing authorities adopt the narrow disability exemption that the CHA adopted, they are likely violating Title II of the Americans with Disabilities Act (ADA) as well.[50] The Minimum Tenant Selection Plan excludes individuals who are "disabled with verification that disability precludes working," but provides no definition of disability.[51] In other tenant selection plans, CHA defines disability narrowly by citing the statutory standard necessary to receive certain disability benefits.[52] Under this standard, individuals must prove that they are unable to work due to a physical or mental impairment that has lasted or is expected to last at least twelve months or is expected to result in death.[53] But many individuals who do not meet this strict standard to receive disability benefits nonetheless have employment-related disabilities.[54] Further, many of these individuals are protected under the much broader definition of disability provided under the ADA, which requires only that they demonstrate that they have a record of, or that they are regarded to have, a physical or mental impairment that substantially limits one or more of the major life activities of such individual.[55] Some subset of individuals protected by the ADA are thus not exempt under the narrow benefits-based exemption provided in the CHA's tenant selection plans.

Since the minimum employment requirements threaten to exclude people with disabilities protected by the ADA, an affected individual may file an ADA challenge. In fact, Title II of the ADA protects a broad range of people with disabilities from exclusion from public benefits owing to their disability: "no qualified individual with a disability shall, by reason of such disability, be excluded from participation in or be denied the benefits of the services, programs, or activities of a public entity, or be subjected to discrimination by any such entity."[56] An ADA implementing regulation more clearly prohibits screening criteria that exclude people with disabilities:

> A public entity shall not impose or apply eligibility criteria that screen out or tend to screen out any individual with a disability or any class of individuals with disabilities from fully and equally enjoying any service, program, or activity, unless such criteria can be shown to be necessary for the provision of the service, program or activity being offered.[57]

Advocates can argue that the employment requirements—which surely are not necessary to the provision of public housing—tend to screen out people who cannot work due to ADA-protected disabilities but who do not meet the stricter definition of disability required to receive public benefits.

Relocation Rights Contract

Finally, in Chicago specifically, advocates could challenge the employment requirements under the relocation rights contract. The relocation rights contract promises that local working groups have the authority to make decisions about screening requirements at each property.[58] But it makes no provision for the CHA to unilaterally adopt the MTSP, which purports to be an absolute floor on the site-specific requirements.[59] By establishing a minimum set of requirements, the CHA has violated the relocation rights contract by usurping power from the local working groups.[60]

The Horner Model

Perhaps a better alternative would be to abandon the rigid hours-based employment requirements and other irrational screening criteria altogether, adopting instead the more reasonable tenant screening process in place at Chicago's Henry Horner Homes. Successful public housing redevelopment can still involve high levels of resident participation, rapidly rising property values, and a large number of former residents returning. In fact, a November 2003 report from the U.S. General Accounting Office found Horner to be an exemplary development by all these measures.[61]

Background on Horner

In 1995, the Horner families won an important consent decree stemming from litigation against the CHA and HUD.[62] Under the Horner consent decree, CHA, the developer, and the managing agent must consult with and attempt to reach agreement with the Horner Residents Committee (HRC)—a group of seven elected building, block, or area presidents at Horner and the Sargent Shriver National Center on Poverty Law as plaintiffs' class counsel—on all matters relating to the redevelopment. If agreement cannot be reached, the matter is resolved by a court-appointed mediator or by the court itself. Accordingly, all demolition was phased so that the vast majority of families would move directly from their high-rises to their new on-site or neighborhood unit.[63] This is in stark contrast to the process at virtually every other CHA development, where most families were forced by CHA to temporarily relocate to the private market in highly segregated and poor areas of the city. Resident involvement has been key to protecting residents in the process of designing a more reasonable tenant screening process at Horner.

The Horner Screening Process

Prior to any tenant screening, under the Horner Amended Consent Decree, all Horner families are allowed to select their choice of replacement housing. In Phase I of the decree, which lasted from 1995 to 2000, four choices of replacement housing were offered: (1) a rehabilitated Horner unit, (2) a newly constructed unit on the site of the demolished high-rises and mid-rises or in the surrounding community of Horner, Chicago's Near West Side, (3) a unit in the private market under the Section 8 certificate/voucher program, or (4) a newly constructed "*Gautreaux* scattered-site" housing unit. In Phase I, roughly one-half of the Horner families elected to remain in the Horner area, either on-site or in the Near West Side, and one-half opted to leave the Horner community through Section 8 or a scattered-site unit. In Phase II, which began in 2000 and is expected to last until 2008, Horner families may select: (1) a newly constructed unit located on the site of the demolished high-rises and mid-rises, or (2) a unit in the private market under the Housing Choice voucher program. This time around, over 75 percent of the families elected to remain at Horner, and only 25 percent of the families elected to leave the community.

As for the screening itself, all assignments to the new units are based on a formula devised by the Horner Residents Committee to ensure fairness. In order to be offered their choice of any of these units, a Horner family must meet five basic requirements: (1) the family must not "voluntarily vacate" its current Horner unit, (2) the family must not be evicted pursuant to court order, (3) the leaseholder must not be convicted of any felony involving physical violence to persons or crimes against property that adversely affect the health, safety, or welfare of other persons, or of the misdemeanors of aggravated assault, unlawful use of a weapon, battery or criminal damage to property, (4) any household member must not be convicted of any of the above felonies or misdemeanors unless the leaseholder agrees to exclude the convicted household member from the household,[64] and (5) the family must not unreasonably refuse to participate in a family needs assessment to determine the family's needs, if any, in terms of employment capabilities, day care, transportation, literacy, parenting skills, gang involvement, housekeeping skills, substance abuse problems, and similar matters.

Importantly, residents are screened only on their behavior on or after

April 4, 1995 (the date that the consent decree was entered). So all the basic eligibility requirements are "prospective," in the sense that nothing in the family's pre-1995 criminal history or other past conduct could be used by the CHA to prohibit a family from being eligible for a replacement unit. The plaintiffs insisted that if the family, at the time of the signing of the decree, was a bona fide Horner leaseholder, the CHA would be prohibited from searching the family's past for information that would disqualify it. Thus, all Horner families were informed that the decree, in effect, operated on a blank slate. All the factors that would disqualify a family from receiving replacement housing could occur only in the future, after the entry of the decree. Accordingly, all Horner families were aware that they themselves controlled whether they would be eligible for a replacement unit. Knowing the eligibility requirements, each family knew what it had to do or not do to remain eligible.

The parties also agreed not to implement work requirements of any kind, hours-based or otherwise, out of respect for Chicago's source-of-income antidiscrimination ordinance. Many Horner families have nonwage income such as public benefits or child support payments. At Horner, the parties agreed that the important thing is that families have the money to pay the rent, not the source of the money. First providing families with decent housing and then assisting them through case-managed social services based on the family needs assessment constitute a more successful way of promoting mixed-income models.

Unsuccessful Horner families may themselves appeal their rejections to a unique grievance panel, consisting of one representative selected by the HRC, one selected by management, and one jointly selected by the HRC and management. In stark contrast to the MTSP's grievance policy[65]—which uses the city of Chicago's administrative hearing officers, who have little accountability and no connection to the community[66]—the Horner model empowers residents, who are uniquely aware of both the challenges that residents face and the types of families that they want living in their communities.

The plaintiffs are allowed to appeal to the HRC any decision on eligibility. Under the decree, the CHA has the duty to consult with and attempt to reach agreement with the HRC on all aspects of the Horner redevelopment effort. If the parties are unable to agree, either party may appeal the disagreement to the U.S. District Court in charge of the Horner litigation (the "Horner court"), which will resolve the issue. Thus, if the HRC thinks that a particular Horner family is eligible for replacement housing under the decree, but the CHA refuses to offer that family a replacement unit, the family, represented by Horner class counsel, could ask the Horner court to review and decide the issue.

Resolving Ambiguities: The Tendering Process

As the Phase I units started to become available, it soon became apparent to the parties that the basic eligibility requirements raised questions about certain situations. For example, if a leaseholder had been arrested but not yet convicted of a disqualifying felony or misdemeanor and it was now the leaseholder's "turn" to receive a new unit, should that leaseholder be provided the unit, subject to the resolution of the criminal case? The parties decided that this would be unfair, both to the leaseholder involved (who would move into the new unit and then have to vacate it if convicted) and to those Horner families passed over in favor of a subsequently disqualified resident.

Accordingly, in June 1997, the parties entered into a Phase I memorandum of agreement (MOA), which gave the CHA the option of seeking a "deferral" for any family under certain circumstances. These circumstances included (1) poor housekeeping, (2) the pendency of a criminal case involving the disqualifying felonies or misdemeanors, (3) the resident's failure to retain custody of household members, (4) the resident's failure to attend replacement unit orientation, and (5) any other specific reason. Again, the parties were able to appeal to the Horner court any case in which agreement on eligibility could not be achieved.

In practice, as the new units became available, plaintiffs' counsel would tender the name of a Horner family to CHA and the management company under contract with CHA to manage Horner ("Horner management") for consideration. The order of the families tendered was governed by the decree and was based on which building the family resided in, the number of bedrooms required, and the priority of the family within the building. CHA and Horner management would then review the tendered named and respond by (1) accepting the family for the unit tendered, (2) rejecting the family if it failed to meet the basic eligibility requirements, or (3) requesting a deferral based on the Phase I MOA. Plaintiffs' counsel would then respond, depending on the circumstances, by either agreeing with the acceptance, rejection, or request for deferral, or in the case of rejection or deferral, disagreeing. The parties would then consult and attempt to reach agreement. If no agreement were reached, either party could appeal the matter to the Horner court. Under this system, all Phase I Horner families were considered by the parties on a case-by-case basis.

Because Phase II involved tax credit and other financing, the parties agreed to a revised memorandum of agreement, the Phase II MOA, signed on December 1, 2002. The Phase II MOA provided CHA and Horner management with additional grounds to seek a deferral: (1) if the household income exceeded the applicable tax credit income limits, (2) if all members of the household were full-time students and no one qualified for an eligibility exemption, or (3) if admission would otherwise violate applicable income restrictions under the tax credit program, HOME Investment Partnership Program funds restrictions, restrictions under the Illinois Low-Income Housing Trust Fund, and certain bond financing rules. In addition the parties agreed to substitute the wording "any other good cause" in the Phase II MOA for "any specific reason" that was contained in the Phase I MOA.

The tendering process for Phase II was the same as described above for Phase I. In addition, if the parties are unable to reach agreement on the issues of eligibility or deferral, the parties agreed to jointly submit the matter to the Horner mediator or the Horner court for resolution.

Conclusion

If the CHA's screening criteria (especially the work requirements) remain unchallenged, advocates estimate that only 12 to 15 percent of the families displaced by the Plan for Transformation will be allowed to return to the resource-rich, mixed-income public housing rebuilt on-site.[67] In stark contrast, the Horner screening process, together with case-managed social services, ensures that nearly 90 percent of the Horner families will actually be able to move into the new units. The Horner model demonstrates that active resident involvement and strong resident protections can create a screening process that is successful at building a mixed-income community that will truly benefit the residents originally displaced by the redevelopment. Advocates who face rigid screening criteria like those proposed in Chicago must use all challenges available to ensure that the criteria will not prohibit displaced residents from returning to the new public housing units rebuilt in their historic communities.

Notes

The authors wish to thank their Sargent Shriver National Center on Poverty Law colleagues for support on this article: staff attorney Kate Walz for her suggestions and ideas throughout; former housing and economic opportunities specialist Marie Claire Tran for research on disability statistics; former legal intern Steve Sharpe for research on the Americans with Disabilities Act; senior attorney Wendy Pollack and advocacy director John Bouman for research and expertise on TANF reform; and legal editor Crystal Ashley for her suggestions and for her patience.

1. As of June 30, 2003, the U.S. General Accounting Office found that 76,393 public housing units were (or were planned to be) demolished under the HOPE VI program, while only 44,781 units would ultimately be rebuilt or renovated. U.S. General Accounting Office, "Public Housing: HOPE VI Resident Issues and Changes in Neighborhoods Surrounding Grant Sites," November 2003, pp. 11–12, www.gao.gov/new.items/d04109.pdf.

2. See, e.g., *Gautreaux v. Chicago Housing Authority/Concerned Residents of ABLA v. Chicago Housing Authority, the U.S. Department of Housing and Urban Development, and the Habitat Co.,* No. 66 C 1459, 2004 U.S. Dist. LEXIS 11501 (N.D. Ill. June 22, 2004) (challenging ABLA HOPE VI redevelopment in Chicago); *Darst-Webbe Tenant Association Board v. St. Louis Housing Authority,* 339 F.3d 702 (8th Cir. 2003) (challenging Darst-Webbe HOPE VI redevelopment in St. Louis); *Reese v. Miami-Dade Co.*, 242 F. Supp. 2d 1292 (S.D. Fla. 2002) (challenging James Scott Homes HOPE VI redevelopment in Miami).

3. See National Housing Law Project et al., "False HOPE: A Critical Assessment of the HOPE VI Public Housing Redevelopment Program," June 2002, p. 25, www.nhlp.org/html/pubhsg/FalseHOPE.pdf (citing "vague, unreasonable screening policies" that prevent former residents from returning to redeveloped HOPE VI sites).

4. Chicago Housing Authority, "Plan for Transformation—Draft Year 6," p. 2 (hereinafter "Draft Year 6," www.thecha.org/transformplan/plans.html).

5. Each mixed-income development will consist of roughly equal numbers of public housing units, affordable units subsidized by the low-income housing tax credit program, and unsubsidized market-rate units, though the precise mix of units varies by development. See Chicago Housing Authority, "Draft Year 6." In all, 6,205 units that are actually available to public housing families will be built in these mixed-income developments.

6. See Chicago Housing Authority, "Draft Year 6," p. 2.

7. See generally Chicago Housing Authority, "Plan for Transformation: Improving Public Housing in Chicago and the Quality of Life," January 6, 2000, www.thecha.org/transformplan/files/plan_for_transformation_year_1_english_final.pdf.

8. See generally Chicago Housing Authority, "Plan for Transformation."

9. Omnibus Consolidated Rescissions and Appropriations Act, Pub. L. No. 104–132, § 202, (April 26, 1996).

10. Chicago Housing Authority, "OCRA 202 Viability Assessment," May 1998 submission, p. 14, finding Dearborn Homes, Cabrini Extension South, Green Homes, Rockwell Gardens, Stateway Gardens, Wells Extension, and Wells Homes subject to the cost test, but finding all of ABLA, Cabrini Extension North, Cabrini Rowhouses, Henry Horner Homes, Robert Taylor A and B, and Washington Park not subject to the cost test.

11. Chicago Housing Authority, "OCRA 202 Viability Assessment."

12. See generally Chicago Housing Authority, "Plan for Transformation."

13. See HUD and CHA, "Memorandum of Approval, Resident Protection Agreement, Moving to Work Agreement," February 2000) (hereinafter "Moving to Work Agreement"), www.hud.gov/offices/pih/programs/ph/mtw/pdfs/agreements/chicago.pdf. See also 110 Stat. 1321–282, 42 U.S.C. § 1437f (statutory authority).

14. See HUD and CHA, "Moving to Work Agreement," pp. 1–7. The CHA cites the Moving to Work Agreement as its authority for implementing many of its screening criteria. See note 37 and text accompanying.

15. See HUD and CHA, "Moving to Work Agreement."

16. Chicago Housing Authority, "CHA Leaseholder Housing Choice and Relocation Rights Contract, 10/1/99," 2000, pp. 5–6 (hereinafter "Relocation Rights Contract").

17. As of July 1, 2004, the CHA family waiting list—which like all Chicago wait-

ing lists is currently closed to new applications—nonetheless contains 34,169 families (consisting of 99,424 individuals), 95 percent of which are considered very low-income families (in that they earn less than 30 percent of the area median income), and 3,875 of which are families including people with disabilities. Another 3,657 families are on the senior housing waiting list; 19,898 families are on the "no preference" waiting list. In all, 57,724 families are seeking housing, 94.3 percent of which are very low-income families and 12,831 of which include people with disabilities. In addition, as of June 30, 2003, the Housing Choice voucher program maintained a separate waiting list with 23,294 applicants. Chicago Housing Authority, "FY 2004 Annual Plan–Plan for Transformation Year 5," pp. 16, 63, www.thecha.org/transformplan/plans.html.

18. For a description of these mixed-income communities, see Chicago Housing Authority, "FY 2006 Moving to Work Annual Plan, Plan for Transformation Year 7," October 31, 2005, pp. 6–34.

19. See Chicago Housing Authority, "FY 2006 Moving to Work Annual Plan, Plan for Transformation Year 7," p. 6.

20. Between January 1, 1995, and August 31, 2002, approximately 3,265 families were so relocated by CHA. See Paul Fischer, "Where Are the Public Housing Families Going? An Update," January 21, 2003, p. 4. Approximately 594 families were moved out of CHA housing in 2003 with vouchers. See Thomas Sullivan, "Independent Monitor's Report to the Chicago Housing Authority and the Central Advisory Council Regarding Phase III-2003 of the Plan for Transformation" February 20, 2004, p. 27. In addition, CHA planned to move out approximately 382 families with vouchers in 2004 and approximately 310 families in 2005. See Chicago Housing Authority, "FY 2005 Annual Plan, Plan for Transformation Year 6" November 1, 2004, ch. 3, p. 9; "FY 2006 Moving to Work Annual Plan, Plan for Transformation Year 7," p. 74. The number of families who actually moved out of public housing with vouchers in 2004 and 2005 is unavailable.

21. See Fischer, "Where Are the Public Housing Families Going?"

22. See Center for Urban Research and Policy, "Chicago Public Housing Transformation: A Research Report," February 2004, p. 6; and see *Wallace v. Chicago Housing Authority,* 298 F. Supp. 2d 710 (N.D. Ill. 2003) (upholding ten of thirteen counts of plaintiffs' complaint alleging resegregation among families leaving CHA with Housing Choice vouchers).

23. Center for Urban Research and Policy, "Chicago Public Housing Transformation," p. 12.

24. See Sullivan, "Independent Monitor's Report," pp. 42–43.

25. Chicago Housing Authority, "Relocation Rights Contract," p. 4.

26. See Chicago Housing Authority, "Relocation Rights Contract," p. 9.

27. See P.L. 104–134, Title I, § 101(e), 110 Stat. 1321–281 (May 2, 1996), *codified at* 42 U.S.C. § 1437f note. True, one express goal of the Moving to Work Demonstration Project is to

give public housing agencies and the Secretary of Housing and Urban Development the flexibility to design and test various approaches for providing and administering housing assistance that: . . . give incentives to families with children where the head of household is working, seeking work, or is preparing for work by participating in job training, educational programs, or programs that assist people to obtain employment and become economically self-sufficient. *Id* at (a).

We question whether the bare threat of exclusion constitutes an "incentive" as envisioned herein, though. Further, this authority expressly does not trump the CHA's mandate to comply with fair housing laws. See "Moving to Work Agreement," p. 5 (providing that the CHA should "administer its programs and activities in a manner affirmatively to further fair housing"). If the work requirements violate fair housing laws, they are not allowable. See the section on "Statutory and Contractual Authority for Legal Challenges" later in this chapter.

Note that in jurisdictions without the Moving to Work designation, public housing authorities lack even this pretense for implementing such criteria. Advocates in such jurisdictions can distinguish the CHA's screening criteria as predicated—if illegitimately—on their Moving to Work designation. But see note 32 (discussing community service requirements that can indirectly mandate work).

28. Families must meet an array of tenant screening criteria beyond these two categories as well.

29. As written, these criteria apply equally to all *renters* at mixed-income developments, whether for very low-income (public) units, affordable (tax credit) units, or market-rate units. See "Chicago Housing Authority, Minimum Tenant Selection Plan 1," September 21, 2004 (on file with authors) (hereinafter MTSP). Families who purchase homes—the vast majority of market-rate families in these mixed-income developments—are exempt from these requirements, though.

30. MTSP, p. 1. But the MTSP does not apply to developments or portions thereof governed by a relevant consent decree—for example, Horner—unless adopted by the parties.

31. Chicago Housing Authority, "Relocation Rights Contract," p. 4. Each development's working group consists of representatives of the CHA, the court-appointed receiver in the *Gautreaux v. Chicago Housing Authority* case, an elected tenant representative (the local advisory council president), a second tenant appointed by the LAC president, representatives of other city of Chicago agencies (e.g., Chicago Department of Planning; Chicago Department of Housing), and a legal representative of the plaintiff class from the *Gautreaux* case; see 296 F. Supp. 907 (N.D. Ill 1969). In addition, other individuals and organizations may be represented on any particular working group, with or without voting authority: the private market developer, a legal representative of the LAC president, local aldermen or other elected officials, hired architects and/or urban planners, and up to two appointed community leaders. *See* Chicago Housing Authority, "Plan for Transformation—Moving to Work Annual Plan FY 2001," December 1, 2000, p. 77, www.thecha.org/transformplan/plans.html.

32. These employment requirements are separate from the community service requirements that have been adopted by the CHA authority-wide, at all mixed-income and nonredeveloped sites. See Chicago Housing Authority, "Admissions and Continued Occupancy Policy," May 2004, p. 30. The CHA requires all nonexempt adults to perform thirty hours of community service per month. Adults who are working at least thirty hours each week (an hours-based work requirement) are exempt from these requirements. So families who meet the hours-based work requirements of the MTSP and various tenant selection plans should be exempt from these community service requirements. Families or family members who are participating in self-sufficiency activities for all or part of thirty hours per week to meet the MTSP or tenant selection plan employment requirements—or who are in the "working to meet" category—can have the time they spend on such self-sufficiency activities count toward their thirty hours of community service requirements.

Public housing authorities have broad statutory discretion in implementing these community service requirements and exclusions thereto. In effect, a public housing authority may implement the community service requirements in a way that creates an indirect work requirement, for example, by establishing a very high community service requirement offset by an exemption for working families. For a complete discussion of the various federal exemptions from the community service requirements, see Judith Goldiner and Risa E. Kaufman, "Community Service Requirement for Public Housing Residents: States' Implementation and Strategies for Advocates," *Clearinghouse Review* 38 (July–August 2004): 126, 127–129.

33. MTSP, p. 3 ("Head or co-head of household must work 120 hours a month [30 hours a week]"). See also Chicago Housing Authority, "ABLA Draft Tenant Selection Plan," February 2004, pp. 14–15 (hereinafter "ABLA TSP"); Chicago Housing Authority, "Robert Taylor Draft Tenant Selection Plan," September 17, 2003, p. 6 (hereinafter Taylor TSP); and Chicago Housing Authority, "Rockwell Draft Tenant Selection Plan," August 2004, p. 7 (hereinafter Rockwell TSP). The Rockwell TSP uniquely provides that its non-statutorily mandated selection criteria are ultimately discretionary, merely "relevant information respecting habits or practices to be considered in making admission determinations." Rockwell TSP, p. 7. No other tenant selection plan provides this broad discretion with regard to the work requirements in particular.

34. MTSP, p. 3. See also ABLA TSP, p. 15; Rockwell TSP, p. 7; Taylor TSP, p. 6.

35. See MTSP, p. 4; Taylor TSP, p. 6 ("head of household *or* co-head of household" required to work, implying that *both* are not) (emphasis added). The Rockwell development has such an exemption as well, but only for families with children under six years of age. Rockwell TSP, p. 7. ABLA has no such exemption. ABLA TSP, p. 14 ("head of household *and* co-head of household" implies that *both* must meet the requirement).

36. MTSP, p. 3; ABLA TSP, pp. 15–16; Rockwell TSP, p. 7; Taylor TSP, p. 6. See also the section of this chapter on "Statutory and Contractual Authority for Legal Challenges" (discussing the inadequate disability exceptions).

37. ABLA TSP, p. 15.

38. Chicago Housing Authority, "Hilliard Homes Draft Tenant Selection Plan / Holsten Screening and Selection Policy," October 2002), p. 2 (hereinafter Hilliard TSP).

39. See Hilliard TSP, p. 12.

40. See MTSP, p. 1. But see "Statutory and Contractual Authority for Legal Challenges" later in this chapter.

41. Mathematica Policy Research Inc., "Families on TANF in Illinois: Employment Assets and Liabilities," June 2003, pp. 3, 10, http://aspe.hhs.gov/hsp/TANF-IL-emp03/.

42. See generally Adam Gross, counsel for *Gautreaux* plaintiffs, letter to Chicago Housing Authority," July 9, 2004 (on file with the authors) (critiquing proposed MTSP in light of TANF studies).

43. See, for example, Adam Gross letter; John Bouman," Shriver Center advocacy director, letter to Chicago Housing Authority, July 9, 2004 (on file with *Clearinghouse Review*) (suggesting that the employment requirements allow for transitional jobs models); Wendy Pollack, senior attorney at the Shriver Center, letter to Chicago Housing Authority, July 9, 2004 (on file with *Clearinghouse Review*) (suggesting numerous improvements to the employment requirements); Robert Wordlaw, executive director of Chicago Jobs Council, letter to Chicago Housing Authority, July 9, 2004 (on file with *Clearinghouse Review*).

44. 42 U.S.C. § 3604(b) (2004).

45. Cf. *Metropolitan Housing Development Corp. v. Village of Arlington Heights*, 558 F.2d 1283 (7th Cir. 1977), *cert. denied* 434 U.S. 1025, 54 L. Ed. 2d 772, 98 S. Ct. 752 (establishing a four-factor test for disparate impact involving proportional disparity on the basis of race); *Betsey v. Turtle Creek Associates*, 736 F. 2d 983 (4th Cir. 1984) (finding disparate impact when eviction notices were sent disproportionately to nonwhite residents). See also Florence Wagman Roisman and Phillip Tegeler, "Improving and Expanding Housing Opportunities for Poor People of Color," *Clearinghouse Review* 24 (1990): 312, 325–337.

46. According to the Bureau of Labor Statistics, African-American or black men seeking work at age sixteen and older had an 11.6 percent unemployment rate in 2003—significantly more than the total unemployment rate (6.3 percent) and more than twice the unemployment rate of white men (5.6 percent). Bureau of Labor Statistics, "Current Population Survey: Annual Averages, Household Data," Table 24, 2004, www.bls.gov/cps/cpsaat24.pdf.

47. Numerous states have source-of-income antidiscrimination statutes—e.g., *Cal. Gov't Code* § 12955 (2003) (California); *Conn. Gen. Stat.* § 46a-64c (2003) (Connecticut); *D.C. Code Ann.* § 2–1402.21 (2002) (District of Columbia); *Me. Rev. Stat. Ann.* tit. 5, § 4582 (West 2002) (Maine); *Mass. Gen. Laws Ann.* ch. 151B, § 4(10) (West 2003) (Massachusetts); *Minn. Stat. Ann.* § 363.03 (West 2002) (Minnesota); 2002 *N.J. Laws* 82 (New Jersey) (recodified September 5, 2002); *Ok. Stat.* tit. 25, § 1452 (2003) (Oklahoma); *Ore. Rev. Stat.* § 659A.421 (2001) (Oregon) (exempting Section 8 vouchers); *Utah Code Ann.* § 57–21–5 (2003) (Utah); *Vt. St. Ann.* tit. 9, § 4503 (2001) (Vermont); and *Wis. Stat. Ann.* § 106.50 (West 2002) (Wisconsin). Numerous cities have enacted similar ordinances—e.g., *Chicago, Ill. Code of Ordinances* § 5–8-010 (2003); *Madison, Wis. Municipal Code* § 3.23(4) (2003); *Minneapolis, Minn. Code of Ordinances* tit. 7 ch. 139 (2002); *St. Paul, Minn. Code of Ordinances* tit. 18, ch. 183 (2002); and *Seattle, Wash. Municipal Code* § 14.08.040(A) (2003).

48. For example, the CHA offers residents a choice between paying a flat, market-based rent and an income-based rent. If they choose the latter, families pay only thirty percent of their monthly adjusted income as rent, or a minimum of $25. See Chicago Housing Authority, "Admissions and Continued Occupancy Policy," pp. 38, 45–46.

49. Few source-of-income discrimination cases have been adjudicated by higher courts, and none of these higher-court decisions has directly addressed whether work requirements themselves constitute source-of-income discrimination. Existing case law provides some guidance on an analogous question: whether source-of-income antidiscrimination statutes prohibit discrimination on the basis of characteristics *related to* having little wage-derived (employment) income. For example, the Connecticut source-of-income statute includes an exception for landlords to deny applicants "solely on the basis of insufficient income." *Conn. Gen. Stat.* § 46a-64c (b)(5). In interpreting that provision, the supreme court of Connecticut looked to the "remedial mandate of [the source-of-income nondiscrimination statute]" in determining that landlords could not arbitrarily define "insufficient income" effectively to exclude all families with Housing Choice vouchers. *Connecticut Human Rights and Opportunities v. Sullivan*, 250 Conn. 763, 789 (Conn. 1999). Connecticut landlords cannot use the fact that all families with vouchers by definition have little wage income as a pretext for rejecting viable applicants who have sufficient effective income to rent the unit (factoring in their vouchers).

Similarly, we argue, the CHA cannot use minimum work or employment requirements as a pretext for excluding from public housing families with little or no wage-related income. But cf. *T.K. v. Landmark West,* 353 N.J. Super 223, 802 A.2d 527 (N.J. App. 2001) (finding that New Jersey's source-of-income antidiscrimination statute does not limit a landlord from refusing to rent an apartment based on another trait common to voucher-holders—the lack of "creditworthiness" of the prospective tenant—so long as that determination is not pretextual).

50. 42 U.S.C. § 12132 (2004).

51. MTSP, p. 4.

52. See ABLA TSP, p. 15 (citing 42 U.S.C. 416(i)(1) or 42 U.S.C. 1382c); Rockwell TSP, p. 7 (same); Taylor TSP, p. 6 (same).

53. See 42 U.S.C. 416(i)(1); 42 U.S.C. 1382c.

54. According to the 2000 census, almost 33.2 million Americans aged sixteen to sixty-four reported having a disability, defined as "a long-lasting physical, mental, or emotional condition [that] can make it difficult for a person to do activities" or may "impede a person from being able to go outside the home alone or to work at a job or business." Census 2000 Summary File 3, Table P42. More than half of these individuals (17.8 million) claim an employment disability (Table P125). In contrast, in 2002, only roughly 3.7 million people of working age received Supplemental Security Income (SSI) payments nationally. United States Social Security Administration, "Annual Statistical Report on the Social Security Disability Insurance Program 2002," Table 7.A9, August 2003, www.ssa.gov/policy/docs/statcomps/di_asr/2002/index.html. In that same year, just over 5.5 million persons under the age of sixty-four received Social Security Death Index (SSDI) (Table 5.A1.2). Assuming little overlap and a fairly steady population of people with disabilities between 2000 and 2002, we can very roughly estimate that only half (9.2 million) of the 17.8 million people with employment-related disabilities collected SSI or SSDI in 2002. A sizable number of persons with employment-related disabilities appear not to receive SSI or SSDI, and presumably some portion of those simply do not qualify under that strict standard. These individuals may be protected by the ADA but not excluded by the strict definition of disability found in the work requirements.

55. 42 U.S.C. § 12102(2). Nor does the ADA on its face require that individuals prove the long-term nature of their disability.

56. 42 U.S.C. § 12102(2).

57. 28 C.F.R. § 35.130(8).

58. See Chicago Housing Authority, "Relocation Rights Contract," p. 4.

59. See MTSP, p. 1.

60. But advocates must decide whether certain exceptions provided by the MTSP might be preferable to site-specific plans. For example, while ambiguous, the MTSP appears to allow heads-of-household to meet the work requirements if they are enrolled as full-time students. MTSP, p. 4. Since this exception is not mirrored by any site-specific tenant selection plan, it is not clear whether it practically survives. Still, advocates might refrain from challenging the MTSP in order to take advantage of its additional exemptions.

61. See U.S. General Accounting Office, "Public Housing."

62. In 1991, the Henry Horner Mothers Guild (a resident organization located at the Henry Horner Annex) and other tenants at the Horner Homes and Horner Extension filed a lawsuit alleging that the CHA and HUD, among other things, were engaged in a process of de facto demolition of Horner, in violation of the National Housing Act, in that Horner's units were 49 percent vacant or otherwise uninhabitable. See *Henry Horner Mothers Guild v. Chicago Housing Authority and the U.S.*

Department of Housing and Urban Development, 780 F. Supp. 511 (N.D. Ill. 1991) (denying the defendants' motion to dismiss); 824 F. Supp. 808 (N.D. Ill. 1993) (denying the parties' cross-motions for summary judgment and setting the case for trial). Under a consent decree and an agreed order in the *Horner* case entered in 1995 and in 2000, the Henry Horner public housing development—which in 1991 consisted of 1,775 units of housing, including eleven sixteen-story high-rises and eight seven-story mid-rise buildings, occupied exclusively by very low-income families—will now consist of 1,325 units of low-rise and mid-rise mixed-income housing both on-site and in the Near West Side community. Of these 1,325 units, 822 will be for public housing families (63 percent of the total newly constructed or rehabilitated units—the highest of any CHA mixed-income development), 132 are affordable units (10 percent of the total), and 361 are market rate units (27 percent of the total). Included among the 822 public housing units are 526 units for very low-income Horner families (or 40 percent of total units—also the highest of any CHA mixed-income development).

63. The latter are scattered-site units built on a site approved by the court in *Gautreaux v. CHA,* 296 F. Supp. 907 (N.D. Ill. 1969).

64. Criminal background screening is distinct from one-strike evictions. In the screening context, the public housing authority looks to prior criminal history to decide whether an applicant may enter these new units. The one-strike provision allows public housing authorities the discretion to evict residents who commit crimes subsequent to their admission. Cf. *Rucker v. Davis,* 535 U.S. 125 (2002); Wendy L. Stasell, "*Rucker v. Davis* and Its Significance for Tenant Advocates," *Clearinghouse Review* 35 (July–August 2001): 144.

65. MTSP, pp. 5–6, citing CHA grievance policy (2004).

66. The city's administrative hearing officers are accountable to the community only in that they are jointly agreed upon by the CHA and the Central Advisory Council prior to their initial appointment. See "Amended Grievance Policy," approved by the CHA Board of Commissioners on January 20, 2004.

67. Preliminary reports are not encouraging. Chicago-based journalist Kate N. Grossman reports that only four of twenty-eight families preliminarily screened at the Ida B. Wells Homes met the screening criteria. Kate N. Grossman, "Many Chicago Tenants Cut Out of Mixed-Income Housing," *Chicago Sun-Times,* October 10, 2004. Further, only eighteen of forty-two families at Rockwell initially met the screening criteria. National studies largely reinforce these estimates as well. See generally U.S. General Accounting Office, "Public Housing" (discussing the expected return rate of HOPE VI developments nationally and the effect of screening criteria).

Part III

LEARNING FROM CHICAGO

PROSPECTS AND CHALLENGES
FOR POLICY MAKERS

9

Gautreaux and Chicago's Public Housing Crisis

The Conflict Between Achieving Integration and Providing Decent Housing for Very Low-Income African Americans

William P. Wilen and Wendy L. Stasell

Nearly forty years ago the Kerner Commission recommended that the United States pursue strategies to improve nonwhite communities and integrate white communities. Over this span of time the country has succeeded in doing little of either. Public housing as well as most residential housing remains overwhelmingly racially segregated,[1] and recent changes in federal housing policies have only exacerbated an existing affordable-housing crisis. Against this backdrop, scholars, public interest attorneys, residents, and community organizers debate the tension between providing adequate housing for very low-income African-Americans and the ideal of integrating them into white communities. Proponents of an integrationist ideal argue that segregation perpetuates poverty within the African-American community.[2] For them, integrated mixed-income communities in cities and suburbs should be the end result of public housing reform. Gentrification is considered positive by these advocates, who point to the perceived social and economic benefits of mixed-income neighborhoods. To these advocates, rebuilding concentrated public housing on-site for very low-income families is both bad public policy and unlawful.[3]

In response, critics of the integrationist approach point to a private market that is both unable and unwilling to accommodate very low-income public housing residents and the general hostility that continues to meet efforts to build scattered-site public housing units in predominately white areas. Even integration proponents agree that deeply ingrained racial and class segregation limits the availability of private housing for low-income African-Americans.[4] While a laudable goal, integration policies have often produced more frustration than housing opportunities.[5] As a consequence, the national effort toward "fair housing" may be of little benefit to very low-income families; just as the Holy Roman Empire was reputed to be neither holy nor Roman, this type of fair housing is in actuality neither "fair" nor "housing."[6]

In this chapter we first present the setting of the debate, the national crisis in affordable housing, as well as the crisis particular to Chicago. Next we examine the forty-year-old public housing desegregation case of *Gautreaux v. Chicago Housing Authority*.[7] In the last section we offer suggestions for resolving the tension between integration and the critical need for low-income housing, a debate that has pitted advocate against advocate and resulted in little tangible benefit to those most in need of housing.

The Affordable Housing Crisis

At a time of national economic growth, that many Americans are suffering through the worst of times is barely in the public consciousness and rarely mentioned in the media. The sad fact is that urban neighborhood poverty has grown dramatically since the 1970s. Between 1970 and 1990 the number of inner-city neighborhoods with a population of at least 40 percent low-income people more than doubled. By 1990 nearly one in seven African-Americans lived in a high-poverty neighborhood, in contrast to only 1 percent of all non-Hispanic whites.[8]

While the need for decent housing is at an all-time high, the number of federally assisted units is not nearly enough to house those in need. In 1996, just as the Chicago Housing Authority (CHA) was beginning to initiate plans that would result in a substantial reduction the local stock of public housing, approximately 15 million households qualified for federal housing assistance, but only 4.5 million families were receiving assistance. Of the more than 10 million poor families not receiving housing assistance, approximately one-half spent at least 50 percent of their income on shelter. These included the disabled, the elderly, and welfare recipients, as well as a surprising number of working families.[9] In 1970 the number of affordable apartments nationwide had exceeded the number of families who needed them by 1 million. By the mid-1990s the affordable housing gap was far greater: "running five million units short, because many of the cheap apartments have been demolished and the number of people who are poor has exploded. In most places, the [public housing] waiting lists are closed, they have become so long."[10]

The local crisis is just as compelling. On the eve of the CHA's launching its Plan for Transformation, in late 1999, more than 28,000 families were on the waiting list for public housing, and more than 30,000 were on the waiting list for Section 8, since renamed the Housing Choice voucher (HCV) program).[11] Further, on any given night, 15,000 people were homeless in Chicago.[12] According to a 1999 rental market study funded in part by the U.S. Department of Housing and Urban Development (HUD) and conducted at the urging of numerous tenant advocacy groups including the Coalition to Protect Public Housing, the Chicago-area vacancy rate was an extremely tight 4 percent. As vacancy rates decreased, rents increased 56 percent more than the consumer price index. According to this 1999 study, the regional rental stock had decreased by 52,000 units, even though the region's population had increased by more than 500,000 during the 1990s. Almost 38 percent of the area's renters paid more than 30 percent of their income for rent.[13] Finally, and most significant to this discussion, the study demonstrated that the Chicago metropolitan area had a deficit of approximately 150,000 units for very low-income families.[14] Thus, not surprisingly, at least 30 percent of the families with Section 8 vouchers were unable to find housing in the Chicago market.[15]

The reason for this huge shortfall in affordable housing units for the poor is that, unlike welfare, public and subsidized housing has never been considered an "entitlement." Even though Congress in 1949 expressed the goal of "a decent home and suitable living environment for every American family," it has never appropriated sufficient funds to house the nation's poor adequately.

Federal Policy Worsens the Crisis

The situation arguably reached an all-time low when the Republicans prevailed in the November 1994 elections and gained control of both the House and the Senate. Beginning in 1995 some Republicans sporadically called for HUD's elimination, but attacking HUD was fortunately not among Congress's highest priorities.[16] Congress did, however, signal its intention to cut back severely on the department's programs, particularly public housing, by rescinding millions of dollars from its budget.[17]

While the funding cuts were devastating, three substantive changes in HUD's public housing programs were even more damaging. First, Congress suspended and then repealed the one-for-one replacement requirement, whereby every public housing unit demolished had to be replaced, thus enabling HUD to embark on its own program to demolish at least 100,000 public housing units by 2000.[18] Second, Congress changed the Homeownership and Opportunity for People Everywhere VI (HOPE VI) program, originally enacted to revitalize severely distressed public housing, into a program that primarily emphasized demolition.[19] Third, Congress enacted the vouchering-out law, which required public housing authorities to perform a two-step viability assessment for all units within their inventories. Under this law many large, troubled developments must be demolished and residents given housing vouchers if this is determined to be more cost-effective than building renovation.[20] HUD initially estimated that in Chicago more than 16,000 units would be lost through vouchering out or through HOPE VI-funded demolition.[21]

Chicago Plans to Raze Housing

In May 1998, pursuant to the vouchering-out law, the Chicago Housing Authority (CHA) submitted its viability assessment to HUD. The number of units to be demolished was staggering. Of the 19,000 units subject to the viability assessment, CHA proposed to demolish slightly more than 11,000 units. It proposed that almost 6,300 units be rehabilitated and that approximately 4,300 new units be built.[22] Only one-half of the new units would be reserved for very-low-income families, who constitute almost all of CHA's current residential population. The rest of the new units would be public housing units for working families and market-rate units, which together would create mixed-income communities. The net result: displacement of 24,000 public housing residents.[23] By early 1999 the scene was shifting again. HUD had been operating the troubled CHA for almost four years and was preparing to return it to local control.[24] Under a memorandum of agreement that Chicago mayor Richard M. Daley and HUD assistant secretary Harold Lucas signed in May 1999, the city and HUD agreed to negotiate a performance compact within the next six months. The performance compact would "establish an action plan and identify the regulatory flexibility, legislative flexibility and resources necessary to achieve performance benchmarks" on which the city and HUD would agree.[25] The vehicle for the regulatory flexibility was the Moving to Work Demonstration Program, authorized by the Omnibus Consolidated Rescissions and Appropriations Act of 1996, which allowed HUD to waive numerous provisions of the U.S. Housing Act.[26] Given Chicago's demonstrable affordable housing crisis, this was an opportunity for the CHA to take the lead in seeking flexibility to create more units, not fewer. However, what soon became apparent was that the performance compact, like the earlier viability assessment, would call for massive demolition without construction of a significant number of new units.

The crux of CHA's draft Plan for Transformation was the demolition of 16,000 units in fifty-one high-rise buildings, including Robert Taylor Homes and Stateway Gardens along the four-mile stretch of public housing known as the State Street Corridor, as well as the displacement of thousands of residents. The plan also called for building or rehabilitating more than 24,000 units (including all of the 9,000 units for the elderly), privatizing management of all of CHA's housing stock, substantially reducing CHA staff, obtaining HUD approval to waive a long list of federal statutory requirements, and funding the plan with $1.5 billion in HUD funds.[27]

The plan angered resident leaders not only because of the massive loss of units but also because it scrapped most of the redevelopment plans that residents had worked out previously in conjunction with the CHA's viability assessments.[28] Critics of the plan also asserted that families moving from the CHA through the Section 8 program were unlikely to be any better off: during the next ten years, nearly all of the CHA's high-rise developments were slated for demolition and redevelopment, displacing more than 11,000 of the city's poorest families. CHA plans call for these families to receive housing vouchers to make the transition to better housing. However, if they do not receive adequate assistance, these families may end up clustered in poor inner-city communities, not much better off in their new housing than before. A 1999 study of more than 1,000 families displaced from the CHA into the Section 8 program confirmed that they were moving primarily to segregated areas with high levels of poverty.[29]

The CHA eventually submitted to HUD its final Plan for Transformation and request for twenty-nine waivers of statutory requirements under the Moving to Work Program.[30] HUD approved twenty-seven of the CHA's requests for waivers in full, approved one waiver in part, and denied one waiver; it also approved a CHA-HUD Resident Protection Agreement and the Moving to Work Agreement.[31] As a result of the approved plan, Chicago's public housing stock will decrease from 39,000 to 25,000 units in ten years.[32] All new development will be market-driven in the sense that new public housing units will be built alongside private housing by developers awarded contracts through competitive bidding. HUD officials had recommended that demolition be tied to the available supply of Section 8 housing, to be determined by an annual market study conducted by HUD; however, HUD's final approval of the plan gave the CHA an out: if HUD fails to conduct a market study, the CHA's demolition plans may still proceed.[33]

Only 4,500 units will be built—mostly at the large Henry Horner, Cabrini-Green, and ABLA (Addams, Brooks, Loomis, and Abbott, four contiguous public housing developments) developments—all located in hot real estate markets. Along the State Street Corridor and in other areas, where approximately 14,000 units will be demolished and thousands of residents involuntarily displaced, the CHA plans to build only a few hundred units.[34] Constructing any new family public housing units on the site of developments slated for demolition will necessarily implicate the *Gautreaux* judgment, which places restrictions on family public housing built in areas with substantial African-American populations.[35] The experience of residents at Horner, Cabrini, and ABLA, where heated disputes have ensued over the *Gautreaux* judgment, does not bode well for other public housing residents who may wish to remain in their communities. To understand these disputes, we need first to understand the history and current operation of the *Gautreaux* judgment.

The Gautreaux *Case*

Nearly forty years ago a group of public housing residents filed the landmark *Gautreaux* case, alleging that the CHA's site-selection and tenant-assignment plans were racially discriminatory. In 1967 the district court found that public housing residents "have the right under the Fourteenth Amendment to have sites selected for public housing projects without regard to the racial composition of either the surrounding neighborhood or the projects themselves."[36] Two years later the court entered a judgment against CHA. The court, finding that CHA had acted intentionally to maintain patterns of racial segregation in family public housing, set forth a comprehensive new plan for site selection and tenant assignment to remedy the discrimination.[37]

In particular, the order divided Cook County into "general areas" (defined as areas with a 70 percent or more white population) and "limited areas" (defined as areas with a 30 percent or more African-American population). For every one new family public housing unit constructed in a limited area, three units had to be built in a general area.[38] The court retained jurisdiction over the case "for all purposes," including enforcement of the decree and the issuance of orders modifying it as necessary to achieve desegregation.

Over the years the ratio of housing to be built in limited and general areas was changed from three to one to one to one.[39] Thus today, for each unit built in a limited area, one unit must be built in a general area. The court added a third neighborhood categorization, a "revitalizing area," defined as a neighborhood that has a large minority population and is undergoing redevelopment such that the area is expected to become integrated within a short period. Revitalizing areas are considered "the most promising neighborhoods for racial and economic integration" because they serve as "buffer" zones between the limited and general areas.[40] If an area is designated as a revitalizing area, units built there do not have to be matched on a one-to-one basis with units in a general area. Henry Horner, part of Cabrini, ABLA, and the Kenwood-Oakland neighborhood on Chicago's South Side have been designated as revitalizing areas.[41]

In the companion case filed against the CHA's funding agency, HUD, the Seventh Circuit determined that "HUD's knowing acquiescence in CHA's admittedly discriminatory housing program violated the Fifth Amendment."[42] The U.S. Supreme Court later determined that a remedial order imposing metropolitan-wide relief was an appropriate remedy for past discrimination.[43]

Following the Supreme Court's decision, HUD and the *Gautreaux* plaintiffs entered into a consent decree under which, among other requirements, HUD was to create and fund a demonstration program using Section 8 rental subsidies to help *Gautreaux* families move to low-poverty neighborhoods throughout the metropolitan area. Under the *Gautreaux* Assisted-Housing Program, as it came to be known, approximately 7,100 families moved, with generally positive results, to low-poverty areas in the city and suburbs. In 1997 the court dismissed HUD from the case after finding that the department had satisfied its obligations under *Gautreaux*.[44]

In the meantime, the CHA and the city of Chicago stalled the construction of scattered-site units in white areas. From 1969 to 1974 the authority built no new public housing at all. The court ultimately ordered it simply to ignore the Illinois statute requiring the city council's site approval. Over the next ten years, however, only a few hundred units were built.[45] Finally, in 1987, finding that the CHA was "simply not up to the task," Judge Marvin E. Aspen appointed a receiver to take over the development of all new family public housing units. The Habitat Company, a private real estate firm, and its chairman, Daniel E. Levin, were appointed as receiver.[46]

Nearly twenty years after the receivership order and more than thirty years after the court entered the *Gautreaux* judgment, public housing in Chicago remains overwhelmingly segregated. As of October 1999, fewer than 3,000 scattered-site housing units had been constructed, while the *Gautreaux* class consists of more than 40,000 families.[47] The CHA built or acquired 1,147 units between 1969 and 1987, two-thirds of which were located in predominantly black neighborhoods. Between 1987 and 1999 the receiver built or purchased 1,822 units, half in predominantly Latino neighborhoods. Only 131 units were built in predominantly white neighborhoods.[48] The receiver has asserted that high land prices have hindered the construction of scattered-site units in such areas; no doubt, strong community opposition played a part as well. Thus desegregation efforts frequently have amounted to little more than "integration on the cheap with the residents often left to barrel through racial barriers on their own."[49]

Research shows that most of the families who are leaving CHA developments with Housing Choice vouchers and who are not participating in the *Gautreaux* Assisted-Housing Program are trading one poor African-American neighborhood for another.[50] For example, between 1995 and 2000, approximately 1,000 families whose public housing developments were slated for closure or demolition took Section 8 vouchers. These families did not receive mobility counseling. Nearly 80 percent relocated to census tracts that were at least 90 percent African-American, and approximately 70 percent relocated to areas with a per capita income below $10,000. Approximately 6,000 more public housing residents are expected to enter the private market with Housing Choice vouchers as the CHA tears down existing developments and replaces them with mixed-income communities.[51] According to Aurie Pennick, former president of the Leadership Council for Metropolitan Open Communities, a fair housing group that administered the *Gautreaux* Assisted-Housing Program, any large-scale expansion of Housing Choice vouchers that does not emphasize integration would undo "all the work we've done over 20 years."[52]

Presumably in light of these grim results, in 1997 the *Gautreaux* plaintiffs unsuccessfully sought to extend the judgment order's one-to-one mandate to the Section 8 (HCV) program. Judge Aspen refused to extend the judgment order without proof that the lingering patterns of segregated family public housing were entirely the result of the CHA's original discrimination.[53] Six months later Judge Aspen made another significant ruling in the case, determining that HOPE VI funds received by the CHA were subject to the *Gautreaux* judgment order.[54] The HOPE VI program, enacted by Congress in 1992, is one of the few remaining funding sources for public housing. Program funds were to be used to demolish and replace some of the nation's worst public housing developments. As a result of Judge Aspen's ruling, the CHA must supply scattered-site housing on a one-to-one basis for each unit built with HOPE VI funds in a limited area or seek designation of the area as revitalizing, as it has done at other CHA developments. If a revitalizing designation is granted, the CHA does not have to build an equal number of units in general areas.

One clear result of this decision will be that, as more CHA developments are demolished through CHA's Plan for Transformation, *Gautreaux* will affect any redevelopment plans that include building on-site family public housing units. Unless Judge Aspen designates the public housing sites as revitalizing, the CHA will not be able to build there without building an equal number of units in white areas. The *Gautreaux* plaintiffs' counsel indicated that he would not agree to a revitalizing designation without reviewing specific plans for each development. In the past he agreed to revitalization designations only when new family public housing units were part of an overall plan for mixed-income developments.

Thus mixed-income housing on the site of former large-scale public housing developments has emerged as *Gautreaux*'s new frontier. Plaintiffs' counsel views mixed-income housing as a way to achieve the racial integration envisioned by *Gautreaux* nearly thirty years ago.[55] The long-term practical effect of these policies, and whether low-income public housing residents will receive a real benefit, remains to be seen. In this next section, we examine the debate and trade-offs related to integration policies and the need for low-income housing.

Integration Versus the Critical Need for Low-Income Housing

In Chicago, remedial efforts to integrate public housing residents—mobility programs and the construction of scattered-site units in nonminority areas—have had the practical result of offering a limited number of participants access to higher-quality municipal services. Meanwhile, most low-income African-American families remain concentrated in segregated areas of the city.[56] In a desire to achieve integration, some advocates have cast aside the more important goal of improving housing conditions for members of previously oppressed groups, thus actually harming the intended beneficiaries of civil rights legislation.[57] To the extent that integration policies require African-Americans to leave their neighborhoods against their will, they are deprived of the freedom to decide where to live, just as they were under former segregation policies.[58]

Indeed, public housing desegregation cases were meant to halt overt racial discrimination against African-Americans. However, some critics assert that the old system of racial discrimination has given way to a new, more insidious one: the peculiar "panacea" of the mixed-income development.[59] Mixed-income housing strategies should be implemented with caution because whether they benefit very low-income African-Americans is debatable:

> Racially mixed neighborhoods tend to represent temporary or token integration when they result from nonwhite influx, and gentrification and displacement when they result from white influx. Herein lies the explosive potential of the fair housing conflict. Regardless of whether the integrating group is white or nonwhite, the benefit accruing to the latter is virtually nonexistent.[60]

Ironically, public housing desegregation cases that support the notion of mixed-income housing are a useful political screen for less benevolent agendas, namely, allowing prime areas such as the Horner, Cabrini, and ABLA public housing land to be privately developed at a substantial profit.[61] As disenchantment with integration remedies grows, the loudest opposition to a civil rights litigation strategy may come from unnamed class members themselves. As one CHA resident stated, "*Gautreaux* discriminates against us in our own communities."[62] Those skeptical of the forced integration ideal, including many public housing residents, ask simply, "Where do poor people move?"

What, then, are the answers? The remedy must lie in both acknowledging discrimination and preserving the right of African-Americans to stay in their communities. The theoretical framework for such a remedy is what John Calmore and Robert Forman call "nonsegregation."[63] As Forman defines it:

> Nonsegregation seems preferable to [the] term desegregation, which tends to emphasize the process of change. Nonsegregation implies both the right of people to remain indefinitely where they are, even if in ghetto areas, and the elimination of restrictions on moving into other areas. Nonsegregation would provide for voluntary ghetto residence, while integration could result in involuntary nonghetto residence. Only white ethnocentrism could lead to the belief that all blacks would want to live in predominately white areas.[64]

The nonsegregation approach is not an attack on integration itself but rather on its "dysfunctional consequences."[65] Presumably all advocates can agree on the ultimate goal: supplying decent housing in stable communities for very low-income persons. How that goal is best achieved is where advocates differ. One of the dysfunctional consequences of the integrationist approach is the dilution of the social and political integrity of African-American communities. Housing, after all, is more than a few rooms in an apartment. Rather, it connotes an enormously complicated idea: "it refers to a whole collection of things that come packaged together, not just four walls and a roof, but a specific location in relation to work and services, neighbors and neighborhood, property rights and privacy provisions, income and investment opportunities, and emotional or psychological symbols and supports."[66]

By forcing African-Americans to leave their communities in order to revitalize them, integrationists are destroying the social networks, the friendships, and the service providers on which residents have come to rely. Forced integration of public housing residents presumes that, in a society free from discrimination, blacks would choose to live dispersed among whites. This belief itself may be considered discriminatory because it implies that the only "proper" residential pattern is one in which African-Americans are submerged within a white majority.[67] W.E.B. DuBois's statement of seventy years ago may be just as true today:

> There [is] no objection to colored people living beside colored people if the surroundings and treatment involve no discrimination, if the streets are well lighted, if there is water, sewerage and police protection, and if anybody of any color who wishes, can live in that neighborhood. . . . But never in the world should our fight be against association with ourselves because

by that very token we give up the whole argument that we are worth associating with.[68]

The choice of some African-Americans to remain in their neighborhoods may be born not out of knee-jerk sentiment but out of valid cultural preferences. Further, it is debatable whether integration efforts bestow on poor African-Americans economic or sociological benefits or, rather, destroy nonwhite political power, sense of community, culture, and neighborhood-based support systems.[69]

While Alexander Polikoff, counsel for the *Gautreaux* plaintiffs, acknowledges that not all residents of ghetto public housing communities want to leave, he also notes that revitalizing inner-city neighborhoods face enormous odds: jobs have shifted from the city to the suburbs, suburbs are a better place to raise children, "enterprise zones" and now "empowerment zones" have generally been unsuccessful, and people still feel oppressed in inner-city public housing communities.[70] As John Calmore states, however,

> fair housing must be reconceptualized to mean not only increased opportunity for blacks to move beyond their socio-territorial disadvantage but also to mean enhanced choice to overcome opportunity-denying circumstances while continuing to live in black communities. . . . Short of this, blacks, as a group, will be left with the inadequate "remedy" of individuals choosing, or being forced, to move to "better" space somewhere else.[71]

And, as we have seen, public housing deconcentration efforts often result in merely reconcentrating poor African-Americans in a different space.

With the rebirth of the inner-city communities in areas such as Horner, Cabrini, and ABLA and the concomitant reinvestment in those communities, "integration" means that poor African-Americans who have suffered through years of neglect, deteriorating housing conditions, gang warfare, and extreme segregation are not able to participate in the revival of their communities. Most of the new housing being built is not for them but for higher-income families in order to achieve a mixed-income community:

> *Gautreaux* is being used to promote a new form of racial exclusion posing as a benign "mixed income" development policy. . . . The redevelopment plans for public housing developments like Cabrini-Green and ABLA, for example, are based on a notion of mixed income determined by the perceived comfort level of the future white or higher income buyers and tenants. To developers, the mix of income is only okay as long as the number of poor households does not exceed some perceived "tipping point," a notion reminiscent of the rationale for racial exclusion at the height of overt racial discriminatory practices of the forties and fifties.[72]

If a nonsegregation policy is to succeed in Chicago, it must consist of both mobility and in-place elements. First, programs that reduce barriers to families who choose or are forced to leave their current homes using Housing Choice vouchers must be expanded, and new strategies must be pursued to change the pattern of resegregation that is occurring. Expanding *Gautreaux*-type mobility counseling to all Housing Choice voucher participants, particularly those forcibly relocated from CHA buildings slated for demolition, would be an important first step.[73] Supply-side measures would include enactment of a statewide prohibition on discrimination based on source of income; this would subject landlords to liability for refusing to rent to tenants simply because the tenants are participating in the Housing Choice voucher program.[74] Further, the newly emerging "regionalism" concept, whereby regional remedies are sought for local problems such as racial segregation or a lack of affordable housing, shows promise in opening up suburban communities to low-income African-Americans. Regional approaches include measures such as inclusionary zoning regulations and tax-base sharing.[75]

Second, more focus is needed on improving housing conditions for low-income African-American families who stay in their neighborhoods. The number of public housing units being supplied in the prime, hot market areas must increase. This is not an admonition simply to turn vertical ghettos into horizontal ghettos. That the practice of concentrating only very low-income families in Chicago's public housing developments has not worked and must not be repeated seems beyond question. However, in the gentrifying neighborhoods discussed here, more than 30 percent public housing could be added to the mix without undue consequences.[76] Lake Parc Place on Chicago's south lakefront, CHA's first foray into the mixed-income arena, is occupied entirely by public housing residents and has been widely praised as a success.[77] Phase I of the Horner redevelopment, with an income mix of public housing residents identical to that at Lake Parc Place (50 percent very low-income and 50 percent low-income), has become a showcase CHA development.[78] These are models that should be followed at revitalization projects in gentrifying areas, where market-rate housing already exists. In these areas, scarce public housing land should not be used to supply housing opportunities for nonpublic housing families.

Third, the court must modify the *Gautreaux* order to allow for the construction of new replacement public housing within the mixed-income context even on sites that are not gentrifying, such as Chicago's State Street Corridor. Such a modification would prevent the involuntary relocation of thousands of CHA residents who do not live in what *Gautreaux* would view as "revitalizing" areas.[79] One potential solution would be for CHA to seek modification of the *Gautreaux* judgment to allow rebuilding on the sites of demolished public housing developments if two conditions are met: (1) the redevelopment is mixed-income in character, with at least one-half of the new units reserved for higher-income, nonpublic housing families, and (2) the improved living conditions for public housing residents are substantially similar to those of other income groups within the redevelopment. This proposal offers two advantages over the present system: the focus would not be on the area where redevelopment occurs but on the type of redevelopment being proposed; and, instead of having to convince the *Gautreaux* court that the proposed redevelopment fits into the "revitalizing" definition, the CHA and private developers would have specific criteria that, if followed, would prevent the *Gautreaux* court from interfering with their plans.[80]

These and other proposals must be implemented if *Gautreaux*'s "dysfunctional consequences" are to be ameliorated. As housing policies begin to take shape in the new millennium, decent housing for very low-income African-Americans must be viewed as a primary goal, not simply a secondary result of integration.

Notes

This chapter is adapted from a longer article with the same title published in the *Journal of Poverty Law and Policy,* July–August 2000. The complete article can be accessed at www.povertylaw.org.

1. See John O. Calmore, "Fair Housing v. Fair Housing: The Problems with Providing Increased Housing Opportunities Through Spatial Deconcentration," *Clearinghouse Review* 14 (May 1980): 7, 17; Douglas S. Massey and Nancy A. Denton, *American Apartheid: Segregation and the Making of the Underclass* (Cambridge, MA: Harvard University Press, 1993). According to Massey and Denton, at least sixteen American cities qualify as hypersegregated: Atlanta, Baltimore, Buffalo, Chicago, Cleveland, Dallas, Detroit, Gary, Indianapolis, Kansas City, Los Angeles, Milwaukee, Newark, New York, Philadelphia, and St. Louis (pp. 75–77). See also Institute on Race and Poverty, University of Minnesota, *Concentrated Poverty: Causes, Effects and Solutions* (Minneapolis: 1999), pp. 8–10.

2. See David Blair-Loy, "A Time to Pull Down, and a Time to Build Up: The Constitutionality of Rebuilding Illegally Segregated Public Housing," *Northwestern University Law Review* 88 (1994): 1537, 1538; William Julius Wilson, *The Truly Disadvantaged: The Inner City, The Underclass, and Public Policy* (Chicago: University of Chicago Press, 1987); Institute on Race and Poverty, *Concentrated Poverty,* pp. 21–34.

3. Alexander Polikoff, "Housing Policy and Urban Poverty," in *New Beginnings Project: A First Report* (Washington, DC: Center for Housing Policy, 1994); Lewis H. Spence, "Rethinking the Social Role of Public Housing," *Housing Policy Debate* 4 (1993): 355, 364–367; see also Alexander Polikoff, *Gautreaux* plaintiffs' counsel, letter to Patricia Wright, associate director of the Nathalie P. Voorhees Center for Neighborhood and Community Improvement, University of Illinois at Chicago, February 4, 2000 (on file with the National Center on Poverty Law), and Calmore, "Fair Housing," p. 7.

4. See Leonard S. Rubinowitz, "Metropolitan Public Housing Desegregation Remedies: Chicago's Privatization Program," *Northern Illinois University Law Review* 12 (1991): 589, 669.

5. Public housing desegregation cases in other cities suggest that *Gautreaux* is not an anomaly and that obtaining integrated housing opportunities through litigation is a long and arduous road. Of particular relevance are cases from Minneapolis, Dallas, and Baltimore, which represent broad-based attempts to desegregate public housing in large metropolitan areas. See *Hollman v. Cisneros,* No. 4–92–712 (D. Minn. filed July 27, 1992) (Clearinghouse No. 48,294); *Walker v. City of Mesquite,* 169 F.3d 973, 976 (5th Cir. 1999); *Thompson v. HUD,* No. MJG 95–309 (D. Md. January 31, 1995) (Clearinghouse No. 51,012). Similar cases nationwide have had varying degrees of success. See, e.g., *Christian Community Action v. Cisneros,* No. 3:91CV00296 (D. Conn. July 16, 1999) (Clearinghouse No. 52,438); *NAACP, Boston Chapter v. Kemp,* No. 78–850-SND (D. Mass. March 8, 1991) (Clearinghouse No. 46,596); *Hawkins v. Kemp,* No. 90–0-55 (D. Neb. November 13, 1991) (Clearinghouse No. 45,485); *United States v. Yonkers,* 624 F. Supp. 1276 (S.D.N.Y. 1985) (Clearinghouse No. 48,674); *Hale v. HUD,* No. C-73 410 (W.D. Tenn. August 23, 1985) (Clearinghouse No. 49,107); *Young v. Pierce,* 628 F. Supp. 1037 (E.D. Tex. 1985) (Clearinghouse No. 41,451); *Hutchins v. Cincinnati Metro. Housing Authority,* No. C1–79–131 (S.D. Ohio June 29, 1984) (Clearinghouse No. 35,010); *United States v. City of Parma,* 504 F. Supp. 913 (N.D. Ohio 1980) (Clearinghouse No. 29,593); *Banks v. Perk,* 341 F. Supp. 1175 (N.D. Ohio 1972).

6. See Calmore, "Fair Housing," p. 7.

7. *Gautreaux v. Chicago Housing Authority,* 265 F. Supp. 582, 583 (N.D. Ill. 1967) (Clearinghouse No. 1969).

8. The number of people living in such neighborhoods increased from 4.1 million to 8 million. See Paul A. Jargowsky, *Poverty and Place: Ghettos, Barrios and the American City* (New York: Russell Sage, 1996), pp. 30 (note 13), 70.

9. See Jason DeParle, "The Year That Housing Died: Slamming the Door," *New York Times Magazine,* October 20, 1996, p. 52. Of these 4.5 million, approximately one-third lived in public housing projects and approximately two-thirds lived in privately owned, federally subsidized units.

10. See National Housing Law Project, "Housing Crisis Finally Makes Front-Page News," *Housing Law Bulletin,* November 1996, pp. 147, 150–151, www.nhlp.org/hlb/1196/1196news.htm.

11. See Office of Budget and Management, City of Chicago, *City of Chicago 5-Year Consolidated Plan* 2000–2004 (February 2000). This strategic planning, established by the U.S. Department of Housing and Urban Development (HUD), combines the planning and reporting requirements for four HUD entitlement programs.

12. See Chicago Coalition for the Homeless, "Homelessness: The Causes and the Facts," 1999, p. 1.

13. See Janet Smith and Thomas Lenz, *For Rent: Housing Options in the Chicago Region* (November 1999), p. 7. This 4.2 percent estimate is significantly lower than the 6 percent threshold that HUD uses to determine whether a tight market exists. See also "Rental Market Study Shows Rent Increases and Low Vacancy Rates Throughout Region" (November 23, 1999) (news release on file with the National Center on Poverty Law).

14. Smith and Lenz, *For Rent,* p. 32 (fig. 34); see also Catholic Charities of the Archdiocese of Chicago, *The Housing Crisis in Our Neighborhoods,* October 1999, p. 1, which cites Jennifer Daskal, *In Search of Shelter: The Growing Shortage of*

Affordable Rental Housing (Washington, DC: Center on Budget and Policy Priorities, June 1998), p. 1, note 2.

15. See Nathalie P. Voorhees Center for Neighborhood and Community Improvement, University of Illinois at Chicago, "The Plan to Voucher Out Public Housing: An Analysis of the Chicago Experience and a Case Study of the Proposal to Redevelop the Cabrini-Green Public Housing Area" (May 1997), p. 9.

16. Although two radical housing authorization bills were introduced and passed their respective chambers in 1995 (the House bill called for the repeal of the U.S. Housing Act of 1937), neither became law due to the conferees' failure to reach an agreement. See David E. Bryson, "How the Clinton Administration and the 104th Congress Impaired Poor People's Rights to Housing," *Clearinghouse Review* 30 (March–April 1997): 1154, 1158.

17. In the 1995 rescission bill, HUD funding was cut by 25 percent, funding for development of new public housing was cut from $600 million to $100 million (and eventually eliminated in 1996), and funding for modernization (repair of existing units) was cut from $3.7 billion to $2.9 billion. Modernization funding was cut even further in 1996 and 1997 to $2.5 billion. See National Housing Law Project, "President Signs FY 1995 Rescission Compromise Package: Bad News for Housing," *Housing Law Bulletin,* August 1995, www.nhlp.org/hlb/895/895rescission.htm.

18. See 62 Fed. Reg. 47740 (September 10, 1997); Quality Housing and Work Responsibility Act of 1998 § 531(c), Pub. L. No. 105–276, 112 Stat. 2461 (October 21, 1998).

19. See Department of Veterans Affairs and Housing and Urban Development and Independent Agencies Appropriations Act, 1996, enacted as part of Pub. L. No. 104–134, 110 Stat. 1321–70 (April 26, 1996). Congress now permits public housing authorities to use modernization funds to construct new units. See 42 U.S.C.A. § 1437g(d) (Lexis through 2000 legislation)

20. § 202, Pub. L. No. 104–134, Conversion of Certain Public Housing Units to Vouchers 110 Stat. 1321–79 (April 26, 1996).

21. See National Housing Law Project, "HUD Issues Implementing Notice for Public Housing Conversion: Public Review and Comment Will Be Crucial," *Housing Law Bulletin,* October 1996, p. 42, also available at www.nhlp.org./hlb/1096/1096notice.htm.

22. Chicago Housing Authority, "OCRA [Omnibus Consolidated Rescission and Appropriations Act] 202 Viability Assessment" (May 1998), p. 4.

23. See "Federal Housing Law Threatens Displacement of Up to 34,000 Chicago Public Housing Residents," *Illinois Welfare News,* September 1998, p. 5.

24. See Evelyn Girardet, "Chicago Housing Authority Returned to Local Control," *A.P. Wire Service,* May 28, 1999. In May 1995 HUD took control of the CHA due to "years of failed attempts to clean up the dismal living conditions" of Chicago's public housing. See James Warren and Patrick T. Reardon, "HUD Tired of CHA Failures; Cisneros Explains Shakeup," *Chicago Tribune,* May 28, 1995. In the year before the takeover, the CHA was stung by a series of scandals, including $37 million missing from an employee pension fund and possible conflicts of interest involving CHA executive director Vincent Lane's private development interests.

25. "City of Chicago-HUD Memorandum of Understanding," May 27, 1999, p. 1 (on file with the National Center on Poverty Law).

26. Omnibus Consolidated Rescissions and Appropriations Act of 1996 § 204, Pub. L. No. 104–134, 110 Stat. 1321 (April 26, 1996).

27. See Curtis Lawrence, "CHA to Raze High-Rises," *Chicago Sun-Times,* October 1, 1999; Melita Marie Garza and Flynn McRoberts, "Leaner, Cleaner CHA Envisioned in Overhaul," *Chicago Tribune,* October 1, 1999.

28. See Melita Marie Garza, "CHA Tenant Leaders Decry Major Makeover," *Chicago Tribune,* October 5, 1999.

29. See Susan J. Popkin, "No Simple Solutions for Housing the Poor," *Chicago Tribune,* May 30, 1999. Almost 80 percent of relocated families are living in census tracts that are more than 90 percent black, and more than 90 percent are in census tracts where the median income is less than $15,000. See Paul Fischer, "Section 8 and the Public Housing Revolution: Where Will the Families Go?" (1999), p. 1.

30. Chicago Housing Authority, "Plan for Transformation: Improving Public Housing in Chicago and the Quality of Life" (January 6, 2000); Chicago Housing Authority, "Commitments, Waivers and Requests" (January 6, 2000).

31. Department of Housing and Urban Development, "Memorandum of Approval, Resident Protection Agreement, and Moving to Work Agreement," February 6, 2000 (hereinafter HUD's "Memorandum of Approval").

32. In February 2000 Chicago's chief financial officer announced that the city would issue $600 million in bonds to finance the Plan for Transformation. See Melita Marie Garza and Andrew Zajac, "Overhaul of CHA Hinges on Investors," *Chicago Tribune,* February 12, 2000. The bond issue, the first of its kind in the nation, was intended to allow the CHA to proceed with its planned demolition, rehabilitation, and rebuilding of 25,000 units.

33. See Harold Lucas, HUD assistant secretary, letter to Richard M. Daley, Mayor of Chicago; Congressmen Danny Davis, Bobby Rush, and Jesse Jackson Jr.; Mamie Bone, Central Advisory Committee President; and Resident Association presidents (November 15, 1999), pp. 4–5 (on file with the National Center on Poverty Law); HUD, "Memorandum of Approval," p. 8.

34. See Chicago Housing Authority, "Plan for Transformation."

35. *Gautreaux v. Chicago Housing Authority,* 265 F. Supp. 582, 583. For a detailed history of the litigation, see Alexander Polikoff, "*Gautreaux* and Institutional Litigation," *Chicago-Kent Law Review* 64 (1988): 451; Joseph Seliga, "*Gautreaux* a Generation Later: Remedying the Second Ghetto or Creating the Third," *Northwestern University Law Review* 94 (2000): p. 1074.

36. *Gautreaux v. Chicago Housing Authority,* 265 F. Supp. p. 584.

37. *Gautreaux v. Chicago Housing Authority,* 296 F. Supp. 907, 909 (N.D. Ill. 1969) (Clearinghouse No. 1969). The CHA argued that the Chicago City Council, which had state-law veto power over all CHA acquisition of real estate, was the entity that had discriminated against African-Americans. See Motion for Summary Judgment and Affidavit of C.E. Humphrey in Support of Defendant's Motion for Summary Judgment, *Gautreaux v. Chicago Housing Authority,* 296 F. Supp. 907 (cited in Polikoff, "*Gautreaux* and Institutional Litigation," pp. 455–456). The court determined that the CHA followed an "unvarying" policy of informally clearing each proposed site with the local aldermen and bowing to the aldermen's veto of white sites. *Gautreaux v. Chicago Housing Authority,* 296 F. Supp. pp. 912–913. Even if the CHA had not participated in this informal site-veto process, CHA officials were constitutionally bound not to build on sites chosen by some other agency based on race.

38. See *Gautreaux v. Landrieu,* 498 F. Supp. 1072, 1073 (N.D. Ill. 1980) (Clearinghouse No. 1969); *Gautreaux v. Chicago Housing Authority,* 4 F. Supp. 2d 757,

758 (N.D. Ill. 1998), *appeal dismissed,* 178 F.3d 951 (7th Cir. 1999) (Clearinghouse No. 1969).

39. See *Gautreaux v. Landrieu,* 498 F. Supp. 1072, 1073 (N.D. Ill. 1980) (Clearinghouse No. 1969); 4 F. Supp. 2d *Gautreaux v. Chicago Housing Authority* 757, 758 (N.D. Ill. 1998), appeal dismissed, 178 F.3d 951 (7th Cir. 1999) (Clearinghouse No. 1969).

40. *Gautreaux v. Landrieu,* 523 F. Supp. 665, 669 (N.D. Ill. 1981) (Clearinghouse No. 1969). The court considers the following factors in determining whether to designate an area as revitalizing: whether the area is (1) undergoing visible redevelopment or evidences impending construction, (2) located along the lakefront, (3) scheduled to receive Community Development Block Grant funds, (4) accessible to transportation, (5) an area with significant stock of housing meeting building code standards, (6) accessible to shopping, (7) located near attractive features, (8) free of a large concentration of assisted housing, (9) not located in a predominately minority area, and (10) not densely populated (p. 671).

41. See *Gautreaux v. Chicago Housing Authority,* No. 66 C 1459, slip. op. and orders (N.D. Ill. March 9, 1995, August 14, 1995, April 15, 1996, and October 22, 1998) (Horner); slip. op. and agreed order (November 11, 1997) (Cabrini); slip op. and order (June 19, 1998) (ABLA); slip op. and order (June 3, 1996) (Kenwood-Oakland) (Clearinghouse No. 1969).

42. *Gautreaux v. Romney,* 448 F.2d 731, 737 (7th Cir. 1971) (Clearinghouse No. 4490).

43. *Hills v. Gautreaux,* 425 U.S. 284, 297–300 (1976) (Clearinghouse No. 1969). The Supreme Court's opinion made clear that metropolitan-wide relief against HUD was appropriate because it would not require consolidation or restructuring local government units. *Id.* at 305. Thus government entities that were not wrongdoers could not be forced to participate in remedial arrangements. See *Milliken v. Bradley,* 418 U.S. 717 (1974) (holding that an "interdistrict violation" must exist for court to order relief crossing school-district boundary lines).

44. *Gautreaux v. Pierce,* 690 F.2d 616 (7th Cir. 1982) (Clearinghouse No. 1969); *Gautreaux v. Chicago Housing Authority,* 981 F. Supp. 1091, 1094 (N.D. Ill. 1997) (Clearinghouse No. 1969). See, e.g., Leonard Rubinowitz and James Rosenbaum, *Crossing the Class and Color Lines* (Chicago: University of Chicago Press, 2000); James Rosenbaum, "Black Pioneers: Do Their Moves to the Suburbs Increase Economic Opportunity for Mothers and Children?" *Housing Policy Debate* 2 (1991): 1179. But see Xavier de Souza Briggs, "Moving Up Versus Moving Out: Neighborhood Effects in Housing Mobility Programs," *Housing Policy Debate* 8 (1997): 195 (suggesting that prior research on mobility programs did not pinpoint the true effects of neighborhoods, apart from the effects of families or social networks, and that assumptions about poor people benefiting from having more affluent neighbors are largely untested).

45. See Polikoff, "*Gautreaux* and Institutional Litigation," pp. 459–460.

46. *Gautreaux v. Pierce,* No. 66 C 1459 and 1460 (consolidated) (N.D. Ill. July 9, 1987) (order appointing receiver) (Clearinghouse No. 1969). The receivership order does not cover senior housing. In addition to being reimbursed for overhead costs for CHA housing, Habitat earns a fee of 3 percent of the dollars spent on new family housing construction. See also Brian Rogal, "Private Firm Keeps Tight Grip on Public Housing," *Chicago Reporter,* November 1999, p. 6 (indicating that HUD has budgeted $21.8 million for Habitat's work, including a fee of more than $6.8 million, of which $17.3 has been paid to Habitat).

47. See *Gautreaux v. Chicago Housing Authority,* 981 F. Supp. p. 1097. The *Gautreaux* class consists of African-American tenants and applicants for Chicago public housing.

48. See Brian Rogal, "Scattered Sites Finally Reach White Areas," *Chicago Reporter,* November 1999, p. 7; see also Andrew Martin and Flynn McRoberts, "Scattered CHA Sites? Hardly," *Chicago Tribune,* December 8, 1998. The court has interpreted the judgment order to allow construction of scattered-site units in low-income Latino neighborhoods because Latinos are not considered "nonwhite." *Gautreaux v. Pierce,* 548 F. Supp. at 1295.

49. Flynn McRoberts, "Move from CHA High-Rise Can Involve a Leap of Faith," *Chicago Tribune,* September 2, 1998, p. 8. See also Rui Kaneya and Danielle Gordon, "Finding Sites for New Public Housing No Easy Task," *Chicago Reporter,* March 1998, p. 15 (describing how hundreds of white residents protested the construction of a single three-flat scattered-site building in their neighborhood); Rogal, "Scattered Sites Finally Reach White Areas"; Garza and McRoberts, "Leaner, Cleaner CHA Envisioned"; Business and Professional People for the Public Interest, "Myths About *Gautreaux*" (November 19, 1999) (on file with the National Center on Poverty Law). Several CHA families that relocated to predominately Latino areas asked to be moved again due to harassment and intimidation by their neighbors.

50. See Brian Rogal, "CHA Residents Moving to Segregated Areas," *Chicago Reporter,* July 1998, p. 3; Fischer, "Section 8 and the Public Housing Revolution," pp. 1–2. See also Paul Fischer, "Racial and Locational Patterns of Subsidized Housing in the Chicago Suburbs," *Geography Journal on Fighting Poverty* 1 (1994): 384, which describes how the Housing Authority of Cook County's administration of the Section 8 program exacerbated segregation in Chicago's south suburbs.

51. See Chicago Housing Authority, "Plan for Transformation," p. 2, and Susan J. Popkin and Mary K. Cunningham, "Where Will We Go? Searching for Housing with Section 8 in Chicago" (Washington, DC: Urban Institute, 1999), which details the unsuccessful efforts of some CHA families to find housing through the Section 8 program.

52. Rogal, "CHA Residents Moving to Segregated Areas," p. 5.

53. See *Gautreaux v. Chicago Housing Authority,* 981 F. Supp. 1094. In October 1999 the *Gautreaux* plaintiffs reached agreement with the CHA authorizing the Leadership Council for Metropolitan Open Communities to give mobility counseling to sixty-five families residing in a CHA development slated for closure. See Memorandum of *Gautreaux* Plaintiffs in Response to ABLA Plaintiffs' Motion to Intervene at exh. 3, *Gautreaux v. Chicago Housing Authority* (No. 66 C 1459) (filed January 10, 2000). See also Phillip Jackson, CHA executive director, letter to Aurie Pennick, president and chief executive officer of the Leadership Council for Metropolitan Open Communities (October 7, 1999) (on file with the National Center on Poverty Law), detailing the mobility counseling agreement between CHA and the Leadership Council.

54. *Gautreaux v. Chicago Housing Authority,* 4 F. Supp. 2d 757.

55. See Cory Oldweiler and Brian J. Rogal, "Public Housing: Reading Between the Lines," *Chicago Reporter,* March 2000, p. 7.

56. See Massey and Denton, *American Apartheid,* pp. 75–77.

57. See Ankur J. Goel, "Maintaining Integration Against Minority Interests: An Anti-Subjugation Theory for Equality in Housing," *Urban Law* 22 (1990): 369, 415.

58. See Michael R. Tein, "Comment: The Devaluation of the Nonwhite Community in Remedies for Subsidized Housing Discrimination," *University of Pennsylvania Law Review* 140 (1992): 1463, 1497; see also Emily Paradise Achtenberg and

Peter Marcuse, "Toward the Decommodification of Housing," *Critical Perspectives on Housing,* in ed. Rachael G. Bratt et al., p. 480 (Philadelphia: Temple University Press, 1986).

59. See David C. Ranney and Patricia Wright, "Where Do Poor People Move?" *Chicago Tribune,* January 26, 2000.

60. Calmore, "Fair Housing," pp. 7, 12.

61. See Nathalie P. Voorhees Center, "The Plan to Voucher Out Public Housing," pp. iii, 46, which estimated that developers of Cabrini-Green stood to make more than $100 million in profits.

62. Chris Chandler, "Court Ruling Poses Threat, Say CHA Residents," *Streetwise,* April 28, 1998 (quoting Wardell Yotaghan, cofounder of the Coalition to Protect Public Housing).

63. See John O. Calmore, "Symposium: The Urban Crisis: The Kerner Commission Report Revisited: Spatial Equality and the Kerner Commission Report: A Back-to-the-Future Essay," *North Carolina Law Review* 71 (June 1993): 1487, 1498; Calmore, "Fair Housing," p. 12; Robert F. Forman, *Black Ghettos, White Ghettos and Slums* (Englewood Cliffs, NJ: Prentice-Hall, 1971).

64. Forman, *Black Ghettos,* p. 46

65. See Calmore, "Fair Housing," p. 8.

66. Roger Montgomery and Daniel R. Mandelker, eds., *Housing in America: Problems and Perspectives,* 2nd ed. (New York: Bobbs-Merrill, 1979), p. 3.

67. See Tein, "Comment," p. 1471.

68. W.E.B. DuBois, "Postscript," *The Crisis,* January 1934, p. 20.

69. See Henry W. McGee, "Afro-American Resistance to Gentrification and the Demise of Integrationist Ideology in the United States," *Urban Law* 23 (1991): 25, 28; Calmore, "Symposium: Urban Crisis," pp. 1501–1508.

70. See Polikoff, "Housing Policy," pp. 97–98, quoting Nicholas Lemann, "the notion of ghetto renewal is untenable," in *The Promised Land: The Great Black Migration and How It Changed America* (New York: Vintage, 1991).

71. Calmore, "Symposium: Urban Crisis," p. 1495.

72. David C. Ranney and Patricia A. Wright, "Perspective on the CHA's Plan for Transformation," *The Coalition to Protect Public Housing's Talking Drum* (newsletter), February 2000, p. 3.

73. See Margery Austin Turner et al., "Section 8 Mobility and Neighborhood Health: Emerging Issues and Policy Challenges" (Washington, DC: Urban Institute, 2000), www.urban.org/community/sec8_mobility.html.

74. Connecticut and New Jersey have enacted such statutes. See *Commission on Human Rights v. Sullivan Assocs.,* No. 941002569, 1998 Conn. Super. *Lexis* 1889 (Conn. Super. Ct. June 8, 1998) (interpreting *Conn. Gen. Stat.* 46a-64c); *Franklin Tower One L.L.C. v. N.M.,* 725 A.2d 1104 (N.J. 1999) (Clearinghouse No. 51,772) (interpreting N.J. Stat. Ann. 2A:42–1000). A court has found that Chicago's fair housing ordinance, which prohibits discrimination based on source of income, applies to Section 8 voucher-holders. *Smith v. Wilmette Real Estate & Mgmt. Co.,* No. 95-H-159 (Chicago Comm. on Human Relations, April 13, 1999) (Clearinghouse No. 52,327). However, because the ordinance does not apply outside Chicago, it is of no help to inner-city residents seeking to move to low-poverty suburban areas.

75. See, e.g., John A. Powell, "Addressing Regional Dilemmas for Minority Communities," in *Reflections on Regionalism,* ed. Bruce Katz, esp. pp. 237–241 (Washington, DC: Brookings Institution, 2000).

76. Even in areas that are not nearly as gentrifying as the areas surrounding Cabrini, ABLA, and Horner, mixed-income public housing has succeeded. At Lake Parc Place on Chicago's South Side, two 141-unit high-rises were completely rehabilitated and converted into mixed-income public housing, with 50 percent of the units reserved for families with incomes between 0 and 50 percent of the area median income and 50 percent for families with incomes between 50 percent and 80 percent of the area median income. When the building reopened in 1991, CHA's renovation effort included substantial improvements in public spaces, exterior landscaping, and other physical amenities, careful tenant screening, private management, and substantial on-site maintenance and support personnel. See Michael H. Schill, "Chicago's Mixed Income New Communities Strategy: The Future Face of Public Housing," in *Affordable Housing and Urban Redevelopment in the United States,* ed. Willem van Vliet, pp. 135–137 (Thousand Oaks, CA: Sage, 1997).

77. For a discussion of Lake Parc's successes, see James E. Rosenbaum et al., "Lake Parc Place: A Study of Mixed Income Housing," *Housing Policy Debate* 9 (1998): 729–731; Maryann Mason, "Mixed Income Public Housing: Outcomes for Tenants and Their Community: A Case Study of the Lake Parc Place Development in Chicago, Illinois" (PhD diss., Loyola University, 1998).

78. See Melita Marie Garza, "Panel Opposed Council's Choice for Management; Horner Residents May Take CHA to Court," *Chicago Tribune,* April 18, 2000.

79. See Brian J. Rogal, "Survey Casts Doubt on CHA Plans," *Chicago Reporter,* June 1999 (reporting that two out of three Robert Taylor Homes residents surveyed opposed CHA's plan to demolish Taylor and move them into the private market with Section 8 vouchers).

80. See Seliga, "*Gautreaux* a Generation Later," pp. 1093–1094.

10

Mixed-Income Communities

Designing Out Poverty or
Pushing Out the Poor?

Janet L. Smith

*The question that we should have asked in 1949, when
the federal urban renewal program started, is long overdue
now: Is it right to deliberately hurt people, to push around
those who are least able to defend themselves, to spend billions
of dollars of the taxpayers' money, so that some people
might be able to enjoy a prettier city?[1]*

The staunch privatist Martin Anderson asked the question above because he
believed "the economic system of free enterprise [was] a viable alternative
to the government program" of urban renewal.[2] The current involvement of
the private sector in public housing transformation appears to be just what
Anderson and other free-market economists wanted. However, public housing proponents are concerned that the approach taken is *too* responsive to
free enterprise and that this new round of urban renewal is doing more harm
than good to those "least able to defend themselves."

At a fundamental level, there was a reason for keeping public housing
"public"—to keep the housing and the land it occupied out of the speculative
influence of the private market.[3] Over the past sixty years, this has assured
that some housing in our communities remained affordable and relatively
available to the poor. While privatization has shown some promise in redeveloping public housing, particularly in finding new sources of funding, it
also presents some challenges for the future of housing for the poor. This
chapter explores the broader logic behind transforming public housing into
mixed-income communities, and how new urbanist design strategies aim to

produce socially and economically viable and sustainable mixed-income communities. It is uncertain whether these strategies, while capable of generating cohesively designed neighborhoods, can actually reduce poverty or will just move the poor out.

The New Frontier: Mixed-Income Development

Trying to rectify previous mistakes in the design and development of public housing, the government requires all new redeveloped public housing sites to be "mixed-income." The federal government hopes that "the intentional mixing of incomes and working status of residents" will "enhance the quality of life for residents while improving the economic viability of multifamily developments, particularly former public housing developments, and strengthen neighborhoods."[4] Income mixing also aims to "promote the economic and social interaction of low-income families within the broader community, thereby providing greater opportunities for the upward mobility of such families."[5]

HOPE VI set the stage for public housing transformation, mandating that these new mixed-income developments should be designed to blend in rather than stand out in a community and to attract higher-income families who would otherwise choose to move into a more conventional community. A manual produced by the Congress for the New Urbanism (CNU) in conjunction with the Department of Housing and Urban Development (HUD) outlines specific design principles for developing these new inner-city communities.[6] Premised on the belief that the neighborhood is the fundamental building block of healthy cities and towns and that neighborhoods should offer a diverse range of housing with services and shopping within walking distance or easily accessed via public transit,[7] the hope is that these new neighborhoods will not only facilitate mixing among the different residents, but also help public housing residents become more self-sufficient. As Secretary of HUD Andrew Cuomo and the CNU's chair, Robert Davis, state in the manual's opening:

> Bringing high quality design to the buildings, streets, parks and public places in HOPE VI communities is critical. The path to self-sufficiency is made easier if a neighborhood is planned to help residents with different incomes interact with one another. The process is enhanced if every home, regardless of the resident's income, is both functional and attractive. Finally, residents can learn real pride when their neighborhood looks and feels like neighborhoods in the surrounding community.[8]

While CNU makes no claims that families are more likely to get out of poverty if they live next to higher-income families, HUD does just that in much of its rhetoric about HOPE VI and now public housing transformation. In broad terms, income mixing is expected to mitigate the "social ills" associated with high concentrations of poverty—crime, unemployment, single mothers, substance abuse.[9]

As discussed in the introduction to this book, recent academic and policy-oriented research assumes that these conditions are the result of poor people living together in isolation and separated from higher-income people. Putting aside for a moment the debates surrounding this particular framing of the problem, we can see how income mixing—whether by bringing higher-income people into a poor community or by relocating poor people into an existing middle-income community—offers a practical way to deconcentrate poverty. Although it is a clear means to an end, there is no certainty that any of the assumed positive spillover effects of mixing will result from either strategy. This includes the assumption that higher-income working families will be good role models for lower-income residents, opening doors to employment opportunities via networking and increasing "social capital" presumed lacking in high-poverty neighborhoods.[10] A second assumption is that as a result of higher-income households' demand for quality neighborhood services, lower-income residents will also benefit because they will receive higher levels of services than they did when they lived in concentrated poverty.

A third assumption is that developing mixed-income housing will improve the overall quality of affordable housing itself as private developers and public officials strive to meet higher standards in order to have a successful development project.[11] Finally, an anticipated result is that with higher-quality public housing, community support for affordable housing is likely to grow and expand into areas that have historically been unwelcoming to rental housing. In other words, the hope is that good examples of mixed-income public housing can mitigate the not-in-my-backyard (NIMBY) problem that often blocks development of subsidized units.

Income mixing through the provision of a range of housing options in a single community has long been a goal of planning and social progressives.[12] Yet in contrast to this progressive policy goal, many scholars and policy makers historically have questioned the viability of "mixed neighborhoods," beginning with the work of sociologists at the University of Chicago in the 1920s. The widely held belief then and for most the twentieth century was that stable or healthy neighborhoods were relatively homogeneous in terms of race, class, and ethnicity, while mixed or heterogeneous neighborhoods were unstable and unhealthy, often in a state of flux.[13] Until the current era of public housing transformation, federal urban policy has generally affirmed this view. A report on neighborhood change produced for HUD in the mid-1970s, for example, assumed that a "healthy" neighborhood was relatively homoge-

Table 10.1

Indicators of a "Healthy" Stable Neighborhood, 1975

Social
- Middle to high social status
- Moderate to upper income levels
- Ethnic homogeneity
- High school graduates and above
- Family oriented or childless adults
- White-collar and/or skilled blue-collar workers
- Pride in neighborhood and house
- Good neighborhood reputation
- Neighborhood perceived as safe
- Socially cohesive

Public services
- Services efficient and appropriate
- Some reliance on private services

Physical
- Good property upkeep
- Sound structural condition
- Good location
- Neighborhood well maintained

Economic
- High owner investment
- Good property values
- Insurance available
- High confidence in future value

Source: James Mitchell, *The Dynamics of Neighborhood Change* (Washington, DC: U.S. Department of Housing and Urban Development, Office of Policy Development and Research, 1974).

neous across income, tenure, race, ethnicity, and even household types and that high income levels and rates of ownership were important to maintaining stability (see Table 10.1). These criteria was developed as part of a model for determining the degree to which neighborhoods were "unhealthy," a declining neighborhood was ethnically or racially mixed and with high proportions of lower-income households as well as renters.

Of course, in the 1960s and 1970s, outright racism coupled with institutional discrimination in the form of blockbusting and redlining helped to generate this impression. While the Fair Housing Act of 1968 made this kind of behavior illegal, annually millions of dollars are given to settle discrimination cases. Further, the overwhelming segregation by income as well as race and ethnicity in many urban areas raises questions about the extent to which different groups of people are willing and able to mix.[14] For example, data from the U.S. census show that, despite slight improvement, the Chicago region continues to be highly segregated by race, ethnicity, and income.[15]

Public officials have also played a role in producing these spatial patterns, with laws and funding criteria also reinforcing racial and ethnic segregation.[16] Until just a few years ago, the Federal government was not willing or able to underwrite mixed-income developments, given the assumption that they would decline and therefore fail. Again, the concern came from the evidence of disinvestment and failing markets found in so many old industrial cities. More recent research suggests that, although they are still the exception and not the rule, mixed neighborhoods can be stable and healthy.[17] Still, when HOPE VI was first introduced, there was no conclusive evidence that mixed-income communities would produce any of the social benefits envisioned.[18] However, the lack of proof was not a deterrent, and income mixing was launched as HUD's ambitious new strategy to transform public housing.

In order to produce these new mixed-income communities, the rules for developing public housing needed to change. In addition to permanently repealing the one-for-one replacement rule, the 1998 Quality Housing and Work Responsibility Act (QHWRA) further restricted how much public housing a public housing agency (PHA) could build back on-site by requiring it to be "significantly fewer than the number of units demolished."[19] While QWHRA does not provide a firm number or ratio for what constitutes "significantly fewer" units, income-targeting guidelines for new tenants do provide some insight on what this might be. The act requires that not less than 40 percent of new families be very low-income (at or below 30 percent of area median income) while the remaining admissions can be higher-income (up to 80 percent of area medium income).[20] A PHA can reduce the number of very low-income residents in a development, but only if it admits an equal proportion (up to 10 percent) of very low-income households into the voucher program (this exchange is referred to as "fungibility"). These formulas are intended to provide for deconcentration of poverty and to promote income mixing. Furthermore, PHAs can offer incentives to higher-income families to move into buildings that are predominantly lower-income. The reciprocal is that they can also offer units to lower-income families in predominantly higher-income developments.

A lesser-known but pivotal change for public housing came when HUD announced its Mixed-Finance Public Housing program and new Federal Housing Administration (FHA) "Mixed-Income Housing Underwriting Guidelines" in 1997.[21] Recognizing that mixed-income development was risky to lenders as well as developers, HUD needed to make it possible to use federal funding as "gap financing" and to have the FHA underwrite the loans. However, mixed-income housing was an area of underwriting historically avoided by the FHA, and the agency would not underwrite the loan unless "these projects can be done without increased risk to the FHA insurance fund."[22] In order to reduce risk and to assure the successful development of "viable" mixed-income housing, new underwriting guidelines required developments:

- to use the surrounding income mix to determine the ratio of market-rate to low-income units—a higher proportion of market-rate units is needed in a predominantly low-income neighborhood to "successfully attract" the market-rate tenants;
- to have adequate amenities and good design in order to "compete against" conventional market-rate units, and the prices must be "very competitive with or, at least initially, even below what the competition is offering for the same level quality and amenities"; and
- to screen all tenants carefully and employ strong "customer-driven" but "even-handed" high-quality management.[23]

While intended to assure investors that new developments would not look like the old public housing, the underwriting requirements also benefit public housing residents, at least by improving the quality of buildings and management. However, requiring a higher proportion of market-rate units to "build a market" clearly aims to assuage higher-income consumers' fear that they are taking a risk. Similarly, this parameter allows a developer to include more market-rate housing to minimize risk and to ensure that the project does not lose money. In part, this practice is justified since mixed-income (and often mixed-tenure and mixed-use) developments are not time-tested real estate ventures. Further, lenders and underwriters are generally less comfortable with projects that require different time periods to service debt, as is the case with public housing sites that are being transformed in stages with both rental and for-sale housing being developed.[24] Generally, these types of projects would sequence the development to begin with the product that allows quick debt retirement (e.g., for-sale housing), followed by the products that have longer debt periods, including rental and commercial property. This is how Harbor Point in Boston was redeveloped in the 1980s.[25] The risk, of course, is that funding will not come through for later phases, leaving a development unfinished. The effect can be detrimental to the project's viability, especially if the later phases include much-needed commercial development. It can also prevent the development from being mixed-income if the rental housing slated for a later phase is not built.

Helping local housing authorities to design and develop these new com-munities is a growing cadre of private sector developers—some very large and well known, others small and local.[26] It is assumed that the knowledge and expertise of these developers will produce a quality product—one that is responsive to the market and attractive to high-income consumers. Under the new rules, these developers are given great flexibility when it comes to de-velopment costs, with the premise that even if the housing costs a great deal up-front, it will be cost-effective in the long run. Private developers are also now allowed to own and manage the sites they develop, including public housing units that are leased by the PHA. The assumption here is that giving private owners this level of control will ensure the long-term viability and quality of the new development, since it is in the owner's best interest to keep property values up and vacancy rates down.

In the United States, income mixing can be considered an experiment that will take some time before we see results from which we can draw valid conclusions. In the meantime, the image of what will happen as a result of deconcentrating poverty has been compelling enough for the government and developers to commit hundreds of millions of public and private dollars to rebuild public housing. We can assume that what makes the whole experi-ment so appealing to investors nationwide (and even internationally via the bond market) is the potential to retrofit whole areas of cities that have borne the negative effects of past policy decisions. While technical changes in FHA underwriting and HUD policy have made it attractive for private sector de-velopers and funders to participate in the transformation of public housing, they do not ensure that these developments will produce the social outcomes that HUD desires—only that the new communities will be mixed-income. To achieve this goal, HUD is relying on new urbanism, which challenges tradi-tional forms of development that segregate people by income and household type, to help with the mixing.

New Urbanism . . . New Directions in Public Housing

Much of the residential development after World War II came in the form of the suburban subdivision—often a large tract of homogeneous and similarly priced homes. Ironically, perhaps, the subdivision is the direct result of changes in building technology that produced public housing in cities. Aimed at mak-ing housing more affordable, both subdivisions and public housing made use of the same mass production techniques, uniform design, and prefabricated components. These allowed developers to respond quickly to demand for inexpensive starter homes and allowed local housing authorities to quickly build high-rise public housing. New urbanists blame modern planning, and zoning in particular, for the separation of land uses typically found in the suburban tract home development.[27] Used to designate the appropriate use of land in a community by classifying large areas according to different codes (residential, commercial, industrial, open space, etc.), zoning aims to produce public benefits by controlling how land is used. Local zoning codes have controlled most development completed in the past sixty years in America. In the case of housing, residential codes (e.g., R-1, R-2, etc.) determine the density of development, as well as whether the site can be used for single-family or multifamily buildings. In many newer suburbs, zoning has restricted or even prohibited high-density residential development, whether owned or rented, resulting in little to no affordable housing options for poor people in these communities.

Upheld by the Supreme Court in 1926, zoning was intended to separate incompatible uses.[28] Over time, zoning has also helped distance the home from work and shopping. Today, a growing number of planners and architects are challenging the American public to think differently about development, and particularly, to support development of mixed-income communities. This shift can be traced to a set of practical problems and ideological changes in recent years. Urban sprawl, for example, with its traffic and congestion, raises questions about the cost of continued metropolitan expansion. More recently, the growing number of Americans paying more than 30 percent of their income for housing, particularly in cities experiencing reinvestment, has drawn attention to the fact that middle-class families are being priced out of many communities. Despite this awareness, however, planners still struggle with the NIMBY attitude that keeps low-income housing out of many communities. Similar tension is seen in the discussion of sprawl: people deplore its impact on the environment as they continue to spread out—an issue in many countries with decentralizing cities—yet are not willing to give up their space or the freedom to distance themselves from things they do not want to live near.

New urbanism, smart growth, and regionalism all promote a mixing of land uses, tenure, and income groups, furthering a movement away from late twentieth-century patterns of housing development. For example, smart growth focuses on (1) promoting neighborhood livability through careful planning to bring together safety, convenience, and affordability; (2) improving access and reducing traffic, giving people choice in their mode of transportation; (3) improving and preserving existing places rather than continuing to build new; (4) making it possible for all to share in the benefits of prosperity; (5) lowering costs and taxes by dealing with problems that generally raise both; and (6) keeping open space for current and future use as parks and nature areas.[29] Regionalism—a term that saw several incarnations during the twentieth century—has become popular again, especially in response to sprawl but also because local economies and social networks do not stop at jurisdictional boundaries. Like smart growth, regionalism speaks of new forms of governance to manage change and to promote mixed use and diversity within urban areas.[30]

New urbanism, which has had the strongest influence on public housing transformation, grew out of desire to reshape the urban landscape and particularly to stop the spread of the homogeneous suburban development by changing the rules for conventional place making. Based on "a belief in the scale and spatial organization of the traditional town as the basic building block for human settlement," the CNU has developed a set of design principles "to guide public policy, development practice, urban planning and design" at the level of the region, the neighborhood, and the block.[31] These new planned developments are regulated by strict codes to ensure appropriate density and control design and aesthetics. Much of the groundwork for translating new urbanist ideas into practice is credited to the architect/planner team of Andrés Duany and Elizabeth Plater-Zyberk and developer Robert Davis, whose pioneering development of Seaside, Florida, became the model for this new form of "traditional" town planning and design. This model includes public green and community space, commercial buildings with housing upstairs, and restricting the flow of automobile traffic through the site.[32]

To complement its efforts to transform "worst case" projects into sites of "promise," HUD worked with the Inner City Task Force of the CNU to develop a set of principles, specifically for use in public housing redevelopment, that were "to be further tested and refined through use."[33] As Table 10.2 illustrates, these principles parallel the community-building language in HOPE VI. Involving a wide range of stakeholders in the redevelopment process is assumed to lead to the design of a space that will facilitate not only a mix of income groups via a range of price levels and housing types but also diversity in age and race. These principles also reproduce the rhetoric and intent of HOPE VI by seeking to "reclaim and repair" the space containing and surrounding public housing. This goal includes making sure that the new site is no longer an isolated project but rather one that blends into the architectural character of its neighborhood. Ideally, these new developments will be mixed-use sites that allow people to work and play close to where they live by reconnecting the site to regional patterns of transportation and land use.

Collectively, these elements aim to produce a positive and cohesive external appearance for the development while simultaneously producing internal clarity about how the space is to be used. Each is important for different reasons. The external appearance is important in changing the image of pub-

Table 10.2

Design Principles of the Congress for the New Urbanism Inner City Task Force

Citizen and community involvement	Engage residents, neighbors, civic leaders, politicians, bureaucrats, developers, and local institutions throughout the process of designing change for neighborhoods.
Economic opportunity	The design of neighborhood development should accommodate management techniques and scales of construction that can be contracted to local and minority businesses.
Diversity	Provide a broad range of housing types and price levels to bring people of diverse ages, races, and incomes into daily interaction—strengthening the personal and civic bonds essential to an authentic community.
Neighborhoods	Neighborhoods are compact, pedestrian-friendly and mixed use with many activities of daily life available within walking distance. New development should help repair existing neighborhoods or create new ones and should not take the form of an isolated "project."
Infill development	Reclaim and repair blighted and abandoned areas within existing neighborhoods by using infill development strategically to conserve economic investment and social fabric.
Mixed use	Promote the creation of mixed-use neighborhoods that support the functions of daily life: employment, recreation, retail, and civic and educational institutions.
Citywide and regional connections	Neighborhoods should be connected to regional patterns of transportation and land use, to open space, and to natural systems.
Streets	The primary task of all urban architecture and landscape design is the physical definition of streets and public space as places of shared use. Neighborhoods should have an interconnected network of streets and public open space.
Public open space	The interconnected network of streets and public open space should provide opportunities for recreation and appropriate settings for civic buildings.
Safety and civic engagement	The relationship of buildings and streets should enable neighbors to create a safe and stable neighborhood by providing "eyes on the street" and should encourage interaction and community identity. Provide a clear definition of public and private realms through block and street design that responds to local tradition.

Dwelling as mirror of self	Recognize the dwelling as the basic element of a neighborhood and as the key to self-esteem and community pride. This includes the clear definition of outdoor space for each dwelling.
Accessibility	Buildings should be designed to be accessible and visitable while respecting the traditional urban fabric.
Local architectural character	The image and character of new development should respond to the best traditions of residential and mixed-use architecture in the area.
Design codes	The economic health and harmonious evolution of neighborhoods can be improved through graphic urban design codes that serve as predictable guides for change.

Source: Congress for the New Urbanism, *Principles for Inner City Neighborhood Design: HOPE VI and the New Urbanism.*

lic housing, which has been an eyesore in so many communities. However, a cohesive look within the development may be even more important since the intention is not to draw attention to differences among its residents. In other words, the facade is just that—it provides no obvious clues about who lives in the home behind it. Instead of looking like public housing, the exterior is to reproduce what would be found in a middle-class development. The external clarity projected by the physical design and orientation of buildings, sidewalks, and roads also aims to change perceptions of public housing, both for residents who have lived in public housing and for new residents of the new mixed-income developments. Typically referred to as "defensible space," the design elements and layout of public areas and pathways are to convey a feeling of safety and security. These elements include lighting, clearly marked paths, places to congregate, fences to keep people from going into certain areas, and even closed-circuit television to monitor areas for illegal behavior.

By design, then, new urbanist sites are expected to prevent or at least minimize uncivil behavior in public and semipublic places. Moreover, both internal and external design aims to remake the existing physical space in such a way that the site itself can ensure neighborhood stability and health by encouraging residents to form interpersonal relationships. For example, a common feature is the inclusion of porches similar to those found in homes built in decades past. Providing a place to congregate, porches offer a way for residents to become neighbors: to greet and welcome each other if not directly into their home, at least onto their private property. Porches also provide a means to observe—to keep "eyes on the street" to see who belongs and who is acting out of place. As the CNU states, "The porch serves a dual purpose: the vestibule to the occupant's private residence, and the occupant's vestibule to the street."[34]

Another strategy is to design homes to fit in with the vernacular architecture, so that regardless of tenure or income, visitors cannot distinguish between adjoining public and private housing. While this goal implies a certain level of uniformity, it by no means requires reproducing the banality often associated with modern suburban developments. Instead, the goal is to give developers and architects guidelines that produce variety, but also space and housing that fit in and fit together. In *Principles for Inner-City Neighborhood Design: HOPE VI and the New Urbanism,* the Congress for the New Urbanism praises designers of the Park DuValle HOPE VI project for developing a pattern book providing "guidelines for massing and placement of houses as well as an inventory of correctly proportioned elements such as windows, doors, porches, and other essential qualities of traditional Louisville architecture."[35] The result is an eclectic set of homes that fit into the surrounding neighborhood, relate well to each other, and do not look like public housing.[36]

Why Does Design Matter in Transforming Public Housing?

Since most redeveloped public housing is still relatively new, we cannot fairly judge how the design of the space affects interpersonal relationships and the potential for poor residents to benefit from living in mixed-income communities. However, observations made by architecture critics and social scientists about more established new urbanist communities suggest that the design approach to building community may have some promise for public housing. For example, Philip Langdon concluded from his visit to Charleston Place in Boca Raton, Florida, that "it succeeded in becoming a place where people are drawn into conversation with their neighbors" and that it stood "a good chance of generating community activity."[37] Michael Southworth reported that homeowners from Kentlands (near Gaithersburg, Maryland) and Laguna West (near Sacramento, California) "sense more neighborliness" there than in conventional suburbs. However, he also found that both sites are "rather rigid architectonic visions that offer instant identity and instant community sense by controlling the built form."[38] Marisa Bartolucci drew a similar conclusion: "It is a well-meaning but futile effort, since such communities are forged not out of quaint architecture and grid schemes (although such elements might help support them), but through the dynamic of place, enterprise and social exchange."[39] Architecture critic Herbert Muschamp is more pointed in his critique:

> The Congress for the New Urbanism also oversells the capacity of its designs to foster a strong sense of community. Clearly if you increase den-

sity, you bring people into closer physical proximity. But as life in any city makes painfully clear, it is by no means certain that proximity guarantees social cohesion or even social contact.[40]

Witold Rybczynski is cautious about overselling the design effects but also a bit more optimistic after his visit to the Walt Disney Corporation's new town, Celebration, Florida. Forgiving of the architectural control, he concludes that while it will take time, this new town will eventually come to replicate the social space of older small towns.[41] Even Andrés Duany acknowledges a need for time to produce the desired form of community. Citing anthropologist Edward LiPuma, Duany assumes that it will take a generation for these new places to really feel urban.[42] For many of the same reasons, transformed public housing also will take time to feel like a community. However, designers may try to speed this time up by engineering positive social relations between new residents. While perhaps logical given the newness of this territory, many of these efforts to build and design community appear to reinforce rather than diminish negative images of public housing residents.

Designing Community for Whom?

New urbanism aims to facilitate interaction among residents through the inclusion of pedestrian pathways, front porches, and pocket parks. Each has the ability to bring people together, either by choice or by chance, in the public realm (or at least outside the house). In turn, these exchanges may build new friendships and establish trust among people who might otherwise remain strangers living within relatively close proximity. Public housing transformation extends this notion of relationship building to include the reduction of poverty. The assumption is that by living near higher-income people, lower-income families will have good role models to emulate. And by forming relationships with higher-income people who are working, poor adults are expected to build positive social capital—networks, relationships—that will get them jobs or, if already employed, better jobs.

In public housing transformation, economic mixing functions as a critical component in creating social capital that, in turn, can help public housing residents get out of poverty. As Milan Ozdinec, deputy assistant secretary of HUD, said about HOPE VI: "It has the very low-income side by side with the family earning 60 percent of median. . . . That's where connections are made, examples are set, and social capital is built."[43] The assumption here is that higher-income neighbors not only have social capital, but also are willing to share it and help their public housing neighbors build it for themselves. Linking social capital directly and positively to the collective economic condition of a community, the rhetoric of public housing transformation expects that lower-income people will become more "civic" as a result of living among higher-income families. In this framework, higher-income families are assumed to be civic as evidenced by their prosperity—a logic that aligns with Robert Putnam's explanation of how social capital produces economic benefits: "these communities did not become civic simply because they were rich. . . . They have become rich because they were civic."[44]

Extending this logic, new urbanism has the potential to produce social capital and help poor residents become civic because the space facilitates the mixing of public housing residents and middle-class owners and renters. Current policy assumes that people are civic if they are either working or doing something equivalent to increase earning potential, assuming that they are old enough and able to work. In Chicago, this means that nondisabled and nonelderly adult tenants must be working at least thirty hours a week, going to school, or attending job training. However, regardless of how or even if the site design helps produce this outcome, there are no assurances that working will actually increase a family's income level so that it, in fact, can get out of poverty, let alone become middle-class. There is no required minimum wage for working public housing residents, only a minimum number of hours that they have to work, which means that a person earning minimum wage (currently $5.15 per hour) could be fulfilling the work requirement and still be in poverty. On the positive side, while still poor, someone in that situation would at least have affordable housing.

New urbanists do not necessarily correlate behavioral outcomes (i.e., social interaction) with site design. Instead, they agree that their design principles can foster equity by creating good-quality places that middle-income families want to live in, which in turn will give all who live there access to the same good schools and other amenities.[45] Although logical, this argument devotes too much attention to the static elements of the site and not enough to the dynamics that will transform these new developments into communities. A place can convey an immediate sense of community through its physical cohesiveness and traditional architecture, and can even address certain conditions that prevent or limit interaction in typical suburban developments (e.g., lack of sidewalks and public gathering places). However, it is not yet known if these sites can produce the degree of social interaction that can in turn develop trusting relationships among people of different income levels and backgrounds.

A practical problem is mobility. Given that on average about one in five households move every year, turnover rates may limit the ability of families in market-rate housing to influence public housing neighbors. In a preliminary evaluation of the mixed-income new communities strategy piloted in Chicago at Lake Parc Place, Michael Schill found that the mobility rate of moderate-income households was three times higher than that of lower-income tenants. Schill concluded that while mixing these different income groups did produce a safer, more stable living environment, it did not necessarily achieve the CHA's goal of "having the more affluent tenants serve as role models for the very low-income households."[46] Analysis of data from other mixed-income developments suggests that if economic mixing is to produce benefits for poor families, then higher-income families should be required to stay a minimum period of time to reduce turnover.[47]

The success of new urbanism in market-rate developments may be a self-fulfilling prophecy, attracting families seeking a place to live that is designed so they can take an immediate, active role in creating community. These same families may react differently, however, in mixed-income public housing developments. Families paying the market rate for their new homes enter redeveloped public housing sites under different terms. While their poor neighbors generally have little choice but to live there, middle-income families have relatively more options in the private housing market. As a result, middle-income families are likely to have different expectations than public housing residents when it comes to housing quality, living conditions, social interaction, and neighborly behavior. Although there is little evidence to work from, research on Lake Parc Place provides some insight into the challenges mixing might present. About three years into the occupancy, Michael Schill looked at how residents interacted and their impressions of the development and each other. The results varied with income. Generally, all distinguished their neighbors as either "working" or "nonworking." However, higher-income (nonpublic housing) tenants "tended to attribute negative characteristics and behaviors, such as laziness, loudness and messiness to the very low-income residents" and "distrusted or disapproved of their very poor neighbors."[48] Of course, while time may have changed these perceptions, the relatively quick turnover rate for higher-income tenants in this development suggests it might not.

A more recent survey of Lake Parc Place residents by James Rosenbaum, Linda Stroh, and Cathy Flynn concluded that most residents were satisfied with their living situation. However, the authors also cautioned that successful mixing of public housing and middle-income households in the same rental complex may rely on higher-income residents, sending a clear message that they will not tolerate unacceptable behavior among public housing residents.[49] In contrast, Philip Nyden argued that the research, when looked at in relation to the previous experience of public housing residents, did not suggest fear as the reason for "positive" behavior. Instead, the public housing residents' behavior derived from being able to act independently because for the first time they had good management that responded to problems and good-quality housing that they actually could maintain.[50]

Rosenbaum, Stroh, and Flynn's interpretation of the data points to an underlying assumption about income mixing that needs some discussion. The design and marketing of these newly redeveloped public housing sites appear to assume that higher-income families have a determinable level of tolerance for differences that, if surpassed, will force them to leave. Just like racial tipping in the past, when whites fled rapidly changing neighborhoods as blacks moved in, the underlying logic in mixed-income public housing is that too many low-income people will make higher-income people flee or at least choose to leave because they can live elsewhere. While fair housing laws make it illegal to set quotas for occupancy based on race or ethnicity, quotas for market-rate housing or requiring a specific ratio of high- to low-income families in the mix is allowed. As noted earlier, the proportion or threshold of lower-income families appears to vary depending on location and surrounding conditions. In Chicago, tenure mix and the range of income levels in the developments also appear to be related. In the case of Lake Parc Place, which is occupied by renters only, public housing makes up about half the mix and the market tenants' income is generally below area median income. In contrast, most of the new developments on the Near North and Near West Sides have market-rate housing listed at prices well above the median for the city; there only about one-third of the total units are occupied by public housing tenants. In the "Plan for Transformation," the CHA describes these sites with the same language used by developers of market-rate housing for higher-income consumers. For example, the three-flat condominium buildings in Old Town Village (part of Cabrini-Green redevelopment area) will include "contemporary kitchen cabinets and appliances, ceramic tiled kitchens and bathrooms, and in-unit laundry hook-ups. Many units will also have iron railings, parking and extensive exterior landscaping."[51] While these features are important to public housing residents, they are not the target audience, which is rather the families that the CHA and its partners are hoping will spend $300,000 or more to buy a home in the new developments.

Building Community for Whom?

The idea of using physical design—scale, density, spatial arrangement—to build community is not new. Ebenezer Howard's garden suburbs a hundred years ago and Clarence Perry's "neighborhood unit" concept in 1929 both offered a means to produce a space for community outside the disorder found in the modern city. Similarly, James Rouse developed the new town of Columbia, Maryland, in the 1960s as "anti-urban and anti-suburban." At the same time plans were being drawn up for Columbia, Jane Jacobs, with the publication of *The Death and Life of Great American Cities* in 1961, was gaining notoriety for her anti–urban renewal and antisuburban position on planning. Jacobs's defense of cities was based on the community that she saw daily in the neighborhoods being torn down and replaced through urban renewal. In her view, planners and public officials had it all wrong. The richness of urban life was in the density, diversity, and variety of land uses found in old central city neighborhoods—these conditions produced an opportunity for community to happen, facilitating interaction and a degree of interdependency among residents.

Of course, Jacobs has been criticized for having a myopic view of the city or at least for being biased toward New York City. Yet the preferences she espoused then are not unlike the proposals of new urbanists and public housing reformers today. However, there is a difference. Jacobs generally favored a higher density than is being produced in redeveloped public housing sites. She also was more protective of the neighborhoods where poor people lived, because she believed that these places were communities and that there were better ways than bulldozing to improve them. Thirty years later, Jacobs reflected on her suggestions to transform public housing in her preface to the 1992 edition of *The Death and Life of Great American Cities:*

> In Chapter Twenty of this book I proposed that the ground levels of self-isolating projects within cities could be radically erased and reconstituted with two objects in view: linking the projects into the normal city by fitting them out with plentiful, new, connecting streets; and converting the projects themselves into urban places at the same time, by adding diverse new facilities along those added streets. The catch here, of course, is that new commercial facilities would need to work out economically, as a measure of their genuine and not fake usefulness. It is disappointing that this sort of radical replanning has not been tried—as far as I know—in the more than thirty years since this book was published. To be sure, with every decade that passes, the task of carrying out the proposal would seem to be more difficult. That is because anticity projects, especially massive public housing projects, tend to cause their city surroundings to deteriorate, so that as time passes, less and less healthy adjoining city is available to tie into.[52]

While she did not like the "massive" projects per se, Jacobs's idea was to improve them by building up the economy and creating opportunities to raise the income levels of poor people living in and around the developments rather than razing the buildings. In other words, she prescribed economic development strategies rather than architectural design principles to solve the problem of poverty.

Of course, the deterioration that she assumed might prevent this solution existed in many cities with distressed public housing when transformation began in the 1990s. The State Street corridor containing Robert Taylor Homes and Stateway Gardens in Chicago was surrounded by poverty and disinvestment. With few exceptions in adjacent communities—the University of Chicago to the southeast and U.S. Cellular Field to the northwest—development had stalled in this area. However, developments in other parts of the city, like Cabrini-Green near the city's revitalizing and expanding downtown, were a different story. As Elvin Wyly and Daniel Hammel have aptly labeled these types of public housing sites, Cabrini was an "island of decay in seas of renewal."[53] As described in previous chapters, renewal was evident in the rapidly changing housing markets surrounding this site in the early 1990s.

Wyly and Hammel argue that in many cases, public housing policy—specifically HOPE VI and privatization—has contributed to and even been a catalyst for gentrification. They hypothesize that in places like Cabrini-Green where there are "sharp boundaries between poverty and wealth . . . gentrification mediates the balance between alternative strategies to reinvent distressed public housing: Private-market gentrification is a necessary, although by no means sufficient, condition for market-rate development and income mixing."[54] If true, they anticipate finding more market-rate housing in the plans for developments near or adjacent to a strong housing market and less market-rate and moderately priced housing included in the plans for developments near poorly performing housing markets. And generally this is what Wyly and Hammel found looking at HOPE VI plans through 1998. This too is the pattern revealed in the different plans for Chicago's sites: there are higher numbers and proportions of market rate housing in already established or active markets, such as around Cabrini-Green and ABLA, and relatively lower numbers and proportions of market-rate housing at various South Side developments where a market is still being established.[55]

Assuming the trend continues, the purpose of including market-rate housing in redevelopment is not to build a market, as the FHA underwriting principles suggest, but rather to take advantage of the market that is already there. Taking the development trends forward a few more years, and depending on how redevelopment is managed, it looks like there will be relatively few poor people living in the neighborhood that once contained ABLA. And while the residents of Cabrini-Green have more control over development in their community, the only affordable housing likely to be there in ten years is the public and subsidized housing the CHA builds. Following this logic, then, we can expect poverty to go down in some of these new mixed-income communities but not necessarily because poor people have escaped poverty—rather because poor people have been moved out and replaced by higher-income families.

The Symbolic Meaning of Community—Modernism Redux?

The rhetoric of new urbanism and community building that is guiding the transformation of public housing conveys a particular image of a mixed-income neighborhood that is stable and healthy. These new communities, as envisioned, will still have poor people as long as there is public housing in the mix, but they will be working and helping to weave the social fabric of the neighborhood rather than tearing it apart. Looking back at Susan Popkin's research findings about HOPE VI in Chapter 3, there is good reason to pause and think about what might be wrong with this image. Not everyone who is poor can work, and even if they can, working does not guarantee that a poor family will get out of poverty. Stepping back from the image of the immaculate new homes, we can see what continues to exist outside these new developments: the larger systemic problems of racism and classism and a long-standing cultural bias against cities that continues to push people farther out rather than pull them in.

Richard Sennett's seminal book *The Uses of Disorder* describes how the powerful symbolism of community could help to create an image of a future state—a society that is somehow "different than it expected to be in the past."[56] The ambitious plans to transform public housing as we know it play this role. The language and imagery are powerful, seemingly capable of changing behavior, as evidenced by risk-averse investors putting up capital, private sector developers building mixed-income housing, and middle-income families buying and renting homes next to public housing. Yet outside these sites—where 98 percent of Americans live—little has changed. The now all-too-common problem of NIMBYism that in the past determined the location of public housing continues to challenge planners, elected officials, and advocates of affordable housing. Whether intentional or not, the strategies used to transform public housing appear to play to these attitudes, fears, and prejudices by ensuring that there is enough market-rate housing in the mix, and by insisting that the few poor people allowed must follow special rules.

New urbanists do not assume that architectural design will change systemic conditions. Still, the rhetoric of transforming public housing into mixed-income communities does suggest this will happen. So how do the imagery and the architectural design connote the symbolism of community that seems to convince people that income mixing will produce specific desired results? Richard Sennett might respond that the purity of the image—single-family homes with front porches and green lawns—helps to condense "all the messy experiences in social life, in order to create a vision of unified community identity."[57] However, it is also the timelessness of the image that is important. The renderings, and now the real places that have been developed, have replaced the existing space of public housing with an architecture that conveys a timeless ideal of community that is outside of change. That is the power of new urbanism in the transformation of public housing. The image of community that these developments convey is, as Iris Marion Young would describe it, an "out of time" ideal type of space in which the effects of time, and not time itself, stand still.[58] The sense of community conveyed by the architecture and layout of these new developments is immediate and constant, and although it is often reminiscent of a previous time, it is also designed to be timeless. The problem with this image, as Young and others point out, is that it completely misses what actually makes a place a community. The static form of architecture or pedestrian pathways does not make a community; rather it is the process of moving forward in time and mediating the experiences of daily life—dealing with the messy issues that build a community.

The aesthetics and look of lower density, economically mixed public housing developments cannot make different income groups mix at social events or help an unemployed worker get a job. These things take time and energy and change and commitment. Yet even if we understand this, the language of public housing reform continues to generate images of unity and authentic social relations that these new communities may or may not be capable of producing. More important, though, this same rhetoric also justifies reducing and privatizing public housing in the United States by favoring new mixed-income public housing (where community is imagined to exist) over old public housing (where community is assumed nonexistent because only the poor live there). This image helps to erase any real experiences and record of the community that still does or did exist in public housing and justifies tearing down the buildings and dispersing the tenants.

If recent history provides any indication of what to expect, it would be easy to assume that the current embrace of antimodernist architecture and planning concepts will produce limited results in public housing. Just as the ideas of modernists were found to be lacking, the influence of new urbanism may also be less than satisfying and therefore in need of retooling in the future. In part, this may be because new urbanism and modernism are so similar. As architecture critic Herbert Muschamp concludes, "Like the modernists, the New Urbanists rely too much on esthetic solutions to solve the social problems created by urban sprawl."[59]

Marginalization of the poor, particularly through housing programs, has become a worldwide theme. In the United States, public housing policy must be looked at in the same context as recent efforts to reform public welfare policy, which rely heavily on the assumption that employment will benefit the very poor. While not an objectionable assumption, it is simplistic. In both cases, the rhetoric tends to gloss over the conditions needed to actually produce the outcomes promised. This includes changing or somehow dealing with the dynamics and volatility of both the job and housing markets, now and in the long run.

Public housing transformation relies on new urbanism to reconfigure physical sites into mixed-income communities. While interpersonal relationships may form as a result of the design and spatial arrangement of the site, the only certain outcome is that the number of public housing units for the very poor will be reduced. In this sense, then, public housing reform is really no different from urban renewal efforts begun in the 1950s: it will do little to benefit the very poor and a lot to benefit the middle-class and private developers.

Notes

1. Martin Anderson, *Federal Bulldozer* (Boston: MIT Press, 1964), p. viii.

2. Anderson, *Federal Bulldozer,* p. viii.

3. Catherine Bauer, "Social Questions in Housing and Community Planning," *Journal of Social Issues* 7 (1951): 1–34; Michael Stone, *Shelter Poverty: New Ideas on Housing Affordability* (Philadelphia: Temple University Press, 1993); Chester Hartman, "The Case for the Right to Housing," *Housing Policy Debate* 9, no. 2 (1998): 223–266.

4. Department of Housing and Urban Development, "FHA's Mixed-Income Housing Underwriting Guidelines," Directive H 97–12, issued March 7, 1997, p. 1.

5. Department of Housing and Urban Development, "Public/Private Partnerships for the Mixed-Finance Development of Public Housing Units," *Federal Register,* 24 CFR Parts 941 and 970, May 2, 1996, pp. 19707–19719.

6. Congress for the New Urbanism, *Principles for Inner City Neighborhood Design: HOPE VI and the New Urbanism* (Washington, DC: Department of Housing and Urban Development, 1996).

7. See www.cnu.org/about/index.cfm for discussion of new urbanism, the principles behind this movement and the Congress for the New Urbanism.

8. Congress for the New Urbanism, *Principles for Inner City Neighborhood Design,* p.1.

9. Alistair Smith, "Mixed Income Housing Developments: Promise and Reality," (Cambridge, MA: Joint Center for Housing Studies of Harvard University, Neighborhood Reinvestment Corporation, October 2002); Jill Khadduri and Marge Martin, "Mixed-Income Housing in the HUD Multifamily Stock," *CityScape* 3, no. 2 (1997): 33–69.

10. Khadduri and Martin, "Mixed-Income Housing."

11. Smith, "Mixed-Income Housing Developments."

12. See, for example, Ebenezer Howard, *Garden Cities of To-Morrow* (Cambridge: MIT Press, 1899); Bauer, "Social Questions in Housing and Community Planning."

13. See Janet L. Smith, "Interpreting Neighborhood Change," PhD diss., Cleveland State University, 1998.

14. Donald Massey and Nancy Denton, *American Apartheid* (Cambridge, MA: Harvard University Press, 1993).

15. Based on analysis of U.S. census data for 1980 to 2000 at the census tract level.

16. Gregory D. Squires, *Capital and Communities in Black and White* (Albany: State University of New York, 1994); Dennis Judd, "Symbolic Politics and Urban Policies: Why African American Got So Little from the Democrats," in *Without Justice for All,* ed. Adolph Reed, pp. 123–150 (Boulder, CO: Westview Press, 1999).

17. Philip Nyden, Michael Maly, and John Lukehart, "The Emergence of Stable Racial and Ethnically Diverse Urban Communities: A Case Study of Nine US Cities," *Housing Policy Debate* 8, no. 2 (1997): 491–534; Michael Maly, *Beyond Segregation: Multiracial and Multiethnic Neighborhoods in the United States* (Philadelphia: Temple University Press, 2005).

18. Alex Schwartz and Kian Tajbakhsh, "Mixed Income Housing: Unanswered Questions," *CityScape* 3, no 2 (1997).

19. Louise Hunt, Mary Schulhof, and Stephen Holmquist, "Summary of the Quality Housing and Work Responsibility Act," Department of Housing and Urban Development, December 1998, p. 11.

20. Current requirements for public housing allow income levels up to 80 percent of area median income.

21. HUD Notice H 97–12, 1997.

22. HUD Notice H 97–12.

23. Department of Housing and Urban Development, "FHA's Mixed-Income Housing Underwriting Guidelines."

24. Joseph Gyourka and Witold Rybczynski, "Financing New Urbanist Projects: Obstacles and Solutions," *Housing Policy Debate* 11, no. 3 (2000).

25. Lawrence Vale, *From Puritans to the Poorhouse* (Cambridge, MA: Harvard University Press, 1996).

26. For a list of consultants, see www.housingresearch.org/hrf/hrf_Consultants.nsf.

27. Andrés Duany, *Suburban Nation* (New York: North Point Press, 2000).

28. See *City of Euclid v. Ambler Real Estate,* 272 U.S. 365 (1926).

29. See "Smart Growth America" at www.smartgrowthamerica.com/.

30. See, for example, Bruce Katz, ed., *Reflections on Regionalism* (Washington, DC: Brookings Institution, 2000).

31. Alex Krieger, *Towns and Town Making Principles* (New York: Rizzoli, 1991), p. 12.

32. See "The Seaside Institute" for more information at www.theseaside institute.org/seaside/.

33. Congress for the New Urbanism, *Principles for Inner City Neighborhood Design,* p. 4.

34. Congress for the New Urbanism, *Principles for Inner City Neighborhood Design,* p. 27.

35. Congress for the New Urbanism, *Principles for Inner City Neighborhood Design,* p. 33.

36. See Urban Design Associates for images and pattern book for Park DuValle and other public housing neighborhoods (www.urbandesignassociates.com/).

37. Philip Langdon, *A Better Place to Live* (Amherst, MA: University of Massachusetts Press, 1994), p. 117.

38. Michael Southworth, "Walkable Suburbs? An Evaluation of Neotraditional Communities on the Edge," *Journal of the American Planning Association* (1997): 43.

39. Marisa Bartolucci, "What Is a Community? *Metropolis* (1997): 76.

40. Herbert Muschamp, "Can New Urbanism Find Room for the Old?" *New York Times,* June 2, 1996.

41. Witold Rybczynski, "Tomorrowland: Living in a Community Planned by Disney has Got to Be a Nightmare, Doesn't It?" *New Yorker,* July 22, 1996, 36–39.

42. Carol Burns et al., "Urban or Suburban? A Roundtable Discussion Among Carol Burns, Robert Campbell, Andres Duany, Jerold Kayden, and Alex Krieger," *Harvard Design Magazine* 1 (Winter/Spring 1997).

43. Howard Hussock, "Public Housing's Hidden Costs to Cities," *New York Sun,* January 7, 2003.

44. Robert Putnam, "The Prosperous Community: Social Capital and Public Life," *American Prospect* 4, no. 13 (1993): 35–42.

45. Emily Talen, "The Social Goals of New Urbanism," *Housing Policy Debate* 13, no. 1 (2002): 165–188.

46. Michael Schill, "Chicago's Mixed-Income New Communities Strategy: The Future of Public Housing?" in *Affordable Housing and Urban Redevelopment in the United States,* ed. Willem Van Vliet (Thousand Oaks, CA: Sage, 1997).

47. Paul Brophy and Rhonda Smith, "Mixed-Income Housing: Factors for Success," *CityScape* 3, no. 2 (1997): 1–31.

48. Schill, "Chicago's Mixed-Income New Communities Strategy," p. 151.

49. James Rosenbaum, Linda Stroh, and Cathy Flynn, "Lake Parc Place: A Study of Mixed-Income Housing," *Housing Policy Debate* 9, no. 4 (1998): 703–740.

50. Philip Nyden, "Comments," *Housing Policy Debate,* 9 (No. 4, 1998): 741–748.

51. Chicago Housing Authority, "FY2005 Annual Plan—Plan for Transformation Year 6," p. 11.

52. Jane Jacobs, *The Death and Life of Great American Cities* (New York: Modern Library, 1992).

53. Elvin Wyly and Daniel Hammel, "Islands of Decay in Seas of Renewal: Urban Policy and the Resurgence of Gentrification," *Housing Policy Debate* 10, no. 4 (1999): 711–771.

54. Wyly and Hammel, "Islands of Decay," p. 725.

55. Sales transaction data for South Side communities that contain or are adjacent to redeveloping public housing show increased activity, but also volatility in the pricing as the market gets established.

56. Richard Sennett, *The Uses of Disorder: Personal Identity and City Life* (New York: Alfred A. Knopf, 1970).

57. Sennett, *Uses of Disorder,* p. 36.

58. Iris Marion Young, "The Ideal of Community and the Politics of Difference," in *Feminism and Community,* ed. Penny A. Weiss and Marilyn Friedman (Philadelphia, PA: Temple University Press, 1995).

59. Muschamp, "Can New Urbanism Find Room for the Old?"

11

Downtown Restructuring and Public Housing in Contemporary Chicago

Fashioning a Better World-Class City

Larry Bennett

From its origins in the 1930s, federal government-sponsored policy seeking to eliminate urban slums, build good-quality affordable housing, and modernize inner-city areas was beset by an underlying paradox: the essentially contradictory aims of public housing advocates versus business-associated proponents of downtown redevelopment. In his comprehensive survey of mid-twentieth century federal urban policy making, historian Mark Gelfand defined these contradictory forces in reference to the frequently paired but not necessarily convergent concepts, "slum" and "blight":

> The campaign against the slum became the preserve of liberal and philan-thropic organizations that found rat-infested tenements detrimental to family welfare. They concentrated their efforts on increasing the supply of decent housing for the bottom third of the population; their crowning achieve-ment was the 1937 Housing Act, which joined a program of slum clear-ance with public construction. In contrast, the anti-blight crusade was led by large landowners and downtown businessmen worried about falling prop-erty values and rising taxes. These people wished to gain government aid to protect their investments in real estate and buildings; for the most part, they opposed public housing as unfair competition with private investment.[1]

For a short time, the passage of the 1949 Housing Act seemed to resolve this contradiction. On the one hand, the public housing program was reautho-rized and funded more generously than during its first decade. On the other hand, Title I of the 1949 Housing Act mandated a new initiative, urban redevelopment, which could be turned to the downtown and near-downtown physical upgrading agenda so dear to the leaders of the "anti-blight crusade."

Over the longer run, the "peace of 1949" was sustained by way of many locally improvised maneuvers. Until its termination in 1974, urban redevelopment (more memorably renamed "urban renewal" in 1954 legislation) often seemed to fall short of its sponsors' dreams. During the 1950s, cities that aggressively demolished inner-city real estate in hopes of attracting new private investment, were greeted, as often as not, by resolute developer indifference.[2] In some cases, urban renewal land was transferred to local public housing agencies, but given the sinking reputation of public housing, the market appeal of the redevelopment agency–held properties that remained was not enhanced by proximity to even newly built low-income communities. Shrewd redevelopment officials, such as New York's Robert Moses, came to realize that the best way to ensure the success of particular urban renewal projects was to anticipate just where private investors would most prefer to rebuild their cities. In this fashion, public housing could be employed as a subordinate redevelopment tool: removing from desirable real estate undesirable incumbent residents.[3] By the late 1950s—and across America—the neighborhoods designated for urban renewal typically were not a city's worst slums, whose demographic makeup, physical infrastructure, and location were unlikely to match up to investors' notions of up-and-comingness. Instead, working-class districts adjoining downtown areas or possessing other under-valued physical attributes often became the targets of urban renewal planners. In the words of historian Robert Fogelson, "Title I did not specify which slums and blighted areas should be designated redevelopment sites. . . . It left the decisions up to local redevelopment agencies, which tended to choose areas that were run down enough to justify demolition, but not so run down as to scare off developers."[4]

As such neighborhoods were gobbled up for urban renewal, cities' most depressed residential quarters were passed over even as demand-side pressure for low-cost housing was amplified. Sociologist Herbert Gans's influential article, "The Failure of Urban Renewal: A Critique and Some Proposals," published just when many cities were pushing ahead with their most ambitious redevelopment schemes, noted that through early 1961, urban renewal had yielded the demolition of four times the number of residential structures as had been produced under its auspices.[5] But this demolition/construction ratio was not simply an unforeseen programmatic breakdown. In their rush to clear away downtown-threatening, blighted neighborhoods, local urban renewal officials "were prepared to ride roughshod over their residents."[6]

The further failings of urban renewal planners—most evidently their penchant for modernist design solutions that never managed to stoke the imagination of hoped-for middle-class urban resettlers, more subtly their misapprehension of the root causes of central city decline—is an oft-told tale. The pages to follow examine the Chicago-centered subplot to this larger narrative, noting how the city's business, civic, and governmental leaders have long sought to promote Chicago as a thriving, postindustrial metropolis. In particular, this analysis focuses on public housing's shifting status as a local policy priority and how—once Chicago's central area real estate market did indeed make the postindustrial turn in the 1990s—the redevelopment/public housing contradiction reemerged. However, at the onset of the twenty-first century, a convergence of trends in federal affordable housing policy, local government's policy aims, and the public's understanding of urban problems appears to have framed an updated resolution to this long-standing policy paradox. As central Chicago expands and transforms itself from a central business district to a multiuse hub accommodating corporate business operations, a kaleidoscope of cultural and entertainment venues, and upscale residence, there is simply no room for public housing as it was configured in the 1950s and 1960s.

Urban Restructuring, Local Response: Chicago Style

Chicago, which English historian Asa Briggs titled the world's "shock city" of the 1890s, rose to prominence as a great metropolis on the shoulders of a three-quarters-of-a-century boom punctuated by the Civil War and the Great Depression.[7] During this era of extraordinary growth, the city's economic might was primarily a function of its centrality within the U.S. railroad network, which made Chicago the bridge linking countless agrarian producers, a host of local agribusiness and industrial giants, and the consumers of myriad manufactured goods spanning the entirety of the greater Mississippi River basin.[8] Although Chicagoans prided themselves on their city's architectural marvels and notable city planning achievements, boomtown Chicago was, for the most part, an unendearing place, excoriated famously by the British writer, Rudyard Kipling, who, following his visit in 1889, "urgently desired never to see it again."[9]

Like those of every other major city in the United States, Chicago's economy and social fabric were shredded by the Great Depression; though the city's manufacturers rebounded during World War II and into the 1950s, the central city's population leveled off, and, increasingly, population growth and economic expansion occurred along the metropolitan periphery.[10] As early as the first decade of the twentieth century, major manufacturers had begun to relocate from the city of Chicago to suburban communities. In the face of what appeared to be inexorable processes of metropolitan expansion and industrial decentralization, by the 1940s civic and business leaders had begun to articulate public policies aimed at transforming Chicago's down-town business district, the Loop, as well as adjoining areas to the north, west, and south, into a corporate center that would also accommodate cultural and educational institutions, and a much larger and more prosperous residential population. Although city leaders invariably characterized the Loop as a sin-gular asset, it was—by the late 1930s—"surrounded by a three-mile-wide band of obsolete, wretched buildings."[11] As one civic leader bluntly phrased it, the purpose of redeveloping the Loop and its environs was "to reattract solvent population and investment to the dying areas of the city."[12]

From the mid-1940s until the 1980s, Chicago's aim to reinvent itself as a postindustrial metropolis was pursued along a number of tracks. The city's business and political leaders won the passage of state legislation in 1947 and 1953 that enabled local redevelopment efforts to proceed. Indeed, histo-rian Arnold Hirsch has described the Illinois Blighted Areas and Redevelop-ment Act of 1947 as a "model for later federal legislation."[13] The direct upshot of this state legislation was the New York Life Insurance Company–financed redevelopment of the Near South Side area lying between Michael Reese Hospital on the lakefront and the Illinois Institute of Technology to the west. In the wake of the U.S. Housing Acts of 1949 and 1954, which put in place the federal urban renewal program, the city of Chicago's redevelopment ac-tivity expanded dramatically. In 1958, the city's recently formed Department of City Planning released its "Development Plan for the Central Area of Chi-cago," whose first section began with this assertion of "major premises":

1. Provision must be made for expansion of regional and administra-tive functions in the Central Commercial District.
2. Proposed and projected development programs for a government center, a university campus, port development, an exposition center, and major residential areas must be considered in the development of a transportation plan.

The "port development," which pertained to improvements at Navy Pier to the northeast of the Loop, was never pursued. Elsewhere in the plan, railroad yards to the south of the downtown—which had been among the principal agents of the city's rise to Midwestern urban hegemony—were character-ized as sources of "blight."[14] In short, civic leaders and planners in Chicago were charting a course of downtown-focused, postindustrial development long before the wave of plant shutdowns and relocations in the late 1970s that recast the "city of the big shoulders" as a historical metaphor.[15]

Fifteen years after the release of the "Development Plan for the Central Area of Chicago," a second important planning document, "Chicago 21: A

Plan for the Central Area Communities," a joint effort of the city of Chicago
and the corporate-anchored Chicago Central Area Committee, more explicitly
laid out the case for physically expanding Chicago's downtown core. Neighborhoods to the south of the Loop, notably Chinatown and Pilsen, were slated
for residential upgrading. Other beyond-the-Loop areas discussed in "Chicago
21" included East Humboldt Park (to the northwest of the downtown area),
Cabrini-Green (where the aim was to "foster a new sense of community"), and
the Near West Side, for which "complete urban renewal" would be the order of
the day.[16] We have discussed the reactions of Near West Side public housing
residents to "Chicago 21" in Chapter 7. Although the waning energies of elderly Mayor Richard J. Daley, combined with the city's sliding economic fortunes in the 1970s, prevented the comprehensive implementation of the
"Chicago 21" plan, this document did yield some significant action. Within a
few years a team of developers and architects seeking to convert the South
Loop to an upscale residential enclave had initiated the rehabilitation and residential conversion of the Printer's Row area and the construction of the Dearborn
Park "new town," both to the south of the Congress Parkway.[17] Coincidently,
some of the same group—joined by other leading figures from corporate Chicago—sought to promote the Near South Side lakefront as the site for a World's
Fair in 1993.[18] Among the aims of this event was to spur spillover development
in nearby neighborhoods such as Pilsen.[19]

During the 1980s, the city's economic development policy under the leadership of Mayor Harold Washington turned away from the single-minded
focus on preserving or, if possible, expanding the Loop. Industrial retention,
as well as commercial and residential development, won the attention of
municipal officials, and economic development initiatives popped up all across
the face of neighborhood Chicago.[20] Nevertheless, the dream of expanding
the Loop and transforming the city's Near North, West, and South Sides did
not disappear, as evidenced by the ongoing rumors pertaining to the Cabrini-
Green development, temptingly situated on the western flank of the exclu-
sive Gold Coast neighborhood.[21] By the 1990s, and in particular once current
Mayor Richard M. Daley had firmly grasped the reins of city government,
new efforts to transform central Chicago quickly shifted into high gear. Moreover, as these initiatives proceeded, they touched down in portions of the city
not so far from the Loop, but for decades presumed to be beyond the pale of
new residential and commercial development.

The Chicago Housing Authority and Central Chicago

The state of Illinois, responding to the federal legislation creating the public
housing program, authorized the Chicago Housing Authority (CHA) in 1937.

Keying the CHA's operations were its state mandates to "make plans in cooperation with any public planning agencies for the redevelopment of substandard areas" and to "plan, build, and operate housing projects."[22] However, as historian Arnold Hirsch has noted, when the Illinois General Assembly passed the Blighted Areas and Redevelopment Act of 1947 (that is, the state legislation authorizing land clearance for redevelopment purposes), this new legislation specified that redevelopment activities would be conducted by a "land clearance commission" rather than a municipality's public housing agency.[23]

Already, by the mid-1940s the CHA was associated with "racial mixes and building in white neighborhoods," and many legislators willing to support municipally sponsored redevelopment action did not trust the intentions of the CHA, in particular those of Executive Director Elizabeth Wood.[24] Though in retrospect Wood's integrationist ambitions appear to have been relatively constrained, and historian Bradford Hunt has argued that Wood's commitment to slum clearance required that much of CHA's construction—even in the absence of the virulent white opposition to public housing that emerged in the 1950s—would have been in already African-American neighborhoods, urban redevelopment in Chicago was a policy shaped far more by the agenda of the city's local growth coalition than by its embattled cadre of public housing advocates.[25]

In any event, following sharp conflicts with the city council over the siting of CHA developments and the agency's intention to integrate previously built developments, Wood was removed as executive director in August 1954. Under her two immediate successors, William B. Kean (1954–1957) and Alvin Rose (1957–1968), the CHA added over 1,000 housing units to its portfolio each year, which in the case of "family" developments (that is, not senior citizen complexes) were inevitably in African-American neighborhoods or areas undergoing racial transition.[26] Moreover, given African-Americans' historical pattern of settlement in Chicago—extending south from the Near South Side in a narrow "Black Belt," after World War II expanding west from initial pockets in the Near West Side—many of the developments constructed in the Kean-Rose era were situated, in fact, rather near the Loop. Among the developments that we have previously discussed in this volume, this group includes the Cabrini Extension buildings and Green Homes at Cabrini-Green, the entirety of the Henry Horner Homes, and the Abbot and Brooks Extension sections of ABLA. Apart from invariably siting new developments in African-American neighborhoods, the CHA also placed many of its buildings in areas thought to be undesirable due to their proximity to major highways, mass transit lines, or industrial facilities.

During the first fifteen years of Richard J. Daley's mayoralty, pushing aggressively forward with public housing development offered a variety of political benefits. For many African-American political and civic leaders, public housing was a desirable improvement over the slum housing occupied by thousands of residents in the oldest portions of the Black Belt. From Daley's standpoint, the multimillion-dollar contracts issued for public housing construction were a surefire method of winning the affection of development interests and the building trades. Within "the projects," moreover, Democratic Party precinct captains could manipulate access to apartments and building services as a means of enforcing voter loyalty.[27] Ultimately, of course, by providing low-cost housing within the boundaries of the original Black Belt and the newer West Side ghetto, the Daley public housing program could also be construed as reducing the likelihood of racial transition in neighborhoods beyond black Chicago. By the mid-1960s—and with the rise of a vigorous civil rights movement in Chicago—such a stance was an essential part of Daley's effort to retain the support of increasingly restive working-class white voters across the city's Northwest, Southwest, and far South Sides.[28]

In the long run, public housing's political uses produced fatal problems on the ground within the CHA's developments. Although historians Hirsch and Hunt disagree on the precise scale of urban redevelopment-generated relocation to public housing, even Hunt's more conservative estimate—that 28 percent of CHA units had to be offered to urban renewal evacuees—would have meant that, by some time in the 1950s, CHA tenant screening efforts were substantially compromised.[29] There is universal agreement that, from the 1950s, CHA construction and maintenance costs were unduly high, by the 1970s producing a fiscal crisis in the agency and the concomitant scaling back of routine maintenance work. Finally, once the CHA stopped building public housing—in the wake of the *Gautreaux* decision and the Nixon administration's reduction in federal aid for public housing—the CHA became an administrative backwater: underfunded, without friends in city hall, and unable to recruit competent managers or rank-and-file staff.[30]

Beyond the crisis deriving from these agency-related problems, by the 1980s Chicago's deindustrialization was yielding an economic crisis in the neighborhoods in which public housing was concentrated.[31] Breakdowns in basic city services, notably police protection and public schools, further contributed to the growing misery within public housing. However, the very forces that were emptying the Near South and West Sides of their warehouses, machine shops, and wholesalers were opening up what geographer Neil Smith calls the "new urban frontier," an aging urban landscape nonetheless amenable to new uses such as residential lofts, "back office" corporate operations, work space for start-up telecommunications firms, and Soho-style retailing.[32] Moreover, recent economic analysis suggests that in the late

1980s or early 1990s, a growth surge in Chicago's advanced corporate services sectors had begun to drive a new boom in the central city economy.[33] As late as the 1980s, the very presence of public housing tended to dampen the enthusiasm of real estate developers eyeing the Near West Side or the fringes of Cabrini-Green, but by the 1990s favorable economic trends, the emerging national policy consensus regarding public housing, and the ambitions of Chicago's new mayor conjoined to sweep away such apprehensions.

Richard M. Daley's New Chicago

Initially gaining the mayoralty for two years in 1989—via a contentious special election to complete the term of office won by Harold Washington a few months before his death by heart attack in late 1987—Richard M. Daley's prospective mayoral agenda and likely longevity in office were the subjects of considerable speculation. During the 1970s Daley had been an aggressive, often abrasive junior member of the state legislature, known by some in Springfield as "dirty little Richie." However, after winning a Cook County post as state's attorney in 1982, Daley demonstrated considerable executive skill and began to form alliances with "independent Democrats" who, in many instances, had been opponents of his father.[34] Campaigning for the mayoralty in 1989, Richard M. Daley presented himself as a managerially minded politician committed to uniting a city whose longstanding racial divisions had been aggravated during the mayoralty of Harold Washington. As such, the Daley agenda baseline, at first, appeared to be a matter of differentiating his program from Washington's. This need, according to political scientist Joel Rast, largely accounted for Daley's initial rejection of the neighborhood economic development and industrial retention programs given so much emphasis in the Washington years.[35]

During Daley's first few years in office, another evident—as well as highly conventional—element in his mayoral agenda was the pursuit of large-scale capital projects, which overtly could be justified as rejuvenating Chicago's image and economy, while covertly offering the mother's milk of urban politics: hundreds of millions of dollars in contracts to be distributed to architects, engineers, and construction firms trickling down to thousands of members of the building trades. Such initiatives included Daley's pressing for the construction of a third airport (in addition to O'Hare and Midway) on the city's far South Side, the development of a gambling casino complex at the southern end of the downtown area, and the construction of a surface rail system to link various destinations in and near the Loop. None of these projects moved beyond architectural renderings, in large part because of Daley's poor working relationship with then-Illinois Governor James Edgar.[36]

However, at about the time that the national economy reignited in the early 1990s and, in its turn, the municipal government's fiscal health began to revive, the Daley administration settled into a core policy track—the physical upgrading of the Loop and adjoining neighborhoods—that has become a hallmark of Daley's decade-and-a-half mayoralty. Downtown beautification is hardly a newcomer to the list of big city mayoral policy priorities, but there are many signs indicating that Mayor Daley has not simply seized on downtown enhancement in a fit of opportunism. The mayor and his wife, Maggie, are committed world travelers, and Daley's preferences in city planning—from the appearance of public sculpture to the details of streetscaping and parks furniture—tend toward European classicism. The mayor's commitment to civic beautification seems to grow out of a real conviction that, as sociologist Terry N. Clark and colleagues argue, "amenities drive urban growth."[37] In Daley's own words:

> I'm very proud of how Chicago's appearance has improved over the last decade or so. Visitors continually tell me the same thing they tell you: "I had no idea Chicago was such a beautiful city." We hear that from people who attended the Democratic National Convention in 1996, and we see it frequently in out-of-town newspapers and national magazines. They expect Nelson Algren and they get Martha Stewart.[38]

In effect, the mayor's passion for civic beautification is a twofold commitment. On the one hand, he seems genuinely determined to redignify the appearance of a city whose fiscal stresses and social conflicts over two generations had yielded a physical infrastructure in many places battered, in countless others merely neglected. On the other hand, Daley views upgrading the local physical environment as a way to increase the city's allure for private investors: "the nice thing is, if you improve the quality of life for the people who live in your city, you will end up attracting new people and new employers."[39] This latter perspective is further reflected in the new "Chicago Central Area Plan": "Central Chicago is poised for dramatic growth with billions of dollars in economic benefits for the city, region and state. This growth, which is good for the city and smart for the region, can only be sustained if the Central Area builds on the special qualities that make it one of the world's greatest places to work, live and play."[40] Interestingly, though the "Central Area Plan" discusses at considerable length new residential development to the north, west, and south of the Loop, there are virtually no direct references to public housing.

The most visible indicator of the Daley administration's commitment to Loop and near-Loop physical upgrading is the series of public works projects that, even as we complete this volume, are recasting the appearance of Chicago's downtown area: the rebuilding of the two-level Wacker Drive paralleling the main channel and south branch of the Chicago River on the Loop's northern and western margins, the development of the Millennium Park complex in the northwestern corner of Grant Park, the rerouting of Lake Shore Drive and creation of a museum campus bounding the Field Museum, Shedd Aquarium, Adler Planetarium, and Soldier Field just southwest of the Loop (as well as the modernization and expansion of each of the latter three facilities), continued expansion of the McCormick Place convention center complex just to the south along Lake Shore Drive, and the rebuilding of the Roosevelt Road bridge as a monumental entrance to the south Loop.[41]

Direct public construction is only a part of the mayor's program to renew and expand the Loop. Given the city's generally solid financial situation over the last decade, the Daley administration has also been able to offer substantial financial incentives to prospective developers. The city's principal development subsidy tool has been tax increment financing (TIF). Between 1996 and the spring of 2002 the Daley administration authorized seventy-seven TIF districts across Chicago.[42] Many of these redevelopment areas have been declared in near-downtown neighborhoods already experiencing significant private real estate activity, though public support via TIF funding presumably makes these areas even more attractive for new development. The Daley administration has also implemented "permit streamlining," simplifying the processes associated with city approvals for development in order to accelerate the planning, financing, and construction of new projects.[43]

When major corporations have beckoned, the Daley administration has also been willing to fashion targeted incentive packages to hold onto or attract headquarters facilities. The Quaker Oats Corporation, before its merger with Pepsico, had negotiated a deal with the Daley administration to support relocation of its headquarters within Chicago's downtown.[44] Clearly the major coup of this sort accomplished by Richard M. Daley's administration was the Boeing Corporation's decision, in the spring of 2001, to move its corporate offices from Seattle to Chicago's west Loop. In this instance, the city of Chicago and the state of Illinois collaborated to offer Boeing a $60 million incentive package.[45]

Another of the Daley administration's citywide initiatives—the support of cultural institutions as a means of generating local investment and neighborhood tourism, as well as infrastructure investments intended to highlight neighborhood cultural heritage—has been given particular attention in the Loop. On several blocks adjoining the intersection of Randolph and Dearborn Streets, the city government has supported the rehabilitation of the Oriental and Palace theaters, as well as the construction of a new Goodman Theater complex housing the city's premier repertory stage company.[46] Whether or not the Loop's reconstituted "theater district" represents a financially or artistically viable initiative remains to be seen.[47] Nonetheless, the city government's underlying aim—to turn the Loop into a cosmopolitan center offering a continuous round of leisure activities—is perfectly evident.

By the mid-1990s, there were tangible signs that the Daley administration's central area enhancement program, in tandem with broader economic and attitudinal trends working to reglamorize inner-city living, was taking hold. In early 1999, the *Chicago Tribune* reported that in the preceding two years, more than 5,000 units of new or newly renovated housing had been sold in near-Loop neighborhoods.[48] Only one-fifth of these sales had occurred in the Near North Side, the community area adjoining the Loop with the busiest residential real estate market in recent decades. A subsequently released Woodstock Institute study found that home purchases in Chicago's four most central community areas (the Loop, Near North, Near West, and Near South Sides) increased from 3,779 in 1993–1994 to 10,660 in 1999–2000. Remarkably, in each of these four community areas, the decennial increase in residential population between 1990 and 2000 was the first since the decade of the 1940s. Moreover, the majority of the 1999–2000 home purchasers, 61 percent, reported annual incomes at or exceeding 120 percent of the metropolitan median income.[49] In short, the repopulating of Chicago's central neighborhoods is also substantially upgrading their socioeconomic profile.

In accounting for the policy initiatives that have contributed to the expansion and redefinition of Chicago's downtown core, one other Daley administration tactic bears mentioning—the effective showcasing of central Chicago via such events as the World Cup soccer matches held at Soldier Field in 1994 and the Democratic National Convention staged at the United Center in the late summer of 1996.[50] In each instance, visitors and journalists from around the world were welcomed by a municipal administration anxious to present not just a tidy central city, but a central city well on the way to reshaping itself as an appealing site for tourism, "new economy" business enterprises, and amenity-rich residential life. Although the tools put to this use by the Richard M. Daley administration have been more subtle and varied than those deployed by Richard J. Daley in the 1950s and 1960s, the younger Mayor Daley's initiatives have, in many respects, produced the postindustrial downtown Chicago that the city's business, civic, and political leaders have been seeking since the years just following World War II.

Chicago's New Chicago Housing Authority

For the CHA, the 1990s represented the public policy equivalent of a roller-coaster ride. Early in the decade, observers of Chicago's long-embattled public housing agency expressed cautious optimism as Executive Director Vincent Lane initiated planning efforts to create mixed-income developments at Lake Parc Place and Cabrini-Green. By the middle of the decade Lane was forced out as head of the CHA, and a new regime—dictated by HUD—sought to press forward with a variant of Lane's program. Within two years, Joseph Shuldiner's CHA was engaged in a Herculean effort to respond to the provisions of the congressionally mandated Omnibus Consolidated Rescissions and Appropriations Act of 1996 (OCRA), which required that the CHA assess the physical "viability" of approximately half of its housing portfolio. At the end of the decade, the CHA was released from direct HUD oversight, and a new local administrative team was putting together the Plan for Transformation.

In contrast to these administrative twists and turns, since the early 1990s CHA officials have sustained a strikingly consistent articulation of their main policy aims: to reduce the "social isolation" of the "distressed communities" that CHA developments had become; to employ the "mixed-income model" of community development to save public housing; to humanize affordable housing through the use of new urbanist design techniques. Though this analytical framework has achieved wide currency among public housing reformers across the United States, much of the intellectual foundation for its first two propositions derives from the work of social scientists conducting research in Chicago. The leading figure in this movement was William Julius Wilson, for many years a member of the Department of Sociology at the University of Chicago.[51] Among Chicago's governmental elite, first Vincent Lane and later Mayor Richard M. Daley (as well as various members of his administration) became aggressive proponents of this agenda.[52]

In respect to Mayor Daley's enthusiasm for public housing reform, the thinning out of the CHA's once-teeming complexes, which in several notable instances are located in up-and-coming near-Loop neighborhoods, has been perfectly consistent with his administration's broader aim of completing the postindustrial transformation and expansion of the downtown core. Moreover, new urbanist public housing redevelopment at once appeals to the mayor's aesthetic preferences and paves the way for new upscale development even as remnant low-income populations are retained in former public housing neighborhoods such as ABLA and Cabrini-Green. As put into practice, the Daley administration drive to downsize CHA developments has produced some telling political inconsistencies and neighborhood conflicts. For example, Daley administration and CHA planners have adopted a notably opportunistic stance in reference to public housing resident consultation. When tenant-selected local advisory councils (LACs) have proved amenable to aggressive downsizing plans—as has been the case with the ABLA LAC, led by Deverra Beverly (see Chapter 7)—administrative support for public housing residents' official representatives has been steadfast. In contrast, once the Cabrini-Green LAC began to question CHA and city plans for neighborhood redevelopment, regular communication between planners and the LAC ceased. CHA and city officials chose to court local influentials, such as Twenty-seventh Ward political figures Jesse White and Walter Burnett, and by way of highly orchestrated public hearings, attempted to sell their vision of the new, mixed-income community directly to the residents of Cabrini-Green.[53]

The redevelopment of several of the CHA's major complexes is occurring in sections of the city, such as the Near West Side, experiencing vigorous private real estate investment. As we have noted in Chapter 7, the principal neighborhood organization in the vicinity of the ABLA development, the University Village Association (UVA), has taken an active role in the discussions of how the new ABLA area will take shape. UVA's position on the ABLA plans has been predictable and perfectly harmonized with CHA and city policy: reduce the number of public housing units, offset new and reha-bilitated public housing with large numbers of market-rate units, and build in an architecturally sensitive way.

In the Oakland community area on Chicago's mid-South Side, a vigorous debate broke out in the mid-1990s over relocation housing for residents of the Lakefront Properties, a CHA development that had been closed for reha-bilitation in 1986. The CHA had never followed through on its commitment to repair the six Lakefront Properties high-rises (though two of these build-ings were renovated as the Lake Parc Place mixed-income development), and by the middle of the next decade considerable gentrification had oc-curred adjoining their site overlooking Lake Michigan. When the CHA, un-der Joseph Shuldiner's leadership, attempted to resolve the Lakefront Properties impasse—by demolishing the remaining four high-rise structures and building smaller-scale public housing developments in the adjoining area—a bitter fight with local homeowners ensued. Ironically, this battle pit-ted African-American neighborhood upgraders against a public housing agency attempting to make good on decade-old promises it had made to African-American public housing residents. Ultimately, the CHA and Oak-land neighborhood residents settled on a compromise whose key provisions included the demolition of the Lakefront Properties buildings and the con-struction of 241 public housing units on various sites in the neighborhood.[54]

Documents describing the transformation of the CHA are loaded with commentary such as this paragraph from Mayor Daley's introduction to the ABLA "Holistic Urban Redevelopment" booklet:

Central to addressing this challenge is successfully transforming deterio-rated public housing enclaves, with overly dense and geographically isolated poor populations, into viable revitalized communities where diverse families can live and prosper. The solution is embodied in developing multicultural, mixed income communities where public housing residents are re-integrated into the community-at-large.[55]

Closer inspection of the CHA's actual redevelopment processes suggests a less uplifting scenario. For most of the 1990s the administration of Richard M. Daley, operating within the city's most favorable economic environment since the 1920s and supported by a Democratic national administration that was bent on divesting itself of unpopular domestic public policy commitments, sought to scale down public housing as part of a broader campaign to redefine Chicago as a revitalized metropolis, poised for the new millennium. Although nominally in conformance with widely accepted planning norms such as local resident consultation, the redevelopment planning of CHA projects has been, in reality, a highly politicized, contentious affair. City and CHA officials have managed rather than solicited resident input, and both broad plans and the particulars of new development have been driven by the aims and working assumptions of the public sector's private investor "collaborators."

Public Housing and the New Geography of Central Chicago

Although the bulk of the social science commentary on public housing redevelopment focuses on a narrow range of more or less technical issues—the effectiveness of former public housing residents as they negotiate the private rental housing market, the impacts of new residential environments on low-income children, the incidence of social pathology among present and former public housing residents—Chicago's experience with public housing transformation may well augur policy consequences of a far more profound nature. For example, efforts to track residential relocation by former CHA dwellers have, so far, been notably uniform in their findings.[56] Armed with Housing Choice vouchers, most CHA relocatees find new dwellings in racial minority neighborhoods characterized by substantial levels of impoverishment. Many of these former CHA residents, in fact, express approval in evaluating their new residential communities, but, objectively speaking, what they have managed to accomplish is to move into only marginally more desirable residential areas. Furthermore, given the skewed geography of CHA siting in the 1950s and 1960s, as near-Loop developments such as Cabrini-Green and ALBA depopulate, their former residents tend to move to neighborhoods such as South Shore, Austin, and Rogers Park, at a far greater distance from Chicago's core neighborhoods.

In effect, the transformation of the CHA and its new approach to providing subsidized housing can be viewed as one element in a broader process by which a European-style social class geography has begun to emerge in Chicago. In sharp contrast to the Chicago School of urban sociology's century-old portrait of a vigorous commercial and industrial core, to which was appended a few upper-income residential enclaves, the geography of the emergent Chicago features a larger central area composed of numerous business, cultural, and leisure-oriented activity centers.[57] This core area is once more experiencing population growth, and by a markedly affluent group of renters and home purchasers. Increasingly—and like many European urban centers—residential areas at considerable distance from the urban core are coming to hold the bulk of Chicago's working-class and low-income populations.[58] Although Mayor Richard M. Daley would never use such terminology to describe his aims for the Loop and its environs, furthering this Europeanization of central Chicago's spatial pattern has been a major accomplishment of his administration. The redevelopment of public housing, as we have described it in this volume, has been among the specific public policy paths used to achieve these aims. In addition to the opening of real estate for new development, the transformation of public housing in Chicago serves to calm the nerves of those newcomers to inner-city Chicago who might otherwise be deterred by lingering fears of neighborhood-level racial conflict or violent street crime.

Perhaps because the emergence of this new central Chicago is a trend of still-recent vintage, relatively little attention has been paid to some of its more disturbing consequences. For instance, although many CHA relocatees are moving into residential areas offering some advantages when compared to the immediate surroundings of their former public housing neighborhoods, neighborhoods such as West Englewood and Austin have not experienced substantially rising prosperity in the wake of the city's booming 1990s. Relocating former public housing residents in these neighborhoods has therefore not solved their "spatial mismatch" liabilities in reference to job centers in the metropolitan area.[59] Ironically, one of the truisms of mass transit use in Chicago is that the Chicago Transit Authority and suburban commuter systems work best for those who live nearest to the central city, where these lines converge. In effect, for those former CHA residents seeking to move up in the workforce, their new neighborhoods represent a curious trade-off: better residential conditions balanced against a greater dependence on the automobile.

Of course, the reorganization of space in central Chicago entails more than moving poor people out. It is also bringing new middle-class and upper-middle-class residents to areas such as the Near North Side environs of Cabrini-Green and the Near West Side borders of ABLA and the Henry Horner

Homes. The more optimistic interpretations of public housing transformation view this new wave of inner-city residents as a source of considerable social capital, mentoring and monitoring their neighbors, networking with those who are occupationally ambitious among the incumbent population. More realistically, many of these "pioneers" are relatively inexperienced in the ways of urban neighborhood life and motivated primarily by the promise of escalating home values and central Chicago's many leisure and recreational attractions. Indeed, a substantial portion of Chicago's new near-downtown residents could learn a principle or two about inner-city living from their neighborhoods' holdover residents. This, of course, is not the line of thinking encountered in most appraisals of how mixed-income community development is supposed to work.

But—whether it is recognized or not—the restructuring of central Chicago, of which the transformation of the CHA and its stock of housing is but one component, is a substantial social experiment. It remains to be seen how steadfast will be the neighborhood commitments of Chicago's new inner-city middle class. At this point, with none of the CHA's developments fully reconfigured as a mixed-income community, we can only speculate as to how effectively interclass and interracial cooperation will develop in these new residential areas. Whether or not the inner-city economic boom of the 1990s will persist is another open matter, whose resolution will have a direct impact on the economic and occupational consequences of public housing resident dispersal. Ultimately, it is incumbent that at least some policy makers, academic researchers, and citizens assess public housing redevelopment by way of these broader perspectives. Not only do the transformation of the CHA and the nationwide restructuring of public housing reflect trends well beyond the parameters of what is conventionally defined as affordable housing policy, but the consequences of these new initiatives in affordable housing provision are likely to spill over to and have a substantial impact on the broader realms of urban development, central city geography, and racial and social class relations across urban America.

Notes

1. Mark I. Gelfand, *A Nation of Cities: The Federal Government and Urban America, 1933–1965* (New York: Oxford University Press, 1975), p. 153.

2. Harold Kaplan, *Urban Renewal Politics* (New York: Columbia University Press, 1963), pp. 10–38.

3. Joel Schwartz, *The New York Approach: Robert Moses, Urban Liberals, and Redevelopment of the Inner City* (Columbus: Ohio State University Press, 1993).

4. Robert M. Fogelson, *Downtown: Its Rise and Fall, 1880–1950* (New Haven, CT: Yale University Press, 2001), p. 378.

5. Herbert J. Gans, "The Failure of Urban Renewal: A Critique and Some Proposals," *Commentary,* April 1965, pp. 29–37.

6. Fogelson, *Downtown,* p. 379.

7. Asa Briggs, *Victorian Cities* (Harmondsworth, UK: Penguin Books, 1980), p. 56.

8. Sam Bass Warner Jr., *The Urban Wilderness: A History of the American City* (New York: Harper & Row, 1972), pp. 85–120; William Cronon, *Nature's Metropolis: Chicago and the Great West* (New York: Norton, 1991).

9. Rudyard Kipling, *American Notes* (Boston: Brown and Co., 1899), p. 91.

10. Gregory D. Squires, Larry Bennett, Kathleen McCourt, and Philip Nyden, *Chicago: Race, Class, and the Response to Urban Decline* (Philadelphia: Temple University Press, 1987), pp. 23–60.

11. Gelfand, *A Nation of Cities,* p. 107.

12. Arnold R. Hirsch, *Making the Second Ghetto: Race and Housing in Chicago, 1940–1960* (New York: Cambridge University Press, 1983), p. 101.

13. Hirsch, *Making the Second Ghetto,* p. 133.

14. Department of City Planning, City of Chicago, "Development Plan for the Central Area of Chicago," August 1958, pp. 3, 19.

15. Larry Bennett, "Postwar Redevelopment in Chicago: The Declining Politics of Party and the Rise of Neighborhood Politics," in *Unequal Partnerships,* ed. Gregory D. Squires, pp. 161–177 (New Brunswick, NJ: Rutgers University Press, 1989); Joel Rast, *Remaking Chicago: The Political Origins of Urban Industrial Change* (DeKalb: Northern Illinois University Press, 1999).

16. Chicago Central Area Committee, "Chicago 21: A Plan for the Central Area Communities," September 1973, pp. 43, 59.

17. Lois Wille, *At Home in the Loop: How Clout and Community Built Chicago's Dearborn Park* (Carbondale: Southern Illinois University Press, 1997).

18. Anne B. Shlay and Robert Giloth, "The Social Organization of a Land-Based Elite: The Case of the Failed Chicago 1992 World's Fair," *Journal of Urban Affairs* 9, no. 4 (1987): 305–324.

19. Robert McClory, "The Fall of the Fair," Chicago: Chicago 1992 Committee, 1986.

20. Rast, *Remaking Chicago.*

21. Ed Marciniak, *Reclaiming the Inner City: Chicago's Near North Revitalization Confronts Cabrini-Green* (Washington, DC: National Center for Urban Ethnic Affairs, 1986); Stanley Ziemba, "Turf Battle Looms Downtown," *Chicago Tribune,* January 27, 1986.

22. Martin Meyerson and Edward C. Banfield, *Politics, Planning, and the Public Interest: The Case of Public Housing in Chicago* (New York: Free Press, 1964), p. 36.

23. Hirsch, *Making the Second Ghetto,* pp. 109–110.

24. Hirsch, *Making the Second Ghetto,* p. 110.

25. Hirsch, *Making the Second Ghetto,* p. 218; D. Bradford Hunt, "Anatomy of a Disaster: Designing and Managing the Second Ghetto," paper presented at the American Historical Association Annual Convention, Chicago, January 9, 2000.

26. Hirsch, *Making the Second Ghetto;* Leonard S. Rubinowitz and James E. Rosenbaum, *Crossing the Class and Color Lines: From Public Housing to White Suburbia* (Chicago: University of Chicago Press, 2000), pp. 17–24.

27. Nicholas Lemann, *The Promised Land: The Great Black Migration and How It Changed America* (New York: Vintage Books, 1992), p. 64; Sudhir Alladi Venkatesh, *American Project: The Rise and Fall of a Modern Ghetto* (Cambridge, MA: Harvard University Press, 2002), p. 102.

28. Roger Biles, *Richard J. Daley: Politics, Race, and the Governing of Chicago* (DeKalb: Northern Illinois University, 1995), pp. 79–83.

29. Hunt, "Anatomy of a Disaster," p. 6.

30. Hunt, "Anatomy of a Disaster"; Metropolitan Planning Council, "Changing the Paradigm: A Call for New Approaches to Public Housing in the Chicago Metropolitan Region," October 1996.

31. Nikolas Theodore and D. Garth Taylor, "The Geography of Opportunity: The Status of African Americans in the Chicago Area Economy," Chicago Urban League, March 1991.

32. Neil Smith, *The New Urban Frontier: Gentrification and the Revanchist City* (New York: Routledge, 1996).

33. Saskia Sassen, *The Global City: New York, London, Tokyo* (Princeton, NJ: Princeton University Press, 2001), pp. 157–162.

34. David Moberg, "Can You Find the Reformers in This Group?" *Chicago Reader,* February 18, 1983.

35. Rast, *Remaking Chicago,* p. 134.

36. Thomas Hardy, "A Schoolyard Kind of Fight," *Chicago Tribune,* December 5, 1996; Ben Joravsky, "Stopped in Its Tracks," *Chicago Reader,* August 22, 1997; Robert Baade and Allen R. Sanderson, "Bearing Down in Chicago," in *Sports, Jobs, and Taxes,* ed. Roger G. Noll and Andrew Zimbalist, pp. 324–354 (Washington, DC: Brookings Institution Press, 1997).

37. Terry Nichols Clark, Richard Lloyd, Kenneth K. Wong, and Pushpam Jain, "Amenities Drive Urban Growth," *Journal of Urban Affairs* 24, no. 5 (2002): 493–515.

38. Richard M. Daley, speech to Chicago Greening Symposium, March 8, 2002, www.ci.chi.il.us on August 27, 2002.

39. Daley, speech to Chicago Greening Symposium, March 8, 2002.

40. City of Chicago, "The Chicago Central Area Plan: Preparing the Central City for the 21st Century," draft final report to the Chicago Plan Commission, May 2003, p. iii.

41. Blair Kamin, "Daley Draws on Architects," *Chicago Tribune,* March 27, 1998; Gary Washburn, "Walk on the Wacker Side," *Chicago Tribune,* June 13, 2000; Andrew Martin and Laurie Cohen, "Millennium Park Flounders as Deadlines, Budget Blown," *Chicago Tribune,* August 5, 2001.

42. Neighborhood Capital Budget Group, "Who Pays for the Only Game in Town," March 2002.

43. Gary Washburn, "Building Permit Delays Spur City Shakeup," *Chicago Tribune,* May 18, 1998.

44. Gary Washburn, "City Deal Persuades Quaker Oats to Stay," *Chicago Tribune,* March 3, 2000.

45. Gary Washburn and Mickey Ciokajlo, "Price Was High, But Was It Worth It?" *Chicago Tribune,* May 11, 2001.

46. Robert Sharoff, "To Draw Traffic, Chicago Bets on Theater," *New York Times,* January 3, 1999.

47. Chris Jones, "Empty Stage," *Chicago Tribune,* January 18, 2000.

48. J. Linn Allen and Cindy Richards, "Making No Plans," *Chicago Tribune,* February 9, 1999.

49. Dan Immergluck and Geoff Smith, "Who's Buying Where?" Chicago: Woodstock Institute, November 2001, p. 2. Although near-Loop residential sales declined in the years after 2000, there was a marked upturn by 2004. See Thomas

A. Corfman, "Downtown Homes Sales Heated," *Chicago Tribune,* February 10, 2005.

50. Blair Kamin, "The Big Fix," *Chicago Tribune Magazine,* August 4, 1996, pp. 13–18.

51. William Julius Wilson, *The Truly Disadvantaged: The Inner City, the Underclass, and Public Policy* (Chicago: University of Chicago Press, 1987), and *When Work Disappears: The World of the New Urban Poor* (New York: Alfred A. Knopf, 1996).

52. Larry Bennett, "Do We Really Wish to Live in a Communitarian City? Communitarian Thinking and the Redevelopment of Chicago's Cabrini-Green Public Housing Complex," *Journal of Urban Affairs* 20, no. 2 (1998): 99–116.

53. Blair Kamin and John Kass, "Daley's Cabrini Dream," *Chicago Tribune,* June 28, 1996; Metropolitan Planning Council, "The Road to Redevelopment: Cabrini of the Future II," August 1996; Andrew Fegelman, "Daley's Cabrini Proposal Ready for Sale," *Chicago Tribune,* February 14, 1997. See also Chapter 6 of this volume.

54. LaRisa Lynch, "Lakefront Battle Scheduled to End," *Chicago Streetwise,* December 8–21, 1998; Abdon M. Pallasch, "4 CHA High-Rises Set for an Explosive End," *Chicago Tribune,* November 9, 1998.

55. City of Chicago, "Holistic Urban Redevelopment: The ABLA Homes Model," n.d.

56. Paul Fischer, "Section 8 and the Public Housing Revolution: Where Will the Families Go?" Chicago: Woods Fund, September 4, 2001, and "Where Are the Public Housing Families Going? An Update," January 2003; Susan J. Popkin and Mary K. Cunningham, "CHA Relocation Counseling Assessment," Washington, DC: Urban Institute, July 2002. See also Chapter 3 of this volume.

57. Robert E. Park, Ernest W. Burgess, and Roderick D. McKenzie, *The City* (Chicago: University of Chicago Press, 1924).

58. Norma Evenson, *Paris: A Century of Change, 1878–1978* (New Haven, CT: Yale University Press, 1979), pp. 232–249; Loïc Wacquant, "The Comparative Structure and Experience of Urban Exclusion: 'Race,' Class, and Space in Chicago and Paris," *Poverty, Inequality and the Future of Social Policy: Western States in the New World Order,* ed. Katharine McFate, Roger Lawson, and William Julius Wilson, pp. 543–570 (New York: Russell Sage Foundation, 1995); Duncan Maclennon, "Decentralization and Residential Choices in European Cities: The Roles of State and Market," in *Urban Change in the United States and Western Europe,* ed. Anita A. Summers, Paul C. Cheshire, and Lanfranco Senn, pp. 515–537 (Washington, DC: Urban Institute, 1999).

59. Edward G. Goetz, *Clearing the Way: Deconcentrating the Poor in Urban America* (Washington, DC: Urban Institute Press, 2003), pp. 27, 76–81.

Epilogue

Larry Bennett, Janet L. Smith, and Patricia A. Wright

Once you tear these high-rise buildings down,
you don't have to know I exist anymore.[1]

On October 19, 2004, the Chicago Housing Authority (CHA) board approved the 2005 Annual Plan to submit to the U.S. Department of Housing and Urban Development (HUD), which marked the beginning of the Plan for Transformation's fifth year. The subheading of the accompanying press release asserted, "Construction underway at or near every major redevelopment site."[2] During the preceding summer, plans and models for most of these sites were on display at city hall in a public preview of the new mixed-income housing that will replace the old high-rise public housing. The brochure for the exhibit donned CHA's new logo: CHAnge. Each page showed renderings or actual buildings at the developments, which have received new designations such as Jazz on the Boulevard and Roosevelt Square. The CHA has also begun advertising on Chicago Transit Authority trains and buses, with posters quoting people's admiration for the progress achieved so far: "Public housing is going to a point I hoped it would—full circle."[3] Several posters profile CHA residents who have made it out of the old public housing and are succeeding in full-time employment or attending school and living in a new unit.

As this book has been written, the CHA began the implementation of its ten-year plan to "transform" public housing in Chicago. Halfway into this process, the CHA can convincingly say that the physical appearance of public housing has been transformed, as evidenced by its new and rehabbed buildings around the city. Less clear, however, is how the residents who were living in CHA housing prior to the onset of the Plan for Transformation have been affected by the many millions of dollars expended thus far. The majority of completed public housing units are in rehabbed senior buildings, which now offer air conditioning and other much-needed amenities. Most of the CHA's scattered-site housing has also been improved, with new windows, new household appliances, and fresh paint. On the other hand, only a few of the sites once dominated by high-rise buildings have reemerged as mixed-income family housing. Most of these developments are still in the planning stage or just beginning construction. As they await the next steps in the trans-formation process, many of the pre-transformation residents of these devel-opments are living in other public housing buildings slated for rehab or functioning as a "relocation resource" with an uncertain future. Many other former public housing residents are using Housing Choice vouchers to rent in the private sector. For some this is a temporary situation as they wait for a new public housing unit. Other families have made the decision to remain in a private rental unit and not return to public housing. Whether or not it is temporary, most such families have found housing that is physically superior to what the CHA had made available, but these families still find themselves in neighborhoods that are highly segregated by race and income.[4]

Since the CHA still has five more years to complete its makeover, it is inappropriate for us to draw conclusions about its ultimate success based on the outcomes to date. Still, we think there is value in looking at what prob-able challenges and opportunities lie ahead. We also think it is important to consider other options and means not only to expand public housing in the Chicago region and elsewhere, but also to change the path that the United States has chosen for dealing with the housing needs of low-income people. This means developing a vision for public housing that relies on different assumptions about the role the federal government and local communities should play in producing and maintaining affordable housing. In this epi-logue we summarize key local and national conditions that warrant close monitoring since they will likely impact the CHA Plan for Transformation and where poor people are going live in the Chicago region of the future. Some of these conditions also present opportunities to think differently about public housing, to move beyond a focus on the simple transformation of buildings and the deconcentration of poverty and, instead, to reassert the human right to good-quality housing and access to economically vibrant, diverse communities.

National and Local Conditions Affecting Public Housing

A lot can happen in five years, especially when there is a change in political leadership. At the national level in the last five years, Republican George W. Bush has been elected and reelected to the presidency. The majorities in both the U.S. Senate and the House of Representatives have become more firmly Republican. In Illinois, Rod Blagojevich was elected governor in the fall of 2002—the first Democrat to win that office in a quarter-century. Of course, some things also remain the same with the passage of time. In Chicago, Mayor Richard M. Daley was reelected for a fifth term in office in 2003. Whether representing continuity or change, all these conditions shape the future of public housing in Chicago, though not all in the same way.

Political leadership, of course, is not the sole determinant of whether or not housing for the poor will be produced or preserved and, if the former, where it will be located. However, it does have tremendous impact on the public expenditure for housing. As was the case seventy years ago, there are still fundamental ideological differences when it comes to public housing, with Democrats generally more willing to support and fund it than Republicans.[5] Yet the terms of even this longstanding political divide have recently shifted. Today, elected officials in both parties tend to look to the private sector to solve what were once viewed as clearly public policy problems. This inclination points political leadership in the direction of providing families with housing vouchers to rent private market units and partnering with private developers to build, own, and manage new mixed-income housing developments. This trend is evident in shifts within the federal budget the past few years. For fiscal year 2004, the total budget for HUD was $34.7 billion, which was about two percent of the entire federal budget. Of this total, about $14.4 billion—nearly half the HUD budget—was allocated to tenant-based rental assistance (vouchers), while public housing received about $6.3 billion for capital and operating expenses.[6] In the 2005 budget passed by the Senate and House, the overall allocation for public housing decreased nearly 20 percent to about $5.1 billion while spending on vouchers increased about 4 percent.[7]

Fiscal support for public housing has been declining for many years. Indeed, the bulk of current funding for public housing and vouchers is used to renew or extend existing commitments and will not help to increase the overall supply of public housing.[8] The low-income housing tax credit, introduced in 1986, has become the primary means for producing affordable rental housing, although not for extremely low-income families (i.e., earning less than 30 percent of area median income). Between 1987 and 2001, tax credits generated more than one million units of affordable rental housing. While tax credits are not a budget item—which is one reason they have strong bipartisan support—their annual fiscal impact equals a direct budget expenditure of $5 billion. It is understandable why politicians like this program. For the same amount of money currently being spent to maintain old public housing, thousands of new units of housing for the working poor are built annually, usually with little long-term obligation required of the government except to honor the tax credit for investors and make sure that building owners are in compliance with the program's requirements (i.e., units remain affordable, occupied, and in relatively good condition).

Since the Great Depression, states and local governments have typically looked to the federal government to finance affordable housing. Thus, when federal appropriations shrink, so does the allocation to lower levels of government. In the 1980s, when federal housing dollars began drying up, state and local government and nonprofit organizations responded by developing new sources of funding, such as housing trust funds.[9] At present, many state and local governments and nonprofits find themselves in a fiscal bind due to the effects of a depressed economy and reduced tax collections. Nevertheless, even in the aftermath of the late 1990s economic bust and the subsequent tightening of state budgets, two Illinois initiatives hold some promise for extending public sector commitments to support affordable housing development. First, through an executive order, Governor Blagojevich established a housing task force to craft a comprehensive statewide housing plan intended to meet the needs of population groups typically underserved by the private housing market. The task force was commissioned to identify the housing needs of various housing consumer categories and propose strategies to meet their needs, including the specification of new funding sources. Second, Governor Blagojevich signed into law the Affordable Housing Planning and Appeal Act (HB 625).[10] The purpose of this legislation is to encourage counties and municipalities to support affordable housing development within their boundaries sufficient to meet the needs of local residents, and to allow builders to seek relief from local regulations inhibiting the construction of affordable housing for low-income and moderate-income households. The act requires any local government in which less than 10 percent of its housing stock is affordable to households with incomes falling below 80 percent of area median income to develop a plan meeting this numerical threshold.[11]

It is too soon to know what practical effect either the task force or the planning act will have in expanding affordable housing in Illinois. At the least, these two initiatives have helped to expand the dialogue about affordable housing. Since all the forty-nine communities with affordable housing shortfalls as defined by the planning act are in the Chicago region, this initiative has provided some leverage for suburban activists to push local governments to become more proactive in the housing development arena and, in some cases, even for individual mayors to prompt fellow mayors to take on their fair share of affordable housing. However, while most observers agree that the task force and the planning act are steps in the right direction, most also agree that neither will directly induce large-scale changes in policy or significant increases in the funding of housing for the poor.

Also within the Chicago region, several trends directly impact the Plan for Transformation. Perhaps the most important involve housing market conditions. When compared to a half-decade ago when the CHA's plan was approved, the rental housing market has softened, though not across all price points. A 2003 HUD study reported a vacancy rate in large rental developments of nearly 10 percent.[12] While rents in such developments vary, these buildings typically are for middle- and upper-income renters. Given the large number of new condominiums and homes that have come on the market in the past five years, the report assumes a relaxation of market demand as more tenants choose owning over renting. Yet even as the market has seemingly adjusted to the tighter conditions of the 1990s, units in such developments are often still priced well above the fair market rent levels and even the allowed exception rents for the area.

Indeed, rents at the lower price points in the local housing market have gone up. Ironically, several neighborhoods on the city's South and West Sides that had a large supply of affordable units in 2000 have seen rents climb as market activity has increased, especially in neighborhoods adjoining sites where public housing was demolished. Many of these same communities had a large number of extremely low-income renters (i.e., income below 30 percent of area median income) that were also extremely rent-burdened (i.e., paying 50 percent or more of their income for rent). Many of the same communities are also enjoying—with the remainder of the city—rising property values. While this a sign of neighborhood improvement, especially after years of disinvestment, property value escalation also means higher taxes for many families. Some homeowners have experienced a near doubling of their property values during the past two three-year tax reassessment periods. Yet among owners and renters alike in these neighborhoods, few have experienced a comparable upward trend in income.

While the for-sale market appears to be strong in Chicago, there are segments that appear to be stalling or at least slowing down when compared to the rapid pace of five years past. This dampening of demand includes homes in the $400,000 to $800,000 price range. Homes listed below and above these prices are still selling well. While this market trend will have no direct impact on the poor, it may affect public housing redevelopment, since at many of the CHA redevelopment sites, private developers are depending on the higher-priced housing sales to make their profit. For example, the higher-end units at Roosevelt Square, which is replacing parts of ABLA, are priced starting at $450,000. This is not out of line with market prices in the area; however, buyers do have other local options in this price range in new developments without public housing. This may also be the situation on Chicago's South Side, where private sector development around public housing sites has been quite active even before CHA redevelopment activity has been completed.

For public housing relocatees, the ability to move to better-quality housing has not meant necessarily moving to less segregated neighborhoods. A lawsuit, *Wallace v. Chicago Housing Authority,* was filed in early 2003 on behalf of relocatees claiming that they have been resegregated into the private market with Housing Choice vouchers—effectively reproducing the same conditions as in public housing. As former U.S. attorney Thomas Sullivan said in an official report on the CHA's relocation program, "vertical ghettos from which the families are being moved are being replaced with horizontal ghettos, located in well-defined, highly segregated neighborhoods on the west and south sides of Chicago."[13] In October 2004, the district court granted the plaintiffs class action status. The class includes all CHA residents who moved into or will move into segregated neighborhoods after October 1, 1999, and all families that moved prior to that date but only if into segregated neighborhoods.[14] In March 2005 the CHA, quite unexpectedly, decided to settle. As a result, there are two new relocation programs:

> (1) CHA's current relocation program, encouraging moves to racially integrated areas of metropolitan Chicago and providing for case-managed social services, would be applied to families initially moving from public housing; and (2) an agreed-upon modified program run by CHA's voucher administrator, CHAC Inc., would encourage former CHA residents to relocate to economically and racially integrated communities and give them increased access to social services.[15]

The CHA was to begin offering these programs soon after the settlement. The lawyers for the plaintiff class are now monitoring relocation and social service programs for public housing families.

Finding quality affordable rental housing in a low-poverty neighborhood is often difficult. In part, this difficulty can be attributed to a limited supply of rental housing in many higher-income communities, especially in the suburbs. However, there is another dimension to this problem. Today, most voucher holders—whether relocatees or not—are living in neighborhoods that are highly racially segregated. Findings in a recent study by the Chicago Area Fair Housing Alliance illustrate this point: "While 19 percent of the households in the region are African-American, 79 percent live in areas with more than 30 percent African-American households. Similarly, 75 percent of the African-American households using vouchers are in areas that have more than 30 percent African-American households."[16]

For Latinos, among whom less than 2 percent are voucher holders, housing market constraints are somewhat different. Still, the majority of Latino voucher holders are concentrated in a few densely populated Latino neighborhoods in the city, despite the fact that nearly 40 percent of all Latinos now live in the suburbs.[17] As such, there is little correlation between concentrations of Latinos using Housing Choice vouchers and concentrations of affordable rental housing. Across the metropolitan area there are quite a number of communities with affordable units that do not have voucher holders. Most of these communities have a majority of white residents.

Efforts to change these patterns include outreach to landlords and helping voucher holders make "mobility moves." However, while both tactics are useful, they only address some of the barriers to the racial and income integration of groups seeking affordable housing. As in most of the country, there is plenty of evidence of NIMBYism (not in my backyard) in both Chicago and the surrounding suburbs. Despite efforts by local affordable housing advocates to mount public education campaigns and build up support for strategies to expand housing opportunities for the poor, protectionist sentiment in many communities continues to block the inclusion of affordable rental housing—even for senior citizens—in plans and proposed developments. Municipal governments respond to local NIMBYism through exclusionary zoning and land use requirements that prevent the construction of multifamily housing. More recently, some communities have restricted development of all forms of family housing in the face of local concerns over increased service expenditures, especially for schools.[18] Interestingly, in Chicago affordable housing activists have been making gains among city council members in their effort to promote inclusionary zoning through a proposed ordinance requiring developers either to set aside a portion of newly built housing units for low-income renters or to put money into an affordable housing fund.[19]

Many of the same groups that worked on the city of Chicago set-aside ordinance have now launched a multimedia marketing campaign targeting that large portion of the metropolitan population that is presumably indifferent (and as such, not actively opposed) to affordable housing. The planned print, radio, and television spots will illustrate who needs affordable housing—teachers, firefighters, nurses, grandparents—presenting images of new, good-quality housing that is accessible to such professionals and population groups within "our" community. The goal of the "Housing Illinois" campaign, which is modeled after a very successful campaign in Minnesota, is to build a broad base of support for affordable housing and new legislation that will expand funds and the communities accessible for such housing development, as well as preserve existing units. This campaign also aims to advance a positive image of public housing by emphasizing the virtues of newly constructed mixed-income developments.

Looking Ahead

As we have traced the story of public housing in Chicago—both in the long and short term—it is evident that there currently is no clear answer to the question: Where are poor people to live? There is no reason to believe that public housing, even in the current environment of public opinion and national political leadership, will be completely eliminated. However, all signs indicate that the scale of public housing, like other longstanding domestic social welfare programs, will be reduced and subject to the continuing claim that a public sector "solution" may not even be necessary. Housing advocates seeking to reverse these trends are further inhibited by fiscal constraints at both the federal and state government levels, which in turn reinforce the disinclination of political elites—Democratic and Republican alike—to reconsider the social welfare rollback of the last two decades. Affordable housing advocates pin their hopes to the prospect of establishing the National Housing Trust Fund, which would have $5 billion to build and rehab over a million units of affordable housing for very poor families, as well as those with more moderate incomes.[20] While the implementation of this program would generate new affordable housing for the poor, it would not improve or preserve existing public housing. At a minimum, at least $40 billion is needed just to deal with deferred maintenance in public housing structures across the country that are not slated for demolition—an amount greater than the entire HUD budget in 2005.

Beyond such fiscal considerations and alternative housing strategies, a more expansive vision of the future of public housing is needed. In Chicago, public housing activists organized by the Coalition to Protect Public Housing (CPPH) are linking the plight of local public housing residents to the international human rights agenda. CPPH is joining forces with activists around the country and the world to build an alternative social vision based on the dignity of human life. It has been successful at soliciting the attention and support of Miloon Kothari, the United Nations Special Rapporteur on Adequate Housing. In his 2004 Human Rights Day solidarity statement to the Chicago public housing activists, Mr. Kothari wrote:

> What we are witnessing in Chicago today is occurring all across the United States, and in fact, across the world. Governments are dismantling social housing, housing subsidies and affirmative actions for low-income people in the name of liberalization and are placing primacy in the market and

privatization as panacea to solve the global crisis of millions living in inadequate and insecure housing. The United States has been the main 'ideologue' behind these policy directives that are increasingly reflected in housing policies and legislations of countries across the world. Such policies are a clear violation of the commitment of States across the world to international human rights instruments.[21]

For obvious reasons, the discourse on human rights in the United States—specifically, the recognition of the barriers limiting universal access to human rights within this country—has been slow to take hold among policy makers and governmental elites. It is, nevertheless, the intention of CPPH to amplify the discussion of human rights in the United States and particularly in the city of Chicago through an educational and organizing campaign based at Cabrini-Green. In the coming years, CPPH will expand its advocacy of the right to adequate housing as laid out in the goals of the Universal Declaration of Human Rights, of which the United States was a principal drafter. As the Universal Declaration states, "Everyone has the right to a standard of living adequate for the health and well-being of himself and his family, including . . . housing." The International Covenant on Economic, Social and Cultural Rights, to which the United States is also a signatory, further "recognize[s] the right of everyone to an adequate standard of living . . . including adequate . . . housing."[22] Building on the principles embodied in these international documents, the CPPH is pressing for a new conversation on housing needs and appropriate policy adjustments at the local level in Chicago and joining forces with other groups throughout the country to eventually effect a national discussion in Washington, DC.

An immediate concern, as expressed by the ongoing CPPH discussions, has been the treatment of public housing residents in conjunction with the redevelopment process. A 2004 report, issued jointly by the Brookings Institution and the Urban Institute, points to a consistent cluster of problems associated with producing mixed-income developments across the United States, mostly involving resident relocations and directly paralleling the experience of CHA residents in Chicago. These problems include (1) the failure of relocation planning to effectively support residents, particularly those who are most impoverished; (2) the mixed experiences of people who have relocated with vouchers: while many are in marginally better communities, they are often still highly segregated by race if not also by income; (3) insufficient relocation options for relocatees, especially large families, people with disabilities, custodial grandparents, and people with multiple problems; and (4) the failure of some public housing authorities to "implement their HOPE VI redevelopment plans effectively."[23] This last finding is illustrated by the experience of the Cabrini-Green development, whose redevelopment has been slowed by lawsuits. Of course, depending on one's point of view, this slowing down may be interpreted as ineffective implementation, but from the perspective of this volume's editors, the on-going and sometimes contentious negotiations between Cabrini-Green resident leaders and public officials have, in fact, produced a better collective outcome for this site's public housing population.

Specific features of the Cabrini-Green experience and legal settlement warrant attention as we think about how to improve the national HOPE VI program. While relocation efforts clearly need to be improved, residents also need to gain more control of the redevelopment process. As with the Henry Horner Homes case, the Cabrini-Green settlement gives residents legally binding powers and prescribes specific outcomes that the parties involved must produce. Both are critical in making sure that public housing residents have a specific level of control over the redevelopment process. One critical component is the *minimum* number of public housing units to be included in the mix, which is independent of the developer's plans or financing needs. Another is that relocation cannot occur until an approved plan is in place and some replacement housing has been built. The Cabrini-Green case also demonstrates that income mixing does not have to stop at the formal redevelopment boundaries of the public housing site. When expanded to include the surrounding neighborhood—about 340 acres—the consent decree requires some replacement public housing units mixed into the new market-rate housing being developed outside the original borders of the Cabrini-Green development.

Ultimately, however, rejuvenating public housing and maintaining good-quality affordable housing—at public housing sites, in mixed-income developments produced by some variety of public-private partnership, and in residential properties developed by the nonprofit sector—requires more than improved planning, consultation, and management procedures. As our preceding discussion has indicated, affordable housing activists in Chicago and elsewhere are engaged in a variety of sophisticated campaigns aimed at broadening public and elite support for new housing construction and existing housing maintenance to meet the needs of the country's very poor and working poor populations. In the current political environment, such efforts would appear to be swimming against a powerful tide of antigovernmental sentiment. Nevertheless, we take some comfort in the consensus among public policy historians that governmental support for the indigent has always been grudging and that even at the peak of popular approval for governmentally sponsored social welfare initiatives, a strong conservative backlash persistently claimed that money was being wasted, socialism was being advanced, and individual moral fiber was being sapped.[24] In short, realism in the face of the current political climate allows us to think strategically about broadening the recognition that Americans cannot forever think of themselves as flourishing when a quarter or more of the nation's population faces day-to-day challenges in obtaining decently paying employment, adequate housing, and routine medical care.

Without question, the high-water mark in public support for government initiatives to protect the poor occurred during the Great Depression, and the partial consensus that sustained the Roosevelt-era social safety net into the 1970s was based on the widespread memory of the economic crisis of the 1930s. We think that a newly emergent crisis—the crisis of American legitimacy across the globe—might be used to leverage broader public commitment for contemporary initiatives to aid America's poor. And we further acknowledge that the particular institutional means used to deliver the bundle of social services once provided by Social Democratic governments in Europe, as well as by the somewhat more complicated system of federal, state, and local service and benefit delivery in the post–New Deal United States, were due for an overhaul probably as early as the 1960s. We are not advocates of public service privatization, but we are proponents of creativity in thinking about the best institutional means to ensure universal access to good schools, housing, and other social services. In a general sense, we view national commitments—that is, federal government legislation—that promote universal access to such programs and benefits as essential. We further think that national funding and administrative oversight of housing, welfare, and medical programs are necessary, both to achieve a reasonable equality of access and to monitor costs and ensure effective program administration. Direct program management—for the moment limiting ourselves to affordable housing development and management—ought to be shared by a constellation of local entities: municipal governments, public-private partnerships, and nonprofit organizations. We recognize that such a mixed system of housing delivery is subject to charges of overcomplexity and possibly of fiscal waste. It is our view that variations in local program structures represent a useful kind of complexity, one that is likely to yield considerable policy innovation, and in addition, will permit more citizen oversight than is available via conventional bureaucratic (governmental or corporate) structures. Moreover, given these prospective benefits, we think that some degree of fiscal duplication is acceptable in a society as wealthy in the United States.

These last comments have been quite broad-stroked, but we direct interested readers to the sketch of an institutionally mixed, national affordable housing policy advanced by sociologist Peter Dreier in 1997.[25] Let us close with our rationale for connecting this version of a progressive, consensus-seeking national housing policy to the global crisis of the early 2000s. In much of the world, the United States has come to be viewed as an arrogant military power whose economic and governmental elites are content to export fast food chains, emotionally and morally stunted popular culture products, and a simpleminded ideology of personal achievement to the residents of Europe, Africa, Asia, and beyond. And when confronted with challenge, such as the emergence of Islamic fundamentalism in the last decade, these same elites are viewed as having offered but one answer, the application of overwhelming military force. This portrait of the United States is a vast oversimplification, but in our view, governmental elites and much of the public that has brought our elites to power have given insufficient attention to the growing reach of this oversimplified picture of America. Even as local activists in Chicago and other cities advance the argument that fundamental human rights have been undermined by recent trends in U.S. public housing policy, thoughtful consideration of the contemporary global context might well become a tool in bringing both the American public at large and governmental elites to the following recognition: that it is time for the United States to recommit itself to its longstanding promise to provide an adequate and hospitable way of life for all its residents including those who are black, brown, yellow, poor, and even recently immigrated. Indeed, by putting its domestic household in order, the United States will be taking the most efficacious of steps to demonstrate to the rest of the world that it remains a beacon in the face of the daunting global problems of poverty, sectarian violence, and worsening environmental conditions. Against this context, using the experience of the last generation to develop new housing programs that meet the needs of America's low-income population via locally sensitive, publicly responsive institutional mechanisms actually looks like a meaningful, manageable step in reconstituting United States public policy. We certainly think so, and we think a rejuvenation of egalitarian public policy within the United States is a potentially popular, worthy way to begin reconstructing our country's international image as well.

Notes

1. Wardell Yotagan, cofounder of the Coalition to Protect Public Housing and resident of Rockwell Gardens on Chicago's West Side, Spring 1998.

2. Chicago Housing Authority, "CHA Board Approves 2005 Annual Plan," press release, October 19, 2004.

3. Charles Pinkston, South Side attorney, CHA advertisement viewed on Chicago Transit Authority train, December 20, 2004.

4. Larry Buron, "An Improved Living Environment? Neighborhood Outcomes for HOPE VI Relocatees" (Washington, DC: Urban Institute, 2004).

5. This difference was evident in the 2004 presidential election. Although housing was not a plank in the platform of either candidate, the Bush-Cheney and Kerry-Edwards campaigns were asked questions about housing by the Campaign for Housing and Community Development Funding (CHCDF). On the topic of public housing, the Kerry-Edwards campaign spoke about retaining public housing and opposed the Bush-Cheney proposal to cut the budget for vouchers and a proposal to voucher out public housing. The Bush-Cheney campaign did not speak to public housing but did speak about vouchers, supporting efforts to promote self-sufficiency and more effective use of subsidies by local housing authorities. See "Presidential Candidate Questionnaire Results: Housing and Community Development," October 11, 2004, www.nlihc.org.

6. National Low-Income Housing Coalition, "Housing Programs Cut in Omnibus Bill," November 22, 2004.

7. See National Low-Income Housing Coalition. "Housing Programs Cut in Omnibus Bill." This excludes $144 million allocated for HOPE VI, which is $5 million less than in 2004.

8. Cushing Dolbeare, Irene Basloe Saraf, and Sheila Crowley, National Low-Income Housing Coalition, "Changing Priorities: The Federal Budget and Housing Assistance 1976–2005," October 2004, pp. 13–14. This does not include funds for other production programs such as HOME, CDBG, or rural housing.

9. Edward Goetz, *Shelter Burden* (Philadelphia: Temple University Press, 1993).

10. The bill was initially much stronger, modeled after a Massachusetts law that was able to generate 30,000 units of housing. See Business and Professional People for the Public Interest at www.bpichicago.org/rah/20031ac.html.

11. The act also creates the State Housing Appeals Board to hear appeals of decisions of a local authority concerning applications for approval of an affordable housing development.

12. Department of Housing and Urban Development, *Quarterly Market Analysis,* February 2003.

13. Cited in "Failed CHA Program Moves Thousands of Families to Racially Segregated, Poor Neighborhoods: Lawsuit Alleges Violation of Civil Rights and Fair Housing Laws and Breach of Contract," press release, Business and Professional People for the Public Interest, January 23, 2003.

14. Sargent Shriver National Center on Poverty Law, "Class Certification Granted in Lawsuit Challenging Displacement of Chicago Public Housing Residents," *Wallace v. Chicago Housing Authority,* No. 03 C 491 (N.D. Ill. October 8, 2004).

15. Sargent Shriver National Center on Poverty Law, "Chicago Housing Authority and Housing Advocates Settle Lawsuit over Resident Relocation," *Wallace v. Chicago Housing Authority,* No. 03 C 491 (N.D. Ill. filed March 15, 2005).

16. Chicago Area Fair Housing Alliance. "Putting the Choice in Housing Choice Vouchers (Part 3): Mapping the Location of Housing Choice Vouchers in the Chicago Region to Demonstrate the Need for Affirmative Efforts to Provide Greater Access to Areas of Opportunity for Families Using Vouchers," July 2004.

17. Chicago Area Fair Housing Alliance, "Putting the Choice in Housing Choice Vouchers."

18. Charise Jones, "Housing Doors Close on Parents; Experts Say Market Is Aiming for Older Clientele and Getting Tighter for Those with Children," *USA Today,* May 6, 2004.

19. Two groups, the Balanced Development Coalition and the Chicago Rehab

Network, worked on this issue and were able to get a majority of council members—incumbent and newly elected—to agree to support a mandatory set-aside in 2003. The bill, which is still sitting in council, would require a 15 percent set-aside in any development of ten or more units.

20. At this time, the National Housing Trust Fund is still a work in progress.

21. Miloon Kothari, "Solidarity Statement," December 10, 2004.

22. "Universal Declaration of Human Rights," adopted and proclaimed by the United Nations General Assembly resolution 217A (III) on December 10, 1948. "International Covenant on Economic, Social and Cultural Rights," adopted and opened for signature, ratification, and accession by the United Nations General Assembly resolution 2200A (XXI) on December 16, 1966; entry into force January 3, 1976.

23. Susan J. Popkin, Bruce Katz, Mary Cunningham, Karen Brown, Jeremy Gustafson, and Margery Turner, "A Decade of HOPE VI: Research Findings and Policy Challenges" (Washington, DC: Urban Institute and Brookings Institution, May 2004).

24. John A. Garraty, *Unemployment in History* (New York: Harper & Row, 1978); Theda Skocpol, *Protecting Soldiers and Mothers* (Cambridge, MA: Harvard University Press, 1992); Michael B. Katz, *In the Shadow of the Poorhouse* (New York: Basic Books, 1996).

25. Peter Dreier, "The New Politics of Housing: How to Rebuild the Constituency for a Progressive Federal Housing Policy," *Journal of the American Planning Association* 63 (Winter 1997): 5–27.

About the Editors and Contributors

Editors

Larry Bennett has taught in the Political Science Department at DePaul University since 1977, having received his PhD in urban planning from Rutgers University. He is author of *Neighborhood Politics: Chicago and Sheffield* (1997) and *It's Hardly Sportin': Stadiums, Neighborhoods, and the New Chicago* (with Costas Spirou, 2003). He is coeditor of the forthcoming *The New Chicago: A Social and Cultural Analysis.* He has worked with Chicago Housing Authority residents and advocacy groups since the mid-1990s.

Janet L. Smith is an associate professor in the Urban Planning and Policy Program and codirector at the Nathalie P. Voorhees Center for Neighborhood and Community Improvement at the University of Illinois at Chicago. Her work specializes in community development with an emphasis on affordable housing preservation and production and on issues of equity and diversity. She has written, coauthored, and edited several articles and book chapters on various aspects of community development, neighborhood revitalization, federal housing policies, and low-income housing.

Patricia A. Wright is the retired director of the Nathalie P. Voorhees Center for Neighborhood and Community Improvement at the University of Illinois at Chicago. From 1980 until 2004, she worked at the Voorhees Center and the Center for Urban Economic Development on numerous housing and community development research projects. She holds a master's in urban planning and policy from the University of Illinois at Chicago.

Contributors

Nancy Hudspeth is a PhD student in urban planning and policy at the University of Illinois at Chicago and has a master's degree in urban planning and policy. She has worked as a research assistant at the Nathalie P. Voorhees Center for three years, providing technical assistance and analysis to community organizations and advocacy groups. She is interested in issues of economic disparity, displacement, and uneven development.

Rajesh D. Nayak worked for two years as an Equal Justice Works fellow/staff attorney at the Sargent Shriver National Center on Poverty Law, where he pursued litigation and legislative advocacy on behalf of families living in public and subsidized housing in Illinois. He currently is an associate counsel at the Brennan Center for Justice at New York University School of Law.

Susan J. Popkin, PhD, is a principal research associate in the Urban Institute's Metropolitan Housing and Communities Policy Center. A nationally recognized expert on assisted housing and mobility, she directs the Urban Institute's "Roof Over Their Heads" research initiative, which examines the impact of the radical changes in public housing policy over the past decade. She is the lead author of *The Hidden War: Crime and the Tragedy of Public Housing in Chicago* and the author of numerous papers and book chapters on housing and poverty-related issues.

Wendy L. Stasell is a graduate of Loyola University School of Law. She previously worked for the Legal Assistance Foundation of Metropolitan Chicago and the National Center on Poverty Law, supporting the rights of low-income persons to quality affordable housing. She is currently a clerk to a federal judge in San Diego, California.

Carol Steele is a resident of the Chicago Housing Authority's Cabrini-Green development. She is president of the Cabrini Rowhouses Resident Management Corporation and past president of the Cabrini-Green Local Advisory Council. In 1996, she, Wardell Yotaghan, and Cora Moore founded the Coalition to Protect Public Housing.

Gretchen Weismann has authored or coauthored a series of reports and articles on community and affordable housing strategies for city, state, public, and private organizations in Massachusetts. Most recently she served as acting deputy director for the City of Boston's Emergency Shelter Commission. Weismann holds a BA from Macalester College in St. Paul and an MPA from

Northeastern University. She is a PhD candidate in the Department of Urban Studies and Planning at the Massachusetts Institute of Technology, where her research focuses on a study of the Moving to Opportunity Program.

Richard M. Wheelock graduated from the University of Wisconsin Law School in 1982. Since 1984 he has worked at the Legal Assistance Foundation of Metropolitan Chicago, a legal aid organization serving the civil legal needs of low-income families in Chicago and Cook County. He has received awards from tenant and legal organizations for outstanding advocacy in housing, including the 2000 Tenant Champion Award from the Metropolitan Tenants Organization and the 2001 Grau Outstanding Housing Advocate Award from the Lawyers' Committee for Better Housing. He currently teaches a Poverty and Housing Law seminar at the University of Chicago Law School.

William P. Wilen, director of housing litigation at the Sargent Shriver National Center on Poverty Law, has thirty-two years of experience in litigation and advocacy on behalf of low-income tenants and homeowners. He is lead attorney in *Henry Horner Mothers Guild v. CHA & HUD*, a landmark public housing case involving construction of new town house units for Horner Homes residents that will contribute to the revitalization of the Near West Side of Chicago. He is also class counsel in *Wallace v. CHA*, a case that challenges CHA's relocation practices. Before joining the Shriver Center in June 1996, he served for twenty-three years at the Legal Assistance Foundation of Chicago, the last fourteen as the supervising attorney of the housing unit. He is a 1973 graduate of Northwestern University School of Law and a member of the Chicago Council of Lawyers.

Yan Zhang earned her PhD in urban studies and planning at the Massachusetts Institute of Technology in 2004. She currently works in the East Europe and Central Asia Infrastructure and Energy Sector Unit of the World Bank.

Index